WORDSWORTH CLASSICS
OF WORLD LITERATURE

General Editor: Tom Griffith

FIVE JACOBEAN TRAGEDIES

praisne (2p

Five Jacobean Tragedies

Middleton(?), The Revenger's Tragedy
Webster, The White Devil
Webster, The Duchess of Malfi
Middleton/Rowley, The Changeling
Middleton, Women beware Women

❖

With Introductions by
Andrew Hadfield

WORDSWORTH CLASSICS
OF WORLD LITERATURE

This edition published 2001 by Wordsworth Editions Limited
Cumberland House, Crib Street, Ware, Hertfordshire SG12 9ET

ISBN 1 84022 106 2

Text © Wordsworth Editions Limited 2001
Introductions © Andrew Hadfield 2001

Wordsworth® is a registered trademark of
Wordsworth Editions Limited

Typeset by Antony Gray
Printed and bound in Great Britain by
Mackays of Chatham, Chatham, Kent

CONTENTS

GENERAL INTRODUCTION

Jacobean tragedy conjures up a number of disturbing and potent images for the contemporary reader or theatregoer. We probably think of such plays as powerfully gloomy, containing a multitude of ghoulish scenes and images, relying at crucial points on supernatural forces, showing a general obsession with madness, death and decay, centred around stories of lust, murder and betrayal, with the constant sense that just below the gaudy surface of Renaissance splendour with the fine and impressive objects and skills on display lies a horror which will remain unexplained at the end of the play. *Hamlet* is in many ways a representative Jacobean tragedy as the action is precipitated by the revelation of a horrible murder which is exposed by a ghost; the plot revolves around madness; behind the celebrations lie guilty secrets; the play ends with a series of murders; and nothing is really explained at the end. Significantly enough, the central character's last words, after he has pointed the way the succession to the Danish throne will undoubtedly go, are 'The rest is silence', leaving the audience to work out the meaning of the play (as legions of readers have attempted ever since).

This volume does indeed contain plays which demonstrate all the features of Jacobean tragedy. Beneath the courtly splendour of *Women Beware Women* and *The Duchess of Malfi* dark, corrupt machinations take place; *The Revenger's Tragedy* opens with the hero holding the skull of his poisoned mistress; *The White Devil* stages the defence of a fallen woman in a hypocritical male world; madmen torment the incarcerated Duchess in *The Duchess of Malfi*; and the sub-plot of *The Changeling* takes place in a mental hospital. The plays all end with the stage littered with bodies and last words which do little to unravel the mysteries which have just been presented.

However, it would be erroneous to suggest that there is no more to the tragedies than these elements of 'gothic' horror and that they simply present a thrilling spectacle for the audience. Tragedy was by no means an ancient art in Engand in the seventeenth century. The first English tragedy on the professional stage, *Gorboduc* (1562), had only been performed some forty years before the advent of the Jacobean era. Accordingly, we should regard Jacobean tragedy as an attempt to experiment with a form of writing which was relatively new and to push what had gone before to new limits.

English Renaissance tragedies do not all follow a simple model and cannot be easily categorised beyond the rather bland observation that tragic action involves a plot in which the main character inevitably has a miserable time and usually dies at the end of the play. Aristotle's relatively recently rediscovered *Poetics* was a huge influence on playwrights, and many clearly followed his conception of tragedy. Aristotle argued that tragedy represented men – and sometimes women – as better than they really were. Tragic action involved the inevitable destruction of a noble hero who had a tragic flaw (*hamartia*) which destroyed him in spite of all his noble qualities. The process of watching tragedy inspired fear and pity in the audience, who recognised faults in the hero which they might have themselves. They felt purged of their sins by seeing the suffering of someone else and could leave the theatre enlightened by what they had seen, a process Aristotle calls *catharsis*. While this model of tragedy had a profound influence on many late sixteenth and early seventeenth-century writers, not many were consistent in applying its dictates in all their work.

Elizabethan tragedy had often been highly moralistic in the conclusions it tended to draw, representing noble characters who repented of their evil actions in the end. However, plays such as Thomas Kyd's *The Spanish Tragedy* (*c.*1589), the story of the murdered ghost Don Andrea's quest for revenge, introduced the supernatural, madness, exciting stage devices, and a foreboding sense of gloom which later dramatists were to develop and exploit. Subsequent Elizabethan and Jacobean tragedy was often dependent on an ethical code. Nevertheless, such plays were never simply tales of moral retribution. They dealt with wider philosophical problems while aiming to entertain through their ingenious, often gaudy, special effects and dramatic cruxes.

ANDREW HADFIELD
The University of Wales, Aberystwyth

SELECT BIBLIOGRAPHY

General

Nicholas Brooke, *Horrid Laughter in Jacobean Tragedy*, Open Books, London 1979

Jonathan Dollimore, *Radical Tragedy: Religion, Ideology and Power in the Drama of Shakespeare and his Contemporaries* (2nd ed.), Harvester, Hemel Hempstead 1989

Alexander Leggatt, *English Drama: Shakespeare to the Restoration, 1590–1660*, Longman, Harlow 1988

J. W. Lever, *The Tragedy of State*, Methuen, London 1971

Duncan Salkeld, *Madness and Drama in the Age of Shakespeare*, Manchester University Press, Manchester 1993

John Webster

Gunnar Boklund, *The Duchess of Malfi: Sources, Themes, Characters*, Harvard University Press, Cambridge, Mass. 1962

Thomas Middleton

Margot Heinemann, *Puritanism and Theatre: Thomas Middleton and Opposition Drama under the Stuarts*, Cambridge University Press, Cambridge 1980

THE REVENGER'S TRAGEDY

INTRODUCTION

The Revenger's Tragedy was first performed in 1606 or 1607. It was long thought to have been the work of Cyril Tourneur (1575?–1626), about whom virtually nothing is known, but is now believed to have been written by Thomas Middleton (*c.*1580–1627), a far more substantial and significant figure, who is considered by many to be the equal of Shakespeare, especially in his portrayal of women. Middleton was the son of a bricklayer. He was probably well educated. He wrote a large number of works including several city-comedies, which satirised the lives of Londoners, and tragedies. After 1613 he was responsible for numerous official pageants performed in London to celebrate significant festivals. In 1624, *A Game at Chess*, his play satirising the behaviour of the Spanish ambassador, Gondomar, caused a huge scandal, and was subsequently banned.

The Revenger's Tragedy has probably the most famous opening scene in Jacobean literature, when Vindice enters holding the skull of his mistress, Gloriana, a beautiful lady who has been murdered by the old duke because she refused to sleep with him. Vindice's speech casts the Duke as a lecherous old vampire who sucks dry the blood of vital youth:

> O, that marrowless age
> Should stuff the hollow bones with damned desires!
> And 'stead of heat, kindle infernal fires
> Within the spendthrift veins of a dry duke,
> A parched and juiceless luxur. O God! One
> That has scarce blood enough to live upon,
> And he to riot it, like a son and heir!
>
> (I, I, 5–11)

The speech introduces a number of themes which assumed importance throughout the Jacobean period. The predominant image is of the old preying on the young and in doing so transposing the two stages of life. Gloriana is transformed into the skull the audience sees, a dead and dry skeleton. The Duke, according to Vindice, has made himself into a young man and is able to 'riot it like a son and heir'. In other words things are really back to front and the young generation has been supplanted by the old in order that the old may relive their youth, a doubly unfair process which Vindice intends to stop.

A commonly expressed feeling in the early 1600s was that the golden age of Elizabeth had passed and that Britain had been left with an unsuitable and unpopular king, James I, who was in fact notorious for his 'rioting' with young men and his passion for pursuits such as hunting. It is hard not to see an allusion to such a sense of bitterness in these lines, especially given their strategic importance in determining the tone and style of the play.

Equally important, Vindice's lines express a fear of an epidemic of sexually transmitted diseases. The description of the Duke as having 'hollow' bones and being 'dry' indicate a venereal infection, one which will clearly spread throughout the court if the Duke carries on in his promiscuous ways. Contemporary woodcuts illustrating the 'Dance of Death' are a relevant sub-text here. In such scenes Death was invariably depicted as a masquer dancing with his victims, who were unaware of his real identity until the fiend removed his mask at the last minute and led them away to their judgment. The victims were usually a varied crowd of young and old, ordinary and aristocratic, striking and plain, but nearly always included one beautiful young woman – like Gloriana – with an expression of pained surprise. The woodcuts served to warn people to be ready to meet their maker at any time because death would strike without regard of time or place and could lead otherwise harmless, or even relatively virtuous, citizens down to hell if they were not careful. Vindice's righteous anger is partly due to his fears for Gloriana's soul. His revenge is designed to make sure that none of his victims has any more chance to repent than Gloriana did, and that they too experience the random brutality of death.

As he watches the duke and his entourage pass by, Vindice vows revenge. The play poses a difficult moral problem for the audience.

While we may sympathise with the embittered Vindice and under-stand his keen sense of loss, we surely cannot condone his actions. Not only did the Bible forbid private revenge ('Vengeance is mine, sayeth the Lord'), but so did contemporary political and religious writings. Nevertheless, the focus of action in the play means that we watch events through the eyes of Vindice, encouraging us to empathise with him, probably against our better judgment. The characters assume names familiar from the morality play tradition; not only is there Vindice (revenge), but the Duke has a legitimate son called Lussurioso (luxurious, lecherous) and an illegitimate one called Spurio, while the Duchess has sons called Ambitioso (ambitious) and Supervacuo (who has no real character and simply tries to ingratiate himself at court). But it would be a mistake to read *The Revenger's Tragedy* as simply a morality play. The audience is tempted to do so and will have to face their complicity with the twisted evil of the play in desiring brutal summary justice for the wrongdoers.

Lussurioso asks Hippolito, Vindice's brother, to recommend him a pimp. Vindice disguises himself as Piato, a malcontent, and assumes the role. Vindice soon realises that the whole family of the Duke is corrupt. The Duke is as unsavoury as his son in his lustfulness; the Duchess, his second wife, is in love with Spurio, the Duke's illegitimate son; the Duchess's unnamed youngest son has raped a nobleman's wife, who has then poisoned herself.

Vindice (Piato) is employed by Lussurioso to procure the services of Vindice's sister, Castiza. He offers his mother money for her, but the virtuous young woman refuses to be tempted. Vindice spurs Lussurioso on with details of the mother's greed. News of the Duchess's desire for Spurio is circulating around the court. Spurio hears of Lussurioso's plans and resolves to murder his brother so that he can inherit the family fortune. Before this can happen, Vindice tells Lussurioso of his brother's affair with his stepmother and Lussurioso tries to confront them in her bedroom. Unfortunately, only the Duke is there and he assumes, not unreasonably given the general behaviour of the family, that Lussurioso plans to murder him and so seize the throne. Lussurioso is detained in prison. Supervacuo and Ambitioso plan to have their brother executed but are fooled by their father who releases Lussurioso before they can reach him; their nameless youngest brother is executed instead.

Vindice is now hired by the Duke to procure him a lady. He dresses up the skull in rich clothes, poisons the lips and with his brother, Hippolito, leads the Duke to a secluded bower ready for the encounter. When the Duke kisses the figure, he falls to his knees only to see Spurio embracing the Duchess, just before he dies.

Lussurioso, disturbed by events and full of suspicions, plots to murder Piato. He approaches Hippolito, who introduces him to Vindice, and the brothers promise to murder the bawd. They dress the Duke in Piato's disguise, and when the body is discovered it is assumed that Piato murdered the Duke before fleeing. Lussurioso succeeds to the throne, but Vindice and Hippolito, now well beyond the former's original plans of avenging Gloriana's death, try to start an uprising against him. A blazing comet signals the evil state of the kingdom. Lussurioso banishes the Duchess and condemns his brother and stepbrothers to death. But various groups are now turning against him and preparing to kill him. The deed is performed by Vindice and Hippolito who thereby frustrate the plans of Spurio, Supervacuo and Ambitioso. In the ensuing conflict, Spurio kills Ambitioso, who is then slain by an unnamed nobleman. Vindice and Hippolito are unable to keep their part in the murders quiet and they are led away to execution. The virtuous Antonio restores order.

In some ways *The Revenger's Tragedy* is a relatively crude play which prepares for the more polished brilliance of later works. However, it should not be taken at face value as a morality tale, which endorses revenge. Rather, the audience is invited to believe that the actions of Vindice can sort problems out until virtue eventually does really triumph. Vindice starts out as an inspired avenger, but soon lapses into the complex and obsessive villainy which has engulfed the court.

CHARACTERS IN THE PLAY

THE DUKE

LUSSURIOSO *the Duke's son*

SPURIO *the Duke's bastard son*

AMBITIOSO *the Duchess's eldest son*

SUPERVACUO *the Duchess's second son*

THE DUCHESS'S YOUNGEST SON

VINDICE *disguised as* PIATO ⎫
HIPPOLITO *also called* CARLO ⎬ *brothers of Castiza*

ANTONIO ⎫
PIERO ⎬ *nobles*

DONDOLO

Judges, Nobles, Gentlemen, Officers, Keeper, Servants

THE DUCHESS

CASTIZA

GRATIANA, *mother of Castiza*

The Scene: a city of Italy

THE REVENGER'S TRAGEDY

ACT I SCENE I

Near the house of Gratiana

Enter VINDICE, *with a skull in his hand.* THE DUKE, DUCHESS,
LUSSURIOSO, SPURIO, *with a train, pass over the stage with torchlight*

VINDICE   Duke! Royal lecher! Go, grey-haired adultery!
And thou his son, as impious steeped as he:
And thou his bastard, true begot in evil:
And thou his duchess, that will do with devil:
Four excellent characters! O, that marrowless age
Should stuff the hollow bones with damned desires!
And, 'stead of heat, kindle infernal fires
Within the spendthrift veins of a dry duke,
A parched and juiceless luxur. O God! One
That has scarce blood enough to live upon,   10
And he to riot it, like a son and heir!
O, the thought of that
Turns my abuséd heart-strings into fret.
[views the skull in his hand]
Thou sallow picture of my poisoned love,
My study's ornament, thou shell of death,
Once the bright face of my betrothéd lady,
When life and beauty naturally filled out
These ragged imperfections;
When two heaven-pointed diamonds were set
In those unsightly rings – then 'twas a face   20
So far beyond the artificial shine
Of any woman's bought complexion,
That the uprightest man (if such there be,
That sin but seven times a day) broke custom,
And made up eight with looking after her.
O, she was able to ha'made a usurer's son
Melt all his patrimony in a kiss;
And what his father fifty yeares told,
To have consumed, and yet his suit been cold.

But, O accursèd palace!   30
Thee, when thou wert apparelled in thy flesh,
The old duke poisonèd,
Because thy purer part would not consent
Unto his palsied lust; for old men lustful
Do show like young men angry, eager, violent,
Outbidden like their limited performances.
O, 'ware an old man hot and vicious!
'Age, as in gold, in lust is covetous.'
Vengeance, thou murder's quit-rent, and whereby
Thou show'st thyself tenant to tragedy,   40
O keep thy day, hour, minute, I beseech,
For those thou hast determined. Hm! Who e'er knew
Murder unpaid? Faith, give revenge her due,
She has kept touch hitherto: be merry, merry,
Advance thee, O thou terror to fat folks,
To have their costly three-piled flesh worn off
As bare as this; for banquets, ease and laughter
Can make great men, as greatness goes by clay;
But wise men little are more great than they.

Enter HIPPOLITO

HIPPOLITO Still sighing o'er death's vizard?
VINDICE   Brother, welcome!   50
What comfort bring'st thou? How go things at court?
HIPPOLITO In silk and silver, brother: never braver.
VINDICE Pooh!
Thou play'st upon my meaning. Prithee, say,
Has that bald madam, Opportunity,
Yet thought upon's? Speak, are we happy yet?
Thy wrongs and mine are for one scabbard fit.
HIPPOLITO It may prove happiness.
VINDICE   What is't may prove?
Give me to taste.
HIPPOLITO   Give me your hearing, then.
You know my place at court?
VINDICE   Ay, the duke's chamber!   60
But 'tis a marvel thou'rt not turned out yet!
HIPPOLITO Faith, I've been shoved at; but 'twas still my hap

To hold by the duchess' skirt: you guess at that:
Whom such a coat keeps up, can ne'er fall flat.
But to the purpose –
Last evening, predecessor unto this,
The duke's son warily inquired for me,
Whose pleasure I attended: he began
By policy to open and unhusk me
About the time and common rumour: 70
But I had so much wit to keep my thoughts
Up in their built houses; yet afforded him
An idle satisfaction without danger.
But the whole aim and scope of his intent
Ended in this: conjuring me in private
To seek some strange-digested fellow forth,
Of ill-contented nature; either disgraced
In former times, or by new grooms displaced,
Since his step-mother's nuptials; such a blood,
A man that were for evil only good –   80
To give you the true word, some base-coined pander.

VINDICE   I reach you; for I know his heat is such,
Were there as many concubines as ladies,
He would not be contained; he must fly out.
I wonder how ill-featured, vile-proportioned,
That one should be, if she were made for woman,
Whom, at the insurrection of his lust,
He would refuse for once. Heart! I think none.
Next to a skull, though more unsound than one,
Each face he meets he strongly doats upon.   90

HIPPOLITO   Brother, y'have truly spoke him.
He knows not you, but I will swear you know him.

VINDICE   And therefore I'll put on that knave for once,
And be a right man then, a man o'the time;
For to be honest is not to be i'the world.
Brother, I'll be that strange-composéd fellow.

HIPPOLITO   And I'll prefer you, brother.

VINDICE   Go to, then:
The smallest advantage fattens wrongéd men:
It may point out occasion; if I meet her,

I'll hold her by the foretop fast enough;   100
Or, like the French mole, heave up hair and all.
I have a habit that will fit it quaintly.
Here comes our mother.

HIPPOLITO   And sister.

VINDICE   We must coin:
Women are apt, you know, to take false money;
But I dare stake my soul for these two creatures,
Only excuse excepted, that they'll swallow,
Because their sex is easy in belief.

Enter GRATIANA *and* CASTIZA

GRATIANA   What news from court, son Carlo?

HIPPOLITO   Faith, mother,
'Tis whispered there the duchess' youngest son
Has played a rape on Lord Antonio's wife.   110

GRATIANA   On that religious lady!

CASTIZA   Royal blood monster! He deserves to die,
If Italy had no more hopes but he.

VINDICE   Sister, y'have sentenced most direct and true.
The law's a woman, and would she were you.
Mother, I must take leave of you.

GRATIANA   Leave for what?

VINDICE   I intend speedy travel.

HIPPOLITO   That he does, madam.

GRATIANA   Speedy indeed!   120

VINDICE   For since my worthy father's funeral,
My life's unnatural to me, e'en compelled;
As if I lived now, when I should be dead.

GRATIANA   Indeed, he was a worthy gentleman,
Had his estate been fellow to his mind.

VINDICE   The duke did much deject him.

GRATIANA   Much?

VINDICE   Too much:
And though disgrace oft smothered in his spirit,
When it would mount, surely I think he died
Of discontent, the noble man's consumption.

GRATIANA   Most sure he did.

VINDICE   Did he, 'lack? You know all —   130

You were his midnight secretary.

GRATIANA   No,
He was too wise to trust me with his thoughts.

VINDICE   I'faith, then, father, thou wast wise indeed;
'Wives are but made to go to bed and feed.'
Come, mother, sister: you'll bring me onward, brother?

HIPPOLITO I will.

VINDICE   [aside] I'll quickly turn into another.

                                              [exeunt

SCENE 2

A Hall of Justice

Enter the DUKE, LUSSURIOSO, *the* DUCHESS, SPURIO,
AMBITIOSO, *and* SUPERVACUO; *the* DUCHESS'S YOUNGEST
SON *brought out by Officers. Two Judges.*

DUKE   Duchess, it is your youngest son. We're sorry
His violent act has e'en drawn blood of honour,
And stained our honours;
Thrown ink upon the forehead of our state,
Which envious spirits will dip their pens into
After our death, and blot us in our tombs:
For that which would seem treason in our lives
Is laughter, when we're dead. Who dares now whisper,
That dares not then speak out, and e'en proclaim
With loud words and broad pens our closest shame?   10

I JUDGE   Your grace hath spoke like to your silver years,
Full of confirmed gravity; for what is't to have
A flattering false insculption on a tomb,
And in men's hearts reproach? The bowelled corpse
May be seared in, but (with free tongue I speak)
The faults of great men through their sear-cloths break.

DUKE   They do; we're sorry for't: it is our fate
To live in fear, and die to live in hate.
I leave him to your sentence; doom him, lords –
The fact is great – whilst I sit by and sigh.   20

DUCHESS   My gracious lord, I pray be merciful:
Although his trespass far exceed his years,

Think him to be your own, as I am yours;
Call him not son-in-law: the law, I fear,
Will fall too soon upon his name and him:
Temper his fault with pity.

LUSSURIOSO   Good my lord,
Then 'twill not taste so bitter and unpleasant
Upon the judges' palate; for offences,
Gilt o'er with mercy, show like fairest women,
Good only for their beauties, which washed off,   30
No sin is uglier.

AMBITIOSO   I beseech your grace,
Be soft and mild; let not relentless law
Look with an iron forehead on our brother.

SPURIO   He yields small comfort yet; hope he shall die;
[aside] And if a bastard's wish might stand in force,
Would all the court were turned into a corse!

DUCHESS   No pity yet? Must I rise fruitless then?
A wonder in a woman! Are my knees
Of such low metal, that without respect –

I JUDGE   Let the offender stand forth: 40
'Tis the duke's pleasure that impartial doom
Shall take fast hold of his unclean attempt.
A rape! Why 'tis the very core of lust –
Double adultery.

YOUNGEST   So, sir.

2 JUDGE   And which was worse,
Committed on the Lord Antonio's wife,
That general-honest lady. Confess, my lord,
What moved you to't?

YOUNGEST   Why, flesh and blood, my lord;
What should move men unto a woman else?

LUSSURIOSO O, do not jest thy doom! Trust not an axe
Or sword too far: the law is a wise serpent,   50
And quickly can beguile thee of thy life.
Though marriage only has made thee my brother,
I love thee so far: play not with thy death.

YOUNGEST I thank you, troth; good admonitions, faith,
If I'd the grace now to make use of them.

I JUDGE   That lady's name has spread such a fair wing

Over all Italy, that if our tongues
Were sparing toward the fact, judgment itself
Would be condemned, and suffer in men's thoughts.

YOUNGEST Well then, 'tis done; and it would please me well   60
Were it to do again: sure, she's a goddess,
For I'd no power to see her and to live.
It falls out true in this, for I must die;
Her beauty was ordained to be my scaffold.
And yet, methinks, I might be easier 'sessed:
My fault being sport, let me but die in jest.

I JUDGE This be the sentence –

DUCHESS O keep't upon your tongue; let it not slip;
Death too soon steals out of a lawyer's lip.
Be not so cruel-wise!

I JUDGE   Your grace must pardon us;   70
'Tis but the justice of the law.

DUCHESS   The law
Is grown more subtle than a woman should be.

SPURIO [aside] Now, now he dies! Rid 'em away.

DUCHESS [aside] O, what it is to have an old cool duke,
To be as slack in tongue as in performance!

I JUDGE Confirmed, this be the doom irrevocable.

DUCHESS O!

I JUDGE Tomorrow early –

DUCHESS   Pray be abed, my lord.

I JUDGE Your grace much wrongs yourself.

AMBITIOSO   No, 'tis that tongue:
Your too much right does do us too much wrong.

I JUDGE Let that offender –

DUCHESS   Live, and be in health.   80

I JUDGE Be on a scaffold –

DUKE   Hold, hold, my lord!

SPURIO [aside]   Pox on't,
What makes my dad speak now?

DUKE We will defer the judgment till next sitting:
In the meantime, let him be kept close prisoner.
Guard, bear him hence.

AMBITIOSO [aside] Brother, this makes for thee;
Fear not, we'll have a trick to set thee free.

YOUNGEST [*aside*] Brother, I will expect it from you both;
And in that hope I rest.

SUPERVACU.   Farewell, be merry.
                              [*exit Youngest with a guard*

SPURIO   Delayed! Deferred! Nay then, if judgment have   90
Cold blood, flattery and bribes will kill it.

DUKE   About it. then, my lords, with your best powers:
More serious business calls upon our hours.
                         [*exeunt, excepting the Duchess*

DUCHESS Was't ever known step-duchess was so mild
And calm as I? Some now would plot his death
With easy doctors, those loose-living men,
And make his withered grace fall to his grave,
And keep church better.
Some second wife would do this, and despatch
Her double-loathéd lord at meat or sleep.   100
Indeed, 'tis true, an old man's twice a child;
Mine cannot speak; one of his single words
Would quite have freed my youngest dearest son
From death or durance, and have made him walk
With a bold foot upon the thorny law,
Whose prickles should bow under him; but 'tis not,
And therefore wedlock-faith shall be forgot:
I'll kill him in his forehead. Hate, there feed;
That wound is deepest, though it never bleed.
And here comes he whom my heart points unto,   110
His bastard son, but my love's true-begot;
Many a wealthy letter have I sent him,
Swelled up with jewels, and the timorous man
Is yet but coldly kind.
That jewel's mine that quivers in his ear,
Mocking his master's chillness and vain fear.
He has spied me now!

                    Enter SPURIO

SPURIO   Madam, your grace so private?
My duty on your hand.

DUCHESS Upon my hand, sir! Troth, I think you'd fear
To kiss my hand too, if my lip stood there.   120

SPURIO   Witness I would not, madam. [*kisses her*]

DUCHESS   'Tis a wonder;
         For ceremony has made many fools!
         It is as easy way unto a duchess,
         As to a hatted dame, if her love answer:
         But that by timorous honours, pale respects,
         Idle degrees of fear, men make their ways
         Hard of themselves. What, have you thought of me?

SPURIO   Madam, I ever think of you in duty,
         Regard, and –

DUCHESS   Pooh! Upon my love, I mean.

SPURIO   I would 'twere love; but 'tis a fouler name   130
         Than lust: you are my father's wife – your grace
         May guess now what I could call it.

DUCHESS   Why, th'art his son but falsely;
         'Tis a hard question whether he begot thee.

SPURIO   I'faith, 'tis true: I'm an uncertain man
         Of more uncertain woman. Maybe, his groom
         O'the stable begot me; you know I know not!
         He could ride a horse well, a shrewd suspicion, marry!
         He was wondrous tall: he had his length, i'faith.
         For peeping over half-shut holyday windows,
         Men would desire him light. When he was afoot   140
         He made a goodly show under a pent-house;
         And when he rid, his hat would check the signs,
         And clatter barbers' basons.

DUCHESS   Nay, set you
         A-horseback once, you'll ne'er light off.

SPURIO   Indeed,
         I am a beggar.

DUCHESS   That's the more sign thou'rt great –
         But to our love:
         Let it stand firm both in thy thought and mind,
         That the duke was thy father, as no doubt then
         He bid fair for't – thy injury is the more;
         For had he cut thee a right diamond,   150
         Thou had'st been next set in the dukedom's ring,
          When his worn self, like age's easy slave,
          Had dropped out of the collet into th'grave.

What wrong can equal this? Canst thou be tame,
And think upon't?

SPURIO   No, mad, and think upon't.

DUCHESS Who would not be revenged of such a father,
E'en in the worst way? I would thank that sin
That could most injure him, and be in league with it.
O, what a grief 'tis that a man should live
But once i'the world, and then to live a bastard –   160
The curse o'the womb, the thief of nature,
Begot against the seventh commandment,
Half-damned in the conception by the justice
Of that unbribèd everlasting law.

SPURIO O, I'd a hot-backed devil to my father.

DUCHESS Would not this mad* e'en patience, make blood rough?
Who but an eunuch would not sin – his bed
By one false minute disinherited?

SPURIO Ay, there's the vengeance that my birth was
                                        wrapped in!
I'll be revenged for all: now, hate, begin;   ·170
I'll call foul incest but a venial sin.

DUCHESS Cold still! In vain then must a duchess woo?

SPURIO Madam, I blush to say what I will do.

DUCHESS Thence flew sweet comfort. Earnest, and farewell.
                                        [kisses him

SPURIO O, one incestuous kiss picks open hell.

DUCHESS Faith, now, old duke, my vengeance shall reach high.
I'll arm thy brow with woman's heraldry.   [exit

SPURIO Duke, thou didst do me wrong; and by thy act
Adultery is my nature.
Faith, if the truth were known, I was begot   180
After some gluttonous dinner; some stirring dish
Was my first father, when deep healths went round,
And ladies' cheeks were painted red with wine,
Their tongues as short and nimble as their heels,
Uttering words sweet and thick; and when they rose,
Were merrily disposed to fall again.
In such a whispering and withdrawing hour,

* madden (verb)

When base male-bawds kept sentinel at stair-head,
Was I stol'n softly. O damnation meet!
The sin of feasts, drunken adultery!   190
I feel it swell me; my revenge is just!
I was begot in impudent wine and lust.
Step-mother, I consent to thy desires;
I love thy mischief well, but I hate thee
And those three cubs thy sons, wishing confusion,
Death and disgrace may be their epitaphs.
As for my brother, the duke's only son,
Whose birth is more beholding to report
Than mine, and yet perhaps as falsely sown
(Women must not be trusted with their own),   200
I'll loose my days upon him, hate-all-I;
Duke, on thy brow I'll draw my bastardy:
For indeed a bastard by nature should make cuckolds
Because he is the son of a cuckold-maker.

                                                      [*exit*

SCENE 3

A part of the city

Enter VINDICE *in disguise, and* HIPPOLITO

VINDICE   What, brother, am I far enough from myself?
HIPPOLITO   As if another man had been sent whole
             Into the world, and none wist how he came.
VINDICE   It will confirm me bold – the child o'the court;
             Let blushes dwell i'the country. Impudence,
             Thou goddess of the palace, mistress of mistresses,
             To whom the costly perfumed people pray,
             Strike thou my forehead into dauntless marble,
             Mine eyes to steady sapphires! Turn my visage;
             And, if I must needs glow, let me blush inward,   10
             That this immodest season may not spy
             That scholar in my cheeks, fool bashfulness;
             That maid in the old time, whose flush of grace
             Would never suffer her to get good clothes.
             Our maids are wiser, and are less ashamed;

Save Grace the bawd, I seldom hear grace named!

HIPPOLITO Nay, brother, you reach out o'the verge now –
'Sfoot, the duke's son! Settle your looks.

VINDICE Pray, let me not be doubted.

HIPPOLITO My lord –

Enter LUSSURIOSO

LUSSURIOSO   Hippolito – (*to Attendants*) Be absent, leave us! 20

HIPPOLITO My lord, after long search, wary inquiries,
And politic siftings, I made choice of yon fellow,
Whom I guess rare for many deep employments:
This our age swims within him; and if Time
Had so much hair, I should take him for Time,
He is so near kin to this present minute.

LUSSURIOSO 'Tis enough;
We thank thee: yet words are but great men's blanks;
Gold, though it be dumb, does utter the best thanks.
[*gives him money*]

HIPPOLITO Your plenteous honour! An excellent fellow, my lord. 30

LUSSURIOSO So, give us leave. [*exit Hippolito*]
           Welcome, be not far off;
We must be better acquainted: pish, be bold
With us – thy hand.

VINDICE With all my heart, i'faith: how dost, sweet muskcat?
When shall we lie together?

LUSSURIOSO   Wondrous knave,
Gather him into boldness! 'Sfoot, the slave's
Already as familiar as an ague,
And shakes me at his pleasure. Friend, I can
Forget myself in private, but elsewhere
I pray do you remember me.   40

VINDICE O, very well, sir – I conster myself saucy.

LUSSURIOSO What hast been? Of what profession?

VINDICE A bone-setter.

LUSSURIOSO   A bone-setter!

VINDICE   A bawd, my lord –
One that sets bones together.

LUSSURIOSO   Notable bluntness!
Fit, fit for me; e'en trained up to my hand:

Thou hast been scrivener to much knavery, then?

VINDICE   'Sfoot, to abundance, sir: I have been witness
To the surrenders of a thousand virgins:
And not so little;
I have seen patrimonies washed a-pieces,   50
Fruit-fields turned into bastards,
And in a world of acres
Not so much dust due to the heir 'twas left to
As would well gravel a petition.

LUSSURIOSO [aside] Fine villain! Troth, I like him wondrously:
He's e'en shaped for my purpose. Then thou know'st
I'th'world strange lust?

VINDICE   O Dutch lust! Fulsome lust!
Drunken procreation! Which begets so many drunkards
Some fathers dread not (gone to bed in wine)
To slide from th'mother, and cling th'daughter-in-law;   60
Some uncles are adulterous with their nieces,
Brothers with brothers' wives. O hour of incest!
Any kin now, next to the rim o'th'sister,
Is men's meat in these days; and in the morning,
When they are up and dressed, and their mask on,
Who can perceive this, save that eternal eye
That sees through flesh and all? Well, if anything
                                                  be damned,
It will be twelve o'clock at night; that twelve
Will never 'scape;
It is the Judas of the hours, wherein   70
Honest salvation is betrayed to sin.

LUSSURIOSO In troth, it is true; but let this talk glide.
It is our blood to err, though hell gape wide.
Ladies know Lucifer fell, yet still are proud.
Now, sir, wert thou as secret as thou'rt subtle,
And deeply fathomed into all estates,
I would embrace thee for a near employment;
And thou shouldst swell in money, and be able
To make lame beggars crouch to thee.

VINDICE   My lord,
Secret! I ne'er had that disease o'the mother,   80
I praise my father: why are men made close,

But to keep thoughts in best? I grant you this,
Tell but some women a secret over night,
Your doctor may find it in the urinal i'the morning.
But, my lord –

LUSSURIOSO   So thou'rt confirmed in me,
And thus I enter thee. [*gives him money*]

VINDICE   This Indian devil
Will quickly enter any man but a usurer;
He prevents that by entering the devil first.

LUSSURIOSO Attend me. I am past my depth in lust,
And I must swim or drown. All my desires   90
Are levelled at a virgin not far from court,
To whom I have conveyed by messenger
Many waxed lines, full of my neatest spirit,
And jewels that were able to ravish her
Without the help of man; all which and more
She (foolish chaste) sent back, the messengers
Receiving frowns for answers.

VINDICE   Possible!
'Tis a rare Phoenix, whosoe'er she be.
If your desires be such, she so repugnant,
In troth, my lord, I'd be revenged and marry her.   100

LUSSURIOSO Pish! The dowry of her blood and of her fortunes
Are both too mean – good enough to be bad withal.
I am one of that number can defend
Marriage is good, yet rather keep a friend.
Give me my bed by stealth – there's true delight;
What breeds a loathing in't, but night by night!

VINDICE   A very fine religion!

LUSSURIOSO   Therefore thus
I'll trust thee in the business of my heart
Because I see thee well-experienced
In this luxurious day wherein we breathe.   110
Go thou, and with a smooth enchanting tongue
Bewitch her ears, and cozen her of all grace:
Enter upon the portion of her soul –
Her honour, which she calls her chastity –
And bring it into expense; for honesty
Is like a stock of money laid to sleep

          Which, ne'er so little broke, does never keep.

VINDICE   You have gi'en it the tang, i'faith, my lord:
          Make known the lady to me, and my brain
          Shall swell with strange invention: I will move it,   120
          Till I expire with speaking, and drop down
          Without a word to save me – but I'll work –

LUSSURIOSO   We thank thee, and will raise thee –
          Receive her name; it is the only daughter
          To Madam Gratiana, the late widow.

VINDICE   [aside] O my sister, my sister!

LUSSURIOSO   Why dost walk aside?

VINDICE   My lord, I was thinking how I might begin:
          As thus, O lady – or twenty hundred devices
          Her very bodkin will put a man in.

LUSSURIOSO   Ay, or the wagging of her hair.   130

VINDICE   No, that shall put you in, my lord.

LUSSURIOSO   Shall't? Why, content. Dost know the daughter then?

VINDICE   O, excellent well by sight.

LUSSURIOSO   That was her brother,
          That did prefer thee to us.

VINDICE   My lord, I think so;
          I knew I had seen him somewhere –

LUSSURIOSO   And therefore, prithee, let thy heart to him
          Be as a virgin close.

VINDICE   O my good lord.

LUSSURIOSO   We may laugh at that simple age within him.

VINDICE   Ha, ha, ha!

LUSSURIOSO   Himself being made the subtle instrument,   140
          To wind up a good fellow.

VINDICE   That's I, my lord.

LUSSURIOSO   That's thou,
          To entice and work his sister.

VINDICE   A pure novice!

LUSSURIOSO   'Twas finely managed.

VINDICE   Gallantly carried!
          A pretty perfumed villain!

LUSSURIOSO   I've bethought me,
          If she prove chaste still and immovable,
          Venture upon the mother; and with gifts,

As I will furnish thee, begin with her.

VINDICE   O, fie, fie! That's the wrong end, my lord.
'Tis mere impossible that a mother, by any gifts,   150
Should become a bawd to her own daughter!

LUSSURIOSO Nay, then, I see thou'rt but a puisne
In the subtle mystery of a woman.
Why, 'tis held now no dainty dish: the name
Is so in league with th'age, that nowadays
It does eclipse three quarters of a mother.

VINDICE   Does it so, my lord?
Let me alone, then, to eclipse the fourth.

LUSSURIOSO Why, well-said. Come, I'll furnish thee, but first
Swear to be true in all.

VINDICE   True!

LUSSURIOSO   Nay, but swear.   160

VINDICE   Swear? I hope your honour little doubts my faith.

LUSSURIOSO Yet, for my humour's sake, 'cause I love swearing –

VINDICE   'Cause you love swearing – 'slud, I will.

LUSSURIOSO   Why, enough!
Ere long look to be made of better stuff.

VINDICE   That will do well indeed, my lord.

LUSSURIOSO   Attend me.   [exit

VINDICE   O!
Now let me burst. I've eaten noble poison;
We are made strange fellows, brother, innocent villains!
Wilt not be angry when thou hear'st on't,
                              think'st thou?
I'faith, thou shalt: swear me to foul my sister!   170
Sword, I durst make a promise of him to thee:
Thou shalt disheir him; it shall be thine honour.
And yet, now angry froth is down in me,
It would not prove the meanest policy,
In this disguise, to try the faith of both.
Another might have had the selfsame office,
Some slave that would have wrought effectually,
Ay, and perhaps o'erwrought 'em; therefore I,
Being thought travelled, will apply myself
Unto the selfsame form, forget my nature,   180
As if no part about me were kin to 'em,

So touch 'em; – though I durst almost for good
Venture my lands in Heaven upon their blood.

[*exit*

SCENE 4

A room in Antonio's house

Enter ANTONIO, *whose* WIFE *the* DUCHESS'S YOUNGEST
SON *ravished, discovering her dead body to* HIPPOLITO,
PIERO, *and* LORDS

ANTONIO   Draw nearer, lords, and be sad witnesses
Of a fair comely building newly fallen,
Being falsely undermined. Violent rape
Has played a glorious act: behold, my lords,
A sight that strikes man out of me.

PIERO   That virtuous lady!

ANTONIO   Precedent for wives!

HIPPOLITO   The blush of many women, whose chaste presence
Would e'en call shame up to their cheeks, and make
Pale wanton sinners have good colours –

ANTONIO   Dead!

Her honour first drank poison, and her life,   10
Being fellows in one house, did pledge her honour.

PIERO   O, grief of many!

ANTONIO   I marked not this before –
A prayer-book, the pillow to her cheek –
This was her rich confection; and another
Placed in her right hand, with a leaf tucked up,
Pointing to these words –
Melius virtute mori, quam per dedecus vivere:
True and effectual it is indeed.

HIPPOLITO   My lord, since you invite us to your sorrows,
Let's truly taste 'em, that with equal comfort,   20
As to ourselves, we may relieve your wrongs:
We have grief too, that yet walks without tongue;
Curae leves loquuntur, majores stupent.

ANTONIO   You deal with truth, my lord;
               Lend me but your attentions, and I'll cut
               Long grief into short words. Last revelling night,
               When torch-light made an artificial noon
               About the court, some courtiers in the masque,
               Putting on better faces than their own,
               Being full of fraud and flattery – amongst whom   30
               The duchess' youngest son (that moth to honour) –
               Filled up a room, and with long lust to eat
               Into my warren, amongst all the ladies
               Singled out that dear form, who ever lived
               As cold in lust as she is now in death.
               Which that step-duchess' monster knew too well,
               And therefore in the height of all the revels,
               When music was heard loudest, courtiers busiest,
               And ladies great with laughter – O vicious minute!
               Unfit but for relation to be spoke of!   40
               Then with a face more impudent than his vizard,
               He harried her amidst a throng of panders,
               That live upon damnation of both kinds,
               And fed the ravenous vulture of his lust.
               O death to think on't! She, her honour forced,
               Deemed it a nobler dowry for her name
               To die with poison than to live with shame.

HIPPOLITO   A wondrous lady! Of rare fire compact;
               She has made her name an empress by that act.

PIERO   My lord, what judgment follows the offender?   50

ANTONIO   Faith, none, my lord; it cools, and is deferred.

PIERO   Delay the doom for rape!

ANTONIO   O, you must note who 'tis should die,
               The duchess' son! She'll look to be a saver:
               'Judgment, in this age, is near kin to favour.'

HIPPOLITO   Nay, then, step forth, thou bribeless officer:
               [draws his sword]
               I'll bind you all in steel, to bind you surely;
               Here let your oaths meet, to be kept and paid,
               Which else will stick like rust, and shame the blade;
               Strengthen my vow that if, at the next sitting,   60
               Judgment speak all in gold, and spare the blood

Of such a serpent, e'en before their seats
To let his soul out, which long since was found
Guilty in Heaven –

ALL   We swear it, and will act it.

ANTONIO   Kind gentlemen, I thank you in mine ire.

HIPPOLITO 'Twere pity
The ruins of so fair a monument
Should not be dipped in the defacer's blood.

PIERO   Her funeral shall be wealthy; for her name
Merits a tomb of pearl. My Lord Antonio,   70
For this time wipe your lady from your eyes;
No doubt our grief and yours may one day court it,
When we are more familiar with revenge.

ANTONIO   That is my comfort, gentlemen, and I joy
In this one happiness above the rest,
Which will be called a miracle at last;
That, being an old man, I'd a wife so chaste.

                                      [*exeunt*

ACT 2 SCENE I

A room in Gratiana's house

Enter CASTIZA

CASTIZA How hardly shall that maiden be beset,
Whose only fortunes are her constant thoughts!
That has no other child's part but her honour,
That keeps her low and empty in estate;
Maids and their honours are like poor beginners;
Were not sin rich, there would be fewer sinners.
Why had not virtue a revenue? Well,
I know the cause, 'twould have impoverished hell.

Enter DONDOLO

How now, Dondolo?

DONDOLO Madonna, there is one as they say, a thing of flesh and   10
blood – a man, I take him by his beard, that would
very desirously mouth to mouth with you.

CASTIZA What's that?

DONDOLO Show his teeth in your company.

CASTIZA I understand thee not.

DONDOLO Why, speak with you, madonna.

CASTIZA Why, say so, madman, and cut off a great deal
Of dirty way; had it not been better spoke
In ordinary words, that one would speak with me?

DONDOLO Ha, ha! That's as ordinary as two shillings. I would strive   20
a little to show myself in my place; a gentleman-usher
scorns to use the phrase and fancy of a serving- man.

CASTIZA Yours be your own, sir; go, direct him hither;

[*exit Dondolo*

I hope some happy tidings from my brother,
That lately travelled, whom my soul affects.
Here he comes.

Enter VINDICE, *disguised*

VINDICE Lady, the best of wishes to your sex –
Fair skins and new gowns.

CASTIZA   O, they shall thank you, sir.

	Whence this?	
VINDICE	O, from a dear and worthy mighty friend.	
CASTIZA	From whom?	30
VINDICE	The duke's son!	
CASTIZA	Receive that. [*boxes his ear*	

CASTIZA   I swore I would put anger in my hand,
And pass the virgin limits of my sex,
To him that next appeared in that base office,
To be his sin's attorney. Bear to him
That figure of my hate upon thy cheek,
Whilst 'tis yet hot, and I'll reward thee for't;
Tell him my honour shall have a rich name,
When several harlots shall share his with shame.   40
Farewell; commend me to him in my hate.   [*exit*

VINDICE   It is the sweetest box that e'er my nose came nigh;
The finest drawn-work cuff that e'er was worn;
I'll love this blow for ever, and this cheek
Shall still henceforward take the wall of this.
O, I'm above my tongue: most constant sister,
In this thou hast right honourable shown.
Many are called by their honour, that have none;
Thou art approved for ever in my thoughts.
It is not in the power of words to taint thee.   50
And yet for the salvation of my oath,
As my resolve in that point, I will lay
Hard siege unto my mother, though I know
A siren's tongue could not bewitch her so.
Mass, fitly here she comes! Thanks, my disguise –
Madam, good afternoon.

Enter GRATIANA

GRATIANA	Y'are welcome, sir.	
VINDICE	The next of Italy commends him to you,	
	Our mighty expectation, the duke's son.	
GRATIANA	I think myself much honoured that he pleases	
	To rank me in his thoughts.	
VINDICE	So may you, lady:	60
	One that is like to be our sudden duke;	
	The crown gapes for him every tide, and then	

Commander o'er us all; do but think on him,
How bless'd were they now that could pleasure him –
E'en with anything almost!

GRATIANA   Ay, save their honour.

VINDICE   Tut, one would let a little of that go too,
And ne'er be seen in't – ne'er be seen in't, mark you;
I'd wink, and let it go.

GRATIANA   Marry, but I would not.

VINDICE   Marry but I would, I hope; I know you would too,
If you'd that blood now, which you gave
                                   your daughter.   70
To her indeed 'tis this wheel comes about;
That man that must be all this, perhaps ere morning
(For his white father does but mould away),
Has long desired your daughter.

GRATIANA   Desired?

VINDICE   Nay, but hear me; he desires now,
That will command hereafter: therefore be wise.
I speak as more a friend to you than him:
Madam, I know you're poor, and, 'lack the day!
There are too many poor ladies already;
Why should you wax the number? 'Tis despised.   80
Live wealthy, rightly understand the world,
And chide away that foolish country girl
Keeps company with your daughter – Chastity.

GRATIANA   O fie, fie! The riches of the world cannot hire
A mother to such a most unnatural task.

VINDICE   No, but a thousand angels can.
Men have no power, angels must work you to't:
The world descends into such baseborn evils,
That forty angels can make fourscore devils.
There will be fools still, I perceive – still fools.   90
Would I be poor, dejected, scorned of greatness,
Swept from the palace, and see others' daughters
Spring with the dew o'the court, having mine own
So much desired and loved by the duke's son?
No, I would raise my state upon her breast,
And call her eyes my tenants; I would count
My yearly maintenance upon her cheeks,

Take coach upon her lip, and all her parts
Should keep men after men, and I would ride
In pleasure upon pleasure.   100
You took great pains for her, once when it was;
Let her requite it now, though it be but some.
You brought her forth: she may well bring you home.

GRATIANA   O Heavens! This o'ercomes me!

VINDICE   [aside]   Not, I hope, already?

GRATIANA   It is too strong for me; men know that know us,
We are so weak their words can overthrow us;
[aside] He touched me nearly, made my virtues bate,
When his tongue struck upon my poor estate.

VINDICE   [aside] I e'en quake to proceed, my spirit turns edge.
I fear me she's unmothered; yet I'll venture.   110
'That woman is all male, whom none can enter.'
What think you now, lady? Speak, are you wiser?
What said advancement to you? Thus it said:
The daughter's fall lifts up the mother's head.
Did it not, madam? But I'll swear it does
In many places: tut, this age fears no man.
''Tis no shame to be bad, because 'tis common.'

GRATIANA   Ay, that's the comfort on't.

VINDICE   The comfort on't!
I keep the best for last – can these persuade you
To forget Heaven, and – [gives her money]

GRATIANA   Ay, these are they –

VINDICE   O!   120

GRATIANA   That enchant our sex. These are the means
That govern our affections – that woman
Will not be troubled with the mother long,
That sees the comfortable shine of you:
I blush to think what for your sakes I'll do.

VINDICE   [aside] O suffering Heaven, with thy invisible finger,
E'en at this instant turn the precious side
Of both mine eyeballs inward, not to see
Myself.

GRATIANA   Look you, sir.

VINDICE   Hollo.

GRATIANA	Let this thank your pains.	
VINDICE	O, you're kind, madam.	130
GRATIANA	I'll see how I can move.	
VINDICE	Your words will sting.	
GRATIANA	If she be still chaste, I'll ne'er call her mine.	
VINDICE	Spoke truer than you meant it.	
GRATIANA	Daughter Castiza.	

Re-enter CASTIZA

CASTIZA   Madam.
VINDICE   O, she's yonder;
Meet her: troops of celestial soldiers guard her heart.
Yon dam has devils enough to take her part.
CASTIZA   Madam, what makes yon evil-officed man
In presence of you?
GRATIANA   Why?
CASTIZA   He lately brought
Immodest writing sent from the duke's son,
To tempt me to dishonourable act.   140
GRATIANA   Dishonourable act! Good honourable fool,
That wouldst be honest, 'cause thou wouldst be so,
Producing no one reason but thy will.
And't has a good report, prettily commended,
But pray, by whom? Poor people, ignorant people;
The better sort, I'm sure, cannot abide it.
And by what rule should we square out our lives,
But by our betters' actions? O, if thou knew'st
What 'twere to lose it, thou wouldst never keep it!
But there's a cold curse laid upon all maids,   150
Whilst others clip the sun, they clasp the shades.
Virginity is paradise locked up.
You cannot come by yourselves without fee,
And 'twas decreed that man should keep the key!
Deny advancement! Treasure! The duke's son!
CASTIZA   I cry you mercy! Lady! I mistook you!
Pray did you see my mother? Which way went you?
Pray God, I have not lost her.
VINDICE   [*aside*]   Prettily put by!
GRATIANA   Are you as proud to me, as coy to him?

Do you not know me now?

CASTIZA   Why, are you she?   160
The world's so changed one shape into another,
It is a wise child now that knows her mother.

VINDICE   [*aside*] Most right, i'faith.

GRATIANA   I owe your cheek my hand
For that presumption now; but I'll forget it.
Come, you shall leave those childish 'haviours,
And understand your time. Fortunes flow to you;
What, will you be a girl?
If all feared drowning that spy waves ashore,
Gold would grow rich, and all the merchants poor.

CASTIZA   It is a pretty saying of a wicked one;   170
But methinks now it does not show so well
Out of your mouth – better in his!

VINDICE   [*aside*] Faith, bad enough in both,
Were I in earnest, as I'll seem no less.
I wonder, lady, your own mother's words
Cannot be taken, nor stand in full force.
'Tis honesty you urge; what's honesty?
'Tis but Heaven's beggar; and what woman is
So foolish to keep honesty,
And be not able to keep herself? No,   180
Times are grown wiser, and will keep less charge.
A maid that has small portion now intends
To break up house, and live upon her friends;
How blessed are you! You have happiness alone;
Others must fall to thousands, you to one,
Sufficient in himself to make your forehead
Dazzle the world with jewels, and petitionary people
Start at your presence.

GRATIANA   O, if I were young, I should be ravished.

CASTIZA   Ay, to lose your honour!   190

VINDICE   'Slid, how can you lose your honour
To deal with my lord's grace?
He'll add more honour to it by his title;
Your mother will tell you how.

GRATIANA   That I will.

VINDICE   O, think upon the pleasure of the palace!

Securéd ease and state! The stirring meats,
Ready to move out of the dishes, that e'en now
Quicken when they are eaten!
Banquets abroad by torchlight! Music! Sports!
Bareheaded vassals, that had ne'er the fortune   200
To keep on their own hats, but let horns wear 'em!
Nine coaches waiting — hurry, hurry, hurry —

CASTIZA   Ay, to the devil.

VINDICE   [aside] Ay, to the devil! [aloud] To the duke, by
                                                    my faith.

GRATIANA   Ay, to the duke: daughter, you'd scorn to think
               O'the devil, an you were there once.

VINDICE   [aside]   True, for most
               There are as proud as he for his heart, i'faith.
               Who'd sit at home in a neglected room,
               Dealing her short-lived beauty to the pictures,
               That are as useless as old men, when those   210
               Poorer in face and fortune than herself
               Walk with a hundred acres on their backs,
               Fair meadows cut into green foreparts? O,
               It was the greatest blessing ever happened to woman
               When farmers' sons agreed and met again,
               To wash their hands, and come up gentlemen!
               The commonwealth has flourished ever since:
               Lands that were mete by the rod, that labour's spared:
               Tailors ride down, and measure 'em by the yard.
               Fair trees, those comely foretops of the field,   220
               Are cut to maintain head-tires — much untold.
               All thrives but Chastity; she lies a-cold.
               Nay, shall I come nearer to you? Mark but this:
               Why are there so few honest women, but because 'tis
               the poorer profession? That's accounted best that's
               best followed; least in trade, least in fashion; and that's
               not honesty, believe it; and do but note the love and
               dejected price of it.
               Lose but a pearl, we search, and cannot brook it:
               But that once gone, who is so mad to look it?   230

GRATIANA   Troth, he says true.

CASTIZA   False! I defy you both:

I have endured you with an ear of fire;
Your tongues have struck hot irons on my face.
Mother, come from that poisonous woman there.

GRATIANA Where?

CASTIZA   Do you not see her? She's too inward, then!
Slave, perish in thy office! You Heavens, please
Henceforth to make the mother a disease,
Which first begins with me: yet I've outgone you.

                                                        [exit

VINDICE [aside] O angels, clap your wings upon the skies,   240
And give this virgin crystal plaudites!

GRATIANA Peevish, coy, foolish! But return this answer:
My lord shall be most welcome, when his pleasure
Conducts him this way. I will sway mine own.
Women with women can work best alone.   [exit

VINDICE Indeed, I'll tell him so.
O, more uncivil, more unnatural
Than those base-titled creatures that look downward;
Why does not Heaven turn black, or with a frown
Undo the world? Why does not earth start up,   250
And strike the sins that tread upon it? O,
Were't not for gold and women, there would be
                                        no damnation.
Hell would look like a lord's great kitchen
                                        without fire in't.
But 'twas decreed, before the world began,
That they should be the hooks to catch at man.

                                                        [exit

SCENE 2

An apartment in the Duke's palace

Enter LUSSURIOSO, *with* HIPPOLITO

LUSSURIOSO I much applaud
                    Thy judgment; thou art well-read in a fellow
                    And 'tis the deepest art to study man.
                    I know this, which I never learnt in schools,
                    The world's divided into knaves and fools.

HIPPOLITO [*aside*] Knave in your face, my lord — behind
                                                    your back —

LUSSURIOSO And I much thank thee, that thou hast preferred
                    A fellow of discourse, well-mingled,
                    And whose brain time hath seasoned.

HIPPOLITO   True, my lord,
                    We shall find season once, I hope. [*aside*] O villain!   10
                    To make such an unnatural slave of me — but —

LUSSURIOSO Mass, here he comes.

HIPPOLITO [*aside*] And now shall I have free leave to depart.

LUSSURIOSO Your absence, leave us.

HIPPOLITO [*aside*]   Are not my thoughts true?
                    I must remove; but, brother, you may stay.
                    Heart, we are both made bawds a new-found way!
                                                                    [*exit*

Enter VINDICE, *disguised*

LUSSURIOSO Now we're an even number, a third man's dangerous,
                    Especially her brother; say, be free,
                    Have I a pleasure toward —

VINDICE   O my lord!

LUSSURIOSO Ravish me in thine answer; art thou rare?   20
                    Hast thou beguiled her of salvation,
                    And rubbed hell o'er with honey? Is she a woman?

VINDICE   In all but in desire.

LUSSURIOSO   Then she's in nothing —
                    I bate in courage now.

VINDICE   The words I brought

     Might well have made indifferent honest naught.
     A right good woman in these days is changed
     Into white money with less labour far;
     Many a maid has turned to Mahomet
     With easier working: I durst undertake,
     Upon the pawn and forfeit of my life,   30
     With half those words to flat a Puritan's wife.
     But she is close and good; yet 'tis a doubt
     By this time – O, the mother, the mother!

LUSSURIOSO I never thought their sex had been a wonder,
     Until this minute. What fruit from the mother?

VINDICE [aside] How must I blister my soul, be forsworn,
     Or shame the woman that received me first!
     I will be true: thou liv'st not to proclaim.
     Spoke to a dying man, shame has no shame.
     My lord.

LUSSURIOSO   Who's that?

VINDICE   Here's none but I, my lord.   40

LUSSURIOSO What would thy haste utter?

VINDICE   Comfort.

LUSSURIOSO   Welcome.

VINDICE The maid being dull, having no mind to travel
     Into unknown lands, what did I straight
     But set spurs to the mother? Golden spurs
     Will put her to a false gallop in a trice.

LUSSURIOSO Is't possible that in this
     The mother should be damned before the daughter?

VINDICE O, that's good manners, my lord; the mother for
     Her age must go foremost, you know.

LUSSURIOSO Thou'st spoke that true! But where comes in
               this comfort?   50

VINDICE In a fine place, my lord – the unnatural mother
     Did with her tongue so hard beset her honour,
     That the poor fool was struck to silent wonder;
     Yet still the maid, like an unlighted taper,
     Was cold and chaste, save that her mother's breath
     Did blow fire on her cheeks. The girl departed;
     But the good ancient madam, half mad, threw me
     These promising words, which I took deeply note of:

'My lord shall be most welcome –

LUSSURIOSO   Faith, I thank her.

VINDICE   'When his pleasure conducts him this way' –   60

LUSSURIOSO That shall be soon, i'faith.

VINDICE   'I will sway mine own –

LUSSURIOSO She does the wiser: I commend her for't.

VINDICE   'Women with women can work best alone.'

LUSSURIOSO By this light, and so they can; give 'em
             Their due, men are not comparable to 'em.

VINDICE   No, that's true; for you shall have one woman
             Knit more in an hour than any man can
             Ravel again in seven-and-twenty year.

LUSSURIOSO Now my desires are happy; I'll make 'em freemen now.
             Thou art a precious fellow; faith, I love thee;   70
             Be wise and make it thy revenue; beg, beg;
             What office couldst thou be ambitious for?

VINDICE   Office, my lord! Marry, if I might have my wish,
             I would have one that was never begged yet.

LUSSURIOSO Nay, then, thou canst have none.

VINDICE   Yes, my lord, I could pick out another office
             Yet; nay, and keep a horse and drab upon't.

LUSSURIOSO Prithee, good bluntness, tell me.

VINDICE   Why, I would desire,
             But this, my lord – to have all the fees behind
             The arras, and all the farthingales that fall   80
             Plump about twelve o'clock at night upon
             The rushes.

LUSSURIOSO   Thou'rt a mad, apprehensive knave;
             Dost think to make any great purchase of that?

VINDICE   O, 'tis an unknown thing, my lord; I wonder't
             Has been missed so long.

LUSSURIOSO Well, this night I'll visit her, and 'tis till then
             A year in my desires – farewell, attend,
             Trust me with thy preferment.

VINDICE   My loved lord! [exit Lussurioso
             O, shall I kill him o'th'wrong side now?
             No! Sword, thou wast never a backbiter yet.
             I'll pierce him to his face; he shall die looking upon me.   90
             Thy veins are swelled with lust, this shall unfill 'em.

Great men were gods, if beggars could not kill 'em.
Forgive me, Heaven, to call my mother wicked!
O, lessen not my days upon the earth,
I cannot honour her. By this, I fear me,
Her tongue has turned my sister unto use.
I was a villain not to be forsworn
To this our lecherous hope, the duke's son;
For lawyers, merchants, some divines, and all,
Count beneficial perjury a sin small.   100
It shall go hard yet, but I'll guard her honour,
And keep the ports sure.

                     [*exit*

SCENE 3

A corridor in the palace

Enter VINDICE, *still disguised, and* HIPPOLITO

HIPPOLITO   Brother, how goes the world? I would know news
Of you. But I have news to tell you.
VINDICE   What, in the name of knavery?
HIPPOLITO   Knavery, faith;
This vicious old duke is worthily abused;
The pen of his bastard writes him cuckold.
VINDICE   His bastard?
HIPPOLITO   Pray, believe it; he and the duchess
By night meet in their linen; they have been seen
By stair-foot panders.
VINDICE   O, sin foul and deep!
Great faults are winked at when the duke's asleep.
See, see, here comes the Spurio.
HIPPOLITO   Monstrous luxur!   10
VINDICE   Unbraced! Two of his valiant bawds with him!
O, there's a wicked whisper; hell's in his ear.
Stay, let's observe his passage –

             Enter SPURIO *and Servants*

SPURIO   O, but are you sure on't?
I SERVANT   My lord, most sure on't; for 'twas spoke by one

	That is most inward with the duke's son's lust,
	That he intends within this hour to steal
	Unto Hippolito's sister, whose chaste life
	The mother has corrupted for his use.
SPURIO	Sweet word! Sweet occasion! Faith, then, brother,
	I'll disinherit you in as short time 20
	As I was when I was begot in haste.
	I'll damn you at your pleasure: precious deed!
	After your lust, O, 'twill be fine to bleed.
	Come, let our passing out be soft and wary.

[exeunt Spurio and Servants

VINDICE   Mark! There; there; that step; now to the duchess!
This their second meeting writes the duke cuckold
With new additions – his horns newly revived.
Night! Thou that look'st like funeral heralds' fees
Torn down betimes i'the morning, thou hang'st fitly
To grace those sins that have no grace at all.   30
Now 'tis full sea abed over the world:
There's juggling of all sides; some that were maids
E'en at sunset, are now perhaps i'the toll-book.
This woman in immodest thin apparel
Lets in her friend by water; here a dame
Cunning nails leather hinges to a door,
To avoid proclamation. Now cuckolds
Are coining, apace, apace, apace, apace!
And careful sisters spin that thread i'the night,
That does maintain them and their bawds i'the day.   40

HIPPOLITO   You flow well, brother.

VINDICE   Pooh! I'm shallow yet;
Too sparing and too modest; shall I tell thee?
If every trick were told that's dealt by night,
There are few here that would not blush outright.

HIPPOLITO   I am of that belief too. Who's this comes?

VINDICE   The duke's son up so late? Brother, fall back,
And you shall learn some mischief. My good lord!

Enter LUSSURIOSO

LUSSURIOSO   Piato! Why, the man I wished for! Come,
I do embrace this season for the fittest

To taste of that young lady.
VINDICE   [aside]   Heart and hell.   50
HIPPOLITO [aside] Damned villain!
VINDICE   [aside] I have no way now to cross it, but to kill him.
LUSSURIOSO Come, only thou and I.
VINDICE   My lord! My lord!
LUSSURIOSO Why dost thou start us?
VINDICE   I'd almost forgot –
            The bastard!
LUSSURIOSO   What of him?
VINDICE   This night, this hour,
            This minute, now –
LUSSURIOSO   What? What?
VINDICE   Shadows the duchess –
LUSSURIOSO Horrible word!
VINDICE   And (like strong poison) eats
            Into the duke your father's forehead.
LUSSURIOSO   O!
VINDICE   He makes horn-royal.
LUSSURIOSO   Most ignoble slave!
VINDICE   This is the fruit of two beds.
LUSSURIOSO   I am mad.   60
VINDICE   That passage he trod warily.
LUSSURIOSO   He did?
VINDICE   And hushed his villains every step he took.
LUSSURIOSO His villains! I'll confound them.
VINDICE   Take 'em finely – finely, now.
LUSSURIOSO The duchess' chamber-door shall not control me.
                              [exeunt Lussurioso and Vindice
HIPPOLITO Good, happy, swift: there's gunpowder i'the court,
            Wildfire at midnight. In this heedless fury
            He may show violence to cross himself.
            I'll follow the event.
                                                    [exit

SCENE 4

The Duke's bedchamber – the DUKE *and* DUCHESS *in bed*

Enter LUSSURIOSO *and* VINDICE, *disguised*

LUSSURIOSO Where is that villain?

VINDICE   Softly, my lord, and you may take 'em twisted.

LUSSURIOSO I care not how.

VINDICE   O! 'Twill be glorious
            To kill 'em doubled, when they're heaped. Be
                                          soft, my lord.

LUSSURIOSO Away!
            My spleen is not so lazy: thus and thus
            I'll shake their eyelids ope, and with my sword
            Shut 'em again for ever. Villain! Strumpet!

DUKE   You upper guard, defend us!

DUCHESS   Treason! Treason!

DUKE   O, take me not in sleep!   10
            I have great sins; I must have days,
            Nay, months, dear son, with penitential heaves,
            To lift 'em out, and not to die unclear.
            O, thou wilt kill me both in Heaven and here.

LUSSURIOSO I am amazed to death.

DUKE   Nay, villain, traitor,
            Worse than the foulest epithet; now I'll
            Gripe thee e'en with the nerves of wrath, and throw
            Thy head amongst the lawyers – Guard!

Enter AMBITIOSO, SUPERVACUO, *and Lords*

I LORD   How comes the quiet of your grace disturbed?

DUKE   This boy, that should be myself after me,   20
            Would be myself before me; and in heat
            Of that ambition bloodily rushed in,
            Intending to depose me in my bed.

2 LORD   Duty and natural loyalty forfend!

DUCHESS   He called his father villain, and me strumpet,
            A word that I abhor to file my lips with.

AMBITIOSO That was not so well done, brother.

LUSSURIOSO [aside]   I am abused —
     I know there's no excuse can do me good.

VINDICE   [aside] 'Tis now good policy to be from sight;
     His vicious purpose to our sister's honour   30
     I crossed beyond our thought.

HIPPOLITO   You little dreamt
     His father slept here.

VINDICE   O, 'twas far beyond me:
     But since it fell so — without frightful words —
     Would he had killed him, 'twould have eased
                               our swords.

DUKE   Be comforted, our duchess, he shall die.

                         [exeunt Vindice and Hippolito

LUSSURIOSO Where's this slave-pander now? Out of mine eye,
     Guilty of this abuse.

                 Enter SPURIO with *Servants*

SPURIO   Y'are villains, fablers!
     You have knaves' chins and harlots' tongues; you lie;
     And I will damn you with one meal a day.

1 SERVANT O good my lord!

SPURIO   'Sblood, you shall never sup.   40

2 SERVANT O, I beseech you, sir!

SPURIO   To let my sword
     Catch cold so long, and miss him!

1 SERVANT   Troth, my lord,
     'Twas his intent to meet there.

SPURIO   Heart! He's yonder.
     Ha, what news here? Is the day out o'the socket,
     That it is noon at midnight? The court up?
     How comes the guard so saucy with his elbows?

LUSSURIOSO The bastard here?
     Nay, then the truth of my intent shall out;
     My lord and father hear me.

DUKE   Bear him hence.

LUSSURIOSO I can with loyalty excuse.   50

DUKE   Excuse? To prison with the villain!
     Death shall not long lag after him.

SPURIO   Good, i'faith: then 'tis not much amiss.

LUSSURIOSO Brothers, my best release lies on your tongues;
            I pray, persuade for me.

AMBITIOSO   It is our duties; make yourself sure of us.

SUPERVACU. We'll sweat in pleading.

LUSSURIOSO   And I may live to thank you.
                                        [exit with Lords

AMBITIOSO   No, thy death shall thank me better.

SPURIO   He's gone; I'll after him,
            And know his trespass; seem to bear a part   60
            In all his ills, but with a puritan heart.
                                        [exit with Servants

AMBITIOSO   Now, brother, let our hate and love be woven
            So subtly together, that in speaking one word
            For his life, we may make three for his death:
            The craftiest pleader gets most gold for breath.

SUPERVACU. Set on, I'll not be far behind you, brother.

DUKE   Is't possible a son
            Should be disobedient as far as the sword?
            It is the highest: he can go no farther.

AMBITIOSO   My gracious lord, take pity –

DUKE   Pity, boys!   70

AMBITIOSO   Nay, we'd be loth to move your grace too much;
            We know the trespass is unpardonable,
            Black, wicked, and unnatural.

SUPERVACU.   In a son!
            O, monstrous!

AMBITIOSO   Yet, my lord, a duke's soft hand
            Strokes the rough head of law, and makes it
                                        lie smooth.

DUKE   But my hand shall ne'er do't.

AMBITIOSO   That as you please, my lord.

SUPERVACU.   We must needs confess.
            Some fathers would have entered into hate
            So deadly-pointed, that before his eyes
            He would ha' seen the execution sound   80
            Without corrupted favour.

AMBITIOSO   But, my lord,
            Your grace may live the wonder of all times,

In pardoning that offence, which never yet
Had face to beg a pardon.

DUKE   Hunny, how's this?

AMBITIOSO Forgive him, good my lord; he's your own son:
And I must needs say, 'twas the viler done.

SUPERVACU. He's the next heir: yet this true reason gathers,
None can possess that dispossess their fathers.
Be merciful!

DUKE   Here's no step-mother's wit;
[aside] I'll try them both upon their love and hate.   90

AMBITIOSO Be merciful – although –

DUKE   You have prevailed.
My wrath, like flaming wax, hath spent itself;
I know 'twas but some peevish moon in him;
Go, let him be released.

SUPERVACU. [aside]   'Sfoot, how now, brother?

AMBITIOSO Your grace doth please to speak beside your spleen;
I would it were so happy.

DUKE   Why, go, release him.

SUPERVACU. O my good lord! I know the fault's too weighty
And full of general loathing: too inhuman,
Rather by all men's voices worthy death.

DUKE   'Tis true too; here, then, receive this signet.   100
Doom shall pass;
Direct it to the judges; he shall die
Ere many days. Make haste.

AMBITIOSO   All speed that may be.
We could have wished his burden not so sore:
We knew your grace did but delay before.
                         [exeunt Ambitioso and Supervacuo

DUKE   Here's envy with a poor thin cover o'er't,
Like scarlet hid in lawn, easily spied through.
This their ambition by the mother's side
Is dangerous, and for safety must be purged.
I will prevent their envies; sure it was   110
But some mistaken fury in our son,
Which these aspiring boys would climb upon:
He shall be released suddenly.

Enter Nobles

I NOBLE	Good morning to your grace.
DUKE	Welcome, my lords.
2 NOBLE	Our knees shall take

        Away the office of our feet for ever,
        Unless your grace bestow a father's eye
        Upon the clouded fortunes of your son,
        And in compassionate virtue grant him that
        Which makes e'en mean men happy – liberty.   120

DUKE   How seriously their loves and honours woo
        For that which I am about to pray them do!
        Arise, my lord; your knees sign his release.
        We freely pardon him.

I NOBLE We owe your grace much thanks, and he much duty.

                          [exeunt Nobles

DUKE   It well becomes that judge to nod at crimes
        That does commit greater himself, and lives.
        I may forgive a disobedient error,
        That expect pardon for adultery,
        And in my old days am a youth in lust.   130
        Many a beauty have I turned to poison
        In the denial, covetous of all.
        Age hot is like a monster to be seen;
        My hairs are white, and yet my sins are green.

ACT 3 SCENE I

A room in the palace

Enter AMBITIOSO *and* SUPERVACUO

SUPERVACU. Brother, let my opinion sway you once;
            I speak it for the best, to have him die
            Surest and soonest; if the signet come
            Unto the judge's hand, why then his doom
            Will be deferred till sittings and court-days,
            Juries, and further. Faiths are bought and sold;
            Oaths in these days are but the skin of gold.

AMBITIOSO In troth, 'tis true too.

SUPERVACU.   Then let's set by the judges,
            And fall to the officers; 'tis but mistaking
            The duke our father's meaning; and where he named   10
            'Ere many days' – 'tis but forgetting that,
            And have him die i'the morning.

AMBITIOSO   Excellent!
            Then am I heir! Duke in a minute!

SUPERVACU. [*aside*]   Nay,
            An he were once puffed out, here is a pin
            Should quickly prick your bladder.

AMBITIOSO   Blessed occasion!
            He being packed we'll have some trick and wile
            To wind our younger brother out of prison,
            That lies in for the rape. The lady's dead,
            And people's thoughts will soon be buried.

SUPERVACU. We may with safety do't, and live and feed;   20
            The duchess' sons are too proud to bleed.

AMBITIOSO We are, i'faith, to say true – come, let's not linger:
            I'll to the officers; go you before,
            And set an edge upon the executioner.

SUPERVACU. Let me alone to grind him.   [*exit*

AMBITIOSO   Meet farewell!
            I am next now; I rise just in that place
            Where thou'rt cut off – upon thy neck, kind brother;
            The falling of one head lifts up another.   [*exit*

SCENE 2

The courtyard of a prison

Enter LUSSURIOSO *with Nobles*

LUSSURIOSO My lords, I am so much indebted to your loves
For this, O, this delivery –

1 NOBLE   Put your
Duties, my lord, unto the hopes that grow in you.

LUSSURIOSO If e'er I live to be myself, I'll thank you.
O liberty, thou sweet and heavenly dame!
But hell for prison is too mild a name.   *[exeunt*

Enter AMBITIOSO *and* SUPERVACUO, *with Officers*

AMBITIOSO Officers, here's the duke's signet, your firm warrant,
Brings the command of present death along with it
Unto our brother, the duke's son; we are sorry
That we are so unnaturally employed   10
In such an unkind office, fitter far
For enemies than brothers.

SUPERVACU.   But, you know,
The duke's command must be obeyed.

1 OFFICER It must and shall, my lord. This morning, then –
So suddenly?

AMBITIOSO   Ay, alas! Poor, good soul!
He must breakfast betimes; the executioner
Stands ready to put forth his cowardly valour.

2 OFFICER Already?

SUPERVACU. Already, i'faith. O sir, destruction hies,
And that is least imprudent, soonest dies.   20

1 OFFICER Troth, you say true. My lord, we take our leaves:
Our office shall be sound; we'll not delay
The third part of a minute.

AMBITIOSO   Therein you show
Yourselves good men and upright. Officers,
Pray, let him die as private as he may;
Do him that favour; for the gaping people
Will but trouble him at his prayers, and make

Him curse and swear, and so die black. Will you
Be so far kind?

1 OFFICER   It shall be done, my lord.

AMBITIOSO   Why, we do thank you; if we live to be –   30
You shall have a better office.

2 OFFICER   Your good lordship –

SUPERVACU.   Commend us to the scaffold in our tears.

1 OFFICER   We'll weep, and do your commendations.

AMBITIOSO   Fine fools in office!   [*exeunt Officers*

SUPERVACU.   Things fall out so fit!

AMBITIOSO   So happily! Come, brother! Ere next clock,
His head will be made serve a bigger block.

                                        [*exeunt*

SCENE 3

Inside a prison

Enter the DUCHESS'S YOUNGEST SON *and Keeper*

YOUNGEST   Keeper!

KEEPER   My lord.

YOUNGEST   No news lately from our brothers?
Are they unmindful of us?

KEEPER   My lord, a messenger came newly in,
And brought this from 'em.

YOUNGEST   Nothing but paper-comforts?
I looked for my delivery before this,
Had they been worth their oaths. Prithee, be from us.

                                        [*exit Keeper*

Now what say you, forsooth? Speak out, I pray.
[*reads the letter*] 'Brother, be of good cheer';
'Slud, it begins like a whore with good cheer.   10
'Thou shalt not be long a prisoner.' Not six
And thirty years, like a bankrupt – I think so.
'We have thought upon a device to get thee out by a
trick.' By a trick! Pox o'your trick, an it be so long a
playing. 'And so rest comforted, be merry, and expect
it suddenly!' Be merry! Hang merry, draw and quarter
merry; I'll be mad. Is't not strange that a man should

lie-in a whole month for a woman? Well, we shall see
how sudden our brothers will be in their promise. I
must expect still a trick: I shall not be long a prisoner. 20
How now, what news?

Re-enter Keeper

KEEPER   Bad news, my lord; I am discharged of you.
YOUNGEST   Slave! Call'st thou that bad news? I thank you, brothers.
KEEPER   My lord, 'twill prove so. Here come the officers,
Into whose hands I must commit you.
YOUNGEST   Ha!
Officers! What? Why?

Enter Officers

1 OFFICER   You must pardon us, my lord:
Our office must be sound: here is our warrant,
The signet from the duke; you must straight suffer.
YOUNGEST   Suffer! I'll suffer you to begone; I'll suffer you
To come no more; what would you have me suffer? 30
2 OFFICER   My lord, those words were better changed to prayers.
The time's but brief with you: prepare to die.
YOUNGEST   Sure, 'tis not so!
3 OFFICER   It is too true, my lord.
YOUNGEST   I tell you 'tis not; for the duke my father
Deferred me till next sitting; and I look,
E'en every minute, threescore times an hour,
For a release, a trick wrought by my brothers.
1 OFFICER   A trick, my lord! If you expect such comfort,
Your hope's as fruitless as a barren woman:
Your brothers were the unhappy messengers   40
That brought this powerful token for your death.
YOUNGEST   My brothers? No, no.
2 OFFICER   'Tis most true, my lord.
YOUNGEST   My brothers to bring a warrant for my death!
How strange this shows!
3 OFFICER   There's no delaying time.
YOUNGEST   Desire 'em hither: call 'em up – my brothers!
They shall deny it to your faces.
1 OFFICER   My lord,
They're far enough by this, at least at court;

And this most strict command they left behind 'em.
When grief swam in their eyes, they showed
like brothers,
Brimful of heavy sorrow – but the duke   50
'Must have his pleasure'.

YOUNGEST His pleasure!

I OFFICER These were the last words, which my memory bears,
'Commend us to the scaffold in our tears.'

YOUNGEST Pox dry their tears! What should I do with tears?
I hate 'em worse than any citizen's son
Can hate salt water. Here came a letter now,
New-bleeding from their pens, scarce stinted yet:
Would I'd been torn in pieces when I tore it:
Look, you officious whoresons, words of comfort,   60
'Not long a prisoner.'

I OFFICER It says true in that, sir; for you must suffer presently.

YOUNGEST A villainous Duns upon the letter! Knavish exposition!
Look, you then here, sir: 'we'll get thee out by a trick,'
says he.

2 OFFICER That may hold too, sir; for you know a trick is commonly four cards, which was meant by us four
officers.

YOUNGEST Worse and worse dealing.

I OFFICER   The hour beckons us.
The headsman waits: lift up your eyes to Heaven.   70

YOUNGEST I thank you, faith; good pretty wholesome counsel!
I should look up to Heaven, as you said,
Whilst he behind me cozens me of my head.
Ay, that's the trick.

3 OFFICER   You delay too long, my lord.

YOUNGEST Stay, good authority's bastards; since I must,
Through brothers' perjury, die, O let me venom
Their souls with curses.

3 OFFICER   Come, 'tis no time to curse.

YOUNGEST Must I bleed then without respect of sign?
Well –
My fault was sweet sport which the world approves,   80
I die for that which every woman loves.
[exeunt

SCENE 4

A lodge in the ducal grounds

Enter VINDICE, *disguised, and* HIPPOLITO

VINDICE   O, sweet, delectable, rare, happy, ravishing!

HIPPOLITO   Why, what's the matter, brother?

VINDICE   O, 'tis able
            To make a man spring up and knock his forehead
            Against yon silver ceiling.

HIPPOLITO   Prithee, tell me;
            Why may not I partake with you? You vowed once
            To give me share to every tragic thought.

VINDICE   By the mass, I think I did too;
            Then I'll divide it to thee. The old duke,
            Thinking my outward shape and inward heart
            Are cut out of one piece (for he that prates   10
            His secrets, his heart stands o'the outside),
            Hires me by price to greet him with a lady –
            In some fit place, veiled from the eyes o'the court,
            Some darkened, blushless angle, that is guilty
            Of his forefather's lust and great folks' riots;
            To which I easily (to maintain my shape)
            Consented, and did wish his impudent grace
            To meet her here in this unsunnéd lodge,
            Wherein 'tis night at noon; and here the rather
            Because, unto the torturing of his soul,   20
            The bastard and the duchess have appointed
            Their meeting too in this luxurious circle;
            Which most afflicting sight will kill his eyes,
            Before we kill the rest of him.

HIPPOLITO   'Twill, i'faith! Most dreadfully digested!
            I see not how you could have missed me, brother.

VINDICE   True; but the violence of my joy forgot it.

HIPPOLITO   Ay, but where's that lady now?

VINDICE   O! At that word
            I'm lost again; you cannot find me yet:

I'm in a throng of happy apprehensions.   30
He's suited for a lady; I have took care
For a delicious lip, a sparkling eye –
You shall be witness, brother:
Be ready; stand with your hat off.   [*exit*

HIPPOLITO Troth, I wonder what lady it should be!
Yet 'tis no wonder, now I think again,
To have a lady stoop to a duke, that stoops
Unto his men.
'Tis common to be common through the world:
And there's more private common shadowing vices,   40
Than those who are known both by their names
                                and prices.
'Tis part of my allegiance to stand bare
To the duke's concubine; and here she comes.

Re-enter VINDICE, *with the skull of his betrothed dressed up in tires*

VINDICE Madam, his grace will not be absent long.
Secret! Ne'er doubt us, madam; 'twill be worth
Three velvet gowns to your ladyship. Known!
Few ladies respect that disgrace: a poor thin shell!
'Tis the best grace you have to do it well.
I'll save your hand that labour: I'll unmask you!
HIPPOLITO Why, brother, brother!   50
VINDICE Art thou beguiled now? Tut, a lady can,
As such all hid, beguile a wiser man.
Have I not fitted the old surfeiter
With a quaint piece of beauty? Age and bare bone
Are e'er allied in action. Here's an eye,
Able to tempt a great man – to serve God:
A pretty hanging lip, that has forgot now to dissemble.
Methinks this mouth should make a swearer tremble;
A drunkard clasp his teeth, and not undo 'em,
To suffer wet damnation to run through 'em.   60
Here's a cheek keeps her colour, let the wind
                                go whistle:
Spout, rain, we fear thee not: be hot or cold,
All's one with us; and is not he absurd,
Whose fortunes are upon their faces set,

That fear no other god but wind and wet?

HIPPOLITO Brother, you've spoke that right: is this the form
That, living, shone so bright?

VINDICE   The very same.
And now methinks I could e'en chide myself
For doating on her beauty, though her death
Shall be revenged after no common action.   70
He imagines her to be speaking, and answers her.
Does the silkworm expend her yellow labours
For thee? For thee does she undo herself?
Are lordships sold to maintain ladyships,
For the poor benefit of a bewildering minute?
Why does yon fellow falsify high ways,
And put his life between the judge's lips,
To refine such a thing – keeps horse and men
To beat their valours for her?
Surely we are all mad people, and they   80
Whom we think are, are not: we mistake those;
'Tis we are mad in sense, they but in clothes.

HIPPOLITO Faith, and in clothes too we, give us our due.

VINDICE Does every proud and self-affecting dame
Camphire her face for this, and grieve her Maker
In sinful baths of milk, when many an infant starves
For her superfluous outside – all for this?
Who now bids twenty pounds a night? Prepares
Music, perfumes, and sweetmeats? All are hushed.
Thou may'st lie chaste now! It were fine, methinks,   90
To have thee seen at revels, forgetful feasts,
And unclean brothels! Sure, 'twould fright the sinner,
And make him a good coward: put a reveller
Out of his antic amble,
And cloy an epicure with empty dishes.
Here might a scornful and ambitious woman
Look through and through herself. See, ladies,
                                        with false forms
You deceive men, but cannot deceive worms.
Now to my tragic business. Look you, brother,
I have not fashioned this only for show   100
And useless property; no, it shall bear a part

E'en in its own revenge. This very skull,
Whose mistress the duke poisoned, with this drug,
The mortal curse of the earth, shall be revenged
In the like strain, and kiss his lips to death.
As much as the dumb thing can, he shall feel:
What fails in poison, we'll supply in steel.

HIPPOLITO Brother, I do applaud thy constant vengeance –
The quaintness of thy malice – above thought.

VINDICE So, 'tis laid on [*he poisons the lips of the skull*]:
                    now come and welcome, duke,   110
I have her for thee. I protest it, brother,
Methinks she makes almost as fair a fine,
As some old gentlewoman in a periwig.
Hide thy face now for shame; thou hadst need
                    have a mask now:
'Tis vain when beauty flows; but when it fleets,
This would become graves better than the streets.

HIPPOLITO You have my voice in that: hark, the duke's come.

VINDICE Peace, let's observe what company he brings,
And how he does absent 'em; for you know
He'll wish all private. Brother, fall you back   120
A little with the bony lady.

HIPPOLITO   That I will.   [*retires*

VINDICE So, so;
Now nine years' vengeance crowd into a minute!

Enter DUKE *and Gentlemen*

DUKE You shall have leave to leave us, with this charge
Upon your lives, if we be missed by the duchess
Or any of the nobles, to give out,
We're privately rid forth.

VINDICE   O happiness!

DUKE With some few honourable gentlemen, you may say –
You may name those that are away from court.

GENT. Your will and pleasure shall be done, my lord.   130
                  [*exeunt Gentlemen*

VINDICE 'Privately rid forth!'
He strives to make sure work on't. [*advances*]
                  Your good grace!

DUKE   Piato, well done, hast brought her! What lady is't?
VINDICE   Faith, my lord, a country lady, a little bashful at first,
            as most of them are; but after the first kiss, my lord,
            the worst is past with them. your grace knows now
            what you have to do; she has somewhat a grave look
            with her – but –
DUKE   I love that best; conduct her.
VINDICE   [aside]   Have at all.
DUKE   In gravest looks the greatest faults seem less.   140
            Give me that sin that's robed in holiness.
VINDICE   [aside] Back with the torch! Brother, raise the
                                                      perfumes.
DUKE   How sweet can a duke breathe! Age has no fault.
            Pleasure should meet in a perfuméd mist.
            Lady, sweetly encountered: I came from court,
            I must be bold with you. [kisses the skull]
                                        O, what's this? O!
VINDICE   Royal villain! White devil!
DUKE   O!
VINDICE   Brother,
            Place the torch here, that his affrighted eyeballs
            May start into those hollows. Duke, dost know
            Yon dreadful vizard? View it well: 'tis the skull   150
            Of Gloriana, whom thou poisonedst last.
DUKE   O! 'T has poisoned me.
VINDICE   Didst not know that till now?
DUKE   What are you two?
VINDICE   Villains all three! The very ragged bone
            Has been sufficiently revenged.
DUKE   O, Hippolito, call treason! [he sinks down]
HIPPOLITO   Yes, my lord;
            Treason! Treason! Treason! [stamping on him]
DUKE   Then I'm betrayed.
VINDICE   Alas! Poor lecher: in the hands of knaves,
            A slavish duke is baser than his slaves.
DUKE   My teeth are eaten out.
VINDICE   Hadst any left?   160
HIPPOLITO   I think but few.

VINDICE   Then those that did eat are eaten.

DUKE   O my tongue!

VINDICE   Your tongue? 'Twill teach you to kiss closer,
Not like a slobbering Dutchman. You have eyes still:
Look, monster, what a lady hast thou made me
                              [*discovers himself*
My once betrothed wife.

DUKE   Is it thou, villain? Nay, then –

VINDICE   'Tis I, 'tis Vindice, 'tis I.

HIPPOLITO   And let this comfort thee: our lord and father
Fell sick upon the infection of thy frowns,
And died in sadness: be that thy hope of life.   170

DUKE   O!

VINDICE   He had his tongue, yet grief made him die speechless.
Pooh! 'Tis but early yet; now I'll begin
To stick thy soul with ulcers. I will make
Thy spirit grievous sore; it shall not rest,
But like some pestilent man toss in thy breast.
Mark me, duke:
Thou art a renownéd, high and mighty cuckold.

DUKE   O!

VINDICE   Thy bastard rides a-hunting in thy brow.   180

DUKE   Millions of deaths!

VINDICE   Nay, to afflict thee more,
Here in this lodge they meet for damned clips.
Those eyes shall see the incest of their lips.

DUKE   Is there a hell besides this, villains?

VINDICE   Villain!
Nay, Heaven is just; scorns are the hire of scorns;
I ne'er knew yet adulterer without horns.

HIPPOLITO   Once, ere they die, 'tis quitted.

VINDICE   Hark! The music:
Their banquet is preparéd, they're coming –

DUKE   O, kill me not with that sight!

VINDICE   Thou shalt not lose that sight for all thy dukedom.   190

DUKE   Traitors! Murderers!

VINDICE   What! Is not thy tongue eaten out yet?
Then we'll invent a silence. Brother, stifle the torch.

DUKE   Treason! Murder!

VINDICE   Nay, faith, we'll have you hushed. Now with
                                                thy dagger
             Nail down his tongue, and mine shall keep possession
             About his heart; if he but gasp, he dies;
             We dread not death to quittance injuries.
             Brother,
             If he but wink, not brooking the foul object,   200
             Let our two other hands tear up his lids,
             And make his eyes like comets shine through blood.
             When the bad bleeds, then is the tragedy good.
HIPPOLITO   Whist, brother! The music's at our ear; they come.

             Enter SPURIO, *meeting the* DUCHESS

SPURIO   Had not that kiss a taste of sin, 'twere sweet.
DUCHESS   Why, there's no pleasure sweet, but it is sinful.
SPURIO   True, such a bitter sweetness fate hath given;
             Best side to us is the worst side to Heaven.
DUCHESS   Pish! Come: 'tis the old duke, thy doubtful father:
             The thought of him rubs Heaven in thy way.   210
             But I protest by yonder waxen fire,
             Forget him, or I'll poison him.
SPURIO   Madam, you urge a thought which ne'er had life.
             So deadly do I loathe him for my birth,
             That if he took me hasped within his bed,
             I would add murder to adultery,
             And with my sword give up his years to death.
DUCHESS   Why, now thou'rt sociable; let's in and feast:
             Loud'st music sound; pleasure is banquet's guest.
                                      [*exeunt Duchess and Spurio*
DUKE   I cannot brook –   [*dies*
VINDICE   The brook is turned to blood.   220
HIPPOLITO   Thanks to loud music.
VINDICE   'Twas our friend, indeed.
             'Tis state in music for a duke to bleed.
             The dukedom wants a head, though yet unknown;
             As fast as they peep up, let's cut 'em down.
                                                    [*exeunt*

SCENE 5

A room in the palace

Enter AMBITIOSO *and* SUPERVACUO

AMBITIOSO Was not his execution rarely plotted?
We are the duke's sons now.

SUPERVACU.   Ay, you may thank
My policy for that.

AMBITIOSO   Your policy
For what?

SUPERVACU.   Why, was't not my invention, brother,
To slip the judges? And in lesser compass
Did I not draw the model of his death,
Advising you to sudden officers
And e'en extemporal execution?

AMBITIOSO Heart! 'Twas a thing I thought on too.

SUPERVACU. You thought on't too! 'Sfoot, slander not
                                    your thoughts   10
With glorious untruth; I know 'twas not from you.

AMBITIOSO Sir, I say, 'twas in my head.

SUPERVACU.   Ay, like your brains then,
Ne'er to come out as long as you lived.

AMBITIOSO You'd have the honour on't, forsooth, that your wit
Led him to the scaffold.

SUPERVACU.   Since it is my due,
I'll publish't, but I'll ha't in spite of you.

AMBITIOSO Methinks, y'are much too bold; you should a little
Remember us, brother, next to be honest duke.

SUPERVACU. [*aside*] Ay, it shall be as easy for you to be duke
As to be honest; and that's never, i'faith.   20

AMBITIOSO Well, cold he is by this time; and because
We're both ambitious, be it our amity,
And let the glory be shared equally.

SUPERVACU. I am content to that.

AMBITIOSO This night our younger brother shall out of prison:

I have a trick.

SUPERVACU.   A trick! Prithee, what is't?

AMBITIOSO We'll get him out by a wile.

SUPERVACU.   Prithee, what wile?

AMBITIOSO No, sir; you shall not know it, till it be done;
For then you'd swear 'twere yours.

Enter an Officer

SUPERVACU.   How now, what's he?

AMBITIOSO One of the officers.

SUPERVACU.   Desiréd news.   30

AMBITIOSO How now, my friend?

OFFICER My lords, under your pardon, I am allotted
To that desertless office, to present you
With the yet bleeding head –

SUPERVACU.   Ha, ha! Excellent.

AMBITIOSO All's sure our own: brother, canst weep, think'st thou?
'Twould grace our flattery much; think of some dame;
'Twill teach thee to dissemble.

SUPERVACU.   I have thought –
Now for yourself.

AMBITIOSO   '   Our sorrows are so fluent,
Our eyes o'erflow our tongues; words spoke in tears
Are like the murmurs of the waters – the sound   40
Is loudly heard, but cannot be distinguished.

SUPERVACU. How died he, pray?

OFFICER   O, full of rage and spleen.

SUPERVACU. He died most valiantly, then; we're glad to hear it.

OFFICER We could not woo him once to pray.

AMBITIOSO He showed himself a gentleman in that:
Give him his due.

OFFICER   But, in the stead of prayer,
He drew forth oaths.

SUPERVACU.   Then did he pray, dear heart,
Although you understood him not.

OFFICER   My lords,
E'en at his last, with pardon be it spoke,
He cursed you both.

SUPERVACU.   He cursed us? 'Las, good soul!   50

AMBITIOSO It was not in our powers, but the duke's pleasure.
            [*aside*] Finely dissembled a'both sides, sweet fate;
            O happy opportunity!

                        Enter LUSSURIOSO

LUSSURIOSO   Now, my lords.
AMBITIOSO & SUPERVACUO   O!
LUSSURIOSO Why do you shun me, brothers?
            You may come nearer now:
            The savour of the prison has forsook me.
            I thank such kind lords as yourselves, I'm free.
AMBITIOSO Alive!
SUPERVACU. In health!
AMBITIOSO Released!   60
            We were both e'en amazed with joy to see it.
LUSSURIOSO I am much to thank to you.
SUPERVACU. Faith, we spared no tongue unto my lord the duke.
AMBITIOSO I know your delivery, brother,
            Had not been half so sudden but for us.
SUPERVACU. O, how we pleaded!
LUSSURIOSO   Most deserving brothers!
            In my best studies I will think of it.   [*exit*
AMBITIOSO O death and vengeance!
SUPERVACU.   Hell and torments!
AMBITIOSO Slave, cam'st thou to delude us?
OFFICER   Delude you, my lords?
SUPERVACU. Ay, villain, where's his head now?
OFFICER   Why, here, my lord; 70
            Just after his delivery, you both came
            With warrant from the duke to behead your brother.
AMBITIOSO Ay, our brother, the duke's son.
OFFICER   The duke's son,
            My lord, had his release before you came.
AMBITIOSO Whose head's that, then?
OFFICER His whom you left command for, your own brother's.
AMBITIOSO Our brother's? O furies.
SUPERVACU.   Plagues!
AMBITIOSO   Confusions!
SUPERVACU.   Darkness!

AMBITIOSO Devils!

SUPERVACU.   Fell it out so accursedly?

AMBITIOSO So damnedly?

SUPERVACU.   Villain, I'll brain thee with it.

OFFICER   O my good lord!

SUPERVACU.   The devil overtake thee!   80

AMBITIOSO O fatal!

SUPERVACU.   O prodigious to our bloods!

AMBITIOSO Did we dissemble?

SUPERVACU. Did we make our tears women for thee?

AMBITIOSO Laugh and rejoice for thee?

SUPERVACU. Bring warrant for thy death?

AMBITIOSO Mock off thy head?

SUPERVACU. You had a trick: you had a wile, forsooth.

AMBITIOSO A murrain meet 'em; there's none of these wiles
          That ever come to good: I see now, there's nothing
          Sure in mortality, but mortality.   90
          Well, no more words: shalt be revenged, i'faith.
          Come, throw off clouds; now, brother, think
                              of vengeance,
          And deeper-settled hate; sirrah, sit fast,
          We'll pull down all, but thou shalt down at last.

                                             [exeunt

ACT 4 SCENE I

The precincts of the palace

Enter LUSSURIOSO *with* HIPPOLITO

LUSSURIOSO Hippolito!

HIPPOLITO My lord,
        Has your good lordship aught to command me in?

LUSSURIOSO I prythee, leave us!

HIPPOLITO   How's this? Come and leave us!

LUSSURIOSO Hippolito!

HIPPOLITO   Your honour, I stand ready
        For any duteous employment.

LUSSURIOSO Heart! What mak'st thou here?

HIPPOLITO   A pretty lordly humour!
        He bids me be present to depart; something
        Has stung his honour.

LUSSURIOSO   Be nearer; draw nearer:
        Ye're not so good, methinks; I'm angry with you.   10

HIPPOLITO With me, my lord? I'm angry with myself for't.

LUSSURIOSO You did prefer a goodly fellow to me:
        'Twas wittily elected; 'twas. I thought
        He had been a villain, and he proves a knave –
        To me a knave.

HIPPOLITO I chose him for the best, my lord:
        'Tis much my sorrow, if neglect in him
        Breed discontent in you.

LUSSURIOSO   Neglect! 'Twas will.
        Judge of it.
        Firmly to tell of an incredible act,   20
        Not to be thought, less to be spoken of,
        'Twixt my step-mother and the bastard; oh!
        Incestuous sweets between 'em.

HIPPOLITO   Fie, my lord!

LUSSURIOSO I, in kind loyalty to my father's forehead,
        Made this a desperate arm; and in that fury
        Committed treason on the lawful bed,

And with my sword e'en rased my father's bosom,
For which I was within a stroke of death.

HIPPOLITO Alack! I'm sorry. [*aside*] 'Sfoot, just upon the stroke,
Jars in my brother; 'twill be villainous music.   30

Enter VINDICE, *disguised*

VINDICE My honoured lord.
LUSSURIOSO   Away! Prithee, forsake us:
Hereafter we'll not know thee.
VINDICE Not know me, my lord! Your lordship
                            cannot choose.
LUSSURIOSO Begone, I say: thou art a false knave.
VINDICE Why, the easier to be known, my lord.
LUSSURIOSO Pish! I shall prove too bitter, with a word
Make thee a perpetual prisoner,
And lay this ironage upon thee.
VINDICE [*aside*]   Mum!
For there's a doom would make a woman dumb.
Missing the bastard – next him – the wind's
                            come about: 40
Now 'tis my brother's turn to stay,
                            mine to go out. [*exit*
LUSSURIOSO He has greatly moved me.
HIPPOLITO   Much to blame, i'faith.
LUSSURIOSO But I'll recover, to his ruin. 'Twas told me lately,
I know not whether falsely, that you'd a brother.
HIPPOLITO Who, I? Yes, my good lord, I have a brother.
LUSSURIOSO How chance the court ne'er saw him? Of what
                            nature?
How does he apply his hours?
HIPPOLITO   Faith, to curse fates
Who, as he thinks, ordained him to be poor –
Keeps at home, full of want and discontent.
LUSSURIOSO [*aside*] There's hope in him; for discontent and want 50
Is the best clay to mould a villain of.
Hippolito, wish him repair to us:
If there be aught in him to please our blood,
For thy sake we'll advance him, and build fair
His meanest fortunes; for it is in us

To rear up towers from cottages.

HIPPOLITO It is so, my lord: he will attend your honour;
But he's a man in whom much melancholy dwells.

LUSSURIOSO Why, the better; bring him to court.

HIPPOLITO With willingness and speed: 60
[*aside*] Whom he cast off e'en now, must now succeed.
Brother, disguise must off;
In thine own shape now I'll prefer thee to him:
How strangely does himself work
                              to undo him! [*exit*

LUSSURIOSO This fellow will come fitly; he shall kill
That other slave, that did abuse my spleen,
And made it swell to treason. I have put
Much of my heart into him; he must die.
He that knows great men's secrets, and proves slight,
That man ne'er lives to see his beard turn white.   70
Ay, he shall speed him: I'll employ the brother;
Slaves are but nails to drive out one another.
He being of black condition, suitable
To want and ill-content, hope of preferment
Will grind him to an edge.

Enter Nobles

I NOBLE Good days unto your honour.

LUSSURIOSO My kind lords, I do return the like.

2 NOBLE Saw you my lord the duke?

LUSSURIOSO My lord and father! Is he from court?

I NOBLE He's sure from court;   80
But where – which way his pleasure took, we
                              know not,
Nor can we hear on't.

LUSSURIOSO   Here come those should tell.
Saw you my lord and father?

3 NOBLE Not since two hours before noon, my lord,
And then he privately rode forth.

LUSSURIOSO O, he's rid forth.

I NOBLE   'Twas wondrous privately.

2 NOBLE There's none i'th'court had any knowledge on't.

LUSSURIOSO His grace is old and sudden: 'tis no treason

To say the duke, my father, has a humour,
Or such a toy about him; what in us   90
Would appear light, in him seems virtuous.

3 NOBLE   'Tis oracle, my lord.

[*exeunt*

SCENE 2

An apartment in the palace

Enter VINDICE, *out of his disguise, and* HIPPOLITO

HIPPOLITO   So, so, all's as it should be, y'are yourself.
VINDICE   How that great villain puts me to my shifts!
HIPPOLITO   He that did lately in disguise reject thee,
            Shall, now thou art thyself, as much respect thee.
VINDICE   'Twill be the quainter fallacy. But, brother,
            'Sfoot, what use will he put me to now, think'st thou?
HIPPOLITO   Nay, you must pardon me in that: I know not.
            He has some employment for you: but what 'tis,
            He and his secretary (the devil) know best.
VINDICE   Well, I must suit my tongue to his desires,   10
            What colour soe'er they be; hoping at last
            To pile up all my wishes on his breast.
HIPPOLITO   Faith, brother, he himself shows the way.
VINDICE   Now the duke is dead, the realm is clad in clay.
            His death being not yet known, under his name
            The people still are governed. Well, thou his son
            Art not long-lived: thou shalt not joy his death.
            To kill thee, then, I should most honour thee;
            For 'twould stand firm in every man's belief,
            Thou'st a kind child, and only died'st with grief.   20
HIPPOLITO   You fetch about well; but let's talk in present.
            How will you appear in fashion different,
            As well as in apparel, to make all things possible?
            If you be but once tripped, we fall for ever.
            It is not the least policy to be doubtful;
            You must change tongue: familiar was your first.
VINDICE   Why, I'll bear me in some strain of melancholy,
            And string myself with heavy-sounding wire,

Like such an instrument, that speaks merry things sadly.

HIPPOLITO Then 'tis as I meant;
I gave you out at first in discontent.

VINDICE I'll tune myself, and then –

HIPPOLITO 'Sfoot, here he comes.
Hast thought upon't?

VINDICE Salute him; fear not me.

Enter LUSSURIOSO

LUSSURIOSO Hippolito!

HIPPOLITO Your lordship –

LUSSURIOSO What's he yonder?

HIPPOLITO 'Tis Vindice, my discontented brother,
Whom, 'cording to your will, I've brought to court.

LUSSURIOSO Is that thy brother? Beshrew me, a good presence;
I wonder he has been from the court so long.
Come nearer.

HIPPOLITO Brother! Lord Lussurioso, the duke's son.

LUSSURIOSO Be more near to us; welcome; nearer yet.

VINDICE How don you? Gi'you good den.
[*takes off his hat and bows*]

LUSSURIOSO We thank thee.
How strangely such a coarse homely salute
Shows in the palace, where we greet in fire,
Nimble and desperate tongues! Should we name
God in a salutation, 'twould ne'er be stood on –
Heaven!
Tell me, what has made thee so melancholy?

VINDICE Why, going to law.

LUSSURIOSO Why, will that make a man melancholy?

VINDICE Yes, to look long upon ink and black buckram. I went me to law in *anno quadragesimo secundo*, and I waded out of it in *anno sexagesimo tertio*.

LUSSURIOSO What, three-and-twenty years in law?

VINDICE I have known those that have been five-and-fifty, and all about pullen and pigs.

LUSSURIOSO May it be possible such men should breathe,
To vex the terms so much?

VINDICE 'Tis food to some, my lord. There are old men at the

present, that are so poisoned with the affectation of 60
law-words (having had many suits canvassed), that
their common talk is nothing but Barbary Latin. They
cannot so much as pray but in law, that their sins may
be removed with a writ of error, and their souls
fetched up to Heaven with a sasarara.

LUSSURIOSO It seems most strange to me;
        Yet all the world meets round in the same bent:
        Where the heart's set, there goes the tongue's consent.
        How dost apply thy studies, fellow?

VINDICE Study? Why, to think how a great rich man lies a- 70
        dying, and a poor cobbler tolls the bell for him. How
        be cannot depart the world, and see the great chest
        stand before him; when he lies speechless, how he
        will point you readily to all the boxes; and when he is
        past all memory, as the gossips guess, then thinks he of
        forfeitures and obligations; nay, when to all men's
        hearings he whurls and rattles in the throat, he's busy
        threatening his poor tenants. And this would last me
        now some seven years' thinking, or thereabouts. But I
        have a conceit a-coming in picture upon this; I draw it 80
        myself, which, i'faith, la, I'll present to your honour;
        you shall not choose but like it, for your honour shall
        give me nothing for it.

LUSSURIOSO Nay, you mistake me, then,
        For I am published bountiful enough.
        Let's taste of your conceit.

VINDICE In picture, my Lord?

LUSSURIOSO Ay, in picture.

VINDICE Marry, this it is – 'A usuring father to be boiling in
        hell, and his son and heir with a whore dancing over 90
        him.'

HIPPOLITO [aside] He has pared him to the quick.

LUSSURIOSO The conceit's pretty, i'faith;
        But, take't upon my life, 'twill ne'er be liked.

VINDICE No? Why I'm sure the whore will be liked well enough.

HIPPOLITO [aside] Aye, if she were out o'the picture, he'd like her
        then himself.

VINDICE And as for the son and heir, he shall be an eyesore to

no young revellers, for he shall be drawn in cloth-of-
gold breeches.   100

LUSSURIOSO And thou hast put my meaning in the pockets,
And canst not draw that out? My thought was this:
To see the picture of a usuring father
Boiling in hell – our rich men would never like it.

VINDICE O, true, I cry you heartily mercy, I know the reason,
for some of them had rather be damned in deed than
damned in colours.

LUSSURIOSO [aside] A parlous melancholy! He has wit enough
To murder any man, and I'll give him means.
I think thou art ill-moneyed?

VINDICE   Money! Ho, ho!   110
'T has been my want so long, 'tis now my scoff:
I've e'en forgot what colour silver's of.

LUSSURIOSO [aside] It hits as I could wish.

VINDICE   I get good clothes
Of those that dread my humour; and for table-room
I feed on those that cannot be rid of me.

LUSSURIOSO Somewhat to set thee up withal.   [gives him money

VINDICE O mine eyes!

LUSSURIOSO   How now, man?

VINDICE   Almost struck blind;
This bright unusual shine to me seems proud;
I dare not look till the sun be in a cloud.

LUSSURIOSO I think I shall affect his melancholy,   120
How are they now?

VINDICE   The better for your asking.

LUSSURIOSO You shall be better yet, if you but fasten
Truly on my intent. Now y'are both present,
I will unbrace such a close private villain
Unto your vengeful swords, the like ne'er heard of,
Who hath disgraced you much, and injured us.

HIPPOLITO Disgracéd us, my lord?

LUSSURIOSO   Ay, Hippolito.
I kept it here till now, that both your angers
Might meet him at once.

VINDICE   I'm covetous to know

The villain.

LUSSURIOSO   You know him: that slave-pander,   130
Piato, whom we threatened last
With irons in perpetual 'prisonment.

VINDICE [*aside*] All this is I.

HIPPOLITO   Is't he, my lord?

LUSSURIOSO I'll tell you; you first preferréd him to me.

VINDICE Did you, brother?

HIPPOLITO   I did indeed.

LUSSURIOSO And the ungrateful villain,
To quit that kindness, strongly wrought with me –
Being, as you see, a likely man for pleasure –
With jewels to corrupt your virgin sister.

HIPPOLITO O villain!

VINDICE   He shall surely die that did it.   140

LUSSURIOSO I, far from thinking any virgin harm,
Especially knowing her to be as chaste
As that part which scarce suffers to be touched –
The eye – would not endure him.

VINDICE   Would you not,
My lord? 'Twas wondrous honourably done.

LUSSURIOSO But with some fine frowns kept him out.

VINDICE   Out, slave!

LUSSURIOSO What did me he, but in revenge of that,
Went of his own free will to make infirm
Your sister's honour (whom I honour with my soul
For chaste respect) and not prevailing there   150
(As 'twas but desperate folly to attempt it),
In mere spleen, by the way, waylays your mother,
Whose honour being a coward as it seems,
Yielded by little force.

VINDICE   Coward indeed!

LUSSURIOSO He, proud of this advantage (as he thought),
Brought me this news for happy. But I, Heaven
                                        forgive me for't –

VINDICE What did your honour?

LUSSURIOSO   In rage pushed him from me,
Trampled beneath his throat, spurned him, and bruised:
Indeed I was too cruel, to say troth.

HIPPOLITO   Most nobly managed!   160
VINDICE   [*aside*] Has not Heaven an ear? Is all the lightning
                                                wasted?
LUSSURIOSO If I now were so impatient in a modest cause,
            What should you be?
VINDICE   Full mad: he shall not live
            To see the moon change.
LUSSURIOSO   He's about the palace;
            Hippolito, entice him this way, that thy brother
            May take full mark of him.
HIPPOLITO   Heart! That shall not need, my lord:
            I can direct him so far.
LUSSURIOSO   Yet for my hate's sake,
            Go, wind him this way. I'll see him bleed myself.
HIPPOLITO   [*aside*] What now, brother?   170
VINDICE   [*aside*] Nay, e'en what you will – y'are put to't,
                                                brother.
HIPPOLITO   [*aside*] An impossible task, I'll swear,
            To bring him hither, that's already here.   [*exit*
LUSSURIOSO Thy name? I have forgot it.
VINDICE   Vindice, my lord.
LUSSURIOSO 'Tis a good name that.
VINDICE   Ay, a revenger.
LUSSURIOSO It does betoken courage; thou shouldst be valiant,
            And kill thine enemies.
VINDICE   That's my hope, my lord.
LUSSURIOSO This slave is one.
VINDICE   I'll doom him.
LUSSURIOSO   Then I'll praise thee.
            Do thou observe me best, and I'll best raise thee.

                        Re-enter HIPPOLITO

VINDICE   Indeed, I thank you.   180
LUSSURIOSO Now, Hippolito, where's the slave-pander?
HIPPOLITO   Your good lordship
            Would have a loathsome sight of him, much offensive.
            He's not in case now to be seen, my lord.
            The worst of all the deadly sins is in him –
            That beggarly damnation, drunkenness.

LUSSURIOSO Then he's a double slave.

VINDICE   [aside]   'Twas well conveyed
          Upon a sudden wit.

LUSSURIOSO   What, are you both
          Firmly resolved? I'll see him dead myself.

VINDICE   Or else let not us live.

LUSSURIOSO   You may direct   190
          Your brother to take note of him.

HIPPOLITO   I shall.

LUSSURIOSO Rise but in this, and you shall never fall.

VINDICE   Your honour's vassals.

LUSSURIOSO [aside]   This was wisely carried.
          Deep policy in us makes fools of such:
          Then must a slave die, when he knows too much.
                                                    [exit

VINDICE   O thou almighty patience! 'Tis my wonder
          That such a fellow, impudent and wicked,
          Should not be cloven as he stood;
          Or with a secret wind burst open!
          Is there no thunder left: or is't kept up   200
          In stock for heavier vengeance? [thunder] There it goes!

HIPPOLITO Brother, we lose ourselves.

VINDICE   But I have found it;
          'Twill hold, 'tis sure; thanks, thanks to any spirit,
          That mingled it 'mongst my inventions.

HIPPOLITO What is't?

VINDICE   'Tis sound and good; thou shalt partake it;
          I'm hired to kill myself.

HIPPOLITO   True.

VINDICE   Prithee, mark it;
          And the old duke being dead, but not conveyed,
          For he's already missed too, and you know
          Murder will peep out of the closest husk –

HIPPOLITO Most true.

VINDICE   What say you then to this device?   210
          If we dressed up the body of the duke –

HIPPOLITO In that disguise of yours?

VINDICE   Y'are quick, y'have reached it.

HIPPOLITO I like it wondrously.

VINDICE   And being in drink, as you have published him.
             To lean him on his elbow, as if sleep had caught him,
             Which claims most interest in such sluggy men?

HIPPOLITO   Good yet; but here's a doubt;
             We, thought by the duke's son to kill that pander,
             Shall, when he is known, be thought to kill the duke.

VINDICE   Neither, O thanks! It is substantial: 220
             For that disguise being on him which I wore,
             It will be thought I, which he calls the pander,
             Did kill the duke, and fled away in his apparel,
             Leaving him so disguiséd to avoid
             Swift pursuit.

HIPPOLITO   Firmer and firmer.

VINDICE   Nay, doubt not,
             'Tis in grain: I warrant it holds colour.

HIPPOLITO   Let's about it.

VINDICE   By the way, too, now I think on't, brother,
             Let's conjure that base devil out of our mother.

                                                        [exeunt

                            SCENE 3

                      A corridor in the palace

              Enter the DUCHESS, arm in arm with SPURIO, looking
              lasciviously on her. After them enter SUPERVACUO,
                  with a rapier, running; AMBITIOSO stops him

SPURIO   Madam, unlock yourself;
             Should it be seen, your arm would be suspected.

DUCHESS   Who is't that dares suspect or this or these?
             May not we deal our favours where we please?

SPURIO   I'm confident you may.   [exeunt Duchess and Spurio

AMBITIOSO   'Sfoot, brother, hold.

SUPERVACU.   Wouldst let the bastard shame us?

AMBITIOSO   Hold, hold, brother!
             There's fitter time than now.

SUPERVACU.   Now, when I see it!

AMBITIOSO 'Tis too much seen already.
SUPERVACU.   Seen and known;
          The nobler she's, the baser is she grown.
AMBITIOSO If she were bent lasciviously (the fault   10
          Of mighty women, that sleep soft) – O death!
          Must she needs choose such an unequal sinner,
          To make all worse? –
SUPERVACU. A bastard! The duke's bastard! Shame heaped
                                        on shame!
AMBITIOSO O our disgrace!
          Most women have small waists the world throughout;
          But their desires are thousand miles about.
SUPERVACU. Come, stay not here, let's after, and prevent,
          Or else they'll sin faster than we'll repent.

                                        [exeunt

                        SCENE 4

                A room in Gratiana's house

          Enter VINDICE *and* HIPPOLITO, *bringing out* GRATIANA
            by the shoulders, and with daggers in their hands

VINDICE   O thou, for whom no name is bad enough!
GRATIANA   What mean my sons? What, will you murder me?
VINDICE   Wicked, unnatural parent!
HIPPOLITO   Fiend of women!
GRATIANA   O! Are sons turned monsters? Help!
VINDICE   In vain.
GRATIANA   Are you so barbarous to set iron nipples
            Upon the breast that gave you suck?
VINDICE   That breast
            Is turned to quarléd poison.
GRATIANA   Cut not your days for't! Am not I your mother?
VINDICE   Thou dost usurp that title now by fraud,
            For in that shell of mother breeds a bawd.   10
GRATIANA   A bawd! O name far loathsomer than hell!
HIPPOLITO   It should be so, knew'st thou thy office well.
GRATIANA   I hate it.

VINDICE   Ah! Is't possible? Thou only? Powers on high,
That women should dissemble when they die!

GRATIANA Dissemble!

VINDICE   Did not the duke's son direct
A fellow of the world's condition hither,
That did corrupt all that was good in thee?
Made thee uncivilly forget thyself,
And work our sister to his lust?

GRATIANA   Who, I?   20
That had been monstrous. I defy that man
For any such intent! None lives so pure,
But shall be soiled with slander.
Good son, believe it not.

VINDICE   [aside]   O, I'm in doubt,
Whether I am myself, or no –
Stay, let me look again upon this face.
Who shall be saved, when mothers have no grace?

HIPPOLITO 'Twould make one half despair.

VINDICE   I was the man.
Defy me now; let's see, do't modestly.

GRATIANA O hell unto my soul!   30

VINDICE   In that disguise, I, sent from the duke's son,
Tried you, and found you base metal,
As any villain might have done.

GRATIANA   O, no,
No tongue but yours could have bewitched me so.

VINDICE   O nimble in damnation, quick in tune!
There is no devil could strike fire so soon:
I am confuted in a word.

GRATIANA   O sons,
Forgive me! To myself I'll prove more true;
You that should honour me, I kneel to you.
                              [kneels and weeps

VINDICE   A mother to give aim to her own daughter!   40

HIPPOLITO True, brother; how far beyond nature 'tis.

VINDICE   Nay, an you draw tears once, go you to bed;
We will make iron blush and change to red.
Brother, it rains. 'Twill spoil your dagger: house it.

HIPPOLITO 'Tis done.

VINDICE   I'faith, 'tis a sweet shower, it does much good.
            The fruitful grounds and meadows of her soul
            Have been long dry: pour down, thou blessed dew!
            Rise, mother; troth, this shower has made you higher!

GRATIANA   O you Heavens!   50
            Take this infectious spot out of my soul,
            I'll rinse it in seven waters of mine eyes!
            Make my tears salt enough to taste of grace.
            To weep is to our sex naturally given:
            But to weep truly, that's a gift from Heaven.

VINDICE   Nay, I'll kiss you now. Kiss her, brother:
            Let's marry her to our souls, wherein's no lust,
            And honourably love her.

HIPPOLITO   Let it be.

VINDICE   For honest women are so seld and rare,
            'Tis good to cherish those poor few that are.   60
            O you of easy wax! Do but imagine,
            Now the disease has left you, how leprously
            That office would have clinged unto your forehead!
            All mothers that had any graceful hue
            Would have worn masks to hide their face at you:
            It would have grown to this – at your foul name,
            Green-coloured maids would have turned red
                                     with shame.

HIPPOLITO   And then our sister, full of hire and baseness –

VINDICE   There had been boiling lead again,
            The duke's son's great concubine!   70
            A drab of state, a cloth-o'-silver slut,
            To have her train borne up, and her soul trail i'the dirt!

HIPPOLITO   Great, to be miserably great; rich, to be
            Eternally wretched.

VINDICE   O common madness!
            Ask but the thrivingest harlot in cold blood,
            She'd give the world to make her honour good.
            Perhaps you'll say 'but only to the duke's son
            In private'; why, she first begins with one,
            Who afterward to thousands proves a whore:
            'Break ice in one place, it will crack in more.'   80

GRATIANA   Most certainly applied!

HIPPOLITO   O brother, you forget our business.

VINDICE   And well-remembered; joy's a subtle elf,
I think man's happiest when he forgets himself.
Farewell, once dry, now holy-watered mead;
Our hearts wear feathers, that before wore lead.

GRATIANA   I'll give you this – that one I never knew
Plead better for and 'gainst the devil than you.

VINDICE   You make me proud on't.

HIPPOLITO   Commend us in all virtue to our sister.   90

VINDICE   Ay, for the love of Heaven, to that true maid.

GRATIANA   With my best words.

VINDICE   Why, that was motherly said.
                    [*exeunt Vindice and Hippolito*

GRATIANA   I wonder now, what fury did transport me!
I feel good thoughts begin to settle in me.
O, with what forehead can I look on her,
Whose honour I've so impiously beset?
And here she comes –

                    Enter CASTIZA

CASTIZA   Now, mother, you have wrought with me so strongly,
That what for my advancement, as to calm
The trouble of your tongue, I am content.   100

GRATIANA   Content, to what?

CASTIZA   To do as you have wished me;
To prostitute my breast to the duke's son,
And put myself to common usury.

GRATIANA   I hope you will not so!

CASTIZA   Hope you I will not?
That's not the hope you look to be saved in.

GRATIANA   Truth, but it is.

CASTIZA   Do not deceive yourself;
I am as you, e'en out of marble wrought.
What would you now? Are ye not pleased yet with me?
You shall not wish me to be more lascivious
Than I intend to be.

GRATIANA   Strike not me cold.   110

CASTIZA   How often have you charged me on your blessing
To be a curséd woman? When you knew

Your blessing had no force to make me lewd,
You laid your curse upon me; that did more,
The mother's curse is heavy; where that fights,
Suns set in storm, and daughters lose their lights.

GRATIANA Good child, dear maid, if there be any spark
Of heavenly intellectual fire within thee,
O, let my breath revive it to a flame!
Put not all out with woman's wilful follies.   120
I am recovered of that foul disease,
That haunts too many mothers; kind, forgive me.
Make me not sick in health! If then
My words prevailed, when they were wickedness,
How much more now, when they are just and good?

CASTIZA I wonder what you mean! Are not you she,
For whose infect persuasions I could scarce
Kneel out my prayers, and had much ado
In three hours' reading to untwist so much
Of the black serpent as you wound about me?   130

GRATIANA 'Tis unfruitful, child, and tedious to repeat
What's past; I'm now your present mother.

CASTIZA Tush! Now 'tis too late.

GRATIANA Bethink again: thou know'st not what thou say'st.

CASTIZA No! Deny advancement? Treasure? The duke's son?

GRATIANA O, see! I spoke those words, and now they poison me!
What will the deed do then?
Advancement? True, as high as shame can pitch!
For treasure, who e'er knew a harlot rich?
Or could build by the purchase of her sin   140
An hospital to keep her bastards in?
The duke's son! O, when women are young courtiers,
They are sure to be old beggars;
To know the miseries most harlots taste,
Thou'dst wish thyself unborn, when thou art unchaste.

CASTIZA O mother, let me twine about your neck,
And kiss you, till my soul melt on your lips!
I did but this to try you.

GRATIANA   O, speak truth!

CASTIZA Indeed I did but; for no tongue has force
To alter me from honest.   150

If maidens would, men's words could have no power;
A virgin's honour is a crystal tower
Which (being weak) is guarded with good spirits;
Until she basely yields, no ill inherits.

GRATIANA   O happy child! Faith, and thy birth hath saved me.
'Mong thousand daughters, happiest of all others:
Be thou a glass for maids, and I for mothers.

                                    [*exeunt*

ACT 5 SCENE I

*A room in the lodge; the Duke's corpse, dressed
in Vindice's disguise, lying on a couch*

Enter VINDICE *and* HIPPOLITO

VINDICE   So, so, he leans well; take heed you wake him not,
            brother.

HIPPOLITO   I warrant you my life for yours.

VINDICE   That's a good lay, for I must kill myself. Brother, that's
            I, that sits for me: do you mark it? And I must stand
            ready here to make away myself yonder. I must sit to
            be killed, and stand to kill myself. I could vary it not so
            little as thrice over again; 't has some eight returns, like
            Michaelmas term.

HIPPOLITO   That's enow, o'conscience.   10

VINDICE   But, sirrah, does the duke's son come single?

HIPPOLITO   No; there's the hell on't: his faith's too feeble to go
            alone. He brings flesh-flies after him, that will buzz
            against supper-time, and hum for his coming out.

VINDICE   Ah, the fly-flap of vengeance beat 'em to pieces! Here
            was the sweetest occasion, the fittest hour, to have
            made my revenge familiar with him: show him the
            body of the duke his father, and how quaintly he
            died – like a politician, in hugger-mugger, made no
            man acquainted with it – and in catastrophe slay him   20
            over his father's breast. O, I'm mad to lose such a sweet
            opportunity!

HIPPOLITO   Nay, tush! Prithee, be content! There's no remedy
            present; may not hereafter times open in as fair faces as
            this?

VINDICE   They may, if they can paint so well.

HIPPOLITO   Come now: to avoid all suspicion, let's forsake this
            room, and be going to meet the duke's son.

VINDICE   Content: I'm for any weather. Heart! Step close: here
            he comes.   30

Enter LUSSURIOSO

HIPPOLITO   My honoured lord!

LUSSURIOSO   O me! You both present?

VINDICE   E'en newly, my lord, just as your lordship entered
          now: about this place we had notice given he should
          be, but in some loathsome plight or other.

HIPPOLITO   Came your honour private?

LUSSURIOSO   Private enough for this; only a few
          Attend my coming out.

HIPPOLITO   [*aside*]   Death rot those few!

LUSSURIOSO   Stay, yonder's the slave.

VINDICE   Mass, there's the slave, indeed, my lord.
          [*aside*] 'Tis a good child: he calls his father a slave!   40

LUSSURIOSO   Ay, that's the villain, the damnéd villain. Softly.
          Tread easy.

VINDICE   Pah! I warrant you, my lord,
          We'll stifle-in our breaths.

LUSSURIOSO   That will do well:
          Base rogue, thou sleepest thy last; 'tis policy
          To have him killed in's sleep; for if he waked,
          He would betray all to them.

VINDICE   But, my lord –

LUSSURIOSO   Ha, what say'st?

VINDICE   Shall we kill him now he's drunk?

LUSSURIOSO   Ay, best of all.

VINDICE   Why, then he will ne'er live
          To be sober.

LUSSURIOSO   No matter, let him reel to hell.

VINDICE   But being so full of liquor, I fear he will   50
          Put out all the fire.

LUSSURIOSO   Thou art a mad beast.

VINDICE   [*aside*] And leave none to warm your lordship's golls
          withal; for he that dies drunk falls into hell-fire like a
          bucket of water – qush, qush!

LUSSURIOSO   Come, be ready: make your swords:
          Think of your wrongs; this slave has injured you.

VINDICE   [*aside*] Troth, so he has, and he has paid well for't.

LUSSURIOSO Meet with him now.

VINDICE   You'll bear us out, my lord?

LUSSURIOSO Pooh! Am I a lord for nothing, think you? Quickly now!

VINDICE [*stabs the Duke's corpse*] Sa, sa, sa, thump! There he lies. 60

LUSSURIOSO Nimbly done. Ha! O villains! Murderers!
          'Tis the old duke, my father.

VINDICE   That's a jest.

LUSSURIOSO What stiff and cold already!
          O, pardon me to call you from your names:
          'Tis none of your deed. That villain Piato,
          Whom you thought now to kill, has murderéd
          And left him thus disguised.

HIPPOLITO   And not unlikely.

VINDICE O rascal! Was he not ashamed
          To put the duke into a greasy doublet?

LUSSURIOSO He has been stiff and cold – who knows how long? 70

VINDICE [*aside*] Marry, that I do.

LUSSURIOSO No words, I pray, of anything intended.

VINDICE O my lord.

HIPPOLITO I would fain have your lordship think that we
          Have small reason to prate.

LUSSURIOSO Faith, thou say'st true; I'll forthwith send to court
          For all the nobles, bastard, duchess; tell
          How here by miracle we found him dead,
          And in his raiment that foul villain fled.

VINDICE That will be the best way, my lord, 80
          To clear us all; let's cast about to be clear.

LUSSURIOSO Ho! Nencio, Sordido, and the rest!

Enter all of them

1 SERVANT My lord.

2 SERVANT My lord.

LUSSURIOSO Be witnesses of a strange spectacle.
          Choosing for private conference that sad room,
          We found the duke my father gealed in blood.

1 SERVANT My lord the duke! Run, hie thee, Nencio.
          Startle the court by signifying so much.

VINDICE [*aside*] Thus much by wit a deep revenger can:
          When murder's known, to be the clearest man. 90

We're farthest off, and with as bold an eye
Survey his body as the standers-by.

LUSSURIOSO My royal father, too basely let blood
By a malevolent slave!

HIPPOLITO [*aside*] Hark! He calls thee slave again.

VINDICE [*aside*] He has lost: he may.

LUSSURIOSO O sight! Look hither, see, his lips are gnawn
With poison.

VINDICE   How? His lips? By the mass, they be.
O villain! O rogue! O slave! O rascal!   100

HIPPOLITO [*aside*] O good deceit! He quits him with like terms.

AMBITIOSO [*within*] Where?

SUPERVACU. [*within*] Which way?

Enter AMBITIOSO *and* SUPERVACUO, *with Nobles and Gentlemen*

AMBITIOSO Over what roof hangs this prodigious comet
In deadly fire?

LUSSURIOSO   Behold, behold, my lords,
The duke my father's murdered by a vassal
That owes this habit, and here·left disguised.

Enter DUCHESS *and* SPURIO

DUCHESS My lord and husband!

1 NOBLE   Reverend majesty!

2 NOBLE I have seen these clothes often attending on him.

VINDICE [*aside*] That nobleman has been i th'country, for he   110
does not lie.

SUPERVACU. [*aside*] Learn of our mother; let's dissemble too:
I am glad he's vanished; so, I hope, are you.

AMBITIOSO [*aside*] Ay, you may take my word for't.

SPURIO [*aside*]   Old dad dead!
I, one of his cast sins, will send the Fates
Most hearty commendations by his own son;
I'll tug in the new stream, till strength be done.

LUSSURIOSO Where be those two that did affirm to us,
My lord the duke was privately rid forth?

1 GENT. O, pardon us, my lords; he gave that charge –   120
Upon our lives, if he were missed at court,
To answer so; he rode not anywhere;
We left him private with that fellow here.

VINDICE   [*aside*] Confirmed.

LUSSURIOSO O Heavens! That false charge was his death.
               Impudent beggars! Durst you to our face
               Maintain such a false answer? Bear him straight
               To execution.

1 GENT.   My lord!

LUSSURIOSO Urge me no more in this!   130
               The excuse may be called half the murder.

VINDICE   [*aside*] You've sentenced well.

LUSSURIOSO   Away; see it be done.

VINDICE   [*aside*] Could you not stick? See what confession doth!
               Who would not lie, when men are hanged for truth?

HIPPOLITO [*aside*] Brother, how happy is our vengeance!

VINDICE   [*aside*]   Why, it hits
               Past th'apprehension of indifferent wits.

LUSSURIOSO My lord, let post-horses be sent
               Into all places to entrap the villain.

VINDICE   [*aside*] Post-horses, ha, ha!

1 NOBLE   My lord, we're something bold to know our duty.   140
               Your father's accidentally departed;
               The titles that were due to him meet you.

LUSSURIOSO Meet me! I'm not at leisure, my good lord.
               I've many griefs to despatch out o'the way.
               [*aside*] Welcome, sweet titles!
                                             Talk to me, my lords,
               Of sepulchres and mighty emperors' bones;
               That's thought for me.

VINDICE   [*aside*]   So one may see by this
               How foreign markets go;
               Courtiers have feet o'the nines, and tongues o'
                                             the twelves;
               They flatter dukes, and dukes flatter themselves.   150

2 NOBLE   My lord, it is your shine must comfort us.

LUSSURIOSO Alas! I shine in tears, like the sun in April.

1 NOBLE   You're now my lord's grace.

LUSSURIOSO My lord's grace! I perceive you'll have it so.

2 NOBLE   'Tis but your own.

LUSSURIOSO Then, Heavens, give me grace to be so!

VINDICE   [*aside*] He prays well for himself.

I NOBLE   Madam, all sorrows
           Must run their circles into joys. No doubt
           But time will make the murderer bring forth   160
           Himself.
VINDICE   [aside] He were an ass then, i'faith.
I NOBLE   In the mean season,
           Let us bethink the latest funeral honours
           Due to the duke's cold body. And withal,
           Calling to memory our new happiness
           Speed in his royal son: lords, gentlemen,
           Prepare for revels.
VINDICE   [aside]   Revels!
I NOBLE   Time hath several falls.
           Griefs lift up joys: feasts put down funerals.
LUSSURIOSO Come then, my lords, my favour's to you all.
           [aside] The duchess is suspected foully bent;   170
           I'll begin dukedom with her banishment.
                        [exeunt Lussurioso, Duchess, and Nobles
HIPPOLITO Revels!
VINDICE   Ay, that's the word: we are firm yet;
           Strike one strain more, and then we crown our wit.
                              [exeunt Vindice and Hippolito
SPURIO   Well, have at the fairest mark – so said the duke
           When he begot me –
           And if I miss his heart, or near about,
           Then have at any; a bastard scorns to be out.   [exit
SUPERVACU. Not'st thou that Spurio, brother?
AMBITIOSO Yes, I note him to our shame.
SUPERVACU. He shall not live: his hair shall not grow much longer. 180
           In this time of revels, tricks may be set afoot. Seest
           thou yon new moon? It shall outlive the new duke by
           much; this hand shall dispossess him. Then we're
           mighty.
           A mask is treason's licence, that build upon:
           'Tis murder's best face, when a vizard's on.   [exit
AMBITIOSO Is't so? 'Tis very good!
           And do you think to be duke then, kind brother?
           I'll see fair play; drop one, and there lies t'other.
                                                    [exit

SCENE 2

A room in Piero's house

Enter VINDICE *and* HIPPOLITO, *with* PIERO *and other Lords*

VINDICE   My lords, be all of music, strike old griefs into
                                  other countries
    That flow in too much milk, and have faint livers,
    Not daring to stab home their discontents.
    Let our hid flames break out as fire, as lightning,
    To blast this villainous dukedom, vexed with sin;
    Wind up your souls to their full height again.

PIERO   How?

1 LORD   Which way?

2 LORD   Any way: our wrongs are such,
    We cannot justly be revenged too much.

VINDICE   You shall have all enough. Revels are toward,
    And those few nobles that have long suppressed you,   10
    Are busied to the furnishing of a masque,
    And do affect to make a pleasant tale on't:
    The masquing suits are fashioning: now comes in
    That which must glad us all. We too take pattern
    Of all those suits, the colour, trimming, fashion,
    E'en to an undistinguished hair almost:
    Then entering first, observing the true form,
    Within a strain or two we shall find leisure
    To steal our swords out handsomely;
    And when they think their pleasure sweet and good,   20
    In midst of all their joys they shall sigh blood.

PIERO   Weightily, effectually!

3 LORD   Before the t'other maskers come –

VINDICE   We're gone, all done and past.

PIERO   But how for the duke's guard?

VINDICE   Let that alone;
    By one and one their strengths shall be drunk down.

HIPPOLITO   There are five hundred gentlemen in the action,
    That will apply themselves, and not stand idle.

PIERO   O, let us hug your bosoms!
VINDICE   Come, my lords,
            Prepare for deeds: let other times have words.   30
                                                    [*exeunt*

SCENE 3

Hall of State in the palace

In a dumb show, the possessing of the young DUKE *with all his Nobles:
sounding music. A furnished table is brought forth; then enter the* DUKE
and his Nobles to the banquet. A blazing star appeareth.

I NOBLE   Many harmonious hours and choicest pleasures
            Fill up the royal number of your years!
LUSSURIOSO   My lords, we're pleased to thank you, though
                                                    we know
            'Tis but your duty now to wish it so.
I NOBLE   That shine makes us all happy.
3 NOBLE   His grace frowns.
2 NOBLE   Yet we must say he smiles.
I NOBLE   I think we must.
LUSSURIOSO   [*aside*] That foul incontinent duchess we have banished;
            The bastard shall not live. After these revels,
            I'll begin strange ones: he and the step-sons
            Shall pay their lives for the first subsidies;   10
            We must not frown so soon, else 't'had been now.
I NOBLE   My gracious lord, please you prepare for pleasure.
            The masque is not far off.
LUSSURIOSO   We are for pleasure.
            Beshrew thee, what art thou? Thou mad'st me start!
            Thou hast committed treason. A blazing star!
I NOBLE   A blazing star! O, where, my lord?
LUSSURIOSO   Spy out.
2 NOBLE   See, see, my lords, a wondrous dreadful one!
LUSSURIOSO   I am not pleased at that ill-knotted fire,
            That bushing, staring star. Am I not duke?
            It should not quake me now. Had it appeared   20
            Before it, I might then have justly feared;

But yet they say, whom art and learning weds,
When stars wear locks, they threaten great men's heads:
Is it so? You are read, my lords.

I NOBLE   May it please your grace,
It shows great anger.

LUSSURIOSO   That does not please our grace.

2 NOBLE   Yet here's the comfort, my lord: many times,
When it seems most near, it threatens farthest off.

LUSSURIOSO   Faith, and I think so too.

I NOBLE   Beside, my lord,
You're gracefully established with the loves
Of all your subjects; and for natural death,   30
I hope it will be threescore years a-coming.

LUSSURIOSO   True? No more but threescore years?

I NOBLE   Fourscore, I hope, my lord.

2 NOBLE   And fivescore, I.

3 NOBLE   But 'tis my hope, my lord, you shall ne'er die.

LUSSURIOSO   Give me thy hand; these others I rebuke:
He that hopes so is fittest for a duke:
Thou shalt sit next me; take your places, lords;
We're ready now for sports; let 'em set on:
You thing! We shall forget you quite anon!

3 NOBLE   I hear 'em coming, my lord.

Enter the Masque of Revengers: VINDICE *and*
HIPPOLITO, *with two Lords*

LUSSURIOSO   Ah, 'tis well!   40
[*aside*] Brothers and bastard, you dance next in hell!
[*they dance; at the end they steal out their swords, and kill
the four seated at the table. Thunder.*]

VINDICE   Mark, thunder!
Dost know thy cue, thou big-voiced crier?
Dukes' groans are thunder's watchwords.

HIPPOLITO   So, my lords, you have enough.

VINDICE   Come, let's away, no lingering.

HIPPOLITO   Follow! Go!
[*exeunt except Vindice*]

VINDICE   No power is angry when the lustful die;
When thunder claps, heaven likes the tragedy.   [*exit*

LUSSURIOSO O, O!

> *Enter the Masque of intended murderers:* AMBITIOSO, SUPER-
> VACUO, SPURIO, *and a Lord, coming in dancing;* LUSSURIOSO
> *recovers a little in voice, groans, and calls, 'A guard! treason!'*
> *At which the Dancers start out of their measure, and, turning*
> *towards the table, find them all to be murdered*

SPURIO   Whose groan was that?

LUSSURIOSO   Treason! A guard!

AMBITIOSO How now? All murdered!

SUPERVACU.   Murdered!

3 LORD   And those his nobles? 50

AMBITIOSO Here's a labour saved;
          I thought to have sped him. 'Sblood, how came this?

SPURIO   Then I proclaim myself; now I am duke.

AMBITIOSO Thou duke! Brother, thou liest.

SPURIO   Slave! So dost thou.
          [*kills Ambitioso*]

3 LORD   Base villain! hast thou slain my lord and master?
                                              [*stabs Spurio*

> *Re-enter* VINDICE *and* HIPPOLITO *and the two Lords*

VINDICE   Pistols! Treason! Murder! Help! Guard my lord the duke!

> *Enter* ANTONIO *and Guard*

HIPPOLITO Lay hold upon this traitor.

LUSSURIOSO O!

VINDICE   Alas! The duke is murdered.

HIPPOLITO   And the nobles.

VINDICE   Surgeons! Surgeons! [*aside*] Heart! Does he breathe
                                              so long? 60

ANTONIO   A piteous tragedy! Able to make
          An old man's eyes bloodshot.

LUSSURIOSO O!

VINDICE   Look to my lord the duke. [*aside*] A vengeance
                                              throttle him!
          Confess, thou murderous and unhallowed man,
          Didst thou kill all these?

3 LORD   None but the bastard, I.

VINDICE   How came the duke slain, then?
3 LORD   We found him so.
LUSSURIOSO O villain!
VINDICE   Hark!
LUSSURIOSO   Those in the masque did murder us.
VINDICE   La you now, sir –
             O marble impudence! Will you confess now?   70
3 LORD   'Sblood, 'tis all false.
ANTONIO   Away with that foul monster,
             Dipped in a prince's blood.
3 LORD   Heart! 'Tis a lie.
ANTONIO   Let him have bitter execution.
VINDICE   New marrow! No, I cannot be expressed.
             How fares my lord the duke?
LUSSURIOSO   Farewell to all;
             He that climbs highest has the greatest fall.
             My tongue is out of office.
VINDICE   Air, gentlemen, air.
             [whispers in his ear]
             Now thou'lt not prate on't, 'twas Vindice
             Murdered thee.
LUSSURIOSO   O!
VINDICE   [whispers]   Murdered thy father.
LUSSURIOSO   O!   [dies
VINDICE   [whispers] And I am he – tell nobody. So, so,   80
             The duke's departed.
ANTONIO   It was a deadly hand that wounded him.
             The rest, ambitious who should rule and sway
             After his death, were so made all away.
VINDICE   My lord was unlikely –
HIPPOLITO   Now the hope
             Of Italy lies in your reverend years.
VINDICE   Your hair will make the silver age again,
             When there were fewer, but more honest, men.
ANTONIO   The burthen's weighty, and will press age down;
             May I so rule, that Heaven may keep the crown!   90
VINDICE   The rape of your good lady has been quitted
             With death on death.
ANTONIO   Just is the law above.

But of all things it puts me most to wonder
How the old duke came murdered!

VINDICE   O my lord!

ANTONIO   It was the strangeliest carried: I've not heard
Of the like.

HIPPOLITO   'Twas all done for the best, my lord.

VINDICE   All for your grace's good. We may be bold
To speak it now, 'twas somewhat witty carried,
Though we say it — 'twas we two murdered him.

ANTONIO   You two?   100

VINDICE   None else, i'faith, my lord. Nay, 'twas well-managed.

ANTONIO   Lay hands upon those villains!

VINDICE   How! On us?

ANTONIO   Bear 'em to speedy execution.

VINDICE   Heart! Was't not for your good, my lord?

ANTONIO   My good!
Away with 'em: such an old man as he!
You, that would murder him, would murder me.

VINDICE   Is't come about?

HIPPOLITO   'Sfoot, brother, you begun.

VINDICE   May not we set as well as the duke's son?
Thou hast no conscience, are we not revenged?
Is there one enemy left alive amongst those?   110
'Tis time to die, when we're ourselves our foes:
When murderers shut deeds close, this curse
                                    does seal 'em:
If none disclose 'em, they themselves reveal 'em!
This murder might have slept in tongueless brass
But for ourselves, and the world died an ass.
Now I remember too, here was Piato
Brought forth a knavish sentence once;
No doubt (said he), but time
Will make the murderer bring forth himself.
'Tis well he died; he was a witch.   120
And now, my lord, since we are in for ever,
This work was ours, which else might have
                                    been slipped!
And if we list, we could have nobles clipped,
And go for less than beggars; but we hate

   To bleed so cowardly: we have enough, i'faith.
   We're well, our mother turned, our sister true,
   We die after a nest of dukes. Adieu!   [exeunt
ANTONIO How subtly was that murder closed! Bear up
   Those tragic bodies: 'tis a heavy season;
   Pray Heaven their blood may wash away all treason! 130
               [exit

THE WHITE DEVIL

INTRODUCTION

The White Devil was first performed between 1609 and 1613. Almost nothing is known of the life of the author, John Webster (*c.*1580–*c.*1634), beyond his success as a playwright. He collaborated with other major dramatists of the time. His plays are notable for the powerful female characters they contain and their ornate, gloomy imagery.

The White Devil contains one of the most sustained and significant female parts (although, of course, a male actor would have taken the role) in English Renaissance theatre. The play tells the story of Vittoria Corombona, notorious strumpet and *femme fatale*, who defends herself ably against the legions of patriarchal power matched against her and proves that they are no better than she. It is based on the real story of Vittoria Accoromboni, who was murdered on 22 December 1585. Several accounts of this story existed but which of them – if any – Webster used is a matter of conjecture. He may have relied on oral reports.

The Duke of Brachiano falls in love with Vittoria while staying at her house with her aged husband, Camillo. The couple no longer love one another, and the Duke is also weary of his virtuous wife, Isabella, who is the sister of Francisco de Medici, Duke of Florence. They embark on an adulterous affair after Vittoria relates the story of a dream she had, and urges the Duke to murder Camillo. This arouses the disapproval of Vittoria's mother, Cornelia, who has overheard her daughter's tale.

Isabella comes to Rome to find her negligent husband. She stays at the house of her brother, the Duke of Florence. The duchess's brothers, Francisco and the Cardinal Monticelso, confront Brachiano and warn him about his behaviour, using fears about his young son, Giovanni. However, their plans do not work, and

Brachiano warns Isabella that they are effectively divorced because he will never sleep with her again. The doting Isabella pretends that she has been the instigator of the separation. The brothers are put off the scent, and Brachiano employs Julio, a doctor, and Flamineo, to murder Camillo and Isabella. Julio poisons the lips of a portrait of Brachiano so that when Isabella kisses his lips she dies. Flamineo breaks Camillo's neck while he is vaulting in the gymnasium, but makes his death seem like an accident. Brachiano is able to watch both killings in the form of a dumb show.

Vittoria is arrested on suspicion of being an accessory to her husband's murder and a trial is held in Rome. The fact that this is the central scene in the play (3, 2) is signalled by the unusual step of placing a title, 'The Arraignment of Vittoria', in the printed text itself. Cardinal Monticelso is the chief prosecutor, accusing Vittoria of being a 'debauched and diversivolent woman', an adulteress and a murderess. She is able to give as good as she gets at the trial, twisting the words of her accusers against them, demonstrating that they are using the law simply to gain a conviction against a woman who is really no worse than they are. When Monticelso accuses her of being a whore, Vittoria asks him to define his terms: 'Ha! Whore! What's that?' Monticelso's answer, a series of metaphors, betrays a crucial ambivalence and is worth quoting at some length:

> Shall I expound whore to you? Sure I shall;
> I'll give their perfect character. They are, first,
> Sweetmeats which rot the eater; in man's nostrils
> Poisoned perfumes: they are cozening alchemy,
> Shipwrecks in calmest weather. What are whores?
> Cold Russian winters, that appear so barren
> As if that nature had forgot the spring:
> They are the true material fire of hell,
> Worse than those tributes i'th'Low Countries paid,
> Exactions upon meat, drink, garments, sleep,
> Ay even on man's perdition, his sin:
> They are those brittle evidences of law
> Which forfeit all a wretched man's estate
> For leaving out one syllable . . .
>   They are worse,

Worse than dead bodies which are begg'd at gallows,
And wrought upon by surgeons, to teach man
Wherein he is imperfect. What's a whore?
She's like the guilty counterfeited coin
Which, whosoe'er first stamps it, brings in trouble
All that receive it.

                                        (3, 2, 80–103)

Monticelso's speech is rhetorically impressive and his examples
possess considerable force. But he has not really made any sort of
argument at all, and when Vittoria responds 'This character scapes
me' she has clearly scored a hit. The last example Monticelso
produces, that of the counterfeit coin, which devalues others
because it is passed from hand to hand in general circulation, is
specifically targeted at women. However, like all the examples he
uses, the relevance to the behaviour of men in the play, especially
his own, is striking. The character escapes Vittoria because she is
no more a whore than those who are so quick to condemn her.
The audience knows that Vittoria is labelled a whore simple
because of her sex. Yet despite her defence she is found guilty,
because Brachiano has to admit that he was at her house the night
that Camillo was killed. She is condemned to be confined in a
nunnery.

To save himself, Flamineo pretends that he has succumbed to
madness. Monticelso and Francisco cannot agree what to do about
the death of their sister. Francisco is wary of provoking war
between the two states by acting hastily, but he is also reluctant to
wait for the right moment to arise as the Cardinal wishes. Francisco
writes a fake love letter to Vittoria, hoping to cause Brachiano to
repudiate her, and planning to use Lodovico to murder her.
However, the plan misfires when, after a serious argument,
Brachiano takes Vittoria out of her prison and marries her.

Monticelso has now been made Pope, and he excommunicates
Vittoria and Brachiano. He disapproves of Francisco's plan to use
Lodovico to murder Vittoria, but when Francisco sends Lodovico
a thousand ducats purporting to come from the Pope, Lodovico is
convinced that his dark deed has the highest blessing.

Francisco arrives at Brachiano's palace disguised as Mulinassar, a
Moorish knight, accompanied by Lodovico and Gasparo, disguised

as Maltese knights, looking for a chance for revenge. Meanwhile, Flamineo murders his virtuous brother Marcello in front of his mother, Cornelia, who goes mad with grief. Lodovico ingeniously murders Brachiano, when a poison is sprinkled on his helmet before he fights in a tournament. Lodovico and Gasparo disguise themselves as Capuchin monks in order to perform the last rites, and when they are free of witnesses they strangle him in front of Vittoria who has run to his bedroom on hearing Brachiano's cries.

The play ends, like most Jacobean tragedies, with the stage strewn with bodies which have all died gruesome deaths. Brachiano's ghost warns Flamineo that he will soon come to a bad end. He threatens to murder Vittoria and her Moorish maid, Zanche, if they do not adequately reward him. They agree a bizarre suicide pact with him dying first. They shoot him with his pistols but he rises unhurt some minutes later when they (understandably) fail to honour their side of the mad bargain. Their screams are overheard, and the fake Capuchins arrive, only to stab all three. Vittoria expires claiming that her greatest sin lay in her blood: 'Now my blood pays for't . . . My soul, like to a ship in a black storm, is driven, I know not whither' (5, 6, 237–245). There is a close resemblance to the death of Beatrice in *The Changeling*, a play written a few years later. The murderers then get their just deserts. They are captured by Giovanni, the young prince. Lodovico confesses, implicating Francisco, and Giovanni promises to bring all to justice. The resemblance to the ending of *The Duchess of Malfi*, when Delio and Antonio's son appear to restore order, should also be noted.

The White Devil, more than any other play included in this volume, is a study of hypocrisy, specifically male hypocrisy towards women. Vittoria is clearly no angel, and is involved in the murder of her husband and her lover's wife. But she is by no means as evil as the two brothers, Monticelso and Francisco, who systematically abuse their positions of power in a way which resembles the two villainous brothers, Ferdinand and the Cardinal, in Webster's other great tragedy, *The Duchess of Malfi*. Nor is she as bad as Lodovico and her own brother, Flamineo. Yet she can be abused as a whore while the men all enjoy a sense of their superior virtue until proved otherwise. The 'White Devil' of the title is a puzzle, which the reader and the audience have to work out to their own satisfaction.

Is the 'White Devil' Vittoria herself, who should be a 'white' woman but is really scarlet? Or is the real devil the Cardinal who should be white as a servant of God, but is really the most evil of the characters in the play because he abuses the sacred office bestowed on him? If it is both of these, then it serves as a comment on the danger of relying on appearances and so criticises man's vicious treatment of women.

The assumption made at her trial, which Vittoria points out with considerable aplomb, is that she must be guilty because she is a scarlet woman. But, to take just one example, the scarlet of the cardinal is far more dangerous and hides much more evil than she is ever capable of. Webster has written a play which challenges easy moral assumptions. He forces the audience to question its sense of moral values and not to reach for apparently straightforward solutions, even when crimes have been committed which seem to reinforce such views. The first murder is indeed committed by the adulterous couple at the instigation of the woman. But, just as the crimes of Vindice in *The Revenger's Tragedy* easily outstrip those committed by the Duke (who has the good grace to admit that he is no innocent when he has Lussurioso released and comments 'It well becomes that judge to nod at crimes, that does commit the greater himself, and lives'), so do those committed by Lodovico, Monticelso, Flamineo and Francisco go well beyond the evil perpetrated by Vittoria, the 'famous Venetian Courtesan'. So the dramatic core of the play, which is quite convoluted and over-elaborate in its overall plot and design, takes place in Act 3 in the Roman courtroom when Vittoria holds centre stage.

CHARACTERS IN THE PLAY

MONTICELSO, *a Cardinal, afterwards Pope*

FRANCISCO DE MEDICI, *Duke of Florence*

BRACHIANO, *otherwise Paulo Giordano Ursini, Duke of Brachiano, husband of* ISABELLA

GIOVANNI, *his son*

COUNT LODOVICO (*sometimes known as Lodowick*)

CAMILLO, *husband of* VITTORIA

FLAMINEO, *brother of* VITTORIA, *secretary to* BRACHIANO

MARCELLO, *brother of* VITTORIA, *attendant on* FRANCISCO DE MEDICI

HORTENSIO

ANTONELLI

GASPARO

FARNESE

CARLO

PEDRO

Doctor

Conjurer

Lawyer

JAQUES

JULIO

CHRISTOPHERO

Ambassadors, Physicians, Officers, Attendants, etc.

ISABELLA, *sister of* FRANCISCO DE MEDICI, *wife of* BRACHIANO

VITTORIA COROMBONA, *married first to* CAMILLO, *afterwards to* BRACHIANO

CORNELIA, *mother of* VITTORIA

ZANCHE, *a Moor, waiting-woman to* VITTORIA

Matron of the House of Convertites

The Scene: Rome and Padua

THE WHITE DEVIL

ACT I SCENE I

A street in Rome

Enter COUNT LODOVICO, ANTONELLI, *and* GASPARO

LODOVICO   Banished!

ANTONELLI   It grieved me much to hear the sentence.

LODOVICO   Ha, ha! O Democritus, thy gods
That govern the whole world! Courtly reward
And punishment. Fortune's a right whore:
If she give aught, she deals it in small parcels,
That she may take away all at one swoop.
This 'tis to have great enemies – God quit them!
Your wolf no longer seems to be a wolf
Than when she's hungry.

GASPARO   You term those enemies
Are men of princely rank.

LODOVICO   O, I pray for them: 10
The violent thunder is adored by those
Are pashed in pieces by it.

ANTONELLI   Come, my lord,
You are justly doomed: look but a little back
Into your former life; you have in three years
Ruined the noblest earldom.

GASPARO   Your followers
Have swallowed you like mummia and, being sick
With such unnatural and horrid physic,
Vomit you up i'the kennel.

ANTONELLI   All the damnable degrees
Of drinkings have you staggered through: one citizen   20
Is lord of two fair manors called you master
Only for caviare.

GASPARO   Those noblemen
Which were invited to your prodigal feasts
(Wherein the phoenix scarce could scape
                                your throats)
Laugh at your misery, as fore-deeming you

An idle meteor, which, drawn forth the earth,
Would be soon lost i'the air.

ANTONELLI   Jest upon you,
And say you were begotten in an earthquake,
You have ruined such fair lordships.

LODOVICO   Very good.
This well goes with two buckets: I must tend   30
The pouring out of either.

GASPARO   ·   Worse than these;
You have acted certain murders here in Rome,
Bloody and full of horror.

LODOVICO   'Las, they were flea-bitings.
Why took they not my head, then?

GASPARO   .   O, my lord,
The law doth sometimes mediate, thinks it good
Not ever to steep violent sins in blood:
This gentle penance may both end your crimes,
And in the example better these bad times.

LODOVICO So; but I wonder, then, some great men scape
This banishment: there's Paulo Giordano   40
Ursini, the Duke of Brachiano, now lives
In Rome, and by close panderism seeks
To prostitute the honour of Vittoria
Corombona – Vittoria, she that might
Have got my pardon for one kiss to the duke.

ANTONELLI Have a full man within you.
We see that trees bear no such pleasant fruit
There where they grew first as where they are new set:
Perfumes, the more they are chafed, the more
                                        they render
Their pleasing scents; and so affliction   50
Expresseth virtue fully, whether true
Or else adulterate.

LODOVICO   Leave your painted comforts:
I'll make Italian cut-works in their guts,
If ever I return.

GASPARO   O, sir!

LODOVICO   I am patient.
I have seen some ready to be executed

Give pleasant looks and money, and grown familiar
With the knave hangman: so do I. I thank them,
And would account them nobly merciful,
Would they despatch me quickly.

ANTONELLI   Fare you well:
We shall find time, I doubt not, to repeal   60
Your banishment.

LODOVICO   I am ever bound to you:
This is the world's alms; pray, make use of it.
Great men sell sheep thus to be cut in pieces,
When first they have shorn them bare and sold
                                        their fleeces.
                                                [*exeunt*

SCENE 2

An apartment in Camillo's house

Sennet. Enter BRACHIANO, CAMILLO, FLAMINEO,
VITTORIA COROMBONA *and Attendants*

BRACHIANO Your best of rest!
VITTORIA   Unto my lord, the duke,
The best of welcome! More lights! Attend the duke.
                        [*exeunt Camillo and Vittoria Corombona*
BRACHIANO Flamineo –
FLAMINEO   My lord?
BRACHIANO   Quite lost, Flamineo.
FLAMINEO Pursue your noble wishes, I am prompt
As lightning to your service. O, my lord,
[*whispers*] The fair Vittoria, my happy sister,
Shall give you present audience – Gentlemen,
Let the caroche go on; and 'tis his pleasure
You put out all your torches, and depart.
                                        [*exeunt Attendants*
BRACHIANO Are we so happy?
FLAMINEO   Can it be otherwise?   10
Observed you not tonight, my honoured lord,
Which way soe'er you went, she threw her eyes?
I have dealt already with her chambermaid,

Zanche the Moor; and she is wondrous proud
To be the agent for so high a spirit.

BRACHIANO We are happy above thought, because 'bove merit.

FLAMINEO 'Bove merit! We may now talk freely. 'Bove merit!
What is't you doubt? Her coyness? That's but the
superficies of lust most women have: yet why should
ladies blush to hear that named which they do not fear   20
to handle? O, they are politic: they know our desire is
increased by the difficulty of enjoying; whereas satiety
is a blunt, weary, and drowsy passion. If the buttery-
hatch at court stood continually open, there would be
nothing so passionate crowding, nor hot suit after the
beverage.

BRACHIANO O, but her jealous husband.

FLAMINEO Hang him! A gilder that hath his brains perished with
quicksilver is not more cold in the liver: the great
barriers moulted not more feathers than he hath shed   30
hairs, by the confession of his doctor: an Irish gamester
that will play himself naked, and then wage all down-
wards at hazard, is not more venturous: so unable to
please a woman that, like a Dutch doublet, all his back
is shrunk into his breeches.
Shroud you within this closet, good my lord:
Some trick now must be thought on to divide
My brother-in-law from his fair bedfellow.

BRACHIANO O, should she fail to come!

FLAMINEO I must not have your lordship thus unwisely amorous.   40
I myself have loved a lady, and pursued her with a
great deal of under-age protestation, whom some
three or four gallants that have enjoyed would with all
their hearts have been glad to have been rid of: 'tis just
like a summer birdcage in a garden; the birds that are
without despair to get in, and the birds that are within
despair, and are in a consumption, for fear they shall
never get out.
Away, away, my lord!   [exit Brachiano
See, here he comes. This fellow by his apparel   50
Some men would judge a politician;
But call his wit in question, you shall find it

Merely an ass in's foot-cloth.

Re-enter CAMILLO

                           How now, brother!
What, travelling to bed to your kind wife?

CAMILLO   I assure you, brother, no; my voyage lies
More northerly, in a far colder clime:
I do not well remember, I protest,
When I last lay with her.

FLAMINEO   Strange you should lose your count.

CAMILLO   We never lay together, but ere morning   60
There grew a flaw between us.

FLAMINEO   'T had been your part
To have made up that flaw.

CAMILLO   True, but she loathes
I should be seen in't.

FLAMINEO   Why, sir, what's the matter?

CAMILLO   The duke, your master, visits me, I thank him;
And I perceive how, like an earnest bowler,
He very passionately leans that way
He should have his bowl run.

FLAMINEO   I hope you do not think –

CAMILLO   That noblemen bowl booty? Faith, his cheek
Hath a most excellent bias; it would fain
Jump with my mistress.

FLAMINEO   Will you be an ass,   70
Despite your Aristotle? Or a cuckold,
Contrary to your Ephemerides,
Which shows you under what a smiling planet
You were first swaddled?

CAMILLO   Pew-wew, sir, tell not me
Of planets nor of Ephemerides:
A man may be made a cuckold in the day-time,
When the stars' eyes are out.

FLAMINEO   Sir, God b'wi'you;
I do commit you to your pitiful pillow
Stuffed with horn-shavings.

CAMILLO   Brother –

FLAMINEO   God refuse me,
Might I advise you now, your only course   80

Were to lock up your wife.

CAMILLO   'Twere very good.

FLAMINEO Bar her the sight of revels.

CAMILLO   Excellent.

FLAMINEO Let her not go to church, but like a hound
In lyam at your heels.

CAMILLO   'Twere for her honour.

FLAMINEO And so you should be certain in one fortnight
Despite her chastity or innocence,
To be cuckolded, which yet is in suspense:
This is my counsel, and I ask no fee for't.

CAMILLO Come, you know not where my night-cap wings me.

FLAMINEO Wear it a'the old fashion; let your large ears come   90
through, it will be more easy: nay, I will be bitter – bar
your wife of her entertainment: women are more
willingly and more gloriously chaste when they are
least restrained of their liberty. It seems you would be
a fine capricious mathematically jealous coxcomb; take
the height of your own horns with a Jacob's staff afore
they are up. These politic inclosures for paltry mutton
make more rebellion in the flesh than all the provoca-
tive electuaries doctors have uttered since last jubilee.

CAMILLO This doth not physic me.   100

FLAMINEO It seems you are jealous: I'll show you the error of it
by a familiar example. I have seen a pair of spectacles
fashioned with such perspective art, that, lay down but
one twelve pence a'the board, 'twill appear as if there
were twenty; now, should you wear a pair of these
spectacles, and see your wife tying her shoe, you
would imagine twenty hands were taking up of your
wife's clothes, and this would put you into a horrible
causeless fury.

CAMILLO The fault there, sir, is not in the eyesight.   110

FLAMINEO True; but they that have the yellow jaundice think all
objects they look on to be yellow. Jealousy is worser;
her fits present to a man, like so many bubbles in a
basin of water, twenty several crabbed faces; many
times makes his own shadow his cuckold-maker. See,
she comes.

Re-enter VITTORIA COROMBONA

What reason have you to be jealous of this creature?
What an ignorant ass or flattering knave might he be
counted, that should write sonnets to her eyes, or call
her brow the snow of Ida or ivory of Corinth, or   120
compare her hair to the blackbird's bill, when 'tis liker
the blackbird's feather! This is all; be wise, I will make
you friends; and you shall go to bed together. Marry,
look you, it shall not be your seeking; do you stand
upon that by any means: walk you aloof; I would not
have you seen in't. [*Camillo retires*] Sister, my lord
attends you in the banqueting-house. Your husband is
wondrous discontented.

VITTORIA   I did nothing to displease him: I carved to him at
supper-time.   130

FLAMINEO   You need not have carved him, in faith; they say he is
a capon already. I must now seemingly fall out with
you. Shall a gentleman so well descended as Camillo –
a lousy slave, that within this twenty years rode with
the black guard in the duke's carriage, 'mongst spits
and dripping-pans –

CAMILLO   Now he begins to tickle her.

FLAMINEO   An excellent scholar, one that hath a head filled with
calves-brains without any sage in them, come crouching
in the hams to you for a night's lodging? That hath an   140
itch in's hams, which like the fire at the glass-house hath
not gone out this seven years. Is he not a courtly
gentleman? When he wears white satin, one would take
him by his black muzzle to be no other creature than a
maggot. You are a goodly foil, I confess, well set out –
but covered with a false stone, yon counterfeit diamond.

CAMILLO   He will make her know what is in me.

FLAMINEO   Come, my lord attends you; thou shalt go to bed
to my lord –

CAMILLO   Now he comes to't.   150

FLAMINEO   With a relish as curious as a vintner going to taste new
wine. [*to Camillo*] I am opening your case hard.

CAMILLO   A virtuous brother, o'my credit!

FLAMINEO   He will give thee a ring with a philosopher's stone in it.

CAMILLO   Indeed, I am studying alchymy.

FLAMINEO   Thou shalt lie in a bed stuffed with turtles' feathers;
           swoon in perfumed linen, like the fellow was smoth-
           ered in roses. So perfect shall be thy happiness, that, as
           men at sea think land and trees and ships go that way
           they go, so both Heaven and earth shall seem to go   160
           your voyage. Shall't meet him; 'tis fixed with nails of
           diamonds to inevitable necessity.

VITTORIA   How shall's rid him hence?

FLAMINEO   I will put the breeze in's tail – set him gadding presently.
           [to Camillo] I have almost wrought her to it, I find her
           coming: but, might I advise you now, for this night I
           would not lie with her; I would cross her humour to
           make her more humble.

CAMILLO   Shall I, shall I?

FLAMINEO   It will show in you a supremacy of judgment.   170

CAMILLO   True, and a mind differing from the tumultuary
           opinion; for, *quae negata, grata.*

FLAMINEO   Right: you are the adamant shall draw her to you,
           though you keep distance off.

CAMILLO   A philosophical reason.

FLAMINEO   Walk by her o'the nobleman's fashion, and tell her
           you will lie with her at the end of the progress.

CAMILLO   [coming forward] Vittoria, I cannot be induced, or, as a
           man would say, incited –

VITTORIA   To do what, sir?   180

CAMILLO   To lie with you tonight. Your silkworm useth to fast
           every third day, and the next following spins the better.
           Tomorrow at night I am for you.

VITTORIA   You'll spin a fair thread, trust to't.

FLAMINEO   But, do you hear, I shall have you steal to her chamber
           about midnight.

CAMILLO   Do you think so? Why, look you, brother, because
           you shall not think I'll gull you, take the key, lock me
           into the chamber, and say you shall be sure of me.

FLAMINEO   In troth, I will; I'll be your gaoler once. But have you 190
           ne'er a false door?

CAMILLO   A pox on't, as I am a Christian. Tell me tomorrow
           how scurvily she takes my unkind parting.

FLAMINEO   I will.

CAMILLO   Didst thou not mark the jest of the silkworm? Good-
night: in faith, I will use this trick often.

FLAMINEO   Do, do, do. [*exit Camillo, and Flamineo locks the door on
him*] So now you are safe. Ha, ha, ha! Thou entanglest
thyself in thine own work like a silkworm. Come,
sister; darkness hides your blush. Women are like curst   200
dogs: civility keeps them tied all daytime, but they are
let loose at midnight; then they do most good, or most
mischief. My lord, my lord!

Re-enter BRACHIANO. ZANCHE *brings out a carpet,*
spreads it, and lays on it two fair cushions

BRACHIANO   Give credit, I could wish time would stand still,
             And never end this interview, this hour:
             But all delight doth itself soon'st devour.

Enter CORNELIA *behind, listening*

             Let me into your bosom, happy lady,
             Pour out, instead of eloquence, my vows:
             Loose me not, madam; for, if you forego me,
             I am lost eternally.

VITTORIA   Sir, in the way of pity,   210
             I wish you heart-whole.

BRACHIANO   You are a sweet physician.

VITTORIA   Sure, sir, a loathéd cruelty in ladies
             Is as to doctors many funerals;
             It takes away their credit.

BRACHIANO   Excellent creature!
             We call the cruel fair: what name for you
             That are so merciful?

ZANCHE   See, now they close.

FLAMINEO   Most happy union.

CORNELIA   My fears are fall'n upon me: O, my heart!
             My son the pander! Now I find our house
             Sinking to ruin. Earthquakes leave behind,   220
             Where they have tyrannised, iron, lead, or stone;
             But, woe to ruin, violent lust leaves none!

BRACHIANO   What value is this jewel?

VITTORIA   'Tis th'ornament

	Of a weak fortune.
BRACHIANO	In sooth, I'll have it; nay, I will but change
	My jewel for your jewel.
FLAMINEO	Excellent!
	His jewel for her jewel – well put in, duke.
BRACHIANO	Nay, let me see you wear it.
VITTORIA	Here, sir?
BRACHIANO	Nay, lower, you shall wear my jewel lower.
FLAMINEO	That's better; she must wear his jewel lower. 230
VITTORIA	To pass away the time, I'll tell your grace
	A dream I had last night.
BRACHIANO	Most wishedly.
VITTORIA	A foolish idle dream.
	Methought I walked about the mid of night
	Into a churchyard, where a goodly yew-tree
	Spread her large root in ground. Under that yew,
	As I sate sadly leaning on a grave
	Chequered with cross sticks, there came stealing in
	Your duchess and my husband: one of them
	A pick-axe bore, the other a rusty spade, 240
	And in rough terms they gan to challenge me
	About this yew.
BRACHIANO	That tree?
VITTORIA	This harmless yew:
	They told me my intent was to root up
	That well-grown yew, and plant i'the stead of it
	A withered blackthorn; and for that they vowed
	To bury me alive. My husband straight
	With pick-axe gan to dig, and your fell duchess
	With shovel, like a Fury, voided out
	The earth, and scattered bones. Lord, how,
	methought,
	I trembled! And yet, for all this terror, 250
	I could not pray.
FLAMINEO	No; the devil was in your dream.
VITTORIA	When to my rescue there arose, methought,
	A whirlwind, which let fall a massy arm
	From that strong plant;
	And both were struck dead by that sacred yew,

In that base shallow grave that was their due.

FLAMINEO   Excellent devil! She hath taught him in a dream
To make away his duchess and her husband.

BRACHIANO   Sweetly shall I interpret this your dream.
You are lodged within his arms who shall protect you   260
From all the fevers of a jealous husband,
From the poor envy of our phlegmatic duchess.
I'll seat you above law, and above scandal,
Give to your thoughts the invention of delight,
And the fruition; nor shall government
Divide me from you longer than a care
To keep you great: you shall to me at once
Be dukedom, health, wife, children, friends, and all.

CORNELIA   [coming forward] Woe to light hearts, they still
                                   fore-run our fall!

FLAMINEO   What Fury raised thee up? Away, away!   [exit Zanche   270

CORNELIA   What make you here, my lord, this dead of night?
Never dropped mildew on a flower here
Till now.

FLAMINEO   I pray, will you go to bed, then,
Lest you be blasted?

CORNELIA   O, that this fair garden
Had with all poisoned herbs of Thessaly
At first been planted; made a nursery
For witchcraft, rather than a burial plot
For both your honours!

VITTORIA   Dearest mother, hear me.

CORNELIA   O, thou dost make my brow bend to the earth,
Sooner than nature! See, the curse of children!   280
In life they keep us frequently in tears;
And in the cold grave leave us in pale fears.

BRACHIANO   Come, come, I will not hear you.

VITTORIA   Dear my lord –

CORNELIA   Where is thy duchess now, adulterous duke?
Thou little dreamd'st this night she is come to Rome.

FLAMINEO   How! Come to Rome!

VITTORIA   The duchess!

BRACHIANO   She had been better –

CORNELIA   The lives of princes should like dials move,

	Whose regular example is so strong,	
	They make the times by them go right or wrong.	
FLAMINEO	So; have you done?	
CORNELIA	Unfortunate Camillo!	290
VITTORIA	I do protest, if any chaste denial,	
	If anything but blood could have allayed	
	His long suit to me –	
CORNELIA	I will join with thee,	
	To the most woeful end e'er mother kneeled:	
	If thou dishonour thus thy husband's bed,	
	Be thy life short as are the funeral tears	
	In great men's –	
BRACHIANO	Fie, fie, the woman's mad.	
CORNELIA	Be thy act Judas-like – betray in kissing:	
	Mayst thou be envied during his short breath,	
	And pitied like a wretch after his death!	300
VITTORIA	O me accursed! [exit	
FLAMINEO	Are you out of your wits, my lord?	
	I'll fetch her back again.	
BRACHIANO	No, I'll to bed:	
	Send Doctor Julio to me presently.	
	Uncharitable woman! Thy rash tongue	
	Hath raised a fearful and prodigious storm:	
	Be thou the cause of all ensuing harm. [exit	
FLAMINEO	Now, you that stand so much upon your honour,	
	Is this a fitting time a'night, think you,	
	To send a duke home without e'er a man?	310
	I would fain know where lies the mass of wealth	
	Which you have hoarded for my maintenance,	
	That I may bear my beard out of the level	
	Of my lord's stirrup.	
CORNELIA	What! Because we are poor	
	Shall we be vicious?	
FLAMINEO	Pray, what means have you	
	To keep me from the galleys or the gallows?	
	My father proved himself a gentleman,	
	Sold all's land, and, like a fortunate fellow,	
	Died ere the money was spent. You brought me up	
	At Padua, I confess, where, I protest,	320

For want of means (the university judge me)
I have been fain to heel my tutor's stockings,
At least seven years: conspiring with a beard,
Made me a graduate, then to this duke's service.
I visited the court, whence I returned
More courteous, more lecherous by far,
But not a suit the richer: and shall I,
Having a path so open and so free
To my preferment, still retain your milk
In my pale forehead? No, this face of mine   330
I'll arm, and fortify with lusty wine,
'Gainst shame and blushing.

CORNELIA   O, that I ne'er had borne thee

FLAMINEO   So would I;
I would the common'st courtesan in Rome
Had been my mother, rather than thyself.
Nature is very pitiful to whores,
To give them but few children, yet those children
Plurality of fathers: they are sure
They shall not want. Go, go,
Complain unto my great lord cardinal;   340
Yet may be he will justify the act.
Lycurgus wondered much men would provide
Good stallions for their mares, and yet would suffer
Their fair wives to be barren.

CORNELIA   Misery of miseries! [exit

FLAMINEO The duchess come to court! I like not that.
We are engaged to mischief, and must on:
As rivers to find out the ocean
Flow with crook bendings beneath forcéd banks,
Or as we see, to aspire some mountain's top,
The way ascends not straight, but imitates   350
The subtle foldings of a winter snake,
So who knows policy and her true aspect,
Shall find her ways winding and indirect.

                                        [exit

ACT 2 SCENE I

A room in Francisco's palace

Enter FRANCISCO DE MEDICI, CARDINAL MONTICELSO,
MARCELLO, ISABELLA, GIOVANNI, *with* JAQUES *the Moor*

FRANCISCO Have you not seen your husband since you arrived?

ISABELLA Not yet, sir.

FRANCISCO   Surely he is wondrous kind.
          If I had such a dove-house as Camillo's,
          I would set fire on't, were't but to destroy
          The pole-cats that haunt to it. My sweet cousin!

GIOVANNI Lord uncle, you did promise me a horse
          And armour.

FRANCISCO   That I did, my pretty cousin –
          Marcello, see it fitted.

MARCELLO My lord, the duke is here.

FRANCISCO   Sister, away!
          You must not yet be seen.

ISABELLA   I do beseech you,   10
          Entreat him mildly; let not your rough tongue
          Set us at louder variance: all my wrongs
          Are freely pardoned; and I do not doubt,
          As men, to try the precious unicorn's horn,
          Make of the powder a preservative circle,
          And in it put a spider, so these arms
          Shall charm his poison, force it to obeying,
          And keep him chaste from an infected straying.

FRANCISCO I wish it may. Be gone, void the chamber.

                  [*exeunt Isabella, Giovanni, and Jaques*

        Enter BRACHIANO *and* FLAMINEO

          You are welcome: will you sit? – I pray, my lord,   20
          Be you my orator, my heart's too full;
          I'll second you anon.

MONTICEL.   Ere I begin,
          Let me entreat your grace forego all passion
          Which may be raiséd by my free discourse.

BRACHIANO As silent as i'the church: you may proceed.

MONTICEL. It is a wonder to your noble friends,
                    That you, having, as 'twere, entered the world
                    With a free sceptre in your able hand,
                    And to the use of nature well applied
                    High gifts of learning, should in your prime age   30
                    Neglect your awful throne for the soft down
                    Of an insatiate bed. O, my lord,
                    The drunkard after all his lavish cups
                    Is dry, and then is sober; so at length,
                    When you awake from this lascivious dream,
                    Repentance then will follow, like the sting
                    Placed in the adder's tail. Wretched are princes
                    When fortune blasteth but a petty flower
                    Of their unwieldy crowns, or ravisheth
                    But one pearl from their sceptres: but, alas,   40
                    When they to wilful shipwreck lose good fame,
                    All princely titles perish with their name!
BRACHIANO You have said, my lord.
MONTICEL.   Enough to give you taste
                    How far I am from flattering your greatness.
BRACHIANO Now you that are his second, what say you?
                    Do not like young hawks fetch a course about:
                    Your game flies fair and for you.
FRANCISCO   Do not fear it:
                    I'll answer you in your own hawking phrase.
                    Some eagles that should gaze upon the sun
                    Seldom soar high, but take their lustful ease,   50
                    Since they from dunghill birds their prey can seize.
                    You know Vittoria!
BRACHIANO   Yes.
FRANCISCO   You shift your shirt there,
                    When you retire from tennis?
BRACHIANO   Happily.
FRANCISCO Her husband is lord of a poor fortune;
                    Yet she wears cloth of tissue.
BRACHIANO   What of this?
                    Will you urge that, my good lord cardinal,
                    As part of her confession at next shrift,
                    And know from whence it sails?
FRANCISCO   She is your strumpet.

BRACHIANO Uncivil sir, there's hemlock in thy breath,
And that black slander. Were she a whore of mine,   60
All thy loud cannons, and thy borrowed Switzers,
Thy galleys, nor thy sworn confederates,
Durst not supplant her.

FRANCISCO   Let's not talk on thunder.
Thou hast a wife, our sister: would I had given
Both her white hands to death, bound and locked fast
In her last winding-sheet, when I gave thee
But one!

BRACHIANO   Thou hadst given a soul to God, then.

FRANCISCO   True:
Thy ghostly father, with all's absolution,
Shall ne'er do so by thee.

BRACHIANO   Spit thy poison.

FRANCISCO I shall not need; lust carries her sharp whip   70
At her own girdle. Look to't, for our anger
Is making thunderbolts.

BRACHIANO   Thunder! In faith,
They are but crackers.

FRANCISCO   We'll end this with the cannon.

BRACHIANO Thou'lt get naught by it but iron in thy wounds,
And gunpowder in thy nostrils.

FRANCISCO   Better that,
Than change perfumes for plasters.

BRACHIANO   Pity on thee:
'Twere good you'd show your slaves or men
                              condemned
Your new-ploughed forehead. Defiance, and I'll
                            meet thee,
Even in a thicket of thy ablest men!

MONTICEL. My lords, you shall not word it any further   80
Without a milder limit.

FRANCISCO   Willingly.

BRACHIANO Have you proclaimed a triumph, that you bait
A lion thus!

MONTICEL.   My lord!

BRACHIANO   I am tame, I am tame, sir.

FRANCISCO We send unto the duke for conference

'Bout levies 'gainst the pirates; my lord duke
Is not at home. We come ourself in person;
Still my lord duke is busied. But we fear,
When Tiber to each prowling passenger
Discovers flocks of wild ducks, then, my lord,
'Bout moulting time I mean, we shall be certain   90
To find you sure enough, and speak with you.

BRACHIANO Ha!

FRANCISCO A mere tale of a tub, my words are idle;
But to express the sonnet by natural reason –
When stags grow melancholic, you'll find the season.

MONTICEL. No more, my lord: here comes a champion
Shall end the difference between you both –

Re-enter GIOVANNI

Your son, the Prince Giovanni. See, my lords,
What hopes you store in him: this is a casket
For both your crowns, and should be held like dear.   100
Now is he apt for knowledge; therefore know,
It is a more direct and even way
To train to virtue those of princely blood
By examples than by precepts: if by examples,
Whom should he rather strive to imitate
Than his own father? Be his pattern, then;
Leave him a stock of virtue that may last,
Should fortune rend his sails and split his mast.

BRACHIANO Your hand, boy: growing to a soldier?

GIOVANNI Give me a pike.   110

FRANCISCO What, practising your pike so young, fair coz?

GIOVANNI Suppose me one of Homer's frogs, my lord,
Tossing my bullrush thus. Pray, sir, tell me,
Might not a child of good discretion
Be leader to an army?

FRANCISCO   Yes, cousin, a young prince
Of good discretion might.

GIOVANNI   Say you so?
Indeed, I have heard, 'tis fit a general
Should not endanger his own person oft,
So that he make a noise when he's o'horseback,

Like a Dansk drummer – O, 'tis excellent!   120
He need not fight – methinks his horse as well
Might lead an army for him. If I live,
I'll charge the French foe in the very front
Of all my troops, the foremost man.

FRANCISCO   What, what!

GIOVANNI And will not bid my soldiers up and follow,
But bid them follow me.

BRACHIANO   Forward, lapwing!
He flies with the shell on's head.

FRANCISCO   Pretty cousin!

GIOVANNI The first year, uncle, that I go to war,
All prisoners that I take I will set free
Without their ransom.

FRANCISCO   Ha, without their ransom!   130
How, then, will you reward your soldiers
That took those prisoners for you?

GIOVANNI   Thus, my lord;
I'll marry them to all the wealthy widows
That fall that year.

FRANCISCO   Why, then, the next year following,
You'll have no men to go with you to war.

GIOVANNI Why, then, I'll press the women to the war,
And then the men will follow.

MONTICEL.   Witty prince!

FRANCISCO See, a good habit makes a child a man,
Whereas a bad one makes a man a beast.
Come, you and I are friends.

BRACHIANO   Most wishedly;   140
Like bones which, broke in sunder, and well set,
Knit the more strongly.

FRANCISCO   Call Camillo hither. [exit Marcello
You have received the rumour, how Count Lodovico
Is turned a pirate?

BRACHIANO   Yes.

FRANCISCO   We are now preparing
Some ships to fetch him in. Behold your duchess.
We now will leave you, and expect from you

Nothing but kind entreaty.

BRACHIANO   You have charmed me.

[*exeunt Francisco de Medici, Monticelso*
and Giovanni. Flamineo retires.

Re-enter ISABELLA

You are in health, we see.

ISABELLA   And above health,
To see my lord well.

BRACHIANO   So. I wonder much
What amorous whirlwind hurried you to Rome.   150

ISABELLA   Devotion, my lord.

BRACHIANO   Devotion!
Is your soul charged with any grievous sin?

ISABELLA   'Tis burdened with too many; and I think,
The oftener that we cast our reckonings up,
Our sleeps will be the sounder.

BRACHIANO   Take your chamber.

ISABELLA   Nay, my dear lord, I will not have you angry:
Doth not my absence from you, now two months,
Merit one kiss?

BRACHIANO   I do not use to kiss:
If that will dispossess your jealousy,
I'll swear it to you.

ISABELLA   O my lovéd lord,   160
I do not come to chide. My jealousy –
I am to learn what that Italian means.
You are as welcome to these longing arms
As I to you a virgin.

BRACHIANO   O, your breath!
Out upon sweetmeats and continued physic –
The plague is in them!

ISABELLA   You have oft, for these two lips,
Neglected cassia or the natural sweets
Of the spring-violet: they are not yet much withered.
My lord, I should be merry: these your frowns
Show in a helmet lovely; but on me,   170
In such a peaceful interview, methinks
They are too-too roughly knit.

BRACHIANO   O, dissemblance!

Do you bandy factions 'gainst me? Have you learnt
The trick of impudent baseness, to complain
Unto your kindred?

ISABELLA   Never, my dear lord.

BRACHIANO Must I be hunted out? Or was't your trick
To meet some amorous gallant here in Rome,
That must supply our discontinuance?

ISABELLA I pray, sir, burst my heart; and in my death
Turn to your ancient pity, though not love.   180

BRACHIANO Because your brother is the corpulent duke,
That is, the great duke, 'sdeath, I shall not shortly
Racket away five hundred crowns at tennis,
But it shall rest upon record! I scorn him
Like a shaved Polack! All his reverend wit
Lies in his wardrobe; he's a discreet fellow
When he is made up in his robes of state.
Your brother, the great duke, because h'as galleys,
And now and then ransacks a Turkish fly-boat,
(Now all the hellish Furies take his soul!)   190
First made this match: accurséd be the priest
That sang the wedding-mass, and even my issue!

ISABELLA O, too too far you have cursed!

BRACHIANO   Your hand I'll kiss;
This is the latest ceremony of my love.
Henceforth I'll never lie with thee; by this,
This wedding-ring, I'll ne'er more lie with thee:
And this divorce shall be as truly kept
As if the judge had doomed it. Fare you well:
Our sleeps are severed.

ISABELLA   Forbid it, the sweet union
Of all things blesséd! Why, the saints in Heaven   200
Will knit their brows at that.

BRACHIANO   Let not thy love
Make thee an unbeliever; this my vow
Shall never, on my soul, be satisfied
With my repentance; let thy brother rage
Beyond a horrid tempest or sea-fight,
My vow is fixéd.

ISABELLA   O my winding-sheet,

Now shall I need thee shortly. Dear my lord,
Let me hear once more what I would not hear:
Never?

BRACHIANO Never.   210

ISABELLA   O my unkind lord! May your sins find mercy,
As I upon a woeful widowed bed
Shall pray for you, if not to turn your eyes
Upon your wretched wife and hopeful son,
Yet that in time you'll fix them upon Heaven!

BRACHIANO No more: go; go, complain to the great duke.

ISABELLA   No, my dear lord; you shall have present witness
How I'll work peace between you. I will make
Myself the author of your curséd vow;
I have some cause to do it, you have none.   220
Conceal it, I beseech you, for the weal
Of both your dukedoms, that you wrought the means
Of such a separation: let the fault
Remain with my supposéd jealousy;
And think with what a piteous and rent heart
I shall perform this sad ensuing part.

Re-enter FRANCISCO DE MEDICI *and* MONTICELSO

BRACHIANO Well, take your course — My honourable brother!

FRANCISCO Sister! This is not well, my lord. Why, sister!
She merits not this welcome.

BRACHIANO   Welcome, say!
She hath given a sharp welcome.

FRANCISCO   Are you foolish?   230
Come, dry your tears: is this a modest course,
To better what is naught, to rail and weep?
Grow to a reconcilement, or, by Heaven,
I'll ne'er more deal between you.

ISABELLA   Sir, you shall not;
No, though Vittoria, upon that condition,
Would become honest.

FRANCISCO   Was your husband loud
Since we departed?

ISABELLA   By my life, sir, no;
I swear by that I do not care to lose.

Are all these ruins of my former beauty
Laid out for a whore's triumph?

FRANCISCO   Do you hear?   240
Look upon other women, with what patience
They suffer these slight wrongs, with what justice
They study to requite them: take that course.

ISABELLA   O, that I were a man, or that I had power
To execute my apprehended wishes!
I would whip some with scorpions.

FRANCISCO   What! Turned Fury!

ISABELLA   To dig the strumpet's eyes out; let her lie
Some twenty months a-dying; to cut off
Her nose and lips, pull out her rotten teeth;
Preserve her flesh like mummia, for trophies   250
Of my just anger! Hell to my affliction
Is mere snow-water. By your favour, sir –
Brother, draw near, and my lord cardinal –
Sir, let me borrow of you but one kiss:
Henceforth I'll never lie with you, by this,
This wedding-ring.

FRANCISCO   How, ne'er more lie with him!

ISABELLA   And this divorce shall be as truly kept
As if in throngéd court a thousand ears
Had heard it, and a thousand lawyers' hands
Sealed to the separation.   260

BRACHIANO Ne'er lie with me!

ISABELLA   Let not my former dotage
Make thee an unbeliever: this my vow
Shall never, on my soul, be satisfied
With my repentance; *manet alta mente repostum.*

FRANCISCO Now, by my birth, you are a foolish, mad,
And jealous woman.

BRACHIANO   You see 'tis not my seeking.

FRANCISCO Was this your circle of pure unicorn's horn
You said should charm your lord? Now, horns
                                        upon thee,
For jealousy deserves them! Keep your vow
And take your chamber.

ISABELLA   No, sir, I'll presently to Padua;   270

                I will not stay a minute.

MONTICEL.   O good madam!

BRACHIANO 'Twere best to let her have her humour:
                Some half day's journey will bring down her stomach,
                And then she'll turn in post.

FRANCISCO   To see her come
                To my lord cardinal for a dispensation
                Of her rash vow, will beget excellent laughter.

ISABELLA   Unkindness, do thy office; poor heart, break:
                Those are the killing griefs which dare not speak.

                                                              [exit

                Re-enter MARCELLO *with* CAMILLO

MARCELLO Camillo's come, my lord.

FRANCISCO   Where's the commission?

MARCELLO 'Tis here.

FRANCISCO   Give me the signet.   280

           FRANCISCO DE MEDICI, MONTICELSO, CAMILLO
           and MARCELLO *retire to the back of the stage*

FLAMINEO My lord, do you mark their whispering? I will com-
                pound a medicine, out of their two heads, stronger
                than garlic, deadlier than stibium: the cantharides,
                which are scarce seen to stick upon the flesh when
                they work to the heart, shall not do it with more
                silence or invisible cunning.

BRACHIANO About the murder?

FLAMINEO They are sending him to Naples, but I'll send him to
                Candy.

                        Enter Doctor

                Here's another property too.   290

BRACHIANO O, the doctor!

FLAMINEO A poor quack-salving knave, my lord; one that should
                have been lashed for's lechery, but that he confessed a
                judgment, had an execution laid upon him, and so put
                the whip to a *non plus*.

DOCTOR   And was cozened, my lord, by an arranter knave than
                myself, and made pay all the colourable execution.

FLAMINEO He will shoot pills into a man's guts shall make them
                have more ventages than a cornet or a lamprey; he will

poison a kiss; and was once minded, for his master- 300
piece, because Ireland breeds no poison, to have
prepared a deadly vapour in a Spaniard's fart, that
should have poisoned all Dublin.

BRACHIANO O, Saint Anthony's fire.

DOCTOR Your secretary is merry, my lord.

FLAMINEO O thou cursed antipathy to nature! Look, his eye's
bloodshed, like a needle a surgeon stitcheth a wound
with. Let me embrace thee, toad, and love thee, O
thou abominable loathsome gargarism, that will fetch
up lungs, lights, heart, and liver, by scruples!   310

BRACHIANO No more. – I must employ thee, honest doctor:
You must to Padua, and by the way,
Use some of your skill for us.

DOCTOR   Sir, I shall.

BRACHIANO But, for Camillo?

FLAMINEO He dies this night, by such a politic strain,
Men shall suppose him by's own engine slain.
But for your duchess' death –

DOCTOR   I'll make her sure.

BRACHIANO Small mischiefs are by greater made secure.

FLAMINEO Remember this, you slave; when knaves come to preferment, they rise as gallowses are raised i'the Low 320
Countries, one upon another's shoulders.

                    [exeunt Brachiano, Flamineo and Doctor

SCENE 2

The same

FRANCISCO DE MEDICI, MONTICELSO, CAMILLO and MARCELLO

MONTICEL. Here is an emblem, nephew, pray peruse it:
'Twas thrown in at your window.

CAMILLO   At my window!
Here is a stag, my lord, hath shed his horns,
And, for the loss of them, the poor beast weeps:
The word, *Inopem me copia fecit*.

MONTICEL.   That is,

Plenty of horns hath made him poor of horns.

CAMILLO What should this mean?

MONTICEL.　　　　　　　　　　　　I'll tell you: 'tis given out
You are a cuckold.

CAMILLO　　　　　　　　　Is it given out so?
I had rather such report as that, my lord,
Should keep within doors.

FRANCISCO　　　　　　　　　　Have you any children?　　10

CAMILLO None, my lord.

FRANCISCO　　　　　　　You are the happier:
I'll tell you a tale.

CAMILLO　　　　　　　Pray, my lord.

FRANCISCO　　　　　　　　　　An old tale.
Upon a time Phoebus, the god of light,
Or him we call the Sun, would needs be married:
The gods gave their consent, and Mercury
Was sent to voice it to the general world.
But what a piteous cry there straight arose
Amongst smiths and felt-makers, brewers and cooks,
Reapers and butterwomen, amongst fishmongers,
And thousand other trades, which are annoyed　　20
By his excessive heat! 'Twas lamentable.
They came to Jupiter all in a sweat,
And do forbid the bans. A great fat cook
Was made their speaker, who entreats of Jove
That Phoebus might be gelded; for, if now,
When there was but one sun, so many men
Were like to perish by his violent heat,
What should they do if he were married,
And should beget more, and those children
Make fire-works like their father? So say I;　　30
Only I will apply it to your wife:
Her issue, should not providence prevent it,
Would make both nature, time, and man repent it.

MONTICEL. Look you, cousin,
Go, change the air, for shame; see if your absence
Will blast your cornucopia. Marcello
Is chosen with you joint commissioner
For the relieving our Italian coast

From pirates.

MARCELLO   I am much honoured in't.

CAMILLO   But, sir,
Ere I return, the stag's horns may be sprouted   40
Greater than those are shed.

MONTICEL.   Do not fear it:
I'll be your ranger.

CAMILLO   You must watch i'the nights;
Then's the most danger.

FRANCISCO   Farewell, good Marcello:
All the best fortunes of a soldier's wish
Bring you a-ship-board!

CAMILLO   Were I not best, now I am turned soldier,
Ere that I leave my wife, sell all she hath,
And then take leave of her?

MONTICEL.   I expect good from you,
Your parting is so merry.

CAMILLO   Merry, my lord! O'the captain's humour right;   50
I am resolvéd to be drunk this night.

                              [exeunt Camillo and Marcello

FRANCISCO So, 'twas well fitted: now shall we discern
How his wished absence will give violent way
To Duke Brachiano's lust.

MONTICEL.   Why, that was it;
To what scorned purpose else should we make choice
Of him for a sea-captain? And, besides,
Count Lodovico, which was rumoured for a pirate,
Is now in Padua.

FRANCISCO   Is't true?

MONTICEL.   Most certain.
I have letters from him, which are suppliant
To work his quick repeal from banishment: 60
He means to address himself for pension
Unto our sister duchess.

FRANCISCO   O, 'twas well:
We shall not want his absence past six days.
I fain would have the Duke Brachiano run
Into notorious scandal; for there's naught
In such cursed dotage to repair his name,

     Only the deep sense of some deathless shame.
MONTICEL. It may be objected, I am dishonourable
     To play thus with my kinsman; but I answer,
     For my revenge I'd stake a brother's life,   70
     That, being wronged, durst not avenge himself.
FRANCISCO Come, to observe this strumpet.
MONTICEL.   Curse of greatness!
     Sure he'll not leave her?
FRANCISCO   There's small pity in't:
     Like mistletoe on sere elms spent by weather,
     Let him cleave to her, and both rot together.

                [*exeunt*

SCENE 3

A room in the house of Camillo

Enter BRACHIANO, *with a Conjurer*

BRACHIANO Now, sir, I claim your promise: 'tis dead midnight,
     The time prefixed to show me, by your art,
     How the intended murder of Camillo
     And our loathed duchess grow to action.
CONJURER You have won me by your bounty to a deed
     I do not often practise. Some there are
     Which by sophistic tricks aspire that name,
     Which I would gladly lose, of necromancer;
     As some that use to juggle upon cards,
     Seeming to conjure, when indeed they cheat;   10
     Others that raise up their confederate spirits
     'Bout wind-mills, and endanger their own necks
     For making of a squib; and some there are
     Will keep a curtal to show juggling tricks,
     And give out 'tis a spirit; besides these,
     Such a whole realm of almanac-makers, figure-fingers,
     Fellows, indeed, that only live by stealth,
     Since they do merely lie about stol'n goods,
     They'd make men think the devil were fast and loose,
     With speaking fustian Latin. Pray, sit down: 20
     Put on this night-cap, sir, 'tis charmed; and now

I'll show you, by my strong commanding art,
The circumstance that breaks your duchess' heart.

A Dumb Show

Enter suspiciously JULIO *and* CHRISTOPHERO: *they draw a curtain where* BRACHIANO'S *picture is, put on spectacles of glass, which cover their eyes and noses, and then burn perfumes before the picture, and wash the lips; that done, quenching the fire, and putting off their spectacles, they depart laughing.*

    Enter ISABELLA *in her night-gown, as to bedward, with lights after her,* COUNT LODOVICO, GIOVANNI, GUIDANTONIO, *and others waiting on her: she kneels down as to prayers, then draws the curtain of the picture, does three reverences to it, and kisses it thrice; she faints, and will not suffer them to come near it; dies: sorrow expressed in* GIOVANNI *and* COUNT LODOVICO: *she is conveyed out solemnly.*

BRACHIANO Excellent! Then she's dead.

CONJURER   She's poisonéd
    By the fumed picture. 'Twas her custom nightly,
    Before she went to bed, to go and visit
    Your picture, and to feed her eyes and lips
    On the dead shadow. Doctor Julio,
    Observing this, infects it with an oil   30
    And other poisoned stuff, which presently
    Did suffocate her spirits.

BRACHIANO   Methought I saw
    Count Lodovico there.

CONJURER   He was: and by my art
    I find he did most passionately dote
    Upon your duchess. Now turn another way,
    And view Camillo's far more politic fate.
    Strike louder, music, from this charméd ground,
    To yield, as fits the act, a tragic sound.

The Second Dumb Show

Enter FLAMINEO, MARCELLO, CAMILLO, *with four others, as Captains; they drink healths, and dance: a vaulting-horse is brought into the room:* MARCELLO *and two others whispered out of the room, while* FLAMINEO *and* CAMILLO *strip themselves to their shirts, to vault; they compliment who shall begin: as* CAMILLO *is about to vault,* FLAMINEO *pitcheth him upon his neck, and, with help of the rest, writhes his neck about; seems to see if it be broke, and lays him folded double, as it were, under the horse; makes signs to call for help:* MARCELLO *comes in, laments; sends for the Cardinal and Duke, who come forth with armed men, wonder at the act, command the body to be carried home, apprehend* FLAMINEO, MARCELLO, *and the rest, and go, as it were, to apprehend* VITTORIA.

BRACHIANO 'Twas quaintly done; but yet each circumstance
    I taste not fully.
CONJURER   O, 'twas most apparent:
    You saw them enter, charged with their deep healths   40
    To their boon voyage; and, to second that,
    Flamineo calls to have a vaulting-horse
    Maintain their sport; the virtuous Marcello
    Is innocently plotted forth the room;
    Whilst your eye saw the rest, and can inform you
    The engine of all.
BRACHIANO It seems Marcello and Flamineo
    Are both committed.
CONJURER   Yes, you saw them guarded;
    And now they are come with purpose to apprehend
    Your mistress, fair Vittoria. We are now   50
    Beneath her roof: 'twere fit we instantly
    Make out by some back–postern.
BRACHIANO   Noble friend,
    You bind me ever to you: this shall stand
    As the firm seal annexéd to my hand;
    It shall enforce a payment.
CONJURER   Sir, I thank you. [*exit Brachiano*
    Both flowers and weeds spring when the sun is warm,
    And great men do great good or else great harm.
               [*exit*

ACT 3 SCENE I

The mansion of Monticelso

Enter FRANCISCO DE MEDICI *and* MONTICELSO,
their Chancellor and Register

FRANCISCO You have dealt discreetly, to obtain the presence
Of all the grave lieger ambassadors,
To hear Vittoria's trial.

MONTICEL.   'Twas not ill;
For, sir, you know we have naught but circumstances
To charge her with, about her husband's death:
Their approbation, therefore, to the proofs
Of her black lust shall make her infamous
To all our neighbouring kingdoms. I wonder
If Brachiano will be here.

FRANCISCO   O fie.
'Twere impudence too palpable.   *[exeunt* 10

Enter FLAMINEO *and* MARCELLO *guarded, and a Lawyer*

LAWYER What, are you in by the week? So, I will try now
whether thy wit be close prisoner. Methinks none
should sit upon thy sister but old whore-masters.

FLAMINEO Or cuckolds; for your cuckold is your most terrible
tickler of lechery. Whore-masters would serve; for none
are judges at tilting but those that have been old tilters.

LAWYER My lord duke and she have been very private.

FLAMINEO You are a dull ass; 'tis threatened they have been very
public.

LAWYER If it can be proved they have but kissed one another –   20

FLAMINEO What then?

LAWYER My lord cardinal will ferret them.

FLAMINEO A cardinal, I hope, will not catch conies.

LAWYER For to sow kisses (mark what I say), to sow kisses is to
reap lechery; and, I am sure, a woman that will endure
kissing is half won.

FLAMINEO True, her upper part, by that rule: if you will win her
nether part too, you know what follows.

LAWYER Hark; the ambassadors are lighted.

FLAMINEO   [*aside*] I do put on this feignéd garb of mirth   30
           To gull suspicion.

MARCELLO   O my unfortunate sister!
           I would my dagger-point had cleft her heart
           When she first saw Brachiano: you, 'tis said,
           Were made his engine and his stalking-horse,
           To undo my sister.

FLAMINEO   I am a kind of path
           To her and mine own preferment.

MARCELLO   Your ruin.

FLAMINEO   Hum! Thou art a soldier,
           Follow'st the great duke, feed'st his victories,
           As witches do their serviceable spirits,
           Even with thy prodigal blood: what hast got,   40
           But, like the wealth of captains, a poor handful,
           Which in thy palm thou bear'st as men hold water?
           Seeking to gripe it fast, the frail reward
           Steals through thy fingers.

MARCELLO   Sir!

FLAMINEO   Thou hast scarce maintenance
           To keep thee in fresh shamois.

MARCELLO   Brother!

FLAMINEO   Hear me:
           And thus, when we have even poured ourselves
           Into great fights, for their ambition
           Or idle spleen, how shall we find reward?
           But as we seldom find the mistletoe
           Sacred to physic, or the builder oak,   50
           Without a mandrake by it, so in our quest of gain,
           Alas, the poorest of their forced dislikes
           At a limb proffers, but at heart it strikes!
           This is lamented doctrine.

MARCELLO   Come, come.

FLAMINEO   When age shall turn thee
           White as a blooming hawthorn –

MARCELLO   I'll interrupt you –
           For love of virtue bear an honest heart,
           And stride o'er every politic respect,
           Which, where they most advance, they most infect.

Were I your father, as I am your brother,   60
I should not be ambitious to leave you
A better patrimony.

FLAMINEO   I'll think on't.
The lord ambassadors.

The Ambassadors pass over the stage severally

LAWYER   O my sprightly Frenchman! Do you know him? He's
an admirable tilter.

FLAMINEO   I saw him at last tilting: he showed like a pewter
candlestick, fashioned like a man in armour, holding a
tilting-staff in his hand, little bigger than a candle of
twelve i'the pound.

LAWYER   O, but he's an excellent horseman.   70

FLAMINEO   A lame one in his lofty tricks: he sleeps a-horse-back,
like a poulter.

LAWYER   La you, my Spaniard!

FLAMINEO   He carries his face in's ruff as I have seen a serving man
carry glasses in a cypress hatband: monstrous steady,
for fear of breaking: he looks like the claw of a blackbird, first salted, and then broiled in a candle.

                                                    [*exeunt*

SCENE 2

The Arraignment of Vittoria

A hall in Monticelso's mansion

Enter FRANCISCO DE MEDICI, MONTICELSO, *the six lieger*
Ambassadors, BRACHIANO, VITTORIA COROMBONA, FLAMINEO,
            MARCELLO, *Lawyer and a Guard*

MONTICEL.   [*to Brachiano*] Forbear, my lord, here is no place
                                        assigned you:
This business by his holiness is left
To our examination.

BRACHIANO   May it thrive with you! [*lays a rich gown under him*]

FRANCISCO   A chair there for his lordship!

BRACHIANO   Forbear your kindness: an unbidden guest
Should travel as Dutchwomen go to church,

Bear their stools with them.

MONTICEL.   At your pleasure, sir.
Stand to the table, gentlewoman – Now, signior,
Fall to your plea.

LAWYER   *Domine judex, converte oculos in hanc pestem, mulierum* 10
corruptissimam.

VITTORIA   What's he?

FRANCISCO   A lawyer that pleads against you.

VITTORIA   Pray, my lord, let him speak his usual tongue:
I'll make no answer else.

FRANCISCO   Why, you understand Latin.

VITTORIA   I do, sir; but amongst this auditory
Which come to hear my cause, the half or more
May be ignorant in't.

MONTICEL.   Go on, sir.

VITTORIA   By your favour,
I will not have my accusation clouded
In a strange tongue; all this assembly
Shall hear what you can charge me with.   20

FRANCISCO Signior,
You need not stand on't much; pray, change
                              your language.

MONTICEL. O, for God sake! Gentlewoman, your credit
Shall be more famous by it.

LAWYER   Well, then, have at you!

VITTORIA   I am at the mark, sir: I'll give aim to you,
And tell you how near you shoot.

LAWYER   Most literated judges, please your lordships
So to connive your judgments to the view
Of this debauched and diversivolent woman;
Who such a black concatenation   30
Of mischief hath effected, that to extirp
The memory of't, must be the consummation
Of her and her projections –

VITTORIA   What's all this?

LAWYER   Hold your peace:
Exorbitant sins must háve exulceration.

VITTORIA   Surely, my lords, this lawyer here hath swallowed
Some 'pothecaries' bills, or proclamations;

And now the hard and undigestible words
Come up, like stones we use give hawks for physic:
Why, this is Welsh to Latin.

LAWYER   My lords, the woman   40
Knows not her tropes nor figures, nor is perfect
In the academic derivation
Of grammatical elocution.

FRANCISCO Sir, your pains
Shall be well spared, and your deep eloquence
Be worthily applauded amongst those
Which understand you.

LAWYER   My good lord —

FRANCISCO   Sir,
[speaks as in scorn] Put up your papers in your
                                        fustian bag —
Cry mercy, sir, 'tis buckram — and accept
My notion of your learned verbosity.   50

LAWYER I most graduatically thank your lordship:
I shall have use for them elsewhere.   [exit

MONTICEL. [to Vittoria] I shall be plainer with you, and paint out
Your follies in more natural red and white
Than that upon your cheek.

VITTORIA   O you mistake:
You raise a blood as noble in this cheek
As ever was your mother's.

MONTICEL. I must spare you, till proof cry 'whore' to that.
Observe this creature here, my honoured lords,
A woman of a most prodigious spirit,   60
In her effected.

VITTORIA   Honourable my lord,
It doth not suit a reverend cardinal
To play the lawyer thus.

MONTICEL. O, your trade instructs your language.
You see, my lords, what goodly fruit she seems;
Yet, like those apples travellers report
To grow where Sodom and Gomorrah stood,
I will but touch her, and you straight shall see
She'll fall to soot and ashes.

VITTORIA   Your envenomed

'Pothecary should do't.

MONTICEL.   I am resolved,   70
Were there a second Paradise to lose,
This devil would betray it.

VITTORIA   O poor charity!
Thou art seldom found in scarlet.

MONTICEL. Who knows not how, when several night by night
Her gates were choked with coaches, and her rooms
Outbraved the stars with several kind of lights;
When she did counterfeit a prince's court
In music, banquets, and most riotous surfeits?
This whore, forsooth, was holy.

VITTORIA   Ha! Whore! What's that!

MONTICEL. Shall I expound whore to you? Sure, I shall;   80
I'll give their perfect character. They are, first,
Sweetmeats which rot the eater; in man's nostrils
Poisoned perfumes: they are cozening alchemy,
Shipwrecks in calmest weather. What are whores?
Cold Russian winters, that appear so barren
As if that nature had forgot the spring:
They are the true material fire of hell,
Worse than those tributes i'th'Low Countries paid,
Exactions upon meat, drink, garments, sleep,
Ay, even on man's perdition, his sin: 90
They are those brittle evidences of law
Which forfeit all a wretched man's estate
For leaving out one syllable. What are whores?
They are those flattering bells have all one tune,
At weddings and at funerals. Your rich whores
Are only treasuries by extortion filled,
And emptied by cursed riot. They are worse,
Worse than dead bodies which are begged at gallows,
And wrought upon by surgeons, to teach man
Wherein he is imperfect. What's a whore?   100
She's like the guilty counterfeited coin
Which, whosoe'er first stamps it, brings in trouble
All that receive it.

VITTORIA This character scapes me.

MONTICEL.   You – gentlewoman!

	Take from all beasts and from all minerals
	Their deadly poison –
VITTORIA	Well, what then?
MONTICEL.	I'll tell thee;
	I'll find in thee a 'pothecary's shop,
	To sample them all.
FR. AMB.	She hath lived ill.
ENG. AMB	True; but the cardinal's too bitter. 110
MONTICEL.	You know what whore is. Next the devil adultery,
	Enters the devil murder.
FRANCISCO	Your unhappy
	Husband is dead.
VITTORIA	O, he's a happy husband:
	Now he owes nature nothing.
FRANCISCO	And by a vaulting-engine.
MONTICEL.	An active plot; he jumped into his grave.
FRANCISCO	What a prodigy was't
	That from some two yards' height a slender man
	Should break his neck!
MONTICEL.	I'the rushes!
FRANCISCO	And what's more,
	Upon the instant lose all use of speech, 120
	All vital motion, like a man had lain
	Wound up three days. Now mark each circumstance.
MONTICEL.	And look upon this creature was his wife.
	She comes not like a widow; she comes armed
	With scorn and impudence: is this a mourning habit?
VITTORIA	Had I foreknown his death, as you suggest,
	I would have bespoke my mourning.
MONTICEL.	O, you are cunning.
VITTORIA	You shame your wit and judgment,
	To call it so. What! Is my just defence
	By him that is my judge called impudence? 130
	Let me appeal, then, from this Christian court
	To the uncivil Tartar.
MONTICEL.	See, my lords,
	She scandals our proceedings.
VITTORIA	Humbly thus,
	Thus low, to the most worthy and respected

Lieger ambassadors, my modesty
And womanhood I tender; but withal,
So entangled in a cursèd accusation,
That my defence, of force, like Perseus,
Must personate masculine virtue. To the point.
Find me but guilty, sever head from body,   140
We'll part good friends: I scorn to hold my life
At yours or any man's entreaty, sir.

ENG. AMB   She hath a brave spirit.

MONTICEL.   Well, well, such counterfeit jewels
Make true ones oft suspected.

VITTORIA   You are deceived:
For know, that all your strict-combinèd heads,
Which strike against this mine of diamonds,
Shall prove but glassen hammers — they shall break.
These are but feignèd shadows of my evils:
Terrify babes, my lord, with painted devils;
I am past such needless palsy. For your names   150
Of whore and murderess, they proceed from you,
As, if a man should spit against the wind,
The filth returns in's face.

MONTICEL. Pray you, mistress, satisfy me one question:
Who lodged beneath your roof that fatal night
Your husband brake his neck?

BRACHIANO   That question
Enforceth me break silence: I was there.

MONTICEL. Your business?

BRACHIANO   Why, I came to comfort her,
And take some course for settling her estate,
Because I heard her husband was in debt   160
To you, my lord.

MONTICEL.   He was.

BRACHIANO   And 'twas strangely feared
That you would cozen her.

MONTICEL.   Who made you overseer?

BRACHIANO Why, my charity, my charity, which should flow
From every generous and noble spirit
To orphans and to widows.

MONTICEL.   Your lust.

BRACHIANO Cowardly dogs bark loudest: sirrah priest,
    I'll talk with you hereafter. Do you hear?
    The sword you frame of such an excellent temper
    I'll sheathe in your own bowels.
    There are a number of thy coat resemble   170
    Your common post-boys.
MONTICEL.   Ha!
BRACHIANO   Your mercenary post-boys:
    Your letters carry truth, but 'tis your guise
    To fill your mouths with gross and impudent lies.
SERVANT My lord, your gown.
BRACHIANO   Thou liest, 'twas my stool:
    Bestow't upon thy master, that will challenge
    The rest o'the household-stuff; for Brachiano
    Was ne'er so beggarly to take a stool
    Out of another's lodging: let him make
    Vallance for his bed on't, or a demi-foot-cloth
    For his most reverent moil. Monticelso,   180
    Nemo me impune lacessit.   [*exit*
MONTICEL. Your champion's gone.
VITTORIA   The wolf may prey the better.
FRANCISCO My lord, there's great suspicion of the murder,
    But no sound proof who did it. For my part,
    I do not think she hath a soul so black
    To act a deed so bloody: if she have,
    As in cold countries husbandmen plant vines,
    And with warm blood manure them, even so
    One summer she will bear unsavoury fruit,
    And ere next spring wither both branch and root. 190
    The act of blood let pass; only descend
    To matter of incontinence.
VITTORIA   I discern poison
    Under your gilded pills.
MONTICEL. Now the duke's gone, I will produce a letter,
    Wherein 'twas plotted he and you should meet
    At an apothecary's summer-house,
    Down by the river Tiber – view't my lords –
    Where, after wanton bathing and the heat
    Of a lascivious banquet – I pray read it,

I shame to speak the rest.

VITTORIA   Grant I was tempted;   200
Temptation to lust proves not the act:
Casta est quam nemo rogavit.
You read his hot love to me, but you want
My frosty answer.

MONTICEL.   Frost i'the dog-days! Strange!

VITTORIA Condemn you me for that the duke did love me!
So may you blame some fair and crystal river
For that some melancholic distracted man
Hath drowned himself in't.

MONTICEL.   Truly drowned, indeed.

VITTORIA Sum up my faults, I pray; and you shall find
That beauty, and gay clothes, a merry heart,   210
And a good stomach to a feast, are all,
All the poor crimes that you can charge me with.
In faith, my lord, you might go pistol flies;
The sport would be more noble.

MONTICEL.   Very good.

VITTORIA But take you your course: it seems you have
                                beggared me first,
And now would fain undo me. I have houses,
Jewels, and a poor remnant of crusadoes:
Would those would make you charitable!

MONTICEL. If the devil
Did ever take good shape, behold his picture.   220

VITTORIA You have one virtue left – You will not flatter me.

FRANCISCO Who brought this letter?

VITTORIA   I am not compelled to tell you.

MONTICEL. My lord duke sent to you a thousand ducats
The twelfth of August.

VITTORIA   'Twas to keep your cousin
From prison: I paid use for't.

MONTICEL. I rather think 'twas interest for his lust.

VITTORIA Who says so but yourself? If you be my accuser,
Pray, cease to be my judge: come from the bench;
Give in your evidence 'gainst me, and let these
Be moderators. My lord cardinal,   230
Were your intelligencing ears as long

As to my thoughts, had you an honest tongue,
I would not care though you proclaimed them all.

MONTICEL. Go to, go to.
    After your goodly and vainglorious banquet,
    I'll give you a choke-pear.

VITTORIA   O'your own grafting?

MONTICEL. You were born in Venice, honourably descended
    From the Vittelli: 'twas my cousin's fate –
    Ill may I name the hour – to marry you:
    He bought you of your father.   240

VITTORIA Ha!

MONTICEL. He spent there in six months
    Twelve thousand ducats, and (to my acquaintance)
    Received in dowry with you not one julio:
    'Twas a hard pennyworth, the ware being so light.
    I yet but draw the curtain; now to your picture:
    You came from thence a most notorious strumpet,
    And so you have continued.

VITTORIA   My lord –

MONTICEL.   Nay, hear me;
    You shall have time to prate. My Lord Brachiano –
    Alas, I make but repetition   250
    Of what is ordinary and Rialto talk,
    And ballated, and would be played o'the stage,
    But that vice many times finds such loud friends
    That preachers are charmed silent.
    You gentlemen, Flamineo and Marcello,
    The court hath nothing now to charge you with:
    Only you must remain upon your sureties
    For your appearance.

FRANCISCO   I stand for Marcello.

FLAMINEO And my lord duke for me.

MONTICEL. For you, Vittoria, your public fault,   260
    Joined to the condition of the present time,
    Takes from you all the fruits of noble pity;
    Such a corrupted trial have you made
    Both of your life and beauty, and been styled
    No less an ominous fate than blazing stars
    To princes: here's your sentence; you are confined

	Unto a house of convertites, and your bawd –
FLAMINEO	[aside] Who, I?
MONTICEL.	The Moor.
FLAMINEO	[aside] O, I am a sound man again.
VITTORIA	A house of convertites! What's that?
MONTICEL.	A house

Of penitent whores.

VITTORIA   Do the noblemen in Rome   270
Erect it for their wives, that I am sent
To lodge there?

FRANCISCO You must have patience.

VITTORIA   I must first have vengeance.
I fain would know if you have your salvation
By patent, that you proceed thus.

MONTICEL.   Away with her!
Take her hence.

VITTORIA A rape! A rape!

MONTICEL.   How!

VITTORIA   Yes, you have ravished justice;
Forced her to do your pleasure.

MONTICEL.   Fie, she's mad!

VITTORIA Die with these pills in your most curséd maw
Should bring you health! Or while you sit o'the bench   280
Let your own spittle choke you!

MONTICEL.   She's turned Fury.

VITTORIA That the last day of judgment may so find you,
And leave you the same devil you were before!
Instruct me, some good horse-leech, to speak treason;
For since you cannot take my life for deeds,
Take it for words: O woman's poor revenge,
Which dwells but in the tongue! I will not weep;
No, I do scorn to call up one poor tear
To fawn on your injustice; bear me hence
Unto this house of – what's your mitigating title?   290

MONTICEL. Of convertites.

VITTORIA It shall not be a house of convertites;
My mind shall make it honester to me
Than the Pope's palace, and more peaceable
Than thy soul, though thou art a cardinal.

Know this, and let it somewhat raise your spite,
Through darkness diamonds spread their richest light.
                    [*exeunt Vittoria Corombona and Guards*

Re-enter BRACHIANO

BRACHIANO Now you and I are friends, sir, we'll shake hands
            In a friend's grave together; a fit place,
            Being the emblem of soft peace, to atone our hatred.   300
FRANCISCO Sir, what's the matter?
BRACHIANO I will not chase more blood from that loved cheek;
            You have lost too much already: fare you well.   [*exit*
FRANCISCO How strange these words sound! What's the
                                        interpretation?
FLAMINEO [*aside*] Good; this is a preface to the discovery of the
            duchess' death: he carries it well. Because now I cannot
            counterfeit a whining passion for the death of my lady,
            I will feign a mad humour for the disgrace of my sister;
            and that will keep off idle questions. Treason's tongue
            hath a villainous palsy in't: I will talk to any man, hear   310
            no man, and for a time appear a politic madman.
                                                    [*exit*

Enter GIOVANNI, COUNT LODOVICO *and Attendant*

FRANCISCO How now, my noble cousin! What, in black!
GIOVANNI Yes, uncle, I was taught to imitate you
            In virtue, and you must imitate me
            In colours of your garments. My sweet mother
            Is —
FRANCISCO How! Where?
GIOVANNI   Is there; no, yonder: indeed, sir,
            I'll not tell you, for I shall make you weep.
FRANCISCO Is dead?
GIOVANNI Do not blame me now,   320
            I did not tell you so.
LODOVICO   She's dead, my lord.
FRANCISCO Dead!
MONTICEL. Blessed lady, thou art now above thy woes!
            Wilt please your lordships to withdraw a little?
                                        [*exeunt Ambassadors*
GIOVANNI What do the dead do, uncle? Do they eat,

Hear music, go a-hunting, and be merry,
As we that live?

FRANCISCO No, coz; they sleep.

GIOVANNI   Lord, Lord, that I were dead!
I have not slept these six nights – When do they wake?

FRANCISCO When God shall please.

GIOVANNI   Good God, let her sleep ever!   330
For I have known her wake an hundred nights,
When all the pillow where she laid her head
Was brine-wet with her tears. I am to complain
                       to you, sir;
I'll tell you how they have used her now she's dead:
They wrapped her in a cruel fold of lead,
And would not let me kiss her.

FRANCISCO   Thou didst love her.

GIOVANNI I have often heard her say she gave me suck,
And it should seem by that she dearly loved me,
Since princes seldom do it.

FRANCISCO O, all of my poor sister that remains!   340
Take him away, for God's sake!

                [*exeunt Giovanni and Attendant*

MONTICEL.   How now, my lord!

FRANCISCO Believe me, I am nothing but her grave;
And I shall keep her blessed memory
Longer than thousand epitaphs.

            [*exeunt Francisco de Medici and Monticelso*

SCENE 3

Enter FLAMINEO *as if distracted* [*with* MARCELLO *and* LODOVICO]

FLAMINEO We endure the strokes like anvils or hard steel,
Till pain itself make us no pain to feel.
Who shall do me right now? Is this the end of service?
I'd rather go weed garlic; travel through France, and
be mine own ostler; wear sheepskin linings, or shoes
that stink of blacking; be entered into the list of the
forty thousand pedlars in Poland.

Re-enter Ambassadors

Would I had rotted in some surgeon's house at Venice,
built upon the pox as well as on piles, ere I had served
Brachiano!   10

SAV. AMB.   You must have comfort.

FLAMINEO   Your comfortable words are like honey; they relish
well in your mouth that's whole, but in mine that's
wounded they go down as if the sting of the bee were
in them. O, they have wrought their purpose cunningly, as if they would not seem to do it of malice! In
this a politician imitates the devil, as the devil imitates
a cannon; wheresoever he comes to do mischief, he
comes with his backside towards you.

FR. AMB.   The proofs are evident.   20

FLAMINEO   Proof! 'Twas corruption. O gold, what a god art thou!
And O man, what a devil art thou to be tempted by
that cursed mineral! Your diversivolent lawyer, mark
him: knaves turn informers, as maggots turn to flies;
you may catch gudgeons with either. A cardinal! I
would he would hear me: there's nothing so holy but
money will corrupt and putrify it, like victual under
the line. You are happy in England, my lord: here
they sell justice with those weights they press men to
death with. O horrible salary!   30

ENG. AMB.   Fie, fie, Flamineo!   [*exeunt Ambassadors*

FLAMINEO   Bells ne'er ring well, till they are at their full pitch; and
I hope yon cardinal shall never have the grace to pray
well till he come to the scaffold. If they were racked
now to know the confederacy – but your noblemen
are privileged from the rack; and well may, for a little
thing would pull some of them a-pieces afore they
came to their arraignment. Religion, O, how it is
commeddled with policy! The first bloodshed in the
world happened about religion. Would I were a Jew!   40

MARCELLO   O, there are too many.

FLAMINEO   You are deceived: there are not Jews enough, priests
enough, nor gentlemen enough.

MARCELLO   How?

FLAMINEO   I'll prove it; for if there were Jews enough, so many

Christians would not turn usurers; if priests enough,
one should not have six benefices; and if gentlemen
enough, so many early mushrooms, whose best growth
sprang from a dunghill, should not aspire to gentility.
Farewell. Let others live by begging; be thou one of   50
them; practise the art of Wolner in England, to swallow
all's given thee; and yet let one purgation make thee as
hungry again as fellows that work in a saw-pit. I'll go
hear the screech-owl.   [*exit*

LODOVICO [*aside*] This was Brachiano's pander and 'tis strange
That, in such open and apparent guilt
Of his adulterous sister, he dare utter
So scandalous a passion. I must wind him.

Re-enter FLAMINEO

FLAMINEO [*aside*] How dares this banished count return to Rome,
His pardon not yet purchased! I have heard   60
The deceased duchess gave him pension,
And that he came along from Padua
I'the train of the young prince. There's somewhat in't:
Physicians, that cure poisons, still do work
With counter-poisons.

MARCELLO   Mark this strange encounter.

FLAMINEO The god of melancholy turn thy gall to poison,
And let the stigmatic wrinkles in thy face,
Like to the boisterous waves in a rough tide,
One still overtake another.

LODOVICO   I do thank thee,
And I do wish ingeniously for thy sake   70
The dog-days all year long.

FLAMINEO   How croaks the raven?
Is our good duchess dead?

LODOVICO   Dead.

FLAMINEO   O fate!
Misfortune comes, like the coroner's business,
Huddle upon huddle.

LODOVICO Shalt thou and I join house-keeping?

FLAMINEO   Yes, content:
Let's be unsociably sociable.

LODOVICO Sit same three days together, and discourse –

FLAMINEO	Only with making faces: lie in our clothes.
LODOVICO	With faggots for our pillows.
FLAMINEO	And be lousy.

LODOVICO In taffeta linings; that's genteel melancholy: 80
          Sleep all day.

FLAMINEO   Yes; and, like your melancholic hare,
          Feed after midnight —

                    Enter ANTONELLI *and* GASPARO

          We are observed: see how yon couple grieve!

LODOVICO What a strange creature is a laughing fool,
          As if man were created to no use
          But only to show his teeth.

FLAMINEO   I'll tell thee what,
          It would do well, instead of looking-glasses,
          To set one's face each morning by a saucer
          Of a witch's congealed blood.

LODOVICO   Precious gue!
          We'll never part.

FLAMINEO   Never, till the beggary of courtiers,   90
          The discontent of churchmen, want of soldiers,
          And all the creatures that hang manacled,
          Worse than strappadoed, on the lowest felly
          Of Fortune's wheel, be taught, in our two lives,
          To scorn that world which life of means deprives.

ANTONELLI My lord, I bring good news. The Pope, on's deathbed,
          At the earnest suit of the Great Duke of Florence,
          Hath signed your pardon, and restored unto you —

LODOVICO I thank you for your news — Look up again,
          Flamineo, see my pardon.

FLAMINEO   Why do you laugh?   100
          There was no such condition in our covenant.

LODOVICO Why!

FLAMINEO You shall not seem a happier man than I:
          You know our vow, sir; if you will be merry,
          Do it i'the like posture as if some great man
          Sate while his enemy were executed;
          Though it be very lechery unto thee,
          Do't with a crabbéd politician's face.

LODOVICO Your sister is a damnable whore.

FLAMINEO   Ha!

LODOVICO Look you, I spake that laughing.   110

FLAMINEO Dost ever think to speak again?

LODOVICO   Do you hear?
          Wilt sell me forty ounces of her blood
          To water a mandrake?

FLAMINEO   Poor lord, you did vow
          To live a lousy creature.

LODOVICO   Yes.

FLAMINEO   Like one
          That had for ever forfeited the daylight
          By being in debt.

LODOVICO Ha, ha!

FLAMINEO I do not greatly wonder you do break;
          Your lordship learned't long since. But I'll tell you –

LODOVICO What?

FLAMINEO   And't shall stick by you –

LODOVICO   I long for it.   120

FLAMINEO This laughter scurvily becomes your face:
          If you will not be melancholy, be angry.
          [strikes him] See, now I laugh too.

MARCELLO You are to blame: I'll force you hence.

LODOVICO   Unhand me.
                    [exeunt Marcello and Flamineo
          That e'er I should be forced to right myself
          Upon a pander!

ANTONELLI My lord –

LODOVICO H'ad been as good met with his fist a thunderbolt.

GASPARO How this shows!

LODOVICO Ud's death, how did my sword miss him?   130
          These rogues that are most weary of their lives
          Still scape the greatest dangers.
          A pox upon him! All his reputation,
          Nay, all the goodness of his family,
          Is not worth half this earthquake:
          I learned it of no fencer to shake thus:
          Come, I'll forget him, and go drink some wine.
                                        [exeunt

ACT 4 SCENE I

An apartment in the palace of Francisco

Enter FRANCISCO DE MEDICI *and* MONTICELSO

MONTICEL. Come, come, my lord, untie your folded thoughts,
And let them dangle loose as a bride's hair.
Your sister's poisoned.

FRANCISCO   Far be it from my thoughts
To seek revenge.

MONTICEL.   What, are you turned all marble?

FRANCISCO Shall I defy him, and impose a war
Most burdensome on my poor subjects' necks,
Which at my will I have not power to end?
You know, for all the murders, rapes, and thefts,
Committed in the horrid lust of war,
He that unjustly caused it first proceed   10
Shall find it in his grave and in his seed.

MONTICEL. That's not the course I'd wish you; pray, observe me.
We see that undermining more prevails
Than doth the cannon. Bear your wrongs concealed,
And, patient as the tortoise, let this camel
Stalk o'er your back unbruised: sleep with the lion,
And let this brood of secure foolish mice
Play with your nostrils, till the time be ripe
For the bloody audit and the fatal gripe:
Aim like a cunning fowler, close one eye,   20
That you the better may your game espy.

FRANCISCO Free me, my innocence, from treacherous acts!
I know there's thunder yonder; and I'll stand
Like a safe valley, which low bends the knee
To some aspiring mountain; since I know
Treason, like spiders weaving nets for flies,
By her foul work is found, and in it dies.
To pass away these thoughts, my honoured lord,
It is reported you possess a book,
Wherein you have quoted, by intelligence,   30
The names of all notorious offenders

Lurking about the city.

MONTICEL.   Sir, I do;
And some there are which call it my black book:
Well may the title hold; for though it teach not
The art of conjuring, yet in it lurk
The names of many devils.

FRANCISCO   Pray, let's see it.

MONTICEL. I'll fetch it to your lordship.   [*exit*

FRANCISCO   Monticelso,
I will not trust thee; but in all my plots
I'll rest as jealous as a town besieged.
Thou canst not reach what I intend to act: 40
Your flax soon kindles, soon is out again;
But gold slow heats, and long will hot remain.

Re-enter MONTICELSO,
presents FRANCISCO DE MEDICI *with a book*

MONTICEL. 'Tis here, my lord.

FRANCISCO First, your intelligencers, pray, let's see.

MONTICEL. Their number rises strangely; and some of them
You'd take for honest men. Next are panders –
These are your pirates; and these following leaves
For base rogues that undo young gentlemen
By taking up commodities; for politic bankrupts;
For fellows that are bawds to their own wives,   50
Only to put off horses, and slight jewels,
Clocks, defaced plate, and such commodities,
At birth of their first children.

FRANCISCO   Are there such?

MONTICEL. These are for impudent bawds
That go in men's apparel; for usurers
That share with scriveners for their good reportage;
For lawyers that will antedate their writs:
And some divines you might find folded there,
But that I slip them o'er for conscience' sake.
Here is a general catalogue of knaves: 60
A man might study all the prisons o'er,
Yet never attain this knowledge.

FRANCISCO   Murderers!
Fold down the leaf, I pray.

Good my lord, let me borrow this strange doctrine.
MONTICEL. Pray, use't, my lord.
FRANCISCO   I do assure your lordship,
You are a worthy member of the state,
And have done infinite good in your discovery
Of these offenders.
MONTICEL.   Somewhat, sir.
FRANCISCO   O God!
Better than tribute of wolves paid in England:
'Twill hang their skins o'the hedge.
MONTICEL.   I must make bold   70
To leave your lordship.
FRANCISCO   Dearly, sir, I thank you:
If any ask for me at court, report
You have left me in the company of knaves.
                                   [exit Monticelso
I gather now by this, some cunning fellow
That's my lord's officer, one that lately skipped
From a clerk's desk up to a justice' chair,
Hath made this knavish summons, and intends,
As the Irish rebels wont were to sell heads,
So to make prize of these. And thus it happens,
Your poor rogues pay for't which have not the means   80
To present bribe in fist: the rest o'the band
Are razed out of the knaves' record; or else
My lord he winks at them with easy will;
His man grows rich, the knaves are the knaves still.
But to the use I'll make of it: it shall serve
To paint me out a list of murderers,
Agents for any villany. Did I want
Ten leash of courtesans, it would furnish me;
Nay, laundress three armies. That in so little paper
Should lie the undoing of so many men!   90
'Tis not so big as twenty declarations.
See the corrupted use some make of books:
Divinity, wrested by some factious blood,
Draws swords, swells battles, and o'erthrows all good.
To fashion my revenge more seriously,
Let me remember my dead sister's face:

Call for her picture? No, I'll close mine eyes,
And in a melancholic thought I'll frame

Enter ISABELLA'S GHOST

Her figure 'fore me. Now I ha't – how strong
Imagination works! How she can frame   100
Things which are not! Methinks she stands afore me,
And by the quick idea of my mind,
Were my skill pregnant, I could draw her picture.
Thought, as a subtle juggler, makes us deem
Things supernatural, which yet have cause
Common as sickness. 'Tis my melancholy –
How cam'st thou by thy death? How idle am I
To question mine own idleness! Did ever
Man dream awake till now? Remove this object;
Out of my brain with't: what have I to do   110
With tombs, or death-beds, funerals, or tears,
That have to meditate upon revenge?   [*exit Ghost*
So, now 'tis ended, like an old wife's story:
Statesmen think often they see stranger sights
Than madmen. Come, to this weighty business:
My tragedy must have some idle mirth in't,
Else it will never pass. I am in love,
In love with Corombona; and my suit
Thus halts to her in verse – [*writes*]
I have done it rarely: O the fate of princes!   120
I am so used to frequent flattery,
That, being alone, I now flatter myself:
But it will serve; 'tis sealéd.

Enter Servant

                          Bear this to
The House of Convertites, and watch your leisure
To give it to the hands of Corombona,
Or to the matron, when some followers
Of Brachiano may be by. Away!   [*exit Servant*
He that deals all by strength, his wit is shallow:
When a man's head goes through, each limb
                                        will follow.
The engine for my business, bold Count Lodovico: 130

'Tis gold must such an instrument procure;
With empty fist no man doth falcons lure.
Brachiano, I am now fit for thy encounter:
Like the wild Irish, I'll ne'er think thee dead
Till I can play at football with thy head.
Flectere si nequeo superos, Acheronta movebo.

                            [*exit*

SCENE 2

A room in the House of Convertites

Enter the Matron and FLAMINEO

MATRON   Should it be known the duke hath such recourse
To your imprisoned sister, I were like
To incur much damage by it.

FLAMINEO   Not a scruple:
The Pope lies on his death-bed, and their heads
Are troubled now with other business
Than guarding of a lady.

Enter Servant

SERVANT   Yonder's Flamineo in conference
With the Matrona – let me speak with you;
I would entreat you to deliver for me
This letter to the fair Vittoria.   10

MATRON   I shall, sir.

SERVANT   With all care and secrecy:
Hereafter you shall know me, and receive
Thanks for this courtesy.   [*exit*

FLAMINEO   How now! What's that?

MATRON   A letter.

FLAMINEO   To my sister? I'll see't delivered.

Enter BRACHIANO

BRACHIANO   What's that you read, Flamineo?

FLAMINEO   Look.

BRACHIANO   Ha!
[*reads*] 'To the most unfortunate, his best respected
Vittoria' –

Who was the messenger?

FLAMINEO   I know not.

BRACHIANO   No!
Who sent it?

FLAMINEO Ud's foot, you speak as if a man should know   20
          What fowl is coffined in a bakéd meat
          Afore you cut it up.

BRACHIANO I'll open't, were't her heart – What's here subscribed?
          'Florence!' This juggling is gross and palpable:
          I have found out the conveyance – read it, read it.

FLAMINEO [reads] 'Your tears I'll turn to triumphs, be but mine:
          Your prop is fall'n: I pity, that a vine,
          Which princes heretofore have longed to gather,
          Wanting supporters, now should fade and wither.'
          Wine, i'faith, my lord, with lees would serve his turn.   30
          'Your sad imprisonment I'll soon uncharm,
          And with a princely uncontrolléd arm
          Lead you to Florence, where my love and care
          Shall hang your wishes in my silver hair.'
          A halter on his strange equivocation!
          'Nor for my years return me the sad willow:
          Who prefer blossoms before fruit that's mellow?'
          Rotten, on my knowledge, with lying too long i'the
          bedstraw.
          'And all the lines of age this line convinces,   40
          The gods never wax old, no more do princes.'
          A pox on't, tear it; let's have no more atheists, for God's
          sake.

BRACHIANO Ud's death, I'll cut her into atomies,
          And let the irregular north wind sweep her up,
          And blow her into his nostrils! Where's this whore?

FLAMINEO That . . . what do you call her?

BRACHIANO   O, I could be mad,
          Prevent the cursed disease she'll bring me to,
          And tear my hair oil! Where's this changeable stuff?

FLAMINEO O'er head and ears in water, I assure you: 50
          She is not for your wearing.

BRACHIANO   No, you pander?

FLAMINEO What, me, my lord, am I your dog?

BRACHIANO A blood-hound: do you brave, do you stand me?

FLAMINEO Stand you! Let those that have diseases run;
I need no plasters.

BRACHIANO Would you be kicked?

FLAMINEO   Would you have your neck broke?
I tell you, duke, I am not in Russia;
My shins must be kept whole.

BRACHIANO   Do you know me?

FLAMINEO O, my lord, methodically:
As in this world there are degrees of evils,   60
So in this world there are degrees of devils.
You're a great duke, I your poor secretary.
I do look now for a Spanish fig, or an Italian
                                    salad, daily.

BRACHIANO Pander, ply your convoy, and leave your prating.

FLAMINEO All your kindness to me is like that miserable courtesy
of Polyphemus to Ulysses; you reserve me to be de-
voured last: you would dig turfs out of my grave to
feed your larks; that would be music to you. Come,
I'll lead you to her.

BRACHIANO Do you face me?   70

FLAMINEO O, sir, I would not go before a politic enemy with my
back towards him, though there were behind me a
whirlpool.

Enter VITTORIA COROMBONA

BRACHIANO Can you read, mistress? Look upon that letter:
There are no characters nor hieroglyphics;
You need no comment: I am grown your receiver.
God's precious! You shall be a brave great lady,
A stately and advancéd whore.

VITTORIA   Say, sir?

BRACHIANO Come, come, let's see your cabinet, discover
Your treasury of love-letters. Death and Furies!   80
I'll see them all.

VITTORIA   Sir, upon my soul,
I have not any. Whence was this directed?

BRACHIANO Confusion on your politic ignorance!
You are reclaimed, are you? I'll give you the bells,
And let you fly to the devil.

FLAMINEO   Ware hawk, my lord.
VITTORIA   'Florence!' This is some treacherous plot, my lord:
              To me he ne'er was lovely, I protest,
              So much as in my sleep.
BRACHIANO   Right! They are plots.
              Your beauty! O, ten thousand curses on't!
              How long have I beheld the devil in crystal!   90
              Thou hast led me, like an heathen sacrifice,
              With music and with fatal yokes of flowers,
              To my eternal ruin. Woman to man
              Is either a god or a wolf.
VITTORIA   My lord –
BRACHIANO   Away!
              We'll be as differing as two adamants;
              The one shall shun the other. What, dost weep?
              Procure but ten of thy dissembling trade,
              Ye'd furnish all the Irish funerals
              With howling past wild Irish.
FLAMINEO   Fie, my lord!
BRACHIANO That hand, that cursed hand, which I have wearied   100
              With doting kisses! O my sweetest duchess,
              How lovely art thou now! My loose thoughts
              Scatter like quicksilver: I was bewitched,
              For all the world speaks ill of thee.
VITTORIA   No matter:
              I'll live so now, I'll make that world recant,
              And change her speeches. You did name
                                          your duchess.
BRACHIANO Whose death God pardon!
VITTORIA   Whose death God revenge
              On thee, most godless duke!
FLAMINEO   Now for two whirlwinds.
VITTORIA   What have I gained by thee but infamy?
              Thou hast stained the spotless honour of my house,   110
              And frighted thence noble society:
              Like those, which, sick o'the palsy, and retain
              Ill-scenting foxes 'bout them, are still shunned
              By those of choicer nostrils. What do you call
                                          this house?

Is this your palace? Did not the judge style it
A house of penitent whores? Who sent me to it?
Who hath the honour to advance Vittoria
To this incontinent college? Is't not you?
Is't not your high preferment? Go, go brag
How many ladies you have undone like me.   120
Fare you well, sir; let me hear no more of you:
I had a limb corrupted to an ulcer,
But I have cut it off; and now I'll go
Weeping to Heaven on crutches. For your gifts,
I will return them all; and I do wish
That I could make you full executor
To all my sins. O, that I could toss myself
Into a grave as quickly! For all thou art worth
I'll not shed one tear more – I will burst first.

> *[she throws herself upon a bed*

BRACHIANO I have drunk Lethe – Vittoria!   130
My dearest happiness! Vittoria!
What do you ail, my love? Why do you weep?

VITTORIA Yes, I now weep poniards, do you see?

BRACHIANO Are not those matchless eyes mine?

VITTORIA   I had rather
They were not matchless.

BRACHIANO   Is not this lip mine?

VITTORIA Yes; thus to bite it off, rather than give it thee.

FLAMINEO Turn to my lord, good sister.

VITTORIA   Hence, you pander!

FLAMINEO Pander! Am I the author of your sin?

VITTORIA Yes; he's a base thief that a thief lets in.

FLAMINEO We are blown up, my lord.

BRACHIANO   Wilt thou hear me?   140
Once to be jealous of thee, is to express
That I will love thee everlastingly,
And never more be jealous.

VITTORIA   O thou fool,
Whose greatness hath by much o'ergrown thy wit!
What dar'st thou do that I not dare to suffer,
Excepting to be still thy whore? For that,
In the sea's bottom sooner thou shalt make

        A bonfire.

FLAMINEO   O, no oaths, for God's sake!

BRACHIANO Will you hear me?

VITTORIA   Never.

FLAMINEO What a damned imposthume is a woman's will!   150
        Can nothing break it? Fie, fie, my lord,
        Women are caught as you take tortoises;
        She must be turned on her back. − Sister, by this hand,
        I am on your side. − Come, come, you have
                                wronged her:
        What a strange credulous man were you, my lord,
        To think the Duke of Florence would love her!
        Will any mercer take another's ware
        When once 'tis toused and sullied? − And yet, sister,
        How scurvily this frowardness becomes you!
        Young leverets stand not long; and women's anger   160
        Should, like their flight, procure a little sport;
        A full cry for a quarter of an hour,
        And then be put to the dead quat.

BRACHIANO   Shall these eyes,
        Which have so long time dwelt upon your face,
        Be now put out?

FLAMINEO   No cruel landlady i'the world,
        Which lends forth groats to broom-men, and takes use
        For them, would do't. −
        Hand her, my lord, and kiss her: be not like
        A ferret, to let go your hold with blowing.

BRACHIANO Let us renew right hands.

VITTORIA   Hence!   170

BRACHIANO Never shall rage or the forgetful wine
        Make me commit like fault.

FLAMINEO Now you are in the way on't, follow't hard.

BRACHIANO Be thou at peace with me, let all the world
        Threaten the cannon.

FLAMINEO   Mark his penitence:
        Best natures do commit the grossest faults,
        When they're given o'er to jealousy, as best wine,
        Dying, makes strongest vinegar. I'll tell you −
        The sea's more rough and raging than calm rivers,

But not so sweet nor wholesome. A quiet woman   180
Is a still water under a great bridge;
A man may shoot her safely.

VITTORIA   O ye dissembling men!

FLAMINEO   We sucked that, sister,
From women's breasts, in our first infancy.

VITTORIA   To add misery to misery!

BRACHIANO   Sweetest –

VITTORIA   Am I not low enough?
Ay, ay, your good heart gathers like a snow-ball,
Now your affection's cold.

FLAMINEO   Ud's foot, it shall melt
To a heart again, or all the wine in Rome
Shall run a'the lees for't.   190

VITTORIA   Your dog or hawk should be rewarded better
Than I have been. I'll speak not one word more.

FLAMINEO   Stop her mouth with a sweet kiss, my lord. So,
Now the tide's turned, the vessel's come about.
He's a sweet armful. O, we curled-haired men
Are still most kind to women! This is well.

BRACHIANO   That you should chide thus!

FLAMINEO   O, sir, your little chimneys
Do ever cast most smoke! I sweat for you.
Couple together with as deep a silence
As did the Grecians in their wooden horse.   200
My lord, supply your promises with deeds;
You know that painted meat no hunger feeds.

BRACHIANO   Stay in ingrateful Rome –

FLAMINEO   Rome! it deserves to be called Barbary
For our villainous usage.

BRACHIANO   Soft! the same project which the Duke of Florence
(Whether in love or gullery I know not)
Laid down for her escape, will I pursue.

FLAMINEO   And no time fitter than this night, my lord:
The Pope being dead, and all the cardinals entered   210
The conclave for the electing a new Pope,
The city in a great confusion,
We may attire her in a page's suit,
Lay her post-horse, take shipping, and amain

For Padua.

BRACHIANO I'll instantly steal forth the Prince Giovanni,
And make for Padua. You two with your old mother,
And young Marcello that attends on Florence,
If you can work him to it, follow me:
I will advance you all: for you, Vittoria,   220
Think of a duchess' title.

FLAMINEO   La you, sister! —
Stay, my lord; I'll tell you a tale. The crocodile, which
lives in the river Nilus, hath a worm breeds i'the teeth
of't, which puts it to extreme anguish: a little bird, no
bigger than a wren, is barber-surgeon to this crocodile;
flies into the jaws of't, picks out the worm, and brings
present remedy. The fish, glad of ease, but ingrateful to
her that did it, that the bird may not talk largely of her
abroad for non-payment, closeth her chaps, intending
to swallow her, and so put her to perpetual silence. But   230
nature, loathing such ingratitude, hath armed this bird
with a quill or prick in the head, the top o'which
wounds the crocodile i'the mouth, forceth her to open
her bloody prison, and away flies the pretty tooth-
picker from her cruel patient.

BRACHIANO Your application is, I have not rewarded
The service you have done me.

FLAMINEO   No, my lord —
You, sister, are the crocodile: you are blemished in your
fame; my lord cures it; and though the comparison hold
not in every particle, yet observe, remember what good   240
the bird with the prick i'the head hath done you, and
scorn ingratitude.
[aside] It may appear to some ridiculous
Thus to talk knave and madman, and sometimes
Come in with a dried sentence, stuffed with sage:
But this allows my varying of shapes;
Knaves do grow great by being great men's apes.
                                        [exeunt

SCENE 3

Before a church

Enter FRANCISCO DE MEDICI, LODOVICO, GASPARO
and six Ambassadors

FRANCISCO So, my lord, I commend your diligence.
Guard well the conclave; and, as the order is,
Let none have conference with the cardinals.

LODOVICO [*aside*] I shall, my lord. Room for the ambassadors!

GASPARO They're wondrous brave today: why do they wear
These several habits?

LODOVICO   O, sir, they are knights
Of several orders:
That lord i'the black cloak, with the silver cross,
Is Knight of Rhodes; the next, Knight of St Michael;
That, of the Golden Fleece; the Frenchman, there,   10
Knight of the Holy Ghost; my lord of Savoy,
Knight of the Annunciation; the Englishman
Is Knight of the honoured Garter, dedicated
Unto their saint, St George. I could describe to you
Their several institutions, with the laws
Annexéd to their orders; but that time
Permits not such discovery.

FRANCISCO   Where's Count Lodovico?

LODOVICO Here, my lord.

FRANCISCO   'Tis o'the point of dinner time:
Marshal the cardinals' service.

LODOVICO   Sir, I shall.

Enter Servants, with several dishes covered

Stand, let me search your dish: who's this for?   20

SERVANT For my Lord Cardinal Monticelso.

LODOVICO Whose this?

SERVANT   For my Lord Cardinal of Bourbon.

FR. AMB. Why doth he search the dishes? To observe
What meat is drest?

ENG. AMB.   No, sir, but to prevent
Lest any letters should be conveyed in,

To bribe or to solicit the advancement
Of any cardinal. When first they enter,
'Tis lawful for the ambassadors of princes
To enter with them, and to make their suit
For any man their prince affecteth best;   30
But after, till a general election,
No man may speak with them.

LODOVICO You that attend on the lord cardinals,
Open the window, and receive their viands!

CARDINAL [at the window] You must return the service:
                                        the lord cardinals
Are busied 'bout electing of the Pope;
They have given over scrutiny, and are fall'n
To admiration.

LODOVICO   Away, away!

FRANCISCO I'll lay a thousand ducats you hear news
Of a Pope presently. Hark! Sure, he's elected: 40
Behold, my Lord of Arragon appears
On the church-battlements.

ARRAGON [on the church battlements] Denuntio vobis gaudium magnum.
Reverendissimus cardinalis Lorenzo de Monticelso electus est
in sedem apostalicam, et elegit sibi nomen Paulum Quartum.

OMNES   Vivat sanctus pater Paulus Quartus!

Enter Servant

SERVANT Vittoria, my lord –

FRANCISCO   Well, what of her?

SERVANT Is fled the city –

FRANCISCO   Ha!

SERVANT   With Duke Brachiano.

FRANCISCO Fled! Where's the Prince Giovanni?

SERVANT   Gone with his father.

FRANCISCO Let the Matrona of the Convertites   50
Be apprehended – Fled! O, damnable!   [exit Servant
How fortunate are my wishes! Why, 'twas this
I only laboured: I did send the letter
To instruct him what to do. Thy fame, fond duke,
I first have poisoned; directed thee the way
To marry a whore: what can be worse? This follows –
The hand must act to drown the passionate tongue:

I scorn to wear a sword and prate of wrong.

Enter MONTICELSO *in state*

MONTICEL. *Concedimus vobis apostolicam benedictionem et remissionem*
peccatorum.   60

[*Francisco speaks to Monticelso*]

MONTICEL. My lord reports Vittoria Corombona
Is stol'n from forth the House of Convertites
By Brachiano, and they're fled the city.
Now, though this be the first day of our state,
We cannot better please the divine power
Than to sequester from the holy church
These curséd persons. Make it therefore known,
We do denounce excommunication
Against them both: all that are theirs in Rome
We likewise banish. Set on.

[*exeunt Monticelso, his train, Ambassadors, etc.*

FRANCISCO   Come, dear Lodovico;   70
You have ta'en the sacrament to prosecute
The intended murder.

LODOVICO   With all constancy.
But, sir, I wonder you'll engage yourself
In person, being a great prince.

FRANCISCO   Divert me not.
Most of his court are of my faction,
And some are of my council. Noble friend,
Our danger shall be like in this design:
Give leave, part of the glory may be mine.

[*exeunt Francisco de Medici and Gasparo*

Re-enter MONTICELSO

MONTICEL. Why did the duke of Florence with such care
Labour your pardon? Say.   80

LODOVICO Italian beggars will resolve you that,
Who, begging of an alms, bid those they beg of,
Do good for their own sakes; or it may be,
He spreads his bounty with a sowing hand,
Like kings, who many times give out of measure,
Not for desert so much as for their pleasure.

MONTICEL. I know you're cunning. Come, what devil was that

That you were raising?

LODOVICO 　　　　　　　　　Devil, my lord!

MONTICEL. 　　　　　　　　　　　　　I ask you,
How doth the duke employ you, that his bonnet
Fell with such compliment unto his knee, 　　　　　　　　90
When he departed from you?

LODOVICO 　　　　　　　　　　　Why, my lord,
He told me of a resty Barbary horse
Which he would fain have brought to the career,
The sault, and the ring-galliard; now, my lord,
I have a rare French rider.

MONTICEL. 　　　　　　　　　　Take you heed
Lest the jade break your neck. Do you put me off
With your wild horse-tricks? Sirrah, you do lie.
O, thou'rt a foul black cloud, and thou dost threat
A violent storm!

LODOVICO 　　　　　　　Storms are i'the air, my lord:
I am too low to storm.

MONTICEL. 　　　　　　　Wretched creature! 　　　　　100
I know that thou art fashioned for all ill,
Like dogs that once get blood, they'll ever kill.
About some murder, was't not?

LODOVICO 　　　　　　　　　　I'll not tell you:
And yet I care not greatly if I do —
Marry, with this preparation: holy father,
I come not to you as an intelligencer,
But as a penitent sinner: what I utter
Is in confession merely — which you know
Must never be revealed.

MONTICEL. 　　　　　　　You have o'erta'en me.

LODOVICO Sir, I did love Brachiano's duchess dearly, 　　　　110
Or rather I pursued her with hot lust,
Though she ne'er knew on't. She was poisonéd;
Upon my soul, she was; for which I have sworn
To avenge her murder.

MONTICEL. 　　　　　　To the Duke of Florence?

LODOVICO To him I have.

MONTICEL. 　　　Miserable creature!
If thou persist in this, 'tis damnable.

Dost thou imagine thou canst slide on blood,
And not be tainted with a shameful fall?
Or, like the black and melancholic yew-tree,
Dost think to root thyself in dead men's graves,   120
And yet to prosper? Instruction to thee
Comes like sweet showers to over-hardened ground;
They wet, but pierce not deep. And so I leave thee,
With all the Furies hanging 'bout thy neck,
Till by thy penitence thou remove this evil,
In conjuring from thy breast that cruel devil.   [*exit*

LODOVICO I'll give it o'er; he says 'tis damnable,
Besides I did expect his suffrage,
By reason of Camillo's death.

Re-enter FRANCISCO DE MEDICI *with a Servant*

FRANCISCO Do you know that count?
SERVANT   Yes, my lord.   130
FRANCISCO Bear him these thousand ducats to his lodging;
Tell him the Pope hath sent them. [*aside*] Happily
That will confirm him more than all the rest.   [*exit*
SERVANT Sir –
LODOVICO   To me, sir?
SERVANT His Holiness hath sent you a thousand crowns,
And wills you, if you travel, to make him
Your patron for intelligence.
LODOVICO His creature ever to be commanded.   [*exit Servant*
Why, now 'tis come about. He railed upon me;
And yet these crowns were told out and laid ready   140
Before he knew my voyage. O the art,
The modest form of greatness! That do sit,
Like brides at wedding-dinners, with their looks turned
From the least wanton jest, their puling stomach
Sick of the modesty, when their thoughts are loose,
Even acting of those hot and lustful sports
Are to ensue about midnight: such his cunning.
He sounds my depth thus with a golden plummet.
I am doubly armed now. Now to the act of blood.
There's but three Furies found in spacious hell,   150
But in a great man's breast three thousand dwell.
                                                            [*exit*

An apartment in a palace at Padua

A passage over the stage of BRACHIANO, FLAMINEO,
MARCELLO, HORTENSIO, VITTORIA COROMBONA,
CORNELIA, ZANCHE *and others*

> [*exeunt all except Flamineo and Hortensio*

FLAMINEO In all the weary minutes of my life,
   Day ne'er broke up till now. This marriage
   Confirms me happy.

HORTENSIO   'Tis a good assurance.
   Saw you not yet the Moor that's come to court?

FLAMINEO Yes, and conferred with him in the duke's closet:
   I have not seen a goodlier personage,
   Nor ever talked with man better experienced
   In state affairs or rudiments of war:
   He hath, by report, servéd the Venetian
   In Candy these twice seven years, and been chief   10
   In many a bold design.

HORTENSIO   What are those two
   That bear him company?

FLAMINEO Two noblemen of Hungary, that, living in the emperor's
   service as commanders, eight years since, contrary to the
   expectation of all the court, entered into religion, into
   the strict order of Capuchins: but, being not well settled
   in their undertaking, they left their order, and returned
   to court; for which, being after troubled in conscience,
   they vowed their service against the enemies of Christ,
   went to Malta, were there knighted, and in their return   20
   back, at this great solemnity, they are resolved for ever to
   forsake the world, and settle themselves here in a house
   of Capuchins in Padua.

HORTENSIO 'Tis strange.

FLAMINEO One thing makes it so: they have vowed for ever to
   wear, next their bare bodies, those coats of mail they
   served in.

HORTENSIO Hard penance! Is the Moor a Christian?

FLAMINEO   He is.

HORTENSIO Why proffers he his service to our duke?

FLAMINEO Because he understands there's like to grow   30
Some wars between us and the Duke of Florence,
In which he hopes employment.
I never saw one in a stern bold look
Wear more command, nor in a lofty phrase
Express more knowing or more deep contempt
Of our slight airy courtiers. He talks
As if he had travelled all the princes' courts
Of Christendom: in all things strives to express,
That all that should dispute with him may know
Glories, like glow-worms, afar off shine bright,   40
But looked to near, have neither heat nor light –
The duke!

Re-enter BRACHIANO, *with* FRANCISCO DE MEDICI *disguised like*
MULINASSAR, LODOVICO, ANTONELLI, GASPARO, FARNESE, CARLO,
and PEDRO, *bearing their swords and helmets; and* MARCELLO

BRACHIANO You are nobly welcome. We have heard at full
Your honourable service 'gainst the Turk.
To you, brave Mulinassar, we assign
A competent pension: and are inly sorry
The vows of those two worthy gentlemen
Make them incapable of our proffered bounty.
Your wish is, you may leave your warlike swords
For monuments in our chapel: I accept it   50
As a great honour done me, and must crave
Your leave to furnish out our duchess' revels.
Only one thing, as the last vanity
You e'er shall view, deny me not to stay
To see a barriers prepared tonight:
You shall have private standings. It hath pleased
The great ambassadors of several princes,
In their return from Rome to their own countries,
To grace our marriage, and to honour me
With such a kind of sport.

FRANCISCO   I shall persuade them   60
To stay, my lord.

BRACHIANO   Set on there to the presence!
                    [*exeunt Brachiano, Flamineo, Marcello and Hortensio*

CORNELIA   Noble my lord, most fortunately welcome:
           [*the conspirators here embrace*]
           You have our vows, sealed with the sacrament,
           To second your attempts.

PEDRO   And all things ready:
           He could not have invented his own ruin
           (Had he despaired) with more propriety.

LODOVICO   You would not take my way.

FRANCISCO   'Tis better ordered.

LODOVICO   To have poisoned his prayer-book, or a pair of beads,
           The pummel of his saddle, his looking-glass,
           Or the handle of his racket – O, that, that!   70
           That while he had been bandying at tennis,
           He might have sworn himself to hell, and strook
           His soul into the hazard! O, my lord,
           I would have our plot be ingenious,
           And have it hereafter recorded for example,
           Rather than borrow example.

FRANCISCO   There's no way
           More speeding than this thought on.

LODOVICO   On, then.

FRANCISCO And yet methinks that this revenge is poor,
           Because it steals upon him like a thief.
           To have ta'en him by the casque in a pitched field,   80
           Led him to Florence!

LODOVICO   It had been rare: and there
           Have crowned him with a wreath of stinking garlic,
           To have shown the sharpness of his government
           And rankness of his lust – Flamineo comes.

                        [*exeunt Lodovico, Antonelli, Gasparo,
                                    Farnese, Carlo and Pedro*

           Re-enter FLAMINEO, MARCELLO, *and* ZANCHE

MARCELLO   Why doth this devil haunt you, say?

FLAMINEO   I know not;
           For, by this light, I do not conjure for her.
           'Tis not so great a cunning as men think,
           To raise the devil; for here's one up already:
           The greatest cunning were to lay him down.

MARCELLO She is your shame.

FLAMINEO   I prithee, pardon her.   90
In faith, you see, women are like to burs,
Where their affection throws them, there they'll stick.

ZANCHE That is my countryman, a goodly person:
When he's at leisure, I'll discourse with him
In our own language.

FLAMINEO   I beseech you do.   [exit Zanche
How is't, brave soldier? O, that I had seen
Some of your iron days! I pray, relate
Some of your service to us.

FRANCISCO 'Tis a ridiculous thing for a man to be his own chronicle:
I did never wash my mouth with mine own praise for   100
fear of getting a stinking breath.

MARCELLO You're too stoical. The duke will expect other discourse
from you.

FRANCISCO I shall never flatter him: I have studied man too much
to do that. What difference is between the duke and I?
No more than between two bricks, all made of one
clay: only't may be one is placed on the top of a turret,
the other in the bottom of a well, by mere chance. If I
were placed as high as the duke, I should stick as fast,
make as fair a show, and bear out weather equally.   110

FLAMINEO [aside] If this soldier had a patent to beg in churches,
then he would tell them stories.

MARCELLO I have been a soldier too.

FRANCISCO How have you thrived?

MARCELLO Faith, poorly.

FRANCISCO That's the misery of peace: only outsides are then respected. As ships seem very great upon the river, which
show very little upon the seas, so some men i'the court
seem colossuses in a chamber, who, if they came into
the field, would appear pitiful pigmies.   120

FLAMINEO Give me a fair room yet hung with arras, and some great
cardinal to lug me by the ears as his endeared minion.

FRANCISCO And thou mayst do the devil knows what villainy.

FLAMINEO And safely.

FRANCISCO Right: you shall see in the country, in harvest-time,
pigeons, though they destroy never so much corn, the

farmer dare not present the fowling-piece to them:
why? Because they belong to the lord of the manor;
whilst your poor sparrows, that belong to the Lord of
Heaven, they go to the pot for't.   130

FLAMINEO   I will now give you some politic instructions. The
duke says he will give you a pension: that's but bare
promise; get it under his hand. For I have known men
that have come from serving against the Turk, for three
or four months they have had pension to buy them
new wooden legs and fresh plasters; but, after, 'twas
not to be had. And this miserable courtesy shows as if a
tormentor should give hot cordial drinks to one three
quarters dead o'the rack, only to fetch the miserable
soul again to endure more dog-days.   140

[exit Francisco de Medici

Re-enter HORTENSIO and ZANCHE, with a Young Lord and two others

How now, gallants! What, are they ready for the barriers?
LORD   Yes; the lords are putting on their armour.
HORTENSIO   What's he?
FLAMINEO   A new upstart; one that swears like a falconer and will
lie in the duke's ear day by day, like a maker of
almanacs: and yet I knew him, since he came to the
court, smell worse of sweat than an under-tennis-
court-keeper.
HORTENSIO   Look you, yonder's your sweet mistress.
FLAMINEO   Thou art my sworn brother: I'll tell thee, I do love   150
that Moor, that witch, very constrainedly. She knows
some of my villainy. I do love her just as a man holds a
wolf by the ears: but for fear of turning upon me and
pulling out my throat, I would let her go to the devil.
HORTENSIO   I hear she claims marriage of thee.
FLAMINEO   Faith, I made to her some such dark promise; and, in
seeking to fly from't, I run on, like a frighted dog with
a bottle at's tail, that fain would bite it off, and yet dares
not look behind him – Now, my precious gipsy.
ZANCHE   Ay, your love to me rather cools than heats.   160
FLAMINEO   Marry, I am the sounder lover: we have many wenches
about the town heat too fast.
HORTENSIO   What do you think of these perfumed gallants, then?

FLAMINEO   Their satin cannot save them: I am confident
            They have a certain spice of the disease;
            For they that sleep with dogs shall rise with fleas.

ZANCHE   Believe it, a little painting and gay clothes make you
            love me.

FLAMINEO   How! Love a lady for painting or gay apparel? I'll
            unkennel one example more for thee. Aesop had a   170
            foolish dog that let go the flesh to catch the shadow: I
            would have courtiers be better divers.

ZANCHE   You remember your oaths?

FLAMINEO   Lovers' oaths are like mariners' prayers, uttered in
            extremity; but when the tempest is o'er, and that the
            vessel leaves tumbling, they fall from protesting to
            drinking. And yet, amongst gentlemen, protesting and
            drinking go together, and agree as well as shoemakers
            and Westphalia bacon: they are both drawers on; for
            drink draws on protestation, and protestation draws on   180
            more drink. Is not this discourse better now than the
            morality of your sunburnt gentleman?

                        Re-enter CORNELIA

CORNELIA   [*striking Zanche*] Is this your perch, you haggard?
                                        Fly to the stews.

FLAMINEO   You should be clapt by the heels now: strike i'the
                                        court! [*exit Cornelia*

ZANCHE   She's good for nothing, but to make her maids
            Catch cold a-nights: they dare not use a bed-staff
            For fear of her light fingers.

MARCELLO   You're a strumpet,
            An impudent one.

FLAMINEO   [*kicking Zanche*]   Why do you kick her, say?
            Do you think that she is like a walnut tree?
            Must she be cudgelled ere she bear good fruit?   190

MARCELLO   She brags that you shall marry her.

FLAMINEO   What then?

MARCELLO   I had rather she were pitched upon a stake
            In some new-seeded garden, to affright
            Her fellow crows thence.

FLAMINEO   You're a boy, a fool:
            Be guardian to your hound; I am of age.

MARCELLO	If I take her near you, I'll cut her throat.
FLAMINEO	With a fan of feathers?
MARCELLO	And, for you, I'll whip

This folly from you.

FLAMINEO   Are you choleric?
I'll purge't with rhubarb.

HORTENSIO   O, your brother!

FLAMINEO   Hang him,
He wrongs me most that ought to offend me least –   200
I do suspect my mother played foul play
When she conceived thee.

MARCELLO   Now, by all my hopes,
Like the two slaughtered sons of Oedipus,
The very flames of our affection
Shall turn two ways. Those words I'll make thee
                                        answer
With thy heart-blood.

FLAMINEO   Do, like the geese in the progress:
You know where you shall find me.

MARCELLO   Very good.
                    [*exit Flamineo*
An thou be'st a noble friend, bear him my sword,
And bid him fit the length on't.

YOUNG LORD   Sir, I shall.
                    [*exeunt Young Lord, Marcello,*
                    Hortensio, and the two others

ZANCHE   He comes. Hence, petty thought of my disgrace!   210

                    Re-enter FRANCISCO DE MEDICI

I ne'er loved my complexion till now,
'Cause I may boldly say, without a blush,
I love you.

FRANCISCO   Your love is untimely sown; there's a spring at
Michaelmas, but 'tis but a faint one: I am sunk in
years, and I have vowed never to marry.

ZANCHE   Alas! Poor maids get more lovers than husbands: yet
you may mistake my wealth. For, as when ambassadors
are sent to congratulate princes, there's commonly sent
along with them a rich present, so that, though the   220
prince like not the ambassador's person nor words, yet

he likes well of the presentment; so I may come to you
in the same manner, and be better loved for my dowry
than my virtue.

FRANCISCO I'll think on the motion.

ZANCHE   Do: I'll now detain you no longer. At your better
leisure I'll tell you things shall startle your blood.
Nor blame me that this passion I reveal;
Lovers die inward that their flames conceal.   [*exit*

FRANCISCO Of all intelligence this may prove the best: 230
Sure, I shall draw strange fowl from this foul nest.
                                                   [*exit*

SCENE 2

Another apartment in the same

Enter MARCELLO *and* CORNELIA

CORNELIA I hear a whispering all about the court:
You are to fight. Who is your opposite?
What is the quarrel?

MARCELLO   'Tis an idle rumour.

CORNELIA Will you dissemble? Sure, you do not well
To fright me thus: you never look thus pale
But when you are most angry. I do charge you,
Upon my blessing — nay, I'll call the duke,
And he shall school you.

MARCELLO   Publish not a fear
Which would convert to laughter: 'tis not so.
Was not this crucifix my father's?

CORNELIA   Yes.   10

MARCELLO I have heard you say, giving my brother suck,
He took the crucifix between his hands,
And broke a limb off.

CORNELIA   Yes; but 'tis mended.

Enter FLAMINEO

FLAMINEO I have brought your weapon back.
[*runs Marcello through*]

CORNELIA   Ha! O my horror!

MARCELLO You have brought it home, indeed.

CORNELIA   Help! O, he's murdered!

FLAMINEO Do you turn your gall up? I'll to sanctuary,
          And send a surgeon to you.   [*exit*

          Enter CARLO, HORTENSIO *and* PEDRO

HORTENSIO How! O'the ground!

MARCELLO O mother, now remember what I told
          Of breaking of the crucifix! Farewell.   20
          There are some sins which Heaven doth duly punish
          In a whole family. This it is to rise
          By all dishonest means! Let all men know,
          That tree shall long time keep a steady foot
          Whose branches spread no wider than the root. [*dies*]

CORNELIA O my perpetual sorrow!

HORTENSIO   Virtuous Marcello!
          He's dead – Pray, leave him, lady: come, you shall.

CORNELIA Alas, he is not dead; he's in a trance.
          Why, here's nobody shall get any thing by his death.
          Let me call him again, for God's sake!   30

CARLO I would you were deceived.

CORNELIA O, you abuse me, you abuse me, you abuse me! How
          many have gone away thus, for lack of tendance! Rear
          up's head, rear up's head: his bleeding inward will kill
          him.

HORTENSIO You see he is departed.

CORNELIA Let me come to him; give me him as he is: if he be
          turned to earth, let me but give him one hearty kiss,
          and you shall put us both into one coffin. Fetch a
          looking glass; see if his breath will not stain it: or pull   40
          out some feathers from my pillow, and lay them to his
          lips. Will you lose him for a little pains-taking?

HORTENSIO Your kindest office is to pray for him.

CORNELIA Alas, I would not pray for him yet. He may live to lay
          me i'the ground, and pray for me, if you'll let me come
          to him.

    Enter BRACHIANO *all armed save the beaver, with* FLAMINEO,
        FRANCISCO DE MEDICI, LODOVICO *and Page*

BRACHIANO Was this your handiwork?

FLAMINEO   It was my misfortune.

CORNELIA   He lies, he lies; he did not kill him: these have killed
            him that would not let him be better looked to.

BRACHIANO   Have comfort, my grieved mother.   50

CORNELIA   O you screech-owl!

HORTENSIO   Forbear, good madam.

CORNELIA   Let me go, let me go. [*she runs to Flamineo with her knife*
            drawn, and, coming to him, lets it fall]
            The God of Heaven forgive thee! Dost not wonder
            I pray for thee? I'll tell thee what's the reason;
            I have scarce breath to number twenty minutes;
            I'd not spend that in cursing. Fare thee well:
            Half of thyself lies there; and mayst thou live
            To fill an hour-glass with his mouldered ashes,
            To tell how thou shouldst spend the time to come   60
            In blest repentance!

BRACHIANO   Mother, pray tell me
            How came he by his death? What was the quarrel?

CORNELIA   Indeed, my younger boy presumed too much
            Upon his manhood, gave him bitter words,
            Drew his sword first; and so, I know not how,
            For I was out of my wits, he fell with's head
            Just in my bosom.

PAGE   This is not true, madam.

CORNELIA   I pray thee, peace.
            One arrow's grazed already: it were vain
            To lose this for that will ne'er be found again.   70

BRACHIANO   Go bear the body to Cornelia's lodging:
            And we command that none acquaint our duchess
            With this sad accident. For you, Flamineo,
            Hark you, I will not grant your pardon.

FLAMINEO   No?

BRACHIANO   Only a lease of your life; and that shall last
            But for one day: thou shalt be forced each evening
            To renew it, or be hanged.

FLAMINEO   At your pleasure.
            [*Lodovico sprinkles Brachiano's beaver with a poison*]
            Your will is law now, I'll not meddle with it.

BRACHIANO   You once did brave me in your sister's lodging;
            I'll now keep you in awe for't – Where's our beaver?   80

FRANCISCO [*aside*] He calls for his destruction. Noble youth,
          I pity thy sad fate! Now to the barriers.
          This shall his passage to the black lake further;
          The last good deed he did, he pardoned murther.

                                       [*exeunt*

SCENE 3

The lists at Padua. Charges and shouts. They fight at barriers;
first single pairs, then three to three.

Enter BRACHIANO, VITTORIA COROMBONA GIOVANNI,
     FRANCISCO DE MEDICI, FLAMINEO, *with others*

BRACHIANO An armorer! Ud's death, an armorer!
FLAMINEO   Armorer! Where's the armorer?
BRACHIANO Tear off my beaver.
FLAMINEO   Are you hurt, my lord?
BRACHIANO O, my brain's on fire!

                 Enter Armorer

                     The helmet is poisonéd.
ARMORER   My lord, upon my soul –
BRACHIANO   Away with him to torture!
          There are some great ones that have hand in this,
          And near about me.
VITTORIA   O my loved lord! Poisoned!
FLAMINEO Remove the bar. Here's unfortunate revels!
          Call the physicians.

               Enter two Physicians

                    A plague upon you!
          We have too much of your cunning here already: 10
          I fear the ambassadors are likewise poisoned.
BRACHIANO O, I am gone already! The infection
          Flies to the brain and heart. O thou strong heart!
          There's such a covenant 'tween the world and it,
          They're loth to break.
GIOVANNI   O my most lovéd father!
BRACHIANO Remove the boy away –
          Where's this good woman? – Had I infinite worlds,
          They were too little for thee: must I leave thee?

What say you, screech-owls, is the venom mortal?
PHYSICIAN Most deadly.
BRACHIANO   Most corrupted politic hangman,   20
You kill without book; but your art to save
Fails you as oft as great men's needy friends.
I that have given life to offending slaves
And wretched murderers, have I not power
To lengthen mine own a twelvemonth?
Do not kiss me, for I shall poison thee.
This unction's sent from the great Duke of Florence.
FRANCISCO Sir, be of comfort.
BRACHIANO O thou soft natural death, that art joint-twin
To sweetest slumber! No rough-bearded comet   30
Stares on thy mild departure; the dull owl
Beats not against thy casement; the hoarse wolf
Scents not thy carrion: pity winds thy corse,
Whilst horror waits on princes.
VITTORIA   I am lost for ever.
BRACHIANO How miserable a thing it is to die
'Mongst women howling!

Enter LODOVICO *and* GASPARO, *in the habit of Capuchins*
                    What are those?
FLAMINEO   Franciscans:
They have brought the extreme unction.
BRACHIANO On pain of death, let no man name death to me:
It is a word infinitely terrible.
Withdraw into our cabinet.   40
          [*exeunt all except Francisco de Medici and Flamineo*
FLAMINEO To see what solitariness is about dying princes! As here-
tofore they have unpeopled towns, divorced friends,
and made great houses unhospitable, so now, O justice!
Where are their flatterers now? Flatterers are but the
shadows of princes' bodies; the least thick cloud makes
them invisible.
FRANCISCO There's great moan made for him.
FLAMINEO Faith, for some few hours salt-water will run most
plentifully in every office o'the court: but, believe it,
most of them do but weep over their stepmothers' graves. 50
FRANCISCO How mean you?

FLAMINEO   Why, they dissemble; as some men do that live within
compass o'the verge.

FRANCISCO   Come, you have thrived well under him.

FLAMINEO   Faith, like a wolf in a woman's breast; I have been fed
with poultry: but, for money, understand me, I had as
good a will to cozen him as e'er an officer of them all;
but I had not cunning enough to do it.

FRANCISCO   What didst thou think of him? Faith, speak freely.

FLAMINEO   He was a kind of statesman that would sooner have   60
reckoned how many cannon-bullets he had discharged
against a town, to count his expense that way, than
how many of his valiant and deserving subjects he lost
before it.

FRANCISCO   O, speak well of the duke.

FLAMINEO   I have done. Wilt hear some of my court-wisdom? To
reprehend princes is dangerous; and to over-commend
some of them is palpable lying.

Re-enter LODOVICO

FRANCISCO   How is it with the duke?

LODOVICO   Most deadly ill.
He's fall'n into a strange distraction: 70
He talks of battles and monopolies,
Levying of taxes; and from that descends
To the most brain-sick language. His mind fastens
On twenty several objects, which confound
Deep sense with folly. Such a fearful end
May teach some men that bear too lofty crest,
Though they live happiest, yet they die not best.
He hath conferred the whole state of the dukedom
Upon your sister, till the prince arrive
At mature age.

FLAMINEO   There's some good luck in that yet.   80

FRANCISCO   See, here he comes.

Enter BRACHIANO, *presented in a bed,* VITTORIA
COROMBONA, GASPARO *and Attendants*

There's death in's face already.

VITTORIA   O my good lord!

BRACHIANO   Away! You have abused me:

[*these speeches are several kinds of distractions, and in the
action should appear so*]
You have conveyed coin forth our territories,
Bought and sold offices, oppressed the poor,
And I ne'er dreamt on't. Make up your accounts:
I'll now be mine own steward.

FLAMINEO   Sir, have patience.

BRACHIANO Indeed, I am to blame:
For did you ever hear the dusky raven
Chide blackness? Or was't ever known the devil
Railed against cloven creatures?

VITTORIA   O my lord!   90

BRACHIANO Let me have some quails to supper.

FLAMINEO   Sir, you shall.

BRACHIANO No, some fried dog-fish; your quails feed on poison.
That old dog-fox, that politician, Florence!
I'll forswear hunting, and turn dog-killer:
Rare! I'll be friends with him; for, mark you, sir,
                                                one dog
Still sets another a-barking. Peace, peace!
Yonder's a fine slave come in now.

FLAMINEO   Where?

BRACHIANO   Why, there,
In a blue bonnet, and a pair of breeches
With a great cod-piece: ha, ha, ha!
Look you, his cod-piece is stuck full of pins,   100
With pearls o'the head of them. Do not you
                                                know him?

FLAMINEO No, my lord.

BRACHIANO   Why, 'tis the devil;
I know him by a great rose he wears on's shoe,
To hide his cloven foot. I'll dispute with him;
He's a rare linguist.

VITTORIA   My lord, here's nothing.

BRACHIANO Nothing! Rare! Nothing! When I want money,
Our treasury is empty, there is nothing:
I'll not be used thus.

VITTORIA   O, lie still, my lord!

BRACHIANO See, see Flamineo, that killed his brother,

Is dancing on the ropes there, and he carries   110
A money-bag in each hand, to keep him even,
For fear of breaking's neck: and there's a lawyer,
In a gown whipt with velvet, stares and gapes
When the money will fall. How the rogue cuts capers!
It should have been in a halter. 'Tis there: what's she?

FLAMINEO Vittoria, my lord.

BRACHIANO Ha, ha, ha! Her hair is sprinkled with arras-powder,
That makes her look as if she had sinned in the
                                             pastry –
What's he?

FLAMINEO A divine, my lord,   120
[*Brachiano seems here near his end: Lodovico and Gasparo,
in the habit of Capuchins, present him in his bed with a
crucifix and hallowed candle*]

BRACHIANO He will be drunk; avoid him: the argument
Is fearful, when churchmen stagger in't.
Look you, six grey rats, that have lost their tails,
Crawl up the pillow: send for a rat-catcher:
I'll do a miracle, I'll free the court
From all foul vermin. Where's Flamineo?

FLAMINEO [*aside*] I do not like that he names me so often,
Especially on's death-bed: 'tis a sign
I shall not live long – See, he's near his end.

LODOVICO Pray, give us leave – *Attende, domine Brachiane.*   130

FLAMINEO See, see how firmly he doth fix his eye
Upon the crucifix.

VITTORIA   O, hold it constant!
It settles his wild spirits; and so his eyes
Melt into tears.

LODOVICO [*by the crucifix*] *Domine Brachiane, solebas in bello tutus esse
tuo clypeo; nunc hunc clypeum hosti tuo opponas infernali.*

GASPARO [*by the hallowed taper*] *Olim hasta valuisti in bello; nunc
hanc sacram hastam vibrabis contra hostem animarum.*

LODOVICO *Attende, domine Brachiane; si nunc quoque probas ea quae
acta sunt inter nos, flecte caput in dextrum.*   140

GASPARO *Esto securus, domine Brachiane; cogita quantum habeas
meritorum; denique memineris meam animam pro tua
oppignoratam si quid esset periculi.*

LODOVICO   *Si nunc quoque probas ea quae acta sunt inter nos, flecte*
           caput in laevum —
           He is departing. Pray, stand all apart,
           And let us only whisper in his ears
           Some private meditations, which our order
           Permits you not to hear.
           [*here, the rest being departed, Lodovico and Gasparo*
           discover themselves]
GASPARO   Brachiano —
LODOVICO   Devil Brachiano, thou art damned.
GASPARO   Perpetually.   50
LODOVICO   A slave condemned and given up to the gallows
           Is thy great lord and master.
GASPARO   True; for thou
           Art given up to the devil.
LODOVICO   O you slave!
           You that were held the famous politician,
           Whose art was poison!
GASPARO   And whose conscience, murder!
LODOVICO   That would have brake your wife's neck down the stairs,
           Ere she was poisoned!
GASPARO   That had your villainous salads!
LODOVICO   And fine embroidered bottles and perfumes,
           Equally mortal with a winter-plague!
GASPARO   Now there's mercury —
LODOVICO   And copperas —
GASPARO   And quicksilver —   60
LODOVICO   With other devilish 'pothecary stuff
           A-melting in your politic brains: dost hear?
GASPARO   This is Count Lodovico.
LODOVICO   This, Gasparo:
           And thou shalt die like a poor rogue.
GASPARO   And stink
           Like a dead fly-blown dog.
LODOVICO   And be forgotten
           Before thy funeral sermon.
BRACHIANO   Vittoria!
           Vittoria!
LODOVICO   O, the cursèd devil

Comes to himself again! We are undone.

GASPARO   Strangle him in private.

Enter VITTORIA COROMBONA, FRANCISCO DE MEDICI,
FLAMINEO and Attendants

What, will you call him again   70
To live in treble torments? For charity,
For Christian charity, avoid the chamber.
                    [*exeunt Vittoria Corombona, Francisco de Medici,
                                        Flamineo and attendants*

LODOVICO   You would prate, sir? This is a true-love knot
Sent from the Duke of Florence.
            [*he strangles Brachiano*]

GASPARO   What, is it done?

LODOVICO   The snuff is out. No woman-keeper i'the world,
Though she had practised seven year at the pest-house,
Could have done't quaintlier.

Re-enter VITTORIA COROMBONA, FRANCISCO DE MEDICI,
FLAMINEO and Attendants

                                My lords, he's dead.

OMNES   Rest to his soul!

VITTORIA   O me! This place is hell.   [*exit*

FRANCISCO   How heavily she takes it!

FLAMINEO   O, yes, yes;
Had women navigable rivers in their eyes,   80
They would dispend them all: surely, I wonder
Why we should wish more rivers to the city,
When they sell water so good cheap. I'll tell thee,
These are but moonish shades of griefs or fears;
There's nothing sooner dry than women's tears.
Why, here's an end of all my harvest; he has
                                given me nothing.
Court promises! Let wise men count them cursed,
For while you live, he that scores best pays worst.

FRANCISCO   Sure, this was Florence' doing.

FLAMINEO   Very likely.
Those are found weighty strokes which come
                                from the hand,   90
But those are killing strokes which come from the head.

> O, the rare tricks of a Machiavellian!
> He doth not come, like a gross plodding slave,
> And buffet you to death: no, my quaint knave,
> He tickles you to death, makes you die laughing,
> As if you had swallowed down a pound of saffron.
> You see the feat, 'tis practised in a trice;
> To teach court honesty, it jumps on ice.

FRANCISCO Now have the people liberty to talk,
> And descant on his vices.

FLAMINEO   Misery of princes,   100
> That must of force be censured by their slaves!
> Not only blamed for doing things are ill,
> But for not doing all that all men will:
> One were better be a thresher.
> Ud's death, I would fain speak with this duke yet.

FRANCISCO Now he's dead?

FLAMINEO I cannot conjure; but if prayers or oaths
> Will get to the speech of him, though forty devils
> Wait on him in his livery of flames,
> I'll speak to him, and shake him by the hand,   110
> Though I be blasted.   [exit

FRANCISCO   Excellent Lodovico!
> What, did you terrify him at the last gasp?

LODOVICO Yes, and so idly, that the duke had like
> To have terrified us.

FRANCISCO   How?

LODOVICO   You shall hear that hereafter.

Enter ZANCHE

> See, yon's the infernal that would make up sport.
> Now to the revelation of that secret
> She promised when she fell in love with you.

FRANCISCO You're passionately met in this sad world.

ZANCHE I would have you look up, sir; these court-tears
> Claim not your tribute to them: let those weep   120
> That guiltily partake in the sad cause.
> I knew last night, by a sad dream I had,
> Some mischief would ensue; yet, to say truth,
> My dream most concerned you.

LODOVICO   Shall's fall a-dreaming?

FRANCISCO   Yes; and for fashion sake I'll dream with her.

ZANCHE   Methought, sir, you came stealing to my bed.

FRANCISCO   Wilt thou believe me, sweeting? By this light,
                 I was a-dreamt on thee too; for methought
                 I saw thee naked.

ZANCHE   Fie, sir! As I told you,
                 Methought you lay down by me.

FRANCISCO   So dreamt I;   130
                 And lest thou shouldst take cold, I covered thee
                 With this Irish mantle.

ZANCHE   Verily, I did dream
                 You were somewhat bold with me: but to come to't –

LODOVICO   How, how! I hope you will not go to't here.

FRANCISCO   Nay, you must hear my dream out.

ZANCHE   Well, sir, forth.

FRANCISCO   When I threw the mantle o'er thee, thou didst laugh
                 Exceedingly, methought.

ZANCHE   Laugh!

FRANCISCO   And cried'st out,
                 The hair did tickle thee.

ZANCHE   There was a dream indeed!

LODOVICO   Mark her, I prithee; she simpers like the suds
                 A collier hath been washed in.   140

ZANCHE   Come, sir, good fortune tends you. I did tell you
                 I would reveal a secret: Isabella,
                 The Duke of Florence' sister, was impoisoned
                 By a fumed picture; and Camillo's neck
                 Was broke by damned Flamineo, the mischance
                 Laid on a vaulting-horse.

FRANCISCO   Most strange!

ZANCHE   Most true.

LODOVICO   The bed of snakes is broke.

ZANCHE   I sadly do confess I had a hand
                 In the black deed.

FRANCISCO   Thou kept'st their counsel?

ZANCHE   Right;
                 For which, urged with contrition, I intend   150
                 This night to rob Vittoria.

LODOVICO   Excellent penitence!

Usurers dream on't while they sleep out sermons.
ZANCHE   To further our escape, I have entreated
Leave to retire me, till the funeral,
Unto a friend i'the country: that excuse
Will further our escape. In coin and jewels
I shall at least make good unto your use
An hundred thousand crowns.
FRANCISCO   O noble wench!
LODOVICO Those crowns we'll share.
ZANCHE   It is a dowry,
Methinks, should make that sun-burnt proverb false,   160
And wash the Aethiop white.
FRANCISCO   It shall. Away!
ZANCHE   Be ready for our flight.
FRANCISCO   An hour 'fore day. [exit Zanche
O strange discovery! Why, till now we knew not
The circumstance of either of their deaths.

                    Re-enter ZANCHE

ZANCHE   You'll wait about midnight in the chapel?
FRANCISCO   There.
                                        [exit Zanche
LODOVICO Why, now our action's justified.
FRANCISCO   Tush for justice!
What harms it justice? We now, like the partridge,
Purge the disease with laurel; for the fame
Shall crown the enterprise, and quit the shame.
                                        [exeunt

SCENE 4

An apartment in a palace at Padua

Enter FLAMINEO *and* GASPARO, *at one door; another way,*
GIOVANNI, *attended*

GASPARO   The young duke: did you e'er see a sweeter prince?

FLAMINEO   I have known a poor woman's bastard better favoured:
this is behind him. Now, to his face, all comparisons
were hateful. Wise was the courtly peacock that, being
a great minion, and being compared for beauty by some
dottrels, that stood by to the kingly eagle, said the
eagle was a far fairer bird than herself, not in respect of
her feathers, but in respect of her long talons: his will
grow out in time – My gracious lord!

GIOVANNI   I pray, leave me, sir.   10

FLAMINEO   Your grace must be merry: 'tis I have cause to mourn;
for, wot you, what said the little boy that rode behind
his father on horseback?

GIOVANNI   Why, what said he?

FLAMINEO   'When you are dead, father,' said he, 'I hope that I
shall ride in the saddle.' O, 'tis a brave thing for a man
to sit by himself! He may stretch himself in the stirrups,
look about, and see the whole compass of the hemi-
sphere. You're now, my lord, i'the saddle.

GIOVANNI   Study your prayers, sir, and be penitent: 20
'Twere fit you'd think on what hath former bin;
I have heard grief named the eldest child of sin.   [*exit*

FLAMINEO   Study my prayers! He threatens me divinely: I am
falling to pieces already. I care not though, like
Anacharsis, I were pounded to death in a mortar: and
yet that death were fitter for usurers, gold and themselves to be beaten together, to make a most cordial
cullis for the devil.
He hath his uncle's villainous look already,
In *decimo-sexto*.   30

Enter Courtier

Now, sir, what are you?

COURTIER   It is the pleasure, sir, of the young duke,
That you forbear the presence, and all rooms
That owe him reverence.

FLAMINEO   So, the wolf and the raven
Are very pretty fools when they are young.
Is it your office, sir, to keep me out?

COURTIER   So the duke wills.

FLAMINEO   Verily, master courtier, extremity is not to be used in all
offices: say that a gentlewoman were taken out of her
bed about midnight, and committed to Castle Angelo,   40
or to the tower yonder, with nothing about her but her
smock, would it not show a cruel part in the gentleman-
porter to lay claim to her upper garment, pull it o'er her
head and ears, and put her in naked?

COURTIER   Very good: you are merry.   [*exit*

FLAMINEO   Doth he make a court-ejectment of me? A flaming
fire-brand casts more smoke without a chimney than
within't. I'll smoor some of them.

Enter FRANCISCO DE MEDICI

How now! Thou art sad.

FRANCISCO   I met even now with the most piteous sight.   50

FLAMINEO   Thou meet'st another here, a pitiful
Degraded courtier.

FRANCISCO   Your reverend mother
Is grown a very old woman in two hours.
I found them winding of Marcello's corse;
And there is such a solemn melody,
'Tween doleful songs, tears, and sad elegies –
Such as old grandams watching by the dead
Were wont to outwear the nights with – that,
                                              believe me,
I had no eyes to guide me forth the room,
They were so o'ercharged with water.

FLAMINEO   I will see them.   60

FRANCISCO   'Twere much uncharity in you; for your sight
Will add unto their tears.

FLAMINEO   I will see them:

> They are behind the traverse; I'll discover
> [*draws the curtain*] Their superstitious howling.

Cornelia, Zanche, and three other ladies discovered
winding Marcello's corse. A song.

CORNELIA   This rosemary is withered; pray, get fresh.
 I would have these herbs grow up in his grave,
 When I am dead and rotten. Reach the bays,
 I'll tie a garland here about his head;
 'Twill keep my boy from lightning. This sheet
 I have kept this twenty year, and every day   70
 Hallowed it with my prayers: I did not think
 He should have wore it.
ZANCHE   Look you who are yonder.
CORNELIA   O, reach me the flowers.
ZANCHE   Her ladyship's foolish.
LADY   Alas, her grief
 Hath turned her child again!
CORNELIA   You're very welcome:
 [*to Flamineo*] There's rosemary for you — and rue
             for you —
 Heart's-ease for you; I pray make much of it:
 I have left more for myself.
FRANCISCO   Lady, who's this?
CORNELIA   You are, I take it, the grave-maker.
FLAMINEO   So.
ZANCHE   'Tis Flamineo.   80
CORNELIA   Will you make me such a fool? Here's a white hand:
 Can blood so soon be washed out? Let me see;
 When screech-owls croak upon the chimney-tops,
 And the strange cricket i'the oven sings and hops,
 When yellow spots do on your hands appear,
 Be certain then you of a corse shall hear.
 Out upon't, how 'tis speckled! H'as handled a
            toad, sure.
 Cowslip-water is good for the memory:
 Pray, buy me three ounces of't.
FLAMINEO   I would I were from hence.
CORNELIA   Do you hear, sir? 90
 I'll give you a saying which my grandmother

Was wont, when she heard the bell toll, to sing o'er
Unto her lute.

FLAMINEO   Do, an you will, do.

CORNELIA [*in several forms of distraction*] 'Call for the robin
                                        red-breast and the wren,
Since o'er shady groves they hover,
And with leaves and flowers do cover
The friendless bodies of unburied men.
Call unto his funeral dole
The ant, the field-mouse, and the mole,
To rear him hillocks that shall keep him warm,   100
And (when gay tombs are robbed) sustain no harm:
But keep the wolf far thence, that's foe to men,
For with his nails he'll dig them up again.'
They would not bury him 'cause he died in a quarrel;
But I have an answer for them:
'Let holy church receive him duly,
Since he paid the church-tithes truly.'
His wealth is summed, and this is all his store,
This poor men get, and great men get no more.
Now the wares are gone, we may shut up shop.   110
Bless you all, good people.

                        [*exeunt Cornelia, Zanche and ladies*

FLAMINEO I have a strange thing in me, to the which
I cannot give a name, without it be
Compassion. I pray, leave me.

                        [*exit Francisco de Medici*

This night I'll know the utmost of my fate;
I'll be resolved what my rich sister means
To assign me for my service. I have lived
Riotously ill, like some that live in court,
And sometimes when my face was full of smiles,
Have felt the maze of conscience in my breast.   120
Oft gay and honoured robes those tortures try:
We think caged birds sing, when indeed they cry.

Enter BRACHIANO's *ghost, in his leather cassock and breeches,*
boots and cowl; in his hand a pot of lily-flowers, with a skull in it

Ha! I can stand thee: nearer, nearer yet.
What a mockery hath death made thee! Thou
                                    look'st sad.
In what place art thou? In yon starry gallery?
Or in the cursed dungeon? No? Not speak?
Pray, sir, resolve me, what religion's best
For a man to die in? Or is it in your knowledge
To answer me how long I have to live?
That's the most necessary question.   130
Not answer? Are you still like some great men
That only walk like shadows up and down,
And to no purpose? Say:
[*the Ghost throws earth upon him, and shows him the skull*]
What's that? O, fatal! He throws earth upon me!
A dead man's skull beneath the roots of flowers!
I pray, speak, sir: our Italian churchmen
Make us believe dead men hold conference
With their familiars, and many times
Will come to bed to them, and eat with them.
                                    [*exit Ghost*

He's gone; and see, the skull and earth are vanished.   140
This is beyond melancholy. I do dare my fate
To do its worst. Now to my sister's lodging,
And sum up all these horrors: the disgrace
The prince threw on me; next the piteous sight
Of my dead brother, and my mother's dotage;
And last this terrible vision: all these
Shall with Vittoria's bounty turn to good,
Or I will drown this weapon in her blood.
                                    [*exit*

SCENE 5

A street in Padua

Enter FRANCISCO DE MEDICI, LODOVICO *and* HORTENSIO

LODOVICO My lord, upon my soul, you shall no further;
         You have most ridiculously engaged yourself
         Too far already. For my part, I have paid
         All my debts; so, if I should chance to fall,
         My creditors fall not with me; and I vow
         To quit all in this bold assembly
         To the meanest follower. My lord, leave the city,
         Or I'll forswear the murder.   [*exit*
FRANCISCO   Farewell, Lodovico:
         If thou dost perish in this glorious act,
         I'll rear unto thy memory that fame   10
         Shall in the ashes keep alive thy name.   [*exit*
HORTENSIO There's some black deed on foot. I'll presently
         Down to the citadel, and raise some force.
         These strong court-factions, that do brook no checks,
         In the career oft break the riders' necks.
                                                        [*exit*

SCENE 6

An apartment in Vittoria's house

Enter VITTORIA COROMBONA *with a book in her hand,
and* ZANCHE; FLAMINEO *following them*

FLAMINEO What, are you at your prayers? Give o'er.
VITTORIA   How, ruffian!
FLAMINEO I come to you 'bout worldly business.
         Sit down, sit down: nay, stay, blouze, you may
                                              hear it —
         The doors are fast enough.
VITTORIA   Ha, are you drunk?

FLAMINEO   Yes, yes, with wormwood-water: you shall taste
            Some of it presently.
VITTORIA   What intends the Fury?
FLAMINEO   You are my lord's executrix; and I claim
            Reward for my long service.
VITTORIA   For your service!
FLAMINEO   Come, therefore, here is pen and ink; set down
            What you will give me.
VITTORIA   [writes]   There.
FLAMINEO   Ha! Have you done already?   10
            'Tis a most short conveyance.
VITTORIA   I will read it:
            [reads] 'I give that portion to thee, and no other,
            Which Cain groaned under, having slain his brother.'
FLAMINEO   A most courtly patent to beg by!
VITTORIA   You are a villain.
FLAMINEO   Is't come to this? They say, affrights cure agues:
            Thou hast a devil in thee; I will try
            If I can scare him from thee. Nay, sit still:
            My lord hath left me yet two case of jewels
            Shall make me scorn your bounty; you shall see them.
                                                    [exit
VITTORIA   Sure, he's distracted.
ZANCHE   O, he's desperate: 20
            For your own safety give him gentle language.

            Re-enter FLAMINEO with two case of pistols

FLAMINEO   Look, these are better far at a dead lift
            Than all your jewel-house.
VITTORIA   And yet, methinks,
            These stones have no air lustre, they are ill set.
FLAMINEO   I'll turn the right side towards you: you shall see
            How they will sparkle.
VITTORIA   Turn this horror from me!
            What do you want? What would you have me do?
            Is not all mine yours? Have I any children?
FLAMINEO   Pray thee, good woman, do not trouble me
            With this vain worldly business; say your prayers: 30
            I made a vow to my deceaséd lord,

Neither yourself nor I should outlive him
The numbering of four hours.

VITTORIA   Did he enjoin it?

FLAMINEO He did; and 'twas a deadly jealousy,
Lest any should enjoy thee after him,
That urged him vow me to it. For my death,
I did propound it voluntarily, knowing,
If he could not be safe in his own court,
Being a great duke, what hope, then, for us?

VITTORIA This is your melancholy and despair.

FLAMINEO   Away!   40
Fool thou art to think that politicians
Do use to kill the effects of injuries
And let the cause live. Shall we groan in irons,
Or be a shameful and a weighty burden
To a public scaffold? This is my resolve;
I would not live at any man's entreaty,
Nor die at any's bidding.

VITTORIA   Will you hear me?

FLAMINEO My life hath done service to other men;
My death shall serve mine own turn. Make you ready.

VITTORIA Do you mean to die indeed?

FLAMINEO   With as much pleasure   50
As e'er my father gat me.

VITTORIA   Are the doors locked?

ZANCHE   Yes, madam.

VITTORIA Are you grown an atheist? Will you turn your body,
Which is the goodly palace of the soul,
To the soul's slaughter-house? O, the cursed devil,
Which doth present us with all other sins
Thrice-candied o'er; despair with gall and stibium;
Yet we carouse it off – [aside to Zanche] Cry out
                                        for help! –
Makes us forsake that which was made for man,
The world, to sink to that was made for devils,
Eternal darkness!

ZANCHE   Help, help!

FLAMINEO   I'll stop your throat   60

	With winter-plums.
VITTORIA	I prithee, yet remember,
	Millions are now in graves, which at last day
	Like mandrakes shall rise shrieking.
FLAMINEO	Leave your prating,
	For these are but grammatical laments,
	Feminine arguments: and they move me,
	As some in pulpits move their auditory,
	More with their exclamation than sense
	Of reason or sound doctrine.
ZANCHE	[aside to Vittoria] Gentle madam,
	Seem to consent, only persuade him teach
	The way to death; let him die first. 70
VITTORIA	'Tis good. I apprehend it,
	To kill one's self is meat that we must take
	Like pills – not chew't, but quickly swallow it;
	The smart o'the wound, or weakness of the hand,
	May else bring treble torments.
FLAMINEO	I have held it
	A wretched and most miserable life
	Which is not able to die.
VITTORIA	O, but frailty!
	Yet I am now resolved: farewell, affliction!
	Behold, Brachiano, I that while you lived
	Did make a flaming altar of my heart 80
	To sacrifice unto you, now am ready
	To sacrifice heart and all – Farewell, Zanche!
ZANCHE	How, madam! Do you think that I'll outlive you;
	Especially when my best self, Flamineo,
	Goes the same voyage?
FLAMINEO	O, most lovéd Moor!
ZANCHE	Only by all my love let me entreat you –
	Since it is most necessary one of us
	Do violence on ourselves – let you or I
	Be her sad taster, teach her how to die.
FLAMINEO	Thou dost instruct me nobly: take these pistols, 90
	Because my hand is stained with blood already:
	Two of these you shall level at my breast,
	The other 'gainst your own, and so we'll die

               Most equally contented: but first swear
               Not to outlive me.

VITTORIA COROMBONA & ZANCHE Most religiously.

FLAMINEO Then here's an end of me; farewell, daylight!
               And, O contemptible physic, that dost take
               So long a study, only to preserve
               So short a life, I take my leave of thee!
               [*showing the pistols*] These are two cupping-glasses
                                                that shall draw   100
               All my infected blood out. Are you ready?

VITTORIA COROMBONA & ZANCHE   Ready.

FLAMINEO Whither shall I go now? O Lucian, thy ridiculous
               purgatory! To find Alexander the Great cobbling shoes,
               Pompey tagging points, and Julius Caesar making hair-
               buttons! Hannibal selling blacking, and Augustus crying
               garlic! Charlemagne selling lists by the dozen, and King
               Pepin crying apples in a cart drawn with one horse!
               Whether I resolve to fire, earth, water, air,
               Or all the elements by scruples, I know not,
               Nor greatly care – Shoot, shoot: 110
               Of all deaths the violent death is best;
               For from ourselves it steals ourselves so fast,
               The pain, once apprehended, is quite past.
               [*they shoot: he falls, and they run to him, and tread upon him*]

VITTORIA What, are you dropt?

FLAMINEO I am mixed with earth already: as you are noble,
               Perform your vows, and bravely follow me.

VITTORIA Whither? To hell?

ZANCHE   To most assured damnation?

VITTORIA O thou most cursed devil!

ZANCHE   Thou art caught –

VITTORIA In thine own engine. I tread the fire out
               That would have been my ruin.   120

FLAMINEO Will you be perjured? What a religious oath was Styx,
               that the gods never durst swear by, and violate! O, that
               we had such an oath to minister, and to be so well kept
               in our courts of justice!

VITTORIA Think whither thou art going.

ZANCHE   And remember

What villainies thou hast acted.

VITTORIA   This thy death
Shall make me like a blazing ominous star:
Look up and tremble.

FLAMINEO   O, I am caught with a springe!

VITTORIA You see the fox comes many times short home;
'Tis here proved true.

FLAMINEO   Killed with a couple of braches!   130

VITTORIA No fitter offering for the infernal Furies
Than one in whom they reigned while he was living.

FLAMINEO O, the way's dark and horrid! I cannot see:
Shall I have no company?

VITTORIA   O, yes, thy sins
Do run before thee to fetch fire from hell,
To light thee thither.

FLAMINEO   O, I smell soot,
Most stinking soot! The chimney is a-fire:
My liver's parboiled, like Scotch holly-bread;
There's a plumber laying pipes in my guts, it scalds –
Wilt thou outlive me?

ZANCHE   Yes, and drive a stake   140
Through thy body; for we'll give it out
Thou didst this violence upon thyself.

FLAMINEO O cunning devils! Now I have tried your love,
And doubled all your reaches. [*rises*] I am not
                                        wounded;
The pistols held no bullets: 'twas a plot
To prove your kindness to me; and I live
To punish your ingratitude. I knew,
One time or other, you would find a way
To give me a strong potion. O men
That lie upon your death-beds, and are haunted   150
With howling wives, ne'er trust them! They'll
                                        re-marry
Ere the worm pierce your winding-sheet, ere the
                                        spider
Make a thin curtain for your epitaphs. –
How cunning you were to discharge! Do you practise
at the Artillery-yard? Trust a woman? Never, never!

Brachiano be my precedent. We lay our souls to pawn
to the devil for a little pleasure, and a woman makes
the bill of sale. That ever man should marry! For one
Hypermnestra that saved her lord and husband, forty-
nine of her sisters cut their husbands' throats all in one   160
night: there was a shoal of virtuous horse-leeches!
Here are two other instruments.

VITTORIA   Help, help!

Enter LODOVICO *and* GASPARO, *disguised*, PEDRO *and* CARLO

FLAMINEO   What noise is that? Ha! False keys i'the court!
LODOVICO   We have brought you a mask.
FLAMINEO   A matachin, it seems
By your drawn swords. Churchmen turned revellers!
CARLO   Isabella! Isabella!
LODOVICO   Do you know us now?
FLAMINEO   Lodovico! And Gasparo!
LODOVICO   Yes, and that Moor the duke gave pension to
Was the great Duke of Florence.
VITTORIA   O, we are lost!   170
FLAMINEO   You shall not take justice from forth my hands –
O, let me kill her! I'll cut my safety
Through your coats of steel. Fate's a spaniel,
We cannot beat it from us. What remains now?
Let all that do ill, take this precedent –
Man may his fate foresee, but not prevent:
And of all axioms this shall win the prize –
'Tis better to be fortunate than wise.
GASPARO   Bind him to the pillar.
VITTORIA   O, your gentle pity!
I have seen a blackbird that would sooner fly   180
To a man's bosom, than to stay the gripe
Of the fierce sparrowhawk.
GASPARO   Your hope deceives you.
VITTORIA   If Florence be i'the court, would he would kill me!
GASPARO   Fool! Princes give rewards with their own hands,
But death or punishment by the hands of others.
LODOVICO   Sirrah, you once did strike me: I'll strike you
Into the centre.

FLAMINEO	Thou'lt do it like a hangman, a base hangman,
	Not like a noble fellow; for thou see'st
	I cannot strike again.
LODOVICO	Dost laugh?
FLAMINEO	Would'st have me die, as I was born, in whining?
GASPARO	Recommend yourself to Heaven.
FLAMINEO	No, I will carry mine own commendations thither.
LODOVICO	O, could I kill you forty times a day,
	And use't four year together, 'twere too little!
	Naught grieves but that you are too few to feed
	The famine of our vengeance. What dost think on?
FLAMINEO	Nothing; of nothing: leave thy idle questions.
	I am i'the way to study a long silence:
	To prate were idle. I remember nothing.
	There's nothing of so infinite vexation
	As man's own thoughts.
LODOVICO	O thou glorious strumpet!
	Could I divide thy breath from this pure air
	When't leaves thy body, I would suck it up,
	And breathe't upon some dunghill.
VITTORIA	You, my death's-man!
	Methinks thou dost not look horrid enough,
	Thou hast too good a face to be a hangman:
	If thou be, do thy office in right form;
	Fall down upon thy knees, and ask forgiveness.
LODOVICO	O, thou hast been a most prodigious comet!
	But I'll cut off your train — kill the Moor first.
VITTORIA	You shall not kill her first; behold my breast:
	I will be waited on in death; my servant
	Shall never go before me.
GASPARO	Are you so brave?
VITTORIA	Yes, I shall welcome death
	As princes do some great ambassadors;
	I'll meet thy weapon half way.
LODOVICO	Thou dost tremble:
	Methinks fear should dissolve thee into air.
VITTORIA	O, thou art deceived, I am too true a woman:
	Conceit can never kill me. I'll tell thee what,
	I will not in my death shed one base tear;

190

200

210

220

	Or if look pale, for want of blood, not fear.
CARLO	Thou art my task, black Fury.
ZANCHE	I have blood

ZANCHE
As red as either of theirs: wilt drink some?
'Tis good for the falling-sickness. I am proud
Death cannot alter my complexion,
For I shall ne'er look pale.

LODOVICO   Strike, strike,
With a joint motion.
[they stab Vittoria, Zanche, and Flamineo]

VITTORIA   'Twas a manly blow:
The next thou giv'st, murder some sucking infant,
And then thou wilt be famous.

FLAMINEO   O, what blade is't?   230
A Toledo, or an English fox?
I ever thought a cutler should distinguish
The cause of my death, rather than a doctor.
Search my wound deeper; tent it with the steel
That made it.

VITTORIA O, my greatest sin lay in my blood!
Now my blood pays for't.

FLAMINEO   Thou'rt a noble sister!
I love thee now: if woman do breed man,
She ought to teach him manhood: fare thee well.
Know, many glorious women that are famed   240
For masculine virtue have been vicious,
Only a happier silence did betide them:
She hath no faults who hath the art to hide them.

VITTORIA My soul, like to a ship in a black storm,
Is driven, I know not whither.

FLAMINEO   Then cast anchor.
Prosperity doth bewitch men, seeming clear;
But seas do laugh, show white, when rocks are near.
We cease to grieve, cease to be fortune's slaves,
Nay, cease to die, by dying. Art thou gone?
And thou so near the bottom? False report,   250
Which says that women vie with the nine Muses
For nine tough durable lives! I do not look
Who went before, nor who shall follow me;

No, at myself I will begin and end.
While we look up to Heaven, we confound
Knowledge with knowledge. O, I am in a mist!
VITTORIA   O, happy they that never saw the court,
Nor ever knew great men but by report!   [*dies*]
FLAMINEO   I recover like a spent taper, for a flash, and instantly go
out. Let all that belong to great men remember the old   260
wives' tradition, to be like the lions i'the Tower on
Candlemas-day: to mourn if the sun shine, for fear of
the pitiful remainder of winter to come.
'Tis well yet there's some goodness in my death;
My life was a black charnel. I have caught
An everlasting cold; I have lost my voice
Most irrecoverably. Farewell, glorious villains!
This busy trade of life appears most vain,
Since rest breeds rest, where all seek pain by pain.
Let no harsh flattering bells resound my knell;   270
Strike, thunder, and strike loud, to my farewell!   [*dies*]
ENG. AMB.   [*within*] This way, this way! Break ope the doors!
                                     This way!

LODOVICO   Ha! Are we betrayed?
Why, then let's constantly die all together;
And having finished this most noble deed,
Defy the worst of fate, not fear to bleed.

          Enter Ambassadors and GIOVANNI

ENG. AMB.   Keep back the prince: shoot, shoot.
    [*they shoot, and Lodovico falls*]
LODOVICO   O, I am wounded!
I fear I shall be ta'en.
GIOVANNI   You bloody villains,
By what authority have you committed
This massacre?
LODOVICO   By thine.
GIOVANNI   Mine?
LODOVICO   Yes; thy uncle,   280
Which is a part of thee, enjoined us to't:
Thou know'st me, I am sure; I am Count Lodovico;
And thy most noble uncle in disguise

Was last night in thy court.

GIOVANNI   Ha!

CARLO   Yes, that Moor
Thy father chose his pensioner.

GIOVANNI   He turned murderer!
Away with them to prison and to torture!
All that have hands in this shall taste our justice,
As I hope Heaven.

LODOVICO   I do glory yet
That I can call this act mine own. For my part,
The rack, the gallows, and the torturing wheel   290
Shall be but sound sleeps to me: here's my rest;
I limned this night-piece, and it was my best.

GIOVANNI Remove the bodies – See, my honoured lords,
What use you ought make of their punishment:
Let guilty men remember, their black deeds
Do lean on crutches made of slender reeds.

                                        [exeunt

Instead of an EPILOGUE, *only this of Martial supplies me:*
                Haec fuerint nobis praemia, si placui.

For the action of the play, 'twas generally well, and I dare
affirm, with the joint testimony of some of their own   300
quality, for the true imitation of life, without striving to
make nature a monster, the best that ever became them:
whereof as I make a general acknowledgment, so in
particular I must remember the well-approved industry
of my friend Master Perkins, and confess the worth of his
action did crown both the beginning and end.

THE DUCHESS OF MALFI

INTRODUCTION

The Duchess of Malfi was first performed in 1613 or 1614, but was not published in a small quarto edition until 1623. It tells the grisly story, adapted from William Painter's *The Palace of Pleasure* (1566–7), a collection of prose tales which was drawn on by many later dramatists, of the duchess of a small corrupt Italian city-state who was cruelly murdered by her two evil brothers, Duke Ferdinand and the Cardinal. The story, like that on which *The White Devil* was based, was true and had taken place in Italy between 1504 and 1513. Other versions exist, notably a prose version by the Italian author, Matteo Bandello, which Webster may have known (Delio may be based on Bandello himself, as the author claimed to have known the chief protagonists). There was an earlier play by the great Spanish playwright, Lope de Vega, *El Mayordomo de la Duquesa de Amalfi*, but Webster is unlikely to have known of this version.

The Duchess is a widow and she marries her virtuous steward, Antonio, who has returned to his native land after spending some time in France. The marriage has to be kept secret because of the Duchess's quite legitimate fears that her brothers will disapprove of a match which will see the succession of the dukedom prised from their grasp, especially when they consider her husband's relatively humble social origins. The couple have two children and the brothers' suspicions are aroused. They employ Bosola, a malcontent who has spent many years as a galley slave to cover for their crimes, to spy on her. He eventually succeeds in discovering her secret, Antonio flees, and the Duchess is imprisoned in Ferdinand's palace. Ferdinand torments the Duchess for her 'crimes', using Bosola to make her confess where her husband and children are hidden (which she resists), releasing madmen into her chambers, and then having her murdered – even though Bosola has started to have doubts about the course of their actions. When he asks Ferdinand for his reward, he is rebuffed and told that the most he can hope for is a pardon for the murders he has helped commit. Ferdinand descends into madness, and Bosola decides to try and help Antonio escape the clutches of his wife's evil family. The play ends with a series of spectacular killings. Ferdinand, the Cardinal, Antonio and Bosola all die, as well as the Cardinal's mistress, Julia. The play ends with Delio, Antonio's loyal friend, and Antonio's son on stage. Delio concludes that the 'wretched eminent things' which have been seen in the play leave nothing behind them, and the best course of action is to be true to oneself:

> Integrity of life is fame's best friend,
> Which nobly, beyond death, shall crown the end.

> (5, 5, 119–20)

The sentiment is admirable, but it scarcely does justice to what the audience has just seen, or explains how one should behave in a duplicitous and evil world.

What type of tragedy is *The Duchess of Malfi*? It is hard to see the Duchess as an Aristotelian heroine, a noble individual who has a tragic flaw which causes her ultimate downfall, the course of which inspires fear and pity in the audience who leave the theatre enlightened by the experience. The play is far more dark and disturbing than this model of tragedy would imply. A helpful approach has been suggested by J. W. Lever, who reads *The Duchess* as 'a tragedy of state' in which the corrupt and vicious power of the brothers' fiefdom snuffs out any hope that the Duchess might have of living the reasonable and happy life to which she should be entitled. The Duchess has to hide her – quite legitimate – marriage and children, and can only snatch brief moments of happiness away from the systematic surveillance and perverse desires of the brothers, who eventually conspire to destroy her. The court is thus a place where every legitimate expression of desire and affection is twisted into an obscene *double entendre*, so that Ferdinand can deliberately lure his sister into thinking that the 'boneless organ' he refers to as the male means of bewitching women is the penis rather than the tongue. Consequently, the Duchess can only express her natural sexuality in secret (her maid,

Cariola, refers to her as 'the sprawlingest bedfellow'). Ferdinand is so twisted in his unnatural desire for his sister that he is able to make wax models of her family in order to convince her that they are already dead and so drive her to despair. In a sense, his aim is to expunge her identity and so cure himself of his obsession for her. However, when he has finally destroyed her, he loses his own sanity and sense of himself and comes to believe that he is really a wolf. The transformation is fitting, for it is clear to us that Ferdinand is scarcely human. We can only feel pity for him as one of the most wretched and unhappy of God's creatures.

The Duchess resists Ferdinand's and Bosola's efforts with admirable fortitude, although she is on the verge of cracking several times. In one of the most justly celebrated passages of the play Bosola almost wins his battle with her when he encourages her to curse the stars, which she duly does. When he confronts her with the stark reality that 'Look you, the stars shine still' (4, 1, 102), he appears to have won the battle and exposed the Duchess as nothing more than a decaying body:

> Thou art a box of worm-seed, at best, but a salvatory of green mummy! What's this flesh? A little cruddled milk, fantastical puff-paste . . . Thou art some great woman, sure, for riot begins to sit on thy forehead, clad in gray hairs, twenty years sooner than on a merry milkmaid's.   (4, 2, 119–132)

Bosola has scored a direct hit here because all the Duchess has ever really wanted is to have a private life undisturbed by the great and troubling affairs of state. The Duchess is able to resist his metaphysical speculations precisely because she refuses to accept that the suffering experienced in the play is the result of the malignity of the gods. As Bosola later puts it, 'We are the stars' tennis balls, / Struck and bandied which way please them' (5, 4, 53–4). When forced to continue her curse by Bosola she returns it to earth again and blames her brothers for the ways in which they have made her and her family suffer so cruelly. A crisis point has passed, and we surely agree with the Duchess that the philosophising of Bosola serves to mask the unbearable reality of suffering in the city-state of Malfi.

However, another perspective should be applied to the play. In William Painter's telling of the story, the Duchess is represented as far more obviously culpable in her behaviour. While she may desire to live a private life as a member of the ruling family, she clearly cannot – and her refusal to take part in public affairs only tightens the grip of her brothers on the state. As a ruling woman her duty is to secure a proper succession for the dynasty, something she risks by refusing to make a stand and effectively handing over power to rulers who will not act in the interests of the people. Indeed, Ferdinand's mad obsession with her prevents him from ruling at all, apart from sending out his spies to control the behaviour of the people. His lust for his sister, which he either cannot or will not recognise, tends to strengthen this reading of the play and qualify our sympathy for the unfortunate Duchess. Ferdinand's condition is a bizarre and distorted recognition of an uncomfortable political fact in the sixteenth century. In a state like Malfi, the succession had to be carefully worked out or else the ruling clique were likely to surrender power through the city-state passing into the hands of a rival family via a bad match; through a weakening of political allegiance and protection if an insufficiently powerful partner was selected; or, most relevant in this case, though the dilution of the aristocratic blood of the dynasty, their consequent fall in status, and the demand for more democratic forms of government. Ferdinand's forbidden passion for his sister is not simply distasteful and mad, but a perverted expression of his desire to keep the family pure by refusing to let her be had by anyone but himself. He has confused and combined the roles of older brother and husband, and of course his depraved concern leads to disaster. But the state is so corrupt and evil precisely because of the familial anxieties of the ruling family, which cause them, and the people they govern, to implode. *The Duchess of Malfi* is accurately described as 'a tragedy of state', providing we remember that the tragedy also begins in the home.

To the RT. HON. GEORGE HARDING

Baron Berkeley of Berkeley Castle
and Knight of the Order of the Bath to the illustrious Prince Charles

My Noble Lord – That I may present my excuse why, being a
stranger to your lordship, I offer this poem to your patronage, I
plead this warrant: men who never saw the sea yet desire to behold
that regiment of waters, choose some eminent river to guide them
thither, and make that, as it were, their conduct or postilion: by the
like ingenious means has your fame arrived at my knowledge,
receiving it from some of worth, who both in contemplation and
practice owe to your honour their clearest service. I do not
altogether look up at your title, the ancientest nobility being but a
relic of time past, and the truest honour indeed being for a man to
confer honour on himself, which your learning strives to propagate,
and shall make you arrive at the dignity of a great example. I am
confident this work is not unworthy your honour's perusal; for by
such poems as this poets have kissed the hands of great princes, and
drawn their gentle eyes to look down upon their sheets of paper
when the poets themselves were bound up in their winding-sheets.
The like courtesy from your lordship shall make you live in your
grave, and laurel spring out of it, when the ignorant scorners of the
Muses, that like worms in libraries seem to live only to destroy
learning, shall wither neglected and forgotten. This work and myself
I humbly present to your approved censure, it being the utmost of
my wishes to have your honourable self my weighty and perspicuous
comment; which grace so done me shall ever be acknowledged

By your lordship's in all duty and observance,

JOHN WEBSTER

Commendatory Verses

In the just worth of that well deserver,
Mr John Webster,
and upon the masterpiece of tragedy

In this thou imitat'st one rich and wise,
That sees his good deeds done before he dies:
As he by works, thou by this work of fame
Hath well provided for thy living name.
To trust to others' honourings is worth's crime,
Thy monument is raised in thy lifetime;
And 'tis most just, for every worthy man
Is his own marble, and his merit can
Cut him to any figure, and express
More art than death's cathedral palaces
Where royal ashes keep their court. Thy note
Be ever plainness; 'tis the richest coat:
Thy epitaph only the title be,
Write Duchess, that will fetch a tear for thee;
For who e'er saw this Duchess live and die,
That could get off under a bleeding eye?

In Tragoediam
Ut lux ex tenebris ictu percussa tonantis,
Illa, ruina malis, claris fit vita poetis.

Thomas Middletonus
Poeta et Chron. Londinensis

To his friend MR JOHN WEBSTER, upon his DUCHESS OF MALFI

I never saw thy Duchess till the day
That she was lively bodied in thy play:
Howe'er she answered her low-rated love,
Her brothers' anger did so fatal prove;
Yet my opinion is, she might speak more,
But never in her life so well before.

WIL. ROWLEY

To the reader of the AUTHOR, and his DUCHESS OF MALFI

Crown him a poet, whom nor Rome nor Greece
Transcend in all theirs for a masterpiece;
In which, whiles words and matter change, and men
Act one another, he, from whose clear pen
They all took life, to memory hath lent
A lasting fame to raise his monument.

JOHN FORD

CHARACTERS IN THE PLAY

FERDINAND, *Duke of Calabria*

the CARDINAL, *his brother*

ANTONIO BOLOGNA, *steward of the Duchess' household*

DELIO, *his Friend*

DANIEL DE BOSOLA, *gentleman of the horse to the Duchess*

CASTRUCCIO

MARQUIS DE PESCARA

COUNT MALATESTI

RODERIGO

SILVIO

GRISOLAN

Doctor

Several Madmen, Pilgrims, Executioners, Officers, Attendants, etc.

DUCHESS OF MALFI, *sister to Ferdinand and the Cardinal*

CARIOLA, *her woman*

JULIA, CASTRUCCIO'*s wife, and the Cardinal's mistress*

Old lady, ladies and children

The Scene: Malfi, Rome and Milan

THE DUCHESS OF MALFI

ACT I SCENE I

The presence-chamber in the Duchess' palace at Malfi

Enter ANTONIO *and* DELIO

DELIO   You are welcome to your country, dear Antonio;
You have been long in France, and you return
A very formal Frenchman in your habit:
How do you like the French court?

ANTONIO   I admire it:
In seeking to reduce both state and people
To a fixed order, their judicious king
Begins at home; quits first his royal palace
Of flattering sycophants, of dissolute
And infamous persons – which he sweetly terms
His master's masterpiece, the work of Heaven;   10
Considering duly that a prince's court
Is like a common fountain, whence should flow
Pure silver drops in general, but if't chance
Some cursed example poison't near the head,
Death and diseases through the whole land spread.
And what is't makes this blessed government
But a most provident council, who dare freely
Inform him the corruption of the times?
Though some o'the court hold it presumption
To instruct princes what they ought to do,   20
It is a noble duty to inform them
What they ought to foresee. Here comes Bosola,
The only court-gall; yet I observe his railing
Is not for simple love of piety:
Indeed, he rails at those things which he wants;
Would be as lecherous, covetous, or proud,
Bloody, or envious, as any man,
If he had means to be so. Here's the Cardinal.

Enter the CARDINAL *and* BOSOLA

BOSOLA   I do haunt you still.

| CARDINAL | So. | 30 |

BOSOLA   I have done you better service than to be slighted thus. Miserable age, where only the reward of doing well is the doing of it!

CARDINAL   You enforce your merit too much.

BOSOLA   I fell into the galleys in your service; where, for two years together, I wore two towels instead of a shirt, with a knot on the shoulder, after the fashion of a Roman mantle. Slighted thus, I will thrive some way! Blackbirds fatten best in hard weather; why not I in these dog-days?   40

CARDINAL   Would you could become honest!

BOSOLA   With all your divinity, do but direct me the way to it. I have known many travel far for it, and yet return as arrant knaves as they went forth, because they carried themselves always along with them. [*exit Cardinal*] Are you gone? Some fellows, they say, are possessed with the devil, but this great fellow were able to possess the greatest devil, and make him worse.

ANTONIO   He hath denied thee some suit?

BOSOLA   He and his brother are like plum-trees that grow 50 crooked over standing-pools; they are rich and o'er-laden with fruit, but none but crows, pies, and caterpillars feed on them. Could I be one of their flattering panders, I would hang on their ears like a horseleech, till I were full, and then drop off. I pray, leave me. Who would rely upon these miserable dependencies, in expectation to be advanced tomorrow? What creature ever fed worse than hoping Tantalus? Nor ever lied any man more fearfully than he that hoped for a pardon. There are rewards for hawks and dogs 60 when they have done us service; but for a soldier that hazards his limbs in a battle, nothing but a kind of geometry is his last supportation.

DELIO   Geometry?

BOSOLA   Ay, to hang in a fair pair' of slings, take his latter swing in the world upon an honourable pair of crutches, from hospital to hospital. Fare ye well, sir: and yet do not you scorn us; for places in the court are but like

beds in the hospital, where this man's head lies at that
man's foot, and so lower and lower.   [*exit* 70

DELIO   I knew this fellow seven years in the galleys
             For a notorious murder; and 'twas thought
             The Cardinal suborned it: he was released
             By the French general, Gaston de Foix,
             When he recovered Naples.

ANTONIO   'Tis great pity
             He should be thus neglected: I have heard
             He's very valiant. This foul melancholy
             Will poison all his goodness; for, I'll tell you,
             If too immoderate sleep be truly said
             To be an inward rust unto the soul,   80
             It then doth follow want of action
             Breeds all black malcontents; and their close rearing,
             Like moths in cloth, do hurt for want of wearing.

DELIO   The presence 'gins to fill: you promised me
             To make me the partaker of the natures
             Of some of your great courtiers.

ANTONIO   The Lord Cardinal's,
             And other strangers' that are now in court?
             I shall – Here comes the great Calabrian Duke.

Enter FERDINAND, CASTRUCCIO, SILVIO, RODERIGO,
             GRISOLAN *and Attendants*

FERDINAND Who took the ring oftenest?
SILVIO   Antonio Bologna, my lord.   90
FERDINAND Our sister Duchess' great-master of her household? Give
             him the jewel. When shall we leave this sportive action,
             and fall to action indeed?
CASTRUC.   Methinks, my lord, you should not desire to go to war
             in person.
FERDINAND Now for some gravity: why, my lord?
CASTRUC.   It is fitting a soldier arise to be a prince, but not
             necessary a prince descend to be a captain.
FERDINAND No?
CASTRUC.   No, my lord; he were far better do it by a deputy.   100
FERDINAND Why should he not as well sleep or eat by a deputy?
             This might take idle, offensive, and base office from

him, whereas the other deprives him of honour.

CASTRUC.   Believe my experience, that realm is never long in quiet where the ruler is a soldier.

FERDINAND   Thou toldest me thy wife could not endure fighting.

CASTRUC.   True, my lord.

FERDINAND   And of a jest she broke of a captain she met full of wounds: I have forgot it.

CASTRUC.   She told him, my lord, he was a pitiful fellow, to lie, 110 like the children of Ismael, all in tents.

FERDINAND   Why, there's a wit were able to undo all the surgeons o'the city; for although gallants should quarrel, and had drawn their weapons, and were ready to go to it, yet her persuasions would make them put up.

CASTRUC.   That she would, my lord. How do you like my Spanish jennet?

RODERIGO   He is all fire.

FERDINAND   I am of Pliny's opinion; I think he was begot by the wind; he runs as if he were ballassed with quicksilver. 120

SILVIO   True, my lord, he reels from the tilt often.

RODERIGO & GRISOLAN   Ha, ha, ha!

FERDINAND   Why do you laugh? Methinks you that are courtiers should be my touchwood, take fire when I give fire; that is, laugh but when I laugh, were the subject never so witty.

CASTRUC.   True, my lord: I myself have heard a very good jest, and have scorned to seem to have so silly a wit as to understand it.

FERDINAND   But I can laugh at your fool, my lord.   130

CASTRUC.   He cannot speak, you know, but he makes faces: my lady cannot abide him.

FERDINAND   No?

CASTRUC.   Nor endure to be in merry company; for she says too much laughing, and too much company, fills her too full of the wrinkle.

FERDINAND   I would, then, have a mathematical instrument made for her face, that she might not laugh out of compass. I shall shortly visit you at Milan, Lord Silvio.

SILVIO   Your grace shall arrive most welcome.   140

FERDINAND   You are a good horseman, Antonio: you have excellent

	riders in France: what do you think of good horse-
	manship?
ANTONIO	Nobly, my lord: as out of the Grecian horse issued
	many famous princes, so out of brave horsemanship
	arise the first sparks of growing resolution that raise the
	mind to noble action.
FERDINAND	You have bespoke it worthily.
SILVIO	Your brother, the Lord Cardinal, and sister Duchess.

Re-enter CARDINAL, *with* DUCHESS, CARIOLA *and* JULIA

CARDINAL	Are the galleys come about? 150
GRISOLAN	They are, my lord.
FERDINAND	Here's the Lord Silvio is come to take his leave.
DELIO	Now, sir, your promise; what's that Cardinal?
	I mean his temper. They say he's a brave fellow,
	Will play his five thousand crowns at tennis, dance,
	Court ladies, and one that hath fought single
	combats.
ANTONIO	Some such flashes superficially hang on him for form;
	but observe his inward character: he is a melancholy
	churchman; the spring in his face is nothing but the
	engendering of toads; where he is jealous of any man, 160
	he lays worse plots for them than ever was imposed on
	Hercules, for he strews in his way flatterers, panders,
	intelligencers, atheists, and a thousand such political
	monsters. He should have been Pope; but instead of
	coming to it by the primitive decency of the church,
	he did bestow bribes so largely and so impudently as if
	he would have carried it away without Heaven's
	knowledge. Some good he hath done –
DELIO	You have given too much of him. What's his brother?
ANTONIO	The Duke there? A most perverse and turbulent
	nature: 170
	What appears in him mirth is merely outside;
	If he laugh heartily, it is to laugh
	All honesty out of fashion.
DELIO	Twins?
ANTONIO	In quality.
	He speaks with others' tongues, and hears men's suits
	With others' ears; will seem to sleep o'the bench

Only to entrap offenders in their answers;
Dooms men to death by information;
Rewards by hearsay.

DELIO   Then the law to him
Is like a foul black cobweb to a spider –
He makes it his dwelling and a prison   180
To entangle those shall feed him.

ANTONIO   Most true:
He never pays debts unless they be shrewd turns,
And those he will confess that he doth owe.
Last, for his brother there, the Cardinal,
They that do flatter him most say oracles
Hang at his lips; and verily I believe them,
For the devil speaks in them.
But for their sister, the right noble Duchess,
You never fixed your eye on three fair medals
Cast in one figure, of so different temper.   190
For her discourse, it is so full of rapture,
You only will begin then to be sorry
When she doth end her speech, and wish, in wonder,
She held it less vainglory to talk much,
Than your penance to hear her: whilst she speaks,
She throws upon a man so sweet a look,
That it were able to raise one to a galliard
That lay in a dead palsy, and to dote
On that sweet countenance; but in that look
There speaketh so divine a continence   200
As cuts off all lascivious and vain hope.
Her days are practised in such noble virtue,
That sure her nights, nay, more, her very sleeps,
Are more in Heaven than other ladies' shrifts.
Let all sweet ladies break their flattering glasses,
And dress themselves in her.

DELIO   Fie, Antonio,
You play the wire-drawer with her commendations.

ANTONIO I'll case the picture up – only thus much:
All her particular worth grows to this sum:
She stains the time past, lights the time to come.   210

CARIOLA You must attend my lady in the gallery,

Some half an hour hence.

ANTONIO   I shall.
                                    [*exeunt Antonio and Delio*

FERDINAND Sister, I have a suit to you.

DUCHESS   To me, sir?

FERDINAND A gentleman here, Daniel de Bosola,
          One that was in the galleys –

DUCHESS   Yes, I know him.

FERDINAND A worthy fellow he is: pray, let me entreat for
          The provisorship of your horse.

DUCHESS   Your knowledge of him
          Commends him and prefers him.

FERDINAND   Call him hither.
                                    [*exit Attendant*
          We are now upon parting. Good Lord Silvio,
          Do us commend to all our noble friends   220
          At the leaguer.

SILVIO   Sir, I shall.

FERDINAND   You are for Milan?

SILVIO   I am.

DUCHESS   Bring the caroches. We'll bring you down to
                                            the haven.
                    [*exeunt Duchess, Silvio, Castruccio, Roderigo,
                        Grisolan, Cariola, Julia and Attendants*

CARDINAL Be sure you entertain that Bosola
          For your intelligence: I would not be seen in't;
          And therefore many times I have slighted him
          When he did court our furtherance, as this morning.

FERDINAND Antonio, the great-master of her household,
          Had been far fitter.

CARDINAL   You are deceived in him:
          His nature is too honest for such business.   230
          He comes: I'll leave you.   [*exit*

                    Re-enter BOSOLA

BOSOLA   I was lured to you.

FERDINAND My brother here, the Cardinal, could never
          Abide you.

BOSOLA   Never since he was in my debt.

FERDINAND May be some oblique character in your face

Made him suspect you.

BOSOLA   Doth he study physiognomy?
There's no more credit to be given to the face
Than to a sick man's urine, which some call
The physician's whore because she cozens him.
He did suspect me wrongfully.

FERDINAND   For that
You must give great men leave to take their times.   240
Distrust doth cause us seldom be deceived:
You see the oft shaking of the cedar-tree
Fastens it more at root.

BOSOLA   Yet, take heed;
For to suspect a friend unworthily
Instructs him the next way to suspect you,
And prompts him to deceive you.

FERDINAND   There's gold.

BOSOLA   So:
What follows? Never rained such showers as these
Without thunderbolts i'the tail of them:
Whose throat must I cut?

FERDINAND Your inclination to shed blood rides post   250
Before my occasion to use you. I give you that
To live i'the court here, and observe the duchess;
To note all the particulars of her haviour,
What suitors do solicit her for marriage,
And whom she best affects. She's a young widow:
I would not have her marry again.

BOSOLA   No, sir?

FERDINAND Do not you ask the reason; but be satisfied
I say I would not.

BOSOLA   It seems you would create me
One of your familiars.

FERDINAND   Familiar! What's that?

BOSOLA Why, a very quaint invisible devil in flesh,   260
An intelligencer.

FERDINAND   Such a kind of thriving thing
I would wish thee; and ere long thou may'st arrive
At a higher place by't.

BOSOLA   Take your devils,

        Which hell calls angels; these cursed gifts would make
        You a corrupter, me an impudent traitor;
        And should I take these, they'd take me to hell.

FERDINAND Sir, I'll take nothing from you that I have given:
        There is a place that I procured for you
        This morning, the provisorship o'the horse;
        Have you heard on't?

BOSOLA   No.

FERDINAND   'Tis yours: is't not worth thanks? 270

BOSOLA   I would have you curse yourself now, that
                              your bounty
        (Which makes men truly noble) e'er should make me
        A villain. O, that to avoid ingratitude
        For the good deed you have done me, I must do
        All the ill man can invent! Thus the devil
        Candies all sins o'er; and what Heaven terms vile,
        That names he complimental.

FERDINAND   Be yourself;
        Keep your old garb of melancholy; 'twill express
        You envy those that stand above your reach,
        Yet strive not to come near 'em: this will gain   280
        Access to private lodgings, where yourself
        May, like a politic dormouse –

BOSOLA   As I have seen some
        Feed in a lord's dish, half asleep, not seeming
        To listen to any talk; and yet these rogues
        Have cut his throat in a dream. What's my place?
        The provisorship o'the horse? Say, then, my
                         corruption
        Grew out of horse-dung: I am your creature.

FERDINAND   Away!

BOSOLA   Let good men, for good deeds, covet good fame,
        Since place and riches oft are bribes of shame:
        Sometimes the devil doth preach.   [*exit* 290

     Re-enter DUCHESS, CARDINAL *and* CARIOLA

CARDINAL We are to part from you; and your own discretion
        Must now be your director.

FERDINAND   You are a widow:
        You know already what man is; and therefore

Let not youth, high promotion, eloquence —

CARDINAL   No,
Nor any thing without the addition — honour —
Sway your high blood.

FERDINAND   Marry! They are most luxurious
Will wed twice.

CARDINAL   O, fie!

FERDINAND   Their livers are more spotted
Than Laban's sheep.

DUCHESS   Diamonds are of most value,
They say, that have passed through most jewellers'
                                      hands. 300

FERDINAND Whores by that rule are precious.

DUCHESS   Will you hear me?
I'll never marry.

CARDINAL   So most widows say;
But commonly that motion lasts no longer
Than the turning of an hour-glass: the funeral sermon
And it end both together.

FERDINAND   Now hear me:
You live in a rank pasture, here, i'the court;
There is a kind of honey-dew that's deadly;
'Twill poison your fame; look to't: be not cunning;
For they whose faces do belie their hearts
Are witches ere they arrive at twenty years,   310
Ay, and give the devil suck.

DUCHESS   This is terrible good counsel.

FERDINAND Hypocrisy is woven of a fine small thread,
Subtler than Vulcan's engine: yet, believe't,
Your darkest actions, nay, your privat'st thoughts,
Will come to light.

CARDINAL   You may flatter yourself,
And take your own choice; privately be married
Under the eyes of night —

FERDINAND   Think't the best voyage
That e'er you made; like the irregular crab,
Which, though't goes backward, thinks that it
                                      goes right
Because it goes its own way; but observe,   320

          Such weddings may more properly be said
          To be executed than celebrated.
CARDINAL   The marriage night
          Is the entrance into some prison.
FERDINAND   And those joys,
          Those lustful pleasures, are like heavy sleeps
          Which do fore-run man's mischief.
CARDINAL   Fare you well.
          Wisdom begins at the end: remember it.   [*exit*
DUCHESS   I think this speech between you both was studied,
          It came so roundly off.
FERDINAND   You are my sister;
          This was my father's poniard, do you see?
          I'd be loth to see't look rusty, 'cause 'twas his.   330
          I would have you give o'er these chargeable revels:
          A visor and a mask are whispering-rooms
          That were never built for goodness – fare ye well;
          And women like that part which, like the lamprey,
          Hath never a bone in't.
DUCHESS   Fie, sir!
FERDINAND   Nay,
          I mean the tongue; variety of courtship:
          What cannot a neat knave with a smooth tale
          Make a woman believe? Farewell, lusty widow.   [*exit*
DUCHESS   Shall this move me? If all my royal kindred
          Lay in my way unto this marriage,   340
          I'd make them my low footsteps: and even now,
          Even in this hate, as men in some great battles,
          By apprehending danger, have achieved
          Almost impossible actions (I have heard soldiers
                                    say so),
          So I through frights and threatenings will assay
          This dangerous venture. Let old wives report
          I winked and chose a husband – Cariola,
          To thy known secrecy I have given up
          More than my life – my fame.
CARIOLA   Both shall be safe;
          For I'll conceal this secret from the world   350
          As warily as those that trade in poison

Keep poison from their children.

DUCHESS   Thy protestation
Is ingenious and hearty: I believe it.
Is Antonio come?

CARIOLA   He attends you.

DUCHESS   Good, dear soul,
Leave me; but place thyself behind the arras,
Where thou mayst overhear us. Wish me good speed;
For I am going into a wilderness
Where I shall find nor path nor friendly clue
To be my guide.   [*Cariola goes behind the arras*]

Enter ANTONIO

                      I sent for you: sit down;
Take pen and ink, and write: are you ready?

ANTONIO   Yes.   360

DUCHESS What did I say?

ANTONIO   That I should write somewhat.

DUCHESS O, I remember.
After these triumphs and this large expense,
It's fit, like thrifty husbands, we inquire
What's laid up for tomorrow.

ANTONIO So please your beauteous excellence.

DUCHESS   Beauteous!
Indeed, I thank you: I look young for your sake;
You have ta'en my cares upon you.

ANTONIO   I'll fetch your grace
The particulars of your revenue and expense.

DUCHESS O, you are   370
An upright treasurer: but you mistook;
For when I said I meant to make inquiry
What's laid up for tomorrow, I did mean
What's laid up yonder for me.

ANTONIO   Where?

DUCHESS   In Heaven.
I am making my will (as 'tis fit princes should,
In perfect memory), and, I pray, sir, tell me,
Were not one better make it smiling, thus,
Than in deep groans and terrible ghastly looks,
As if the gifts we parted with procured

        That violent distraction?

ANTONIO   O, much better.   380

DUCHESS   If I had a husband now, this care were quit:
        But I intend to make you overseer.
        What good deed shall we first remember? Say.

ANTONIO   Begin with that first good deed began i'the world
        After man's creation, the sacrament of marriage:
        I'd have you first provide for a good husband;
        Give him all.

DUCHESS   All!

ANTONIO   Yes, your excellent self.

DUCHESS   In a winding-sheet?

ANTONIO   In a couple.

DUCHESS   Saint Winifred, that were a strange will!

ANTONIO   'Twere stranger if there were no will in you   390
        To marry again.

DUCHESS   What do you think of marriage?

ANTONIO   I take't, as those that deny purgatory,
        It locally contains or heaven or hell;
        There's no third place in't.

DUCHESS   How do you affect it?

ANTONIO   My banishment, feeding my melancholy,
        Would often reason thus.

DUCHESS   Pray, let's hear it.

ANTONIO   Say a man never marry, nor have children,
        What takes that from him? Only the bare name
        Of being a father, or the weak delight
        To see the little wanton ride a-cock-horse   400
        Upon a painted stick, or hear him chatter
        Like a taught starling.

DUCHESS   Fie, fie, what's all this?
        One of your eyes is blood-shot; use my ring to't,
        They say 'tis very sovereign: 'twas my wedding-ring,
        And I did vow never to part with it
        But to my second husband.

ANTONIO   You have parted with it now.

DUCHESS   Yes, to help your eyesight.

ANTONIO   You have made me stark blind.

DUCHESS   How?

ANTONIO   There is a saucy and ambitious devil
          Is dancing in this circle.
DUCHESS   Remove him.
ANTONIO   How?   410
DUCHESS   There needs small conjuration, when your finger
          May do it: thus; is it fit?
          [she puts the ring upon his finger: he kneels]
ANTONIO   What said you?
DUCHESS   Sir,
          This goodly roof of yours is too low built;
          I cannot stand upright in't nor discourse,
          Without I raise it higher: raise yourself;
          Or, if you please, my hand to help you: so.   [raises him]
ANTONIO   Ambition, madam, is a great man's madness,
          That is not kept in chains and close-pent rooms,
          But in fair lightsome lodgings, and is girt
          With the wild noise of prattling visitants,   420
          Which makes it lunatic beyond all cure.
          Conceive not I am so stupid but I aim
          Whereto your favours tend: but he's a fool
          That, being a-cold, would thrust his hands i'the fire
          To warm them.
DUCHESS   So, now the ground's broke,
          You may discover what a wealthy mine
          I make you lord of.
ANTONIO   O my unworthiness!
DUCHESS   You were ill to sell yourself:
          This darkening of your worth is not like that
          Which tradesmen use i'the city; their false lights   430
          Are to rid bad wares off: and I must tell you,
          If you will know where breathes a complete man
          (I speak it without flattery), turn your eyes,
          And progress through yourself.
ANTONIO   Were there nor heaven nor hell,
          I should be honest: I have long served virtue,
          And ne'er ta'en wages of her.
DUCHESS   Now she pays it.
          The misery of us that are born great!
          We are forced to woo, because none dare woo us;

And as a tyrant doubles with his words,   440
And fearfully equivocates, so we
Are forced to express our violent passions
In riddles and in dreams, and leave the path
Of simple virtue, which was never made
To seem the thing it is not. Go, go brag
You have left me heartless; mine is in your bosom:
I hope 'twill multiply love there. You do tremble:
Make not your heart so dead a piece of flesh,
To fear more than to love me. Sir, be confident:
What is't distracts you? This is flesh and blood, sir;   450
'Tis not the figure cut in alabaster
Kneels at my husband's tomb. Awake, awake, man!
I do here put off all vain ceremony,
And only do appear to you a young widow
That claims you for her husband, and, like a widow,
I use but half a blush in't.

ANTONIO   Truth speak for me;
I will remain the constant sanctuary
Of your good name.

DUCHESS   I thank you, gentle love:
And 'cause you shall not come to me in debt,
Being now my steward, here upon your lips   460
I sign your *Quietus est*. This you should have
                                        begged now:
I have seen children oft eat sweetmeats thus,
As fearful to devour them too soon.

ANTONIO   But for your brothers?

DUCHESS   Do not think of them:
All discord without this circumference
Is only to be pitied, and not feared:
Yet, should they know it, time will easily
Scatter the tempest.

ANTONIO   These words should be mine,
And all the parts you have spoke, if some part of it
Would not have savoured flattery.

DUCHESS   Kneel.
[*Cariola comes from behind the arras*]

ANTONIO   Ha!   470

DUCHESS   Be not amazed; this woman's of my counsel:
          I have heard lawyers say, a contract in a chamber
          Per verba de praesenti is absolute marriage.
          [*she and Antonio kneel*]
          Bless, Heaven, this sacred gordian, which let violence
          Never untwine!

ANTONIO   And may our sweet affections, like the spheres,
          Be still in motion!

DUCHESS   Quickening, and make
          The like soft music!

ANTONIO   That we may imitate
          The loving palms, best emblem of a peaceful
          Marriage, that never bore fruit, divided!   480

DUCHESS   What can the church force more?

ANTONIO   That fortune may not know an accident,
          Either of joy or sorrow, to divide
          Our fixéd wishes!

DUCHESS   How can the church build faster?
          We now are man and wife, and 'tis the church
          That must but echo this – Maid, stand apart:
          I now am blind.

ANTONIO   What's your conceit in this?

DUCHESS   I would have you lead your fortune by the hand
          Unto your marriage bed
          (You speak in me this, for we now are one):   490
          We'll only lie, and talk together, and plot
          To appease my humorous kindred; and if you please,
          Like the old tale in Alexander and Lodovico,
          Lay a naked sword between us, keep us chaste.
          O, let me shroud my blushes in your bosom,
          Since 'tis the treasury of all my secrets!
                              [*exeunt Duchess and Antonio*

CARIOLA   Whether the spirit of greatness or of woman
          Reign most in her, I know not; but it shows
          A fearful madness: I owe her much of pity.
                                                      [*exit*

An apartment in the palace of the Duchess

Enter BOSOLA *and* CASTRUCCIO

BOSOLA   You say you would fain be taken for an eminent
            courtier?

CASTRUC.   'Tis the very main of my ambition.

BOSOLA   Let me see: you have a reasonable good face for't already,
            and your night-cap expresses your ears sufficient largely.
            I would have you learn to twirl the strings of your band
            with a good grace, and in a set speech, at the end of every
            sentence, to hum three or four times, or blow your nose
            till it smart again, to recover your memory. When you
            come to be a president in criminal causes, if you smile 10
            upon a prisoner, hang him; but if you frown upon him
            and threaten him, let him be sure to scape the gallows.

CASTRUC.   I would be a very merry president.

BOSOLA   Do not sup o' nights; 'twill beget you an admirable
            wit.

CASTRUC.   Rather it would make me have a good stomach to
            quarrel; for they say, your roaring boys eat meat seldom,
            and that makes them so valiant. But how shall I know
            whether the people take me for an eminent fellow?

BOSOLA   I will teach a trick to know it: give out you lie a-dying, 20
            and if you hear the common people curse you, be sure
            you are taken for one of the prime night-caps.

Enter an Old Lady

            You come from painting now.

OLD LADY   From what?

BOSOLA   Why, from your scurvy face-physic. To behold thee not
            painted inclines somewhat near a miracle; these in thy
            face here were deep ruts and foul sloughs the last
            progress. There was a lady in France that, having had the
            small-pox, flayed the skin off her face to make it more
            level; and whereas before she looked like a nutmeg- 30
            grater, after she resembled an abortive hedgehog.

OLD LADY   Do you call this painting?

BOSOLA   No, no, but you call it careening of an old morphewed
            lady, to make her disembogue again; there's rough-
            cast phrase to your plastic.

OLD LADY   It seems you are well acquainted with my closet.

BOSOLA   One would suspect it for a shop of witchcraft, to find in
            it the fat of serpents, spawn of snakes, Jews' spittle, and
            their young children's ordure; and all these for the face.
            I would sooner eat a dead pigeon taken from the soles   40
            of the feet of one sick of the plague than kiss one of you
            fasting. Here are two of you, whose sin of your youth is
            the very patrimony of the physician; makes him renew
            his foot-cloth with the spring, and change his high-
            priced courtesan with the fall of the leaf. I do wonder
            you do not loathe yourselves. Observe my meditation
            now.
            What thing is in this outward form of man,
            To be beloved? We account it ominous
            If nature do produce a colt, or lamb,   50
            A fawn, or goat, in any limb resembling
            A man, and fly from't as a prodigy:
            Man stands amazed to see his deformity
            In any other creature but himself.
            But in our own flesh, though we bear diseases
            Which have their true names only ta'en from beasts –
            As the most ulcerous wolf and swinish measle –
            Though we are eaten up of lice and worms,
            And though continually we bear about us
            A rotten and dead body, we delight   60
            To hide it in rich tissue: all our fear,
            Nay, all our terror, is lest our physician
            Should put us in the ground to be made sweet –
            Your wife's gone to Rome: you two couple, and get
            you to the wells at Lucca to recover your aches.
                                [exeunt Castruccio and Old Lady
            I have other work on foot.
                                    I observe our duchess
            Is sick a–days, she pukes, her stomach seethes,
            The fins of her eye–lids look most teeming blue,
            She wanes i'the cheek, and waxes fat i'the flank,

And, contrary to our Italian fashion,   70
Wears a loose-bodied gown: there's somewhat in't.
I have a trick may chance discover it,
A pretty one; I have bought some apricocks,
The first our spring yields.

Enter ANTONIO *and* DELIO

DELIO   And so long since married!
You amaze me.

ANTONIO   Let me seal your lips for ever:
For, did I think that any thing but the air
Could carry these words from you, I should wish
You had no breath at all –

                              Now, sir, in your contemplation?
You are studying to become a great wise fellow.

BOSOLA   O, sir, the opinion of wisdom is a foul tether that runs 80
all over a man's body: if simplicity direct us to have no
evil, it directs us to a happy being; for the subtlest folly
proceeds from the subtlest wisdom: let me be simply
honest.

ANTONIO   I do understand your inside.

BOSOLA   Do you so?

ANTONIO   Because you would not seem to appear to the world
Puffed up with your preferment, you continue
This out-of-fashion melancholy: leave it, leave it.

BOSOLA   Give me leave to be honest in any phrase, in any 90
compliment whatsoever. Shall I confess myself to you?
I look no higher than I can reach: they are the gods
that must ride on winged horses. A lawyer's mule of a
slow pace will both suit my disposition and business;
for, mark me, when a man s mind rides faster than his
horse can gallop, they quickly both tire.

ANTONIO   You would look up to Heaven, but I think
The devil, that rules i'the air, stands in your light.

BOSOLA   O, sir, you are lord of the ascendant, chief man with the
duchess; a duke was your cousin-german removed. Say 100
you are lineally descended from King Pepin, or he
himself, what of this? Search the heads of the greatest
rivers in the world, you shall find them but bubbles of
water. Some would think the souls of princes were

brought forth by some more weighty cause than those of
meaner persons: they are deceived, there's the same hand
to them; the like passions sway them; the same reason
that makes a vicar to go to law for a tithe-pig, and undo
his neighbours, makes them spoil a whole province, and
batter down goodly cities with the cannon.   110

Enter DUCHESS *and* LADIES

DUCHESS   Your arm, Antonio; do I not grow fat?
I am exceeding short-winded – Bosola,
I would have you, sir, provide for me a litter,
Such a one as the Duchess of Florence rode in.

BOSOLA   The duchess used one when she was great with child.

DUCHESS   I think she did – Come hither, mend my ruff;
Here! When? Thou art such a tedious lady; and
Thy breath smells of lemon-pills; would thou
                            hadst done!
Shall I swoon under thy fingers! I am
So troubled with the mother!

BOSOLA   [*aside*]   I fear too much.   120

DUCHESS   I have heard you say that the French courtiers
Wear their hats on 'fore the king.

ANTONIO   I have seen it.

DUCHESS   In the presence?

ANTONIO   Yes.

DUCHESS   Why should not we bring up that fashion?
'Tis ceremony more than duty that consists
In the removing of a piece of felt:
Be you the example to the rest o' the court;
Put on your hat first.

ANTONIO   You must pardon me:
I have seen, in colder countries than in France,   130
Nobles stand bare to the prince; and the distinction
Methought showed reverently.

BOSOLA   I have a present for your grace.

DUCHESS   For me, sir?

BOSOLA   Apricocks, madam.

DUCHESS   O, sir, where are they?
I have heard of none to-year.

BOSOLA   [*aside*]   Good; her colour rises.

DUCHESS   Indeed, I thank you: they are wondrous fair ones.
         What an unskilful fellow is our gardener!
         We shall have none this month.

BOSOLA   Will not your grace pare them?

DUCHESS   No: they taste of musk, methinks; indeed they do.

BOSOLA   I know not: yet I wish your grace had pared 'em.   140

DUCHESS   Why?

BOSOLA   I forgot to tell you, the knave gardener,
         Only to raise his profit by them the sooner,
         Did ripen them in horse-dung.

DUCHESS   O, you jest –
         You shall judge: pray taste one.

ANTONIO   Indeed, madam,
         I do not love the fruit.

DUCHESS   Sir, you are loth
         To rob us of our dainties: 'tis a delicate fruit;
         They say they are restorative.

BOSOLA   'Tis a pretty art,
         This grafting.

DUCHESS   'Tis so; bettering of nature.

BOSOLA   To make a pippin grow upon a crab,
         A damson on a blackthorn – [aside] How greedily
                     she eats them!   150
         A whirlwind strike off these bawd farthingales!
         For, but for that and the loose-bodied gown,
         I should have discovered apparently
         The young springal cutting a caper in her belly.

DUCHESS   I thank you, Bosola: they are right good ones,
         If they do not make me sick.

ANTONIO   How now, madam!

DUCHESS   This green fruit and my stomach are not friends:
         How they swell me!

BOSOLA   [aside]   Nay, you are too much swelled already.

DUCHESS   O, I am in an extreme cold sweat!

BOSOLA   I am very sorry.

DUCHESS   Lights to my chamber! O good Antonio,   160
         I fear I am undone!

DELIO   Lights there, lights!
       [exeunt Duchess and ladies; exit, on the other side, Bosola

ANTONIO   O my most trusty Delio, we are lost!
          I fear she's fall'n in labour; and there's left
          No time for her remove.
DELIO   Have you prepared
          Those ladies to attend her? And procured
          That politic safe conveyance for the midwife
          Your duchess plotted?
ANTONIO   I have.
DELIO   Make use, then, of this forced occasion:
          Give out that Bosola hath poisoned her
          With these apricocks; that will give some colour   170
          For her keeping close.
ANTONIO   Fie, fie, the physicians
          Will then flock to her.
DELIO   For that you may pretend
          She'll use some prepared antidote of her own,
          Lest the physicians should re-poison her.
ANTONIO   I am lost in amazement: I know not what to
                                              think on't.
                                              [exeunt

                         SCENE 2

                  A hall in the same palace

                       Enter BOSOLA

BOSOLA   So, so, there's no question but her tetchiness and most
          vulturous eating of the apricocks are apparent signs of
          breeding.

                     Enter an Old Lady

          Now?
OLD LADY I am in haste, sir.
BOSOLA   There was a young waiting-woman had a monstrous
          desire to see the glass-house –
OLD LADY Nay, pray let me go.
BOSOLA   And it was only to know what strange instrument it
          was should swell up a glass to the fashion of a woman's   10
          belly.

OLD LADY   I will hear no more of the glass-house. You are still
           abusing women?
BOSOLA   Who, I? No; only, by the way now and then, mention
           your frailties. The orange-tree bears ripe and green fruit
           and blossoms all together; and some of you give enter-
           tainment for pure love, but more for more precious
           reward. The lusty spring smells well; but drooping
           autumn tastes well. If we have the same golden showers
           that rained in the time of Jupiter the thunderer, you   20
           have the same Danaës still, to hold up their laps to
           receive them. Didst thou never study the mathematics?
OLD LADY   What's that, sir?
BOSOLA   Why to know the trick how to make a-many lines
           meet in one centre. Go, go, give your foster-daughters
           good counsel: tell them, that the devil takes delight to
           hang at a woman's girdle, like a false rusty watch, that
           she cannot discern how the time passes. [exit Old Lady

           Enter ANTONIO, RODERIGO *and* GRISOLAN

ANTONIO   Shut up the court-gates.
RODERIGO   Why, sir? What's the danger?
ANTONIO   Shut up the posterns presently, and call   30
           All the officers o'the court.
GRISOLAN   I shall instantly.   [exit
ANTONIO   Who keeps the key o'the park-gate?
RODERIGO   Forobosco.
ANTONIO   Let him bring't presently.   [exit Roderigo

           Re-enter GRISOLAN *with Servants*

SERVANT   O, gentlemen o'the court, the foulest treason!
BOSOLA   [aside] If that these apricocks should be poisoned now,
           Without my knowledge!
1 SERVANT There was taken even now a Switzer in the duchess'
           bed-chamber –
2 SERVANT A Switzer!
1 SERVANT With a pistol in his great cod-piece.   40
BOSOLA   Ha, ha, ha!
1 SERVANT The cod-piece was the case for't.
2 SERVANT There was a cunning traitor: who would have
           searched his cod-piece?

I SERVANT	True, if he had kept out of the ladies' chambers: and all the moulds of his buttons were leaden bullets.
2 SERVANT	O wicked cannibal! A fire-lock in's cod-piece!
I SERVANT	'Twas a French plot, upon my life.
2 SERVANT	To see what the devil can do!
ANTONIO	Are all the officers here?
SERVANTS	We are.
ANTONIO	Gentlemen, 50
	We have lost much plate you know; and but this evening
	Jewels, to the value of four thousand ducats,
	Are missing in the duchess' cabinet.
	Are the gates shut?
SERVANTS	Yes.
ANTONIO	'Tis the duchess' pleasure
	Each officer be locked into his chamber
	Till the sun-rising; and to send the keys
	Of all their chests and of their outward doors
	Into her bed-chamber. She is very sick.
RODERIGO	At her pleasure.
ANTONIO	She entreats you take't not ill: the innocent 60
	Shall be the more approved by it.
RODERIGO	Gentleman o'the wood-yard, where's your Switzer now?
I SERVANT	By this hand, 'twas credibly reported by one o'the black guard. [exeunt all except Antonio and Delio
DELIO	How fares it with the duchess?
ANTONIO	She's exposed
	Unto the worst of torture, pain and fear.
DELIO	Speak to her all happy comfort.
ANTONIO	How I do play the fool with mine own danger!
	You are this night, dear friend, to post to Rome:
	My life lies in your service.
DELIO	Do not doubt me. 70
ANTONIO	O, 'tis far from me: and yet fear presents me
	Somewhat that looks like danger.
DELIO	Believe it,
	'Tis but the shadow of your fear, no more:
	How superstitiously we mind our evils!

The throwing down salt, or crossing of a hare,
Bleeding at nose, the stumbling of a horse,
Or singing of a cricket, are of power
To daunt whole man in us. Sir, fare you well:
I wish you all the joys of a blessed father:
And, for my faith, lay this unto your breast –   80
Old friends, like old swords, still are trusted best. [*exit*

Enter CARIOLA

CARIOLA   Sir, you are the happy father of a son:
Your wife commends him to you.

ANTONIO   Blessed comfort!
For Heaven' sake tend her well: I'll presently
Go set a figure for's nativity.

                                    [*exeunt*

SCENE 3

The court of the same palace

Enter BOSOLA, *with a dark lantern*

BOSOLA   Sure I did hear a woman shriek: list, ha!
And the sound came, if I received it right,
From the duchess' lodgings. There's some stratagem
In the confining all our courtiers
To their several wards: I must have part of it;
My intelligence will freeze else. List, again!
It may be 'twas the melancholy bird,
Best friend of silence and of solitariness,
The owl, that screamed so – Ha! Antonio!

Enter ANTONIO

ANTONIO   I heard some noise – Who's there? What art
                                   thou? Speak.   10

BOSOLA   Antonio, put not your face nor body
To such a forced expression of fear:
I am Bosola, your friend.

ANTONIO   Bosola!
[*aside*] This mole does undermine me – Heard you not

A noise even now?

BOSOLA   From whence?

ANTONIO   From the duchess' lodging.

BOSOLA   Not I: did you?

ANTONIO   I did, or else I dreamed.

BOSOLA   Let's walk towards it.

ANTONIO   No: it may be 'twas
But the rising of the wind.

BOSOLA   Very likely.
Methinks 'tis very cold, and yet you sweat:
You look wildly.

ANTONIO   I have been setting a figure   20
For the duchess' jewels.

BOSOLA   Ah, and how falls your question?
Do you find it radical?

ANTONIO   What's that to you?
'Tis rather to be questioned what design,
When all men were commanded to their lodgings,
Makes you a night-walker.

BOSOLA   In sooth, I'll tell you:
Now all the court's asleep, I thought the devil
Had least to do here; I came to say my prayers;
And if it do offend you I do so,
You are a fine courtier.

ANTONIO   [aside]   This fellow will undo me –
You gave the duchess apricocks today: 30
Pray Heaven they were not poisoned!

BOSOLA   Poisoned! A Spanish fig
For the imputation.

ANTONIO   Traitors are ever confident
Till they are discovered. There were jewels stol'n too:
In my conceit, none are to be suspected
More than yourself.

BOSOLA   You are a false steward.

ANTONIO   Saucy slave, I'll pull thee up by the roots.

BOSOLA   May be the ruin will crush you to pieces.

ANTONIO   You are an impudent snake indeed, sir:
Are you scarce warm, and do you show your sting?
You libel well, sir.   40

BOSOLA   No, sir: copy it out,
          And I will set my hand to't.
ANTONIO   [aside]   My nose bleeds.
          One that were superstitious would count
          This ominous, when it merely comes by chance:
          Two letters, that are wrote here for my name,
          Are drowned in blood!
          Mere accident — For you, sir, I'll take order
          I'the morn you shall be safe — [aside] 'tis that
                                          must colour
          Her lying-in — sir, this door you pass not:
          I do not hold it fit that you come near   50
          The duchess' lodgings, till you have quit yourself —
          [aside] The great are like the base, nay, they are
                                          the same,
          When they seek shameful ways to avoid shame.   [exit
BOSOLA   Antonio hereabout did drop a paper —
          Some of your help, false friend — O, here it is.
          What's here? A child's nativity calculated!
          [reads] 'The duchess was delivered of a son, 'tween the
          hours twelve and one in the night, *Anno Dom.*' — that's
          this year — '*decimo nono Decembris*' — that's this night —
          'taken according to the meridian of Malfi,' — that's our 60
          duchess: happy discovery! — 'The lord of the first
          house being combust in the ascendant, signifies short
          life; and Mars being in a human sign, joined to the tail
          of the Dragon, in the eighth house, doth threaten a
          violent death. *Cetera non scrutantur.*'
          Why, now 'tis most apparent: this precise fellow
          Is the duchess' bawd: I have it to my wish!
          This is a parcel of intelligency
          Our courtiers were cased up for: it needs must follow
          That I must be committed on pretence   70
          Of poisoning her; which I'll endure, and laugh at.
          If one could find the father now! But that
          Time will discover. Old Castruccio
          I'the morning posts to Rome: by him I'll send
          A letter that shall make her brothers' galls
          O'erflow their livers. This was a thrifty way.

> . Though lust do mask in ne'er so strange disguise,
> She's oft found witty, but is never wise.

[exit

SCENE 4

An apartment in the palace of the Cardinal at Rome

Enter CARDINAL *and* JULIA

CARDINAL Sit: thou art my best of wishes. Prithee, tell me
What trick didst thou invent to come to Rome
Without thy husband.

JULIA   Why, my lord, I told him
I came to visit an old anchorite
Here for devotion.

CARDINAL   Thou art a witty false one –
I mean, to him.

JULIA   You have prevailed with me
Beyond my strongest thoughts: I would not now
Find you inconstant.

CARDINAL   Do not put thyself
To such a voluntary torture, which proceeds
Out of your own guilt.

JULIA   How, my lord!

CARDINAL   You fear   10
My constancy, because you have approved ·
Those giddy and wild turnings in yourself.

JULIA Did you e'er find them?

CARDINAL   Sooth, generally for women,
A man might strive to make glass malleable,
Ere he should make them fixéd.

JULIA   So, my lord.

CARDINAL We had need go borrow that fantastic glass
Invented by Galileo the Florentine
To view another spacious world i'the moon,
And look to find a constant woman there.

JULIA This is very well, my lord.

CARDINAL   Why do you weep?   20
Are tears your justification? The self-same tears

Will fall into your husband's bosom, lady,
With a loud protestation that you love him
Above the world. Come, I'll love you wisely;
That's jealously, since I am very certain
You cannot make me cuckold.

JULIA   I'll go home
To my husband.

CARDINAL   You may thank me, lady,
I have taken you off your melancholy perch,
Bore you upon my fist, and showed you game,
And let you fly at it – I pray thee, kiss me –   30
When thou wast with thy husband, thou
                                        wast watched
Like a tame elephant – still you are to thank me –
Thou hadst only kisses from him and high feeding;
But what delight was that? 'Twas just like one
That hath a little fingering on the lute,
Yet cannot tune it – still you are to thank me.

JULIA   You told me of a piteous wound i'the heart
And a sick liver, when you wooed me first,
And spake like one in physic.

CARDINAL   Who's that? –

Enter Servant

Rest firm, for my affection to thee,   40
Lightning moves slow to't.

SERVANT   Madam, a gentleman,
That's come post from Malfi, desires to see you.

CARDINAL Let him enter: I'll withdraw.   [*exit*

SERVANT   He says
Your husband, old Castruccio, is come to Rome,
Most pitifully tired with riding post.   [*exit*

Enter DELIO

JULIA   Signior Delio! [*aside*] 'Tis one of my old suitors.

DELIO   I was bold to come and see you.

JULIA   Sir, you are welcome.

DELIO   Do you lie here?

JULIA   Sure, your own experience
Will satisfy you no: our Roman prelates

Do not keep lodging for ladies.

DELIO   Very well: 50
I have brought you no commendations from
                              your husband,
For I know none by him.

JULIA   I hear he's come to Rome.

DELIO   I never knew man and beast, of a horse and a knight,
So weary of each other: if he had had a good back,
He would have undertook to have borne his horse,
His breech was so pitifully sore.

JULIA   Your laughter
Is my pity.

DELIO   Lady, I know not whether
You want money, but I have brought you some.

JULIA   From my husband?

DELIO   No, from mine own allowance.

JULIA   I must hear the condition, ere I be bound to take it.   60

DELIO   Look on't, 'tis gold: hath it not a fine colour?

JULIA   I have a bird more beautiful.

DELIO   Try the sound on't.

JULIA   A lute-string far exceeds it:
It hath no smell, like cassia or civet;
Nor is it physical, though some fond doctors
Persuade us seethe't in cullises. I'll tell you,
This is a creature bred by —

                        Re-enter Servant

SERVANT   Your husband's come,
Hath delivered a letter to the Duke of Calabria
That, to my thinking, hath put him out of his wits.
                                        [*exit*

JULIA   Sir, you hear: 70
Pray, let me know your business and your suit
As briefly as can be.

DELIO   With good speed: I would wish you,
At such time as you are non-resident
With your husband, my mistress.

JULIA   Sir, I'll go ask my husband if I shall,
And straight return your answer.   [*exit*

DELIO   Very fine!

Is this her wit, or honesty, that speaks thus?
I heard one say the Duke was highly moved
With a letter sent from Malfi. I do fear
Antonio is betrayed: how fearfully   80
Shows his ambition now! Unfortunate fortune!
They pass through whirlpools, and deep woes
                           do shun,
Who the event weigh ere the action's done.

                                [*exit*

SCENE 5

Another apartment in the same palace

Enter CARDINAL *and* FERDINAND *with a letter*

FERDINAND I have this night digged up a mandrake.
CARDINAL   Say you?
FERDINAND And I am grown mad with't.
CARDINAL   What's the prodigy?
FERDINAND Read there – a sister damned: she's loose i'the hilts;
     Grown a notorious strumpet.
CARDINAL   Speak lower.
FERDINAND   Lower!
     Rogues do not whisper't now, but seek to publish't
     (As servants do the bounty of their lords)
     Aloud, and with a covetous searching eye,
     To mark who note them. O, confusion seize her!
     She hath had most cunning bawds to serve her turn,
     And more secure conveyances for lust   10
     Than towns of garrison for service.
CARDINAL   Is't possible?
     Can this be certain?
FERDINAND   Rhubarb! O, for rhubarb
     To purge this choler! Here's the curséd day
     To prompt my memory; and here't shall stick
     Till of her bleeding heart I make a sponge
     To wipe it out.
CARDINAL   Why do you make yourself

So wild a tempest?

FERDINAND   Would I could be one,
That I might toss her palace 'bout her ears,
Root up her goodly forests, blast her meads,
And lay her general territory as waste   20
As she hath done her honours.

CARDINAL   Shall our blood,
The royal blood of Aragon and Castile,
Be thus attainted?

FERDINAND   Apply desperate physic:
We must not now use balsamum, but fire,
The smarting cupping-glass, for that's the mean
To purge infected blood, such blood as hers.
There is a kind of pity in mine eye —
I'll give it to my handkercher; and now 'tis here,
I'll bequeath this to her bastard.

CARDINAL   What to do?

FERDINAND Why, to make soft lint for his mother's wounds,   30
When I have hewed her to pieces.

CARDINAL   Curséd creature!
Unequal nature, to place women's hearts
So far upon the left side!

FERDINAND   Foolish men,
That e'er will trust their honour in a bark
Made of so slight weak bulrush as is woman,
Apt every minute to sink it!

CARDINAL   Thus
Ignorance, when it hath purchased honour,
It cannot wield it.

FERDINAND   Methinks I see her laughing —
Excellent hyena! Talk to me somewhat quickly,
Or my imagination will carry me   40
To see her in the shameful act of sin.

CARDINAL With whom?

FERDINAND Happily with some strong-thighed bargeman,
Or one o'the woodyard that can quoit the sledge,
Or toss the bar, or else some lovely squire
That carries coals up to her privy lodgings.

CARDINAL   You fly beyond your reason.

FERDINAND   Go to, mistress!
     'Tis not your whore's milk that shall quench
                                my wild fire,
     But your whore's blood.

CARDINAL   How idly shows this rage, which carries you,   50
     As men conveyed by witches through the air,
     On violent whirlwinds! This intemperate noise
     Fitly resembles deaf men's shrill discourse,
     Who talk aloud, thinking all other men
     To have their imperfection.

FERDINAND   Have not you
     My palsy?

CARDINAL   Yes, but I can be angry
     Without this rupture: there is not in nature
     A thing that makes man so deformed, so beastly,
     As doth intemperate anger. Chide yourself.
     You have divers men who never yet expressed   60
     Their strong desire of rest but by unrest,
     By vexing of themselves. Come, put yourself
     In tune.

FERDINAND   So I will only study to seem
     The thing I am not. I could kill her now,
     In you or in myself; for I do think
     It is some sin in us Heaven doth revenge
     By her.

CARDINAL   Are you stark mad?

FERDINAND   I would have their bodies
     Burnt in a coal-pit with the ventage stopped,
     That their cursed smoke might not ascend to Heaven;
     Or dip the sheets they lie in in pitch or sulphur,   70
     Wrap them in't, and then light them like a match;
     Or else to boil their bastard to a cullis,
     And give't his lecherous father to renew
     The sin of his back.

CARDINAL   I'll leave you.

FERDINAND   Nay, I have done.
     I am confident, had I been damned in hell,
     And should have heard of this, it would have put me

Into a cold sweat. In, in; I'll go sleep.
Till I know who leaps my sister, I'll not stir:
That known, I'll find scorpions to string my whips,
And fix her in a general eclipse.   80

                                              [*exeunt*

ACT 3 SCENE I

An apartment in the palace of the Duchess

Enter ANTONIO *and* DELIO

ANTONIO   Our noble friend, my most belovéd Delio!
          O, you have been a stranger long at court;
          Came you along with the Lord Ferdinand?

DELIO   I did, sir: and how fares your noble Duchess?

ANTONIO   Right fortunately well: she's an excellent
          Feeder of pedigrees; since you last saw her,
          She hath had two children more, a son and daughter.

DELIO   Methinks 'twas yesterday: let me but wink,
          And not behold your face, which to mine eye
          Is somewhat leaner, verily I should dream   10
          It were within this half hour.

ANTONIO   You have not been in law, friend Delio,
          Nor in prison, nor a suitor at the court,
          Nor begged the reversion of some great man's place,
          Nor troubled with an old wife, which doth make
          Your time so insensibly hasten.

DELIO   Pray, sir, tell me,
          Hath not this news arrived yet to the ear
          Of the lord Cardinal?

ANTONIO   I fear it hath:
          The Lord Ferdinand, that's newly come to court,
          Doth bear himself right dangerously.

DELIO   Pray, why?   20

ANTONIO   He is so quiet that he seems to sleep
          The tempest out, as dormice do in winter:
          Those houses that are haunted are most still
          Till the devil be up.

DELIO   What say the common people?

ANTONIO   The common rabble do directly say
          She is a strumpet.

DELIO   And your graver heads
          Which would be politic, what censure they?

ANTONIO   They do observe I grow to infinite purchase,

The left hand way, and all suppose the Duchess
Would amend it, if she could; for, say they,   30
Great princes, though they grudge their officers
Should have such large and unconfinéd means
To get wealth under them, will not complain,
Lest thereby they should make them odious
Unto the people; for other obligation
Of love or marriage between her and me
They never dream of.

DELIO   The Lord Ferdinand
Is going to bed.

Enter DUCHESS, FERDINAND *and Attendants*

FERDINAND   I'll instantly to bed,
For I am weary – I am to bespeak
A husband for you.

DUCHESS   For me, sir! Pray, who is't?   40

FERDINAND The great Count Malatesti.

DUCHESS   Fie upon him!
A count! He's a mere stick of sugar-candy;
You may look quite through him. When I choose
A husband, I will marry for your honour.

FERDINAND You shall do well in't – How is't, worthy Antonio?

DUCHESS   But, sir, I am to have private conference with you
About a scandalous report is spread
Touching mine honour.

FERDINAND   Let me be ever deaf to't:
One of Pasquil's paper bullets, court-calumny,
A pestilent air, which princes' palaces   50
Are seldom purged of. Yet say that it were true,
I pour it in your bosom, my fixed love
Would strongly excuse, extenuate, nay, deny
Faults, were they apparent in you. Go, be safe
In your own innocency.

DUCHESS   [*aside*]   O blessed comfort!
This deadly air is purged.

                    [*exeunt Duchess, Antonio, Delio and Attendants*

FERDINAND   Her guilt treads on
Hot-burning coulters.

Enter BOSOLA

                    Now, Bosola,
How thrives our intelligence?

BOSOLA   Sir, uncertainly:
'Tis rumoured she hath had three bastards, but
By whom we may go read i'the stars.

FERDINAND   Why, some   60
Hold opinion all things are written there.

BOSOLA Yes, if we could find spectacles to read them.
I do suspect there hath been some sorcery
Used on the duchess.

FERDINAND   Sorcery! To what purpose?

BOSOLA To make her dote on some desertless fellow
She shames to acknowledge.

FERDINAND   Can your faith give way
To think there's power in potions or in charms,
To make us love whether we will or no?

BOSOLA Most certainly.

FERDINAND Away! These are mere gulleries, horrid things,   70
Invented by some cheating mountebanks
To abuse us. Do you think that herbs or charms
Can force the will? Some trials have been made
In this foolish practice, but the ingredients
Were lenitive poisons, such as are of force
To make the patient mad; and straight the witch
Swears by equivocation they are in love.
The witchcraft lies in her rank blood. This night
I will force confession from her. You told me
You had got, within these two days, a false key   80
Into her bed-chamber.

BOSOLA   I have.

FERDINAND   As I would wish.

BOSOLA What do you intend to do?

FERDINAND   Can you guess?

BOSOLA   No.

FERDINAND Do not ask, then:
He that can compass me, and know my drifts,
May say he hath put a girdle 'bout the world,

And sounded all her quicksands.

BOSOLA   I do not
Think so.

FERDINAND   What do you think, then, pray?

BOSOLA   That you
Are your own chronicle too much, and grossly
Flatter yourself.

FERDINAND   Give me thy hand; I thank thee:
I never gave pension but to flatterers,   90
Till I entertained thee. Farewell.
That friend a great man's ruin strongly checks,
Who rails into his belief all his defects.

                                            [*exeunt*

SCENE 2

The bed-chamber of the Duchess

Enter DUCHESS, ANTONIO, *and* CARIOLA

DUCHESS   Bring me the casket hither, and the glass –
You get no lodging here tonight, my lord.

ANTONIO   Indeed, I must persuade one.

DUCHESS   Very good:
I hope in time 'twill grow into a custom,
That noblemen shall come with cap and knee
To purchase a night's lodging of their wives.

ANTONIO   I must lie here.

DUCHESS   Must! You are a lord of mis-rule.

ANTONIO   Indeed, my rule is only in the night.

DUCHESS   To what use will you put me?

ANTONIO   We'll sleep together.

DUCHESS   Alas,   10
What pleasure can two lovers find in sleep!

CARIOLA   My lord, I lie with her often; and I know
She'll much disquiet you.

ANTONIO   See, you are complained of.

CARIOLA   For she's the sprawling'st bedfellow.

ANTONIO   I shall like her the better for that.

CARIOLA   Sir, shall I ask you a question?

ANTONIO	Ay, pray thee, Cariola.
CARIOLA	Wherefore still, when you lie with my lady,
	Do you rise so early?
ANTONIO	Labouring men

ANTONIO   Labouring men
Count the clock oftenest, Cariola,   20
Are glad when their task's ended.

DUCHESS   I'll stop your mouth. [*kisses him*]

ANTONIO Nay, that's but one; Venus had two soft doves
To draw her chariot; I must have another —
[*she kisses him again*]
When wilt thou marry, Cariola?

CARIOLA   Never, my lord.

ANTONIO O, fie upon this single life! Forego it.
We read how Daphne, for her peevish flight,
Became a fruitless bay-tree; Syrinx turned
To the pale empty reed; Anaxarete
Was frozen into marble: whereas those
Which married, or proved kind unto their friends,   30
Were by a gracious influence transhaped
Into the olive, pomegranate, mulberry,
Became flowers, precious stones, or eminent stars.

CARIOLA This is a vain poetry: but I pray you tell me,
If there were proposed me, wisdom, riches,
                      and beauty,
In three several young men, which should I choose.

ANTONIO 'Tis a hard question: this was Paris' case,
And he was blind in't, and there was great cause;
For how was't possible he could judge right,
Having three amorous goddesses in view,   40
And they stark naked? 'Twas a motion
Were able to benight the apprehension
Of the severest counsellor of Europe.
Now I look on both your faces so well formed,
It puts me in mind of a question I would ask.

CARIOLA What is't?

ANTONIO   I do wonder why hard-favoured ladies,
For the most part, keep worse-favoured
                      waiting-women
To attend them, and cannot endure fair ones.

DUCHESS   O, that's soon answered.
           Did you ever in your life know an ill painter   50
           Desire to have his dwelling next door to the shop
           Of an excellent picture-maker? 'Twould disgrace
           His face-making, and undo him. I prithee,
           When were we so merry? – My hair tangles.
ANTONIO   Pray thee, Cariola, let's steal forth the room,
           And let her talk to herself: I have divers times
           Served her the like, when she hath chafed extremely.
           I love to see her angry. Softly, Cariola.
                              [*exeunt Antonio and Cariola*
DUCHESS   Doth not the colour of my hair 'gin to change?
           When I wax gray, I shall have all the court   60
           Powder their hair with arras, to be like me.
           You have cause to love me; I entered you into
                                                my heart
           Before you would vouchsafe to call for the keys.

                    Enter FERDINAND *behind*

           We shall one day have my brothers take you napping;
           Methinks his presence, being now in court,
           Should make you keep your own bed; but you'll say
           Love mixed with fear is sweetest. I'll assure you,
           You shall get no more children till my brothers
           Consent to be your gossips. Have you lost
                                          your tongue?
           'Tis welcome: 70
           For know, whether I am doomed to live or die,
           I can do both like a prince.
FERDINAND [*giving her a poniard*]   Die, then, quickly!
           Virtue, where art thou hid? What hideous thing
           Is it that doth eclipse thee?
DUCHESS   Pray, sir, hear me.
FERDINAND Or is it true thou art but a bare name,
           And no essential thing?
DUCHESS   Sir –
FERDINAND   Do not speak.
DUCHESS   No, sir:
           I will plant my soul in mine ears, to hear you.

FERDINAND   O most imperfect light of human reason,
            That mak'st us so unhappy to foresee   80
            What we can least prevent! Pursue thy wishes,
            And glory in them: there's in shame no comfort
            But to be past all bounds and sense of shame.

DUCHESS   I pray, Sir, hear me: I am married.

FERDINAND   So!

DUCHESS   Haply, not to your liking: but for that,
            Alas, your shears do come untimely now
            To clip the bird's wing that's already flown!
            Will you see my husband?

FERDINAND   Yes, if I could change
            Eyes with a basilisk.

DUCHESS   Sure, you came hither
            By his confederacy.

FERDINAND   The howling of a wolf   90
            Is music to thee, screech-owl: prithee, peace –
            Whate'er thou art that hast enjoyed my sister,
            For I am sure thou hear'st me, for thine own sake
            Let me not know thee. I came hither prepared
            To work thy discovery; yet am now persuaded
            It would beget such violent effects
            As would damn us both. I would not for ten millions
            I had beheld thee: therefore use all means
            I never may have knowledge of thy name;
            Enjoy thy lust still, and a wretched life,   100
            On that condition – And for thee, vile woman,
            If thou do wish thy lecher may grow old
            In thy embracements, I would have thee build
            Such a room for him as our anchorites
            To holier use inhabit. Let not the sun
            Shine on him till he's dead; let dogs and monkeys
            Only converse with him, and such dumb things
            To whom nature denies use to sound his name;
            Do not keep a paraquito, lest she learn it.
            If thou do love him, cut out thine own tongue,   110
            Lest it bewray him.

DUCHESS   Why might not I marry?
            I have not gone about in this to create

Any new world or custom.

FERDINAND   Thou art undone;
And thou hast ta'en that massy sheet of lead
That hid thy husband's bones, and folded it
About my heart.

DUCHESS   Mine bleeds for't.

FERDINAND   Thine! Thy heart!
What should I name't unless a hollow bullet
Filled with unquenchable wild-fire?

DUCHESS   You are in this
Too strict; and were you not my princely brother,
I would say, too wilful: my reputation   120
Is safe.

FERDINAND   Dost thou know what reputation is?
I'll tell thee – to small purpose, since the instruction
Comes now too late.
Upon a time Reputation, Love, and Death,
Would travel o'er the world; and it was concluded
That they should part, and take three several ways.
Death told them, they should find him in
                                great battles,
Or cities plagued with plagues: Love gives
                                them counsel
To inquire for him 'mongst unambitious shepherds,
Where dowries were not talked of, and sometimes   130
'Mongst quiet kindred that had nothing left
By their dead parents: 'Stay,' quoth Reputation,
'Do not forsake me; for it is my nature,
If once I part from any man I meet,
I am never found again.' And so for you:
You have shook hands with Reputation,
And made him invisible. So, fare you well:
I will never see you more.

DUCHESS   Why should only I,
Of all the other princes of the world,
Be cased up, like a holy relic? I have youth   140
And a little beauty.

FERDINAND   So you have some virgins
That are witches. I will never see thee more.   [exit

Re-enter ANTONIO, *with a pistol, and* CARIOLA

DUCHESS   You saw this apparition?
ANTONIO   Yes: we are
Betrayed. How came he hither? I should turn
This to thee, for that.
CARIOLA   Pray, sir, do; and when
That you have cleft my heart, you shall read there
Mine innocence.
DUCHESS   That gallery gave him entrance.
ANTONIO   I would this terrible thing would come again,
That, standing on my guard, I might relate
My warrantable love – [*she shows the poniard*]
                                  Ha! What means this?   150
DUCHESS   He left this with me.
ANTONIO   And it seems did wish
You would use it on yourself.
DUCHESS   His action
Seemed to intend so much.
ANTONIO   This hath a handle to't,
As well as a point: turn it towards him,
And so fasten the keen edge in his rank gall.
[*knocking within*]
How now! Who knocks? More earthquakes?
DUCHESS   I stand
As if a mine beneath my feet were ready
To be blown up.
CARIOLA   'Tis Bosola.
DUCHESS   Away!
O misery! Methinks unjust actions
Should wear these masks and curtains, and not we.   160
You must instantly part hence: I have fashioned
                                  it already.
                                  [*exit Antonio*

Enter BOSOLA

BOSOLA   The duke your brother is ta'en up in a whirlwind;
Hath took horse, and's rid post to Rome.
DUCHESS   So late?
BOSOLA   He told me, as he mounted into the saddle,

You were undone.

DUCHESS   Indeed, I am very near it.

BOSOLA   What's the matter?

DUCHESS   Antonio, the master of our household,
Hath dealt so falsely with me in's accounts:
My brother stood engaged with me for money
Ta'en up of certain Neapolitan Jews,   170
And Antonio lets the bonds be forfeit.

BOSOLA   Strange! – [*aside*] This is cunning.

DUCHESS   And hereupon
My brother's bills at Naples are protested
Against. Call up our officers.

BOSOLA   I shall.   [*exit*

Re-enter ANTONIO

DUCHESS   The place that you must fly to is Ancona:
Hire a house there; I'll send after you
My treasure and my jewels. Our weak safety
Runs upon enginous wheels: short syllables
Must stand for periods. I must now accuse you
Of such a feignéd crime as Tasso calls   180
Magnanima menzogna, a noble lie,
'Cause it must shield our honours – Hark! They
                            are coming.

Re-enter BOSOLA *and Officers*

ANTONIO   Will your grace hear me?

DUCHESS   I have got well by you; you have yielded me
A million of loss: I am like to inherit
The people's curses for your stewardship.
You had the trick in audit-time to be sick,
Till I had signed your *quietus*; and that cured you
Without help of a doctor – Gentlemen,
I would have this man be an example to you all;   190
So shall you hold my favour. I pray, let him;
For h'as done that, alas, you would not think of,
And, because I intend to be rid of him,
I mean not to publish – Use your fortune elsewhere.

ANTONIO   I am strongly armed to brook my overthrow,
As commonly men bear with a hard year:

I will not blame the cause on't; but do think
The necessity of my malevolent star
Procures this, not her humour. O, the inconstant
And rotten ground of service! You may see,   200
'Tis even like him, that in a winter night,
Takes a long slumber o'er a dying fire,
A–loth to part from't; yet parts thence as cold
As when he first sat down.

DUCHESS   We do confiscate,
Towards the satisfying of your accounts,
All that you have.

ANTONIO   I am all yours; and 'tis very fit
All mine should be so.

DUCHESS   So, sir, you have your pass.

ANTONIO You may see, gentlemen, what 'tis to serve
A prince with body and soul.   [*exit*

BOSOLA Here's an example for extortion: what moisture is 210
drawn out of the sea, when foul weather comes, pours
down, and runs into the sea again.

DUCHESS I would know what are your opinions
Of this Antonio.

2 OFFICER He could not abide to see a pig's head gaping: I
thought your grace would find him a Jew.

3 OFFICER I would you had been his officer, for your own sake.

4 OFFICER You would have had more money.

4 OFFICER He stopped his ears with black wool, and to those
came to him for money said he was thick of hearing.   220

2 OFFICER Some said he was an hermaphrodite, for he could not
abide a woman.

4 OFFICER How scurvy proud he would look when the treasury
was full! Well, let him go.

1 OFFICER Yes, and the chippings of the buttery fly after him, to
scour his gold chain.

DUCHESS Leave us.   [*exeunt Officers*
What do you think of these?

BOSOLA That these are rogues that in's prosperity,
But to have waited on his fortune, could have wished
His dirty stirrup riveted through their noses,   230
And followed after's mule, like a bear in a ring;

Would have prostituted their daughters to his lust;
Made their first-born intelligencers; thought
                      none happy
But such as were born under his blest planet,
And wore his livery: and do these lice drop off now?
Well, never look to have the like again:
He hath left a sort of flattering rogues behind him;
Their doom must follow. Princes pay flatterers
In their own money: flatterers dissemble their vices,
And they dissemble their lies; that's justice.   240
Alas, poor gentleman!

DUCHESS   Poor! He hath amply filled his coffers.

BOSOLA   Sure, he was too honest. Pluto, the god of riches,
When he's sent by Jupiter to any man,
He goes limping, to signify that wealth
That comes on God's name comes slowly; but
                      when he's sent
On the devil's errand, he rides post and comes in
                      by scuttles.
Let me show you what a most unvalued jewel
You have in a wanton humour thrown away,
To bless the man shall find him. He was an excellent   250
Courtier and most faithful; a soldier that thought it
As beastly to know his own value too little
As devilish to acknowledge it too much.
Both his virtue and form deserved a far better fortune:
His discourse rather delighted to judge itself
                    than show itself:
His breast was filled with all perfection,
And yet it seemed a private whispering-room,
It made so little noise of't.

DUCHESS   But he was basely descended.

BOSOLA   Will you make
Yourself a mercenary herald, rather to examine   260
Men's pedigrees than virtues? You shall want him:
For know an honest statesman to a prince
Is like a cedar planted by a spring;
The spring bathes the tree's root, the grateful tree
Rewards it with his shadow: you have not done so.

　　　　　　I would sooner swim to the Bermudas on
　　　　　　Two politicians' rotten bladders, tied
　　　　　　Together with an intelligencer's heart-string,
　　　　　　Than depend on so changeable a prince's favour.
　　　　　　Fare thee well, Antonio! Since the malice of the world　270
　　　　　　Would needs down with thee, it cannot be said yet
　　　　　　That any ill happened unto thee, considering thy fall
　　　　　　Was accompanied with virtue.
DUCHESS　　O, you render me excellent music!
BOSOLA　　　　　　　　　　　　　　　　　Say you?
DUCHESS　　This good one that you speak of is my husband.
BOSOLA　　Do I not dream! Can this ambitious age
　　　　　　Have so much goodness in't as to prefer
　　　　　　A man merely for worth, without these shadows
　　　　　　Of wealth and painted honours? Possible?
DUCHESS　　I have had three children by him.
BOSOLA　　　　　　　　　　　　　　Fortunate lady!　280
　　　　　　For you have made your private nuptial bed
　　　　　　The humble and fair seminary of peace.
　　　　　　No question but many an unbeneficed scholar
　　　　　　Shall pray for you for this deed, and rejoice
　　　　　　That some preferment in the world can yet
　　　　　　Arise from merit. The virgins of your land
　　　　　　That have no dowries shall hope your example
　　　　　　Will raise them to rich husbands. Should you want
　　　　　　Soldiers, 'twould make the very Turks and Moors
　　　　　　Turn Christians, and serve you for this act.　290
　　　　　　Last, the neglected poets of your time,
　　　　　　In honour of this trophy of a man,
　　　　　　Raised by that curious engine, your white hand,
　　　　　　Shall thank you, in your grave, for't; and make that
　　　　　　More reverend than all the cabinets
　　　　　　Of living princes. For Antonio,
　　　　　　His fame shall likewise flow from many a pen,
　　　　　　When heralds shall want coats to sell to men.
DUCHESS　　As I taste comfort in this friendly speech,
　　　　　　So would I find concealment.
BOSOLA　　　　　　　　　　　　O, the secret of my prince,　300
　　　　　　Which I will wear on the inside of my heart!

DUCHESS   You shall take charge of all my coin and jewels
           And follow him; for he retires himself
           To Ancona.
BOSOLA   So.
DUCHESS   Whither, within few days,
           I mean to follow thee.
BOSOLA   Let me think:
           I would wish your grace to feign a pilgrimage
           To our Lady of Loretto, scarce seven leagues
           From fair Ancona; so may you depart
           Your country with more honour, and your flight
           Will seem a princely progress, retaining   310
           Your usual train about you.
DUCHESS   Sir, your direction
           Shall lead me by the hand.
CARIOLA   In my opinion,
           She were better progress to the baths at Lucca,
           Or go visit the Spa
           In Germany; for, if you will believe me,
           I do not like this jesting with religion,
           This feigned pilgrimage.
DUCHESS   Thou art a superstitious fool:
           Prepare us instantly for our departure.
           Past sorrows, let us moderately lament them;
           For those to come, seek wisely to prevent them.   320
                            [*exeunt Duchess and Cariola*
BOSOLA   A politician is the devil's quilted anvil:
           He fashions all sins on him, and the blows
           Are never heard: he may work in a lady's chamber,
           As here for proof. What rests but I reveal
           All to my lord? O, this base quality
           Of intelligencer! Why, every quality i'the world
           Prefers but gain or commendation:
           Now for this act I am certain to be raised,
           And men that paint weeds to the life are praised.
                                                      [*exit*

SCENE 3

An apartment in the Cardinal's palace at Rome

Enter CARDINAL, FERDINAND, MALATESTI, PESCARA,
DELIO *and* SILVIO.

CARDINAL Must we turn soldier, then?

MALATESTI   The emperor,
    Hearing your worth that way, ere you attained
    This reverend garment, joins you in commission
    With the right fortunate soldier the Marquis
                             of Pescara,
    And the famous Lannoy.

CARDINAL   He that had the honour
    Of taking the French king prisoner?

MALATESTI   The same.
    Here's a plot drawn for a new fortification
    At Naples.

FERDINAND This great Count Malatesti, I perceive,
    Hath got employment?

DELIO   No employment, my lord;   10
    A marginal note in the muster-book, that he is
    A voluntary lord.

FERDINAND   He's no soldier.

DELIO He has worn gunpowder in's hollow tooth for the
    toothache.

SILVIO He comes to the leaguer with a full intent
    To eat fresh beef and garlic, means to stay
    Till the scent be gone, and straight return to court.

DELIO He hath read all the late service
    As the city chronicle relates it;
    And keeps two pewterers going, only to express   20
    Battles in model.

SILVIO   Then he'll fight by the book.

DELIO By the almanac, I think,
    To choose good days and shun the critical;
    That's his mistress' scarf.

SILVIO   Yes, he protests
    He would do much for that taffeta.

DELIO	I think he would run away from a battle,
	To save it from taking prisoner.
SILVIO	He is horribly afraid
	Gunpowder will spoil the perfume on't.
DELIO	I saw a Dutchman break his pate once
	For calling him pot-gun; he made his head
	Have a bore in't like a musket.
SILVIO	I would he had made a touchhole to't.
	He is indeed a guarded sumpter-cloth,
	Only for the remove of the court.

Enter BOSOLA

PESCARA	Bosola arrivéd! What should be the business?
	Some falling-out amongst the cardinals.
	These factions amongst great men, they are like
	Foxes, when their heads are divided,
	They carry fire in their tails, and all the country
	About them goes to wreck for't.
SILVIO	What's that Bosola?
DELIO	I knew him in Padua – a fantastical scholar, like such who study to know how many knots was in Hercules' club, of what colour Achilles' beard was, or whether Hector were not troubled with the toothache. He hath studied himself half blear-eyed to know the true symmetry of Caesar's nose by a shoeing-horn; and this he did to gain the name of a speculative man.
PESCARA	Mark Prince Ferdinand:
	A very salamander lives in's eye,
	To mock the eager violence of fire.
SILVIO	That Cardinal hath made more bad faces with his oppression than ever Michael Angelo made good ones: he lifts up's nose, like a foul porpoise before a storm.
PESCARA	The Lord Ferdinand laughs.
DELIO	Like a deadly cannon
	That lightens ere it smokes.
PESCARA	These are your true pangs of death,
	The pangs of life, that struggle with great statesmen.
DELIO	In such a deformed silence witches whisper their charms.
CARDINAL	Doth she make religion her riding-hood

30

40

50

60

To keep her from the sun and tempest?

FERDINAND   That,
That damns her. Methinks her fault and beauty,
Blended together, show like leprosy –
The whiter, the fouler. I make it a question
Whether her beggarly brats were ever christened.

CARDINAL I will instantly solicit the state of Ancona
To have them banished.

FERDINAND   You are for Loretto:
I shall not be at your ceremony; fare you well –
Write to the Duke of Malfi, my young nephew
She had by her first husband, and acquaint him   70
With's mother's honesty.

BOSOLA   I will.

FERDINAND   Antonio!
A slave that only smelled of ink and counters,
And never in's life looked like a gentleman,
But in the audit-time – Go, go presently,
Draw me out an hundred and fifty of our horse,
And meet me at the fort-bridge.

                                                        [*exeunt*

SCENE 4

The shrine of our Lady of Loretto

Enter two Pilgrims

1 PILGRIM I have not seen a goodlier shrine than this;
Yet I have visited many.

2 PILGRIM   The Cardinal of Arragon
Is this day to resign his cardinal's hat:
His sister Duchess likewise is arrived
To pay her vow of pilgrimage. I expect
A noble ceremony.

1 PILGRIM   No question – They come.

*Here the ceremony of the Cardinal's instalment in the habit
of a soldier, is performed by his delivering up his cross, hat,
robes and ring, at the shrine, and the investing of him with
sword, helmet, shield and spurs; then Antonio, the Duchess,*

and their children, having presented themselves at the shrine,
are, by a form of banishment in dumb-show expressed
towards them by the Cardinal and the state of Ancona,
banished: during all which ceremony, this ditty is
sung, to very solemn music, by divers churchmen.

Arms and honours deck thy story,
To thy fame's eternal glory!
Adverse fortune ever fly thee;
No disastrous fate come nigh thee!   10
I alone will sing thy praises,
Whom to honour virtue raises;
And thy study, that divine is,
Bent to martial discipline is.
Lay aside all those robes lie by thee;
Crown thy arts with arms, they'll beautify thee.
O worthy of worthiest name, adorned in this manner,
Lead bravely thy forces on under war's warlike
                                                   banner!
O mayst thou prove fortunate in all martial courses!
Guide thou still by skill in arts and forces!   20
Victory attend thee nigh, whilst fame sings loud
                                              thy powers;
Triumphant conquest crown thy head, and
                              blessings pour down showers!
                    [*exeunt all except the two Pilgrims*

1 PILGRIM Here's a strange turn of state! Who would
                                              have thought
           So great a lady would have matched herself
           Unto so mean a person? Yet the Cardinal
           Bears himself much too cruel.
2 PILGRIM   They are banished.
1 PILGRIM But I would ask what power hath this state
           Of Ancona to determine of a free prince?
2 PILGRIM They are a free state, sir, and her brother showed
           How that the Pope, fore-hearing of her looseness,   30
           Hath seized into the protection of the church
           The dukedom which she held as dowager.
1 PILGRIM But by what justice?
2 PILGRIM   Sure, I think by none,

Only her brother's instigation.

I PILGRIM   What was it with such violence he took
Off from her finger?

2 PILGRIM   'Twas her wedding-ring;
Which he vowed shortly he would sacrifice
To his revenge.

I PILGRIM   Alas, Antonio!
If that a man be thrust into a well,
No matter who sets hand to't, his own weight   40
Will bring him sooner to the bottom. Come,
                            let's hence.
Fortune makes this conclusion general,
All things do help the unhappy man to fall.

                                   [*exeunt*

SCENE 5

Near Loretto

Enter DUCHESS, ANTONIO, *Children*, CARIOLA *and Servants*

DUCHESS   Banished Ancona!

ANTONIO   Yes, you see what power
Lightens in great men's breath.

DUCHESS   Is all our train
Shrunk to this poor remainder?

ANTONIO   These poor men,
Which have got little in your service, vow
To take your fortune: but your wiser buntings,
Now they are fledged, are gone.

DUCHESS   They have done wisely.
This puts me in mind of death: physicians thus,
With their hands full of money, use to give o'er
Their patients.

ANTONIO   Right the fashion of the world:
From decayed fortunes every flatterer shrinks;   10
Men cease to build where the foundation sinks.

DUCHESS   I had a very strange dream tonight.

ANTONIO   What was't?

DUCHESS   Methought I wore my coronet of state,

	And on a sudden all the diamonds
	Were changed to pearls.
ANTONIO	My interpretation
	Is, you'll weep shortly; for to me the pearls
	Do signify your tears.
DUCHESS	The birds that live i'the field
	On the wild benefit of nature live
	Happier than we; for they may choose their mates, 20
	And carol their sweet pleasures to the spring.

Enter BOSOLA *with a letter*

BOSOLA	You are happily o'erta'en.
DUCHESS	From my brother?
BOSOLA	Yes, from the Lord Ferdinand your brother
	All love and safety.
DUCHESS	Thou dost blanch mischief,
	Wouldst make it white. See, see, like to
	calm weather
	At sea before a tempest, false hearts speak fair
	To those they intend most mischief.
	[*reads*] 'Send Antonio to me; I want his head
	In a business.' A politic equivocation!
	He doth not want your counsel, but your head; 30
	That is, he cannot sleep till you be dead.
	And here's another pitfall that's strewed o'er
	With roses; mark it, 'tis a cunning one:
	[*reads*] 'I stand engaged for your husband for several
	debts at Naples: let not that trouble him; I had rather
	have his heart than his money' –
	And I believe so too.
BOSOLA	What do you believe?
DUCHESS	That he so much distrusts my husband's love,
	He will by no means believe his heart is with him
	Until he sees it: the devil is not cunning enough 40
	To circumvent us in riddles.
BOSOLA	Will you reject that noble and free league
	Of amity and love which I present you?
DUCHESS	Their league is like that of some politic kings,
	Only to make themselves of strength and power
	To be our after-ruin: tell them so.

BOSOLA	And what from you?
ANTONIO	Thus tell him; I will not come.
BOSOLA	And what of this?
ANTONIO	My brothers have dispersed

ANTONIO (cont.)
Blood-hounds abroad; which till I hear are muzzled,
No truce, though hatched with ne'er such
                          politic skill,   50
Is safe, that hangs upon our enemies' will.
I'll not come at them.

BOSOLA   This proclaims your breeding:
Every small thing draws a base mind to fear,
As the adamant draws iron. Fare you well, sir:
You shall shortly hear from's.   [*exit*

DUCHESS   I suspect some ambush:
Therefore by all my love I do conjure you
To take your eldest son, and fly towards Milan.
Let us not venture all this poor remainder
In one unlucky bottom.

ANTONIO   You counsel safely.
Best of my life, farewell, since we must part: 60
Heaven hath a hand in't; but no otherwise
Than as some curious artist takes in sunder
A clock or watch, when it is out of frame,
To bring't in better order.

DUCHESS   I know not which is best,
To see you dead, or part with you – Farewell, boy:
Thou art happy that thou hast not understanding
To know thy misery; for all our wit
And reading brings us to a truer sense
Of sorrow – In the eternal church, sir,
I do hope we shall not part thus.

ANTONIO   O, be of comfort!   70
Make patience a noble fortitude,
And think not how unkindly we are used:
Man, like to cassia, is proved best being bruised.

DUCHESS Must I, like a slave-born Russian,
Account it praise to suffer tyranny?
And yet, O Heaven, thy heavy hand is in't!
I have seen my little boy oft scourge his top,

And compared myself to't: naught made me e'er
Go right but Heaven's scourge-stick.

ANTONIO   Do not weep:
Heaven fashioned us of nothing, and we strive   80
To bring ourselves to nothing – Farewell, Cariola,
And thy sweet armful – If I do never see thee more,
Be a good mother to your little ones,
And save them from the tiger: fare you well.

DUCHESS   Let me look upon you once more, for that speech
Came from a dying father: your kiss is colder
Than that I have seen an holy anchorite
Give to a dead man's skull.

ANTONIO   My heart is turned to a heavy lump of lead,
With which I sound my danger: fare you well.   90
                                    [exeunt Antonio and his son

DUCHESS   My laurel is all withered.

CARIOLA   Look, madam, what a troop of arméd men
Make towards us.

DUCHESS   O, they are very welcome:
When Fortune's wheel is over-charged with princes,
The weight makes it move swift: I would have
                                                    my ruin
Be sudden.

          Re-enter BOSOLA *visarded, with a guard*

                    I am your adventure, am I not?

BOSOLA   You are: you must see your husband no more.

DUCHESS   What devil art thou that counterfeit'st Heaven's
                                                    thunder?

BOSOLA   Is that terrible? I would have you tell me whether
Is that note worse that frights the silly birds   100
Out of the corn, or that which doth allure them
To the nets? You have hearkened to the last
                                              too much.

DUCHESS   O misery! Like to a rusty o'er-charged cannon,
Shall I never fly in pieces? Come, to what prison?

BOSOLA   To none.

DUCHESS   Whither, then?

BOSOLA   To your palace.

DUCHESS   I have heard

That Charon's boat serves to convey all o'er
The dismal lake, but brings none back again.

BOSOLA   Your brothers mean you safety and pity.

DUCHESS   Pity!
With such a pity men preserve alive
Pheasants and quails, when they are not fat enough   110
To be eaten.

BOSOLA   These are your children?

DUCHESS   Yes.

BOSOLA   Can they prattle?

DUCHESS   No;
But I intend, since they were born accursed,
Curses shall be their first language.

BOSOLA   Fie, madam!
Forget this base, low fellow –

DUCHESS   Were I a man,
I'd beat that counterfeit face into thy other.

BOSOLA   One of no birth.

DUCHESS   Say that he was born mean,
Man is most happy when's own actions
Be arguments and examples of his virtue.   120

BOSOLA   A barren, beggarly virtue.

DUCHESS   I prithee, who is greatest? Can you tell?
Sad tales befit my woe: I'll tell you one.
A salmon, as she swam unto the sea,
Met with a dog-fish, who encounters her
With this rough language: 'Why art thou so bold
To mix thyself with our high state of floods,
Being no eminent courtier, but one
That for the calmest and fresh time o'the year
Dost live in shallow rivers, rank'st thyself
With silly smelts and shrimps? And darest thou   130
Pass by our dog-ship without reverence?'
'O!' quoth the salmon, 'sister, be at peace:
Thank Jupiter we both have passed the net!
Our value never can be truly known
Till in the fisher's basket we be shown:
I'the market then my price may be the higher,
Even when I am nearest to the cook and fire.'

So to great men the moral may be stretchéd;
Men oft are valued high, when they're most
                                        wretched –
But come, whither you please. I am armed
                                    'gainst misery;   140
Bent to all sways of the oppressor's will:
There's no deep valley but near some great hill.
                                                    [*exeunt*

ACT 4 SCENE I

An apartment in the Duchess' palace at Malfi

Enter FERDINAND *and* BOSOLA

FERDINAND How doth our sister Duchess bear herself
　　　　　In her imprisonment?
BOSOLA 　　　　　　　　　　Nobly: I'll describe her.
　　　　　She's sad as one long used to't, and she seems
　　　　　Rather to welcome the end of misery
　　　　　Than shun it; a behaviour so noble
　　　　　As gives a majesty to adversity:
　　　　　You may discern the shape of loveliness
　　　　　More perfect in her tears than in her smiles:
　　　　　She will muse four hours together; and her silence,
　　　　　Methinks, expresseth more than if she spake.　　　10
FERDINAND Her melancholy seems to be fortified
　　　　　With a strange disdain.
BOSOLA 　　　　　　　　　　'Tis so; and this restraint,
　　　　　Like English mastiffs that grow fierce with tying,
　　　　　Makes her too passionately apprehend
　　　　　Those pleasures she's kept from.
FERDINAND 　　　　　　　　　　　　Curse upon her!
　　　　　I will no longer study in the book
　　　　　Of another's heart. Inform her what I told you.

　　　　　　　　　　　　　　　　　　　　　[*exit*

Enter DUCHESS

BOSOLA 　All comfort to your grace!
DUCHESS 　　　　　　　　　　I will have none.
　　　　　Pray thee, why dost thou wrap thy poisoned pills
　　　　　In gold and sugar?　　　　　　　　　　　　　20
BOSOLA 　Your elder brother, the Lord Ferdinand,
　　　　　Is come to visit you, and sends you word,
　　　　　'Cause once he rashly made a solemn vow
　　　　　Never to see you more, he comes i'the night;
　　　　　And prays you gently neither torch nor taper
　　　　　Shine in your chamber: he will kiss your hand,
　　　　　And reconcile himself; but for his vow

He dares not see you.

DUCHESS   At his pleasure –
Take hence the lights. He's come.

Enter FERDINAND

FERDINAND   Where are you?
DUCHESS   Here, sir.
FERDINAND This darkness suits you well.
DUCHESS   I would ask you pardon. 30
FERDINAND You have it;
For I account it the honorabl'st revenge,
Where I may kill, to pardon – Where are your cubs?
DUCHESS Whom?
FERDINAND Call them your children;
For though our national law distinguish bastards
From true legitimate issue, compassionate nature
Makes them all equal.
DUCHESS   Do you visit me for this?
You violate a sacrament o'the church
Shall make you howl in hell for't.   40
FERDINAND It had been well,
Could you have lived thus always; for, indeed,
You were too much i'the light – but no more;
I come to seal my peace with you. Here's a hand
[*gives her a dead man's hand*] To which you have
                         vowed much love; the ring upon't
You gave.
DUCHESS   I affectionately kiss it.
FERDINAND Pray, do, and bury the print of it in your heart.
I will leave this ring with you for a love-token;
And the hand as sure as the ring; and do not doubt
But you shall have the heart too: when you need
                              a friend, 50
Send it to him that owned it; you shall see
Whether he can aid you.
DUCHESS   You are very cold:
I fear you are not well after your travel –
Ha! Lights! O, horrible!
FERDINAND   Let her have lights enough.
                                        [*exit*

DUCHESS   What witchcraft doth he practise, that he hath left
           A dead man's hand here?
           [*here is discovered, behind a traverse, the artificial figures of*
           ANTONIO *and his children, appearing as if they were dead*]

BOSOLA   Look you, here's the piece from which 'twas ta'en.
           He doth present you this sad spectacle,
           That, now you know directly they are dead,
           Hereafter you may wisely cease to grieve   60
           For that which cannot be recovered.

DUCHESS   There is not between heaven and earth one wish
           I stay for after this: it wastes me more
           Than were't my picture, fashioned out of wax,
           Stuck with a magical needle, and then buried
           In some foul dunghill; and yond's an excellent
                                                        property
           For a tyrant, which I would account mercy.

BOSOLA   What's that?

DUCHESS   If they would bind me to that lifeless trunk,
           And let me freeze to death.

BOSOLA   Come, you must live.   70

DUCHESS   That's the greatest torture souls feel in hell,
           In hell, that they must live, and cannot die.
           Portia, I'll new kindle thy coals again,
           And revive the rare and almost dead example
           Of a loving wife.

BOSOLA   O, fie! Despair? Remember
           You are a Christian.

DUCHESS   The church enjoins fasting:
           I'll starve myself to death.

BOSOLA   Leave this vain sorrow.
           Things being at the worst begin to mend: the bee
           When he hath shot his sting into your hand,
           May then play with your eyelid.

DUCHESS   Good comfortable fellow,   80
           Persuade a wretch that's broke upon the wheel
           To have all his bones new set; entreat him live
           To be executed again. Who must despatch me?
           I account this world a tedious theatre,
           For I do play a part in't 'gainst my will.

BOSOLA	Come, be of comfort; I will save your life.
DUCHESS	Indeed, I have not leisure to attend
	So small a business.
BOSOLA	Now, by my life, I pity you.
DUCHESS	Thou art a fool, then,

DUCHESS
To waste thy pity on a thing so wretched   90
As cannot pity itself. I am full of daggers.
Puff, let me blow these vipers from me.

Enter Servant

What are you?

SERVANT   One that wishes you long life.

DUCHESS I would thou wert hanged for the horrible curse
Thou hast given me: I shall shortly grow one
Of the miracles of pity. I'll go pray –
No, I'll go curse.

BOSOLA   O, fie!

DUCHESS   I could curse the stars.

BOSOLA O, fearful.

DUCHESS And those three smiling seasons of the year
Into a Russian winter: nay, the world   100
To its first chaos.

BOSOLA Look you, the stars shine still.

DUCHESS   O, but you must
Remember, my curse hath a great way to go. –
Plagues, that make lanes through largest families,
Consume them!

BOSOLA   Fie, lady!

DUCHESS   Let them, like tyrants,
Never be remembered but for the ill they have done;
Let all the zealous prayers of mortified
Churchmen forget them!

BOSOLA   O, uncharitable!

DUCHESS Let Heaven a little while cease crowning martyrs,
To punish them!   110
Go, howl them this, and say, I long to bleed:
It is some mercy when men kill with speed.   [*exit*

Re-enter FERDINAND

FERDINAND Excellent, as I would wish; she's plagued in art:

These presentations are but framed in wax
By the curious master in that quality,
Vincentio Lauriola, and she takes them
For true substantial bodies.

BOSOLA   Why do you do this?

FERDINAND To bring her to despair.

BOSOLA   Faith, end here,
And go no farther in your cruelty:
Send her a penitential garment to put on   120
Next to her delicate skin, and furnish her
With beads and prayer-books.

FERDINAND   Damn her! That body of hers,
While that my blood ran pure in't, was more worth
Than that which thou wouldst comfort, called a soul.
I will send her masques of common courtesans,
Have her meat served up by bawds and ruffians,
And, 'cause she'll needs be mad, I am resolved
To remove forth the common hospital
All the mad-folk, and place them near her lodging;
There let them practise together, sing and dance,   130
And act their gambols to the full o'the moon:
If she can sleep the better for it, let her.
Your work is almost ended.

BOSOLA   Must I see her again?

FERDINAND Yes.

BOSOLA   Never.

FERDINAND   You must.

BOSOLA   Never in mine own shape;
That's forfeited by my intelligence
And this last cruel lie: when you send me next,
The business shall be comfort.

FERDINAND   Very likely;
Thy pity is nothing of kin to thee. Antonio
Lurks about Milan: thou shalt shortly thither,
To feed a fire as great as my revenge,   140
Which never will slack till it have spent his fuel:
Intemperate agues make physicians cruel.

                              [exeunt

SCENE 2

Another room in the Duchess's lodging

Enter DUCHESS *and* CARIOLA

DUCHESS   What hideous noise was that?

CARIOLA   'Tis the wild consort
Of madmen, lady, which your tyrant brother
Hath placed about your lodging: this tyranny,
I think, was never practised till this hour.

DUCHESS   Indeed, I thank him: nothing but noise and folly
Can keep me in my right wits; whereas reason
And silence make me stark mad. Sit down;
Discourse to me some dismal tragedy.

CARIOLA   O, 'twill increase your melancholy.

DUCHESS   Thou art deceived:
To hear of greater grief would lessen mine.   10
This is a prison?

CARIOLA   Yes, but you shall live
To shake this durance off.

DUCHESS   Thou art a fool:
The robin-redbreast and the nightingale
Never live long in cages.

CARIOLA   Pray, dry your eyes.
What think you of, madam?

DUCHESS   Of nothing;
When I muse thus, I sleep.

CARIOLA   Like a madman, with your eyes open?

DUCHESS   Dost thou think we shall know one another
In the other world?

CARIOLA   Yes, out of question.

DUCHESS   O, that it were possible we might   20
But hold some two days' conference with the dead!
From them I should learn somewhat, I am sure,
I never shall know here. I'll tell thee a miracle;
I am not mad yet, to my cause of sorrow:
The heaven o'er my head seems made of
                                              molten brass,

The earth of flaming sulphur, yet I am not mad.
I am acquainted with sad misery
As the tanned galley-slave is with his oar;
Necessity makes me suffer constantly,
And custom makes it easy. Who do I look like now?   30

CARIOLA Like to your picture in the gallery,
A deal of life in show, but none in practice;
Or rather like some reverend monument
Whose ruins are even pitied.

DUCHESS   Very proper;
And Fortune seems only to have her eyesight
To behold my tragedy. How now! What noise is that?

Enter Servant

SERVANT I am come to tell you
Your brother hath intended you some sport.
A great physician, when the Pope was sick
Of a deep melancholy, presented him   40
With several sorts of madmen, which wild object
Being full of change and sport, forced him to laugh,
And so the imposthume broke: the self-same cure
The duke intends on you.

DUCHESS   Let them come in.

SERVANT There's a mad lawyer; and a secular priest;
A doctor that hath forfeited his wits
By jealousy; an astrologian
That in his works said such a day o'the month
Should be the day of doom, and, failing of 't,
Ran mad; an English tailor crazed i'the brain   50
With the study of new fashions; a gentleman-usher
Quite beside himself with care to keep in mind
The number of his lady's salutations
Or 'How do you' she employed him in each morning;
A farmer, too, an excellent knave in grain,
Mad 'cause he was hindered transportation:
And let one broker that's mad loose to these,
You'd think the devil were among them.

DUCHESS Sit, Cariola – Let them loose when you please,
For I am chained to endure all your tyranny.   60

Enter Madmen

Here this song is sung to a dismal kind of music by a Madman

> O, let us howl some heavy note,
>   Some deadly dogged howl,
> Sounding as from the threatening throat
>   Of beasts and fatal fowl!
> As ravens, screech-owls, bulls and bears,
>   We'll bell, and bawl our parts,
> Till irksome noise have cloyed your ears
>   And corrosived your hearts.
> At last, whenas our quire wants breath,
>   Our bodies being blest,   70
> We'll sing, like swans, to welcome death,
>   And die in love and rest.

1 MADMAN Doom's-day not come yet! I'll draw it nearer by a perspective, or make a glass that shall set all the world on fire upon an instant. I cannot sleep; my pillow is stuffed with a litter of porcupines.

2 MADMAN Hell is a mere glass-house, where the devils are continually blowing up women's souls on hollow irons, and the fire never goes out.

3 MADMAN I will lie with every woman in my parish the tenth 80 night; I will tythe them over like haycocks.

4 MADMAN Shall my pothecary out-go me because I am a cuckold? I have found out his roguery; he makes alum of his wife's urine, and sells it to Puritans that have sore throats with overstraining.

1 MADMAN I have skill in heraldry.

2 MADMAN Hast?

1 MADMAN You do give for your crest a woodcock's head with the brains picked out on't; you are a very ancient gentleman.   90

3 MADMAN Greek is turned Turk: we are only to be saved by the Helvetian translation.

1 MADMAN Come on, sir, I will lay the law to you.

2 MADMAN O, rather lay a corrosive: the law will eat to the bone.

3 MADMAN He that drinks but to satisfy nature is damned.

4 MADMAN   If I had my glass here, I would show a sight should make all the women here call me mad doctor.

1 MADMAN   What's he? A rope-maker?

2 MADMAN   No, no, no, a snuffling knave that, while he shows the tombs, will have his hand in a wench's placket.   100

3 MADMAN   Woe to the caroche that brought home my wife from the masque at three o'clock in the morning! It had a large feather-bed in it.

4 MADMAN   I have pared the devil's nails forty times, roasted them in raven's eggs, and cured agues with them.

3 MADMAN   Get me three hundred milchbats, to make possets to procure sleep.

4 MADMAN   All the college may throw their caps at me: I have made a soap-boiler costive; it was my masterpiece.
[here a dance of eight Madmen, with music answerable thereto; after which, BOSOLA, like an Old Man, enters]

DUCHESS   Is he mad too?

SERVANT   Pray, question him. I'll leave you.   110
                     [exeunt Servant and Madmen

BOSOLA   I am come to make thy tomb.

DUCHESS   Ha! My tomb!
Thou speak'st as if I lay upon my deathbed,
Gasping for breath: dost thou perceive me sick?

BOSOLA   Yes, and the more dangerously, since thy sickness is insensible.

DUCHESS   Thou art not mad, sure: dost know me?

BOSOLA   Yes.

DUCHESS   Who am I?

BOSOLA   Thou art a box of worm-seed, at best but a salvatory of green mummy. What's this flesh? A little crudded   120 milk, fantastical puff-paste. Our bodies are weaker than those paper-prisons boys use to keep flies in; more contemptible, since ours is to preserve earth-worms. Didst thou ever see a lark in a cage? Such is the soul in the body: this world is like her little turf of grass, and the heaven o'er our heads, like her looking-glass, only gives us a miserable knowledge of the small compass of our prison.

DUCHESS   Am not I thy Duchess?

BOSOLA	Thou art some great woman, sure, for riot begins to sit 130 on thy forehead (clad in grey hairs) twenty years sooner than on a merry milkmaid's. Thou sleepest worse than if a mouse should be forced to take up her lodging in a cat's ear: a little infant that breeds its teeth, should it lie with thee, would cry out, as if thou wert the more unquiet bedfellow.
DUCHESS	I am Duchess of Malfi still.
BOSOLA	That makes thy sleeps so broken: Glories, like glow-worms, afar off shine bright, But looked to near, have neither heat nor light. 140
DUCHESS	Thou art very plain.
BOSOLA	My trade is to flatter the dead, not the living; I am a tomb-maker.
DUCHESS	And thou com'st to make my tomb?
BOSOLA	Yes.
DUCHESS	Let me be a little merry – of what stuff wilt thou make it?
BOSOLA	Nay, resolve me first, of what fashion?
DUCHESS	Why do we grow fantastical in our deathbed? Do we affect fashion in the grave?
BOSOLA	Most ambitiously. Princes' images on their tombs do 150 not lie, as they were wont, seeming to pray up to Heaven; but with their hands under their cheeks, as if they died of the toothache: they are not carved with their eyes fixed upon the stars; but as their minds were wholly bent upon the world, the self-same way they seem to turn their faces.
DUCHESS	Let me know fully therefore the effect Of this thy dismal preparation, This talk fit for a charnel.
BOSOLA	Now I shall –

Enter Executioners with a coffin, cords and a bell

	Here is a present from your princely brothers; 160 And may it arrive welcome, for it brings Last benefit, last sorrow.
DUCHESS	Let me see it: I have so much obedience in my blood,

I wish it in their veins to do them good.

BOSOLA   This is your last presence-chamber.

CARIOLA   O my sweet lady!

DUCHESS   Peace; it affrights not me.

BOSOLA   I am the common bellman,
That usually is sent to condemned persons
The night before they suffer.

DUCHESS   Even now thou said'st
Thou wast a tomb-maker.

BOSOLA   'Twas to bring you   170
By degrees to mortification. Listen.
Hark, now every thing is still;
The screech-owl and the whistler shrill
Call upon our dame aloud,
And bid her quickly don her shroud!
Much you had of land and rent;
Your length in clay's now competent:
A long war disturbéd your mind;
Here your perfect peace is signed.
Of what is't fools make such vain keeping?   180
Sin their conception, their birth weeping,
Their life a general mist of error,
Their death a hideous storm of terror.
Strew your hair with powders sweet,
Don clean linen, bathe your feet,
And (the foul fiend more to check)
A crucifix let bless your neck:
'Tis now full tide 'tween night and day;
End your groan, and come away.

CARIOLA   Hence, villains, tyrants, murderers! Alas!   190
What will you do with my lady? – Call for help.

DUCHESS   To whom? To our next neighbours? They are
                                        madfolks.

BOSOLA   Remove that noise.

DUCHESS   Farewell, Cariola.
In my last will I have not much to give:
A-many hungry guests have fed upon me;
Thine will be a poor reversion.

CARIOLA   I will die with her.

DUCHESS   I pray thee, look thou giv'st my little boy
         Some syrup for his cold, and let the girl
         Say her prayers ere she sleep.
         [*Cariola is forced out by the executioners*]
                       Now what you please:
         What death?   200

BOSOLA   Strangling; here are your executioners.

DUCHESS   I forgive them:
         The apoplexy, catarrh, or cough o'the lungs,
         Would do as much as they do.

BOSOLA   Doth not death fright you?

DUCHESS   Who would be afraid on't,
         Knowing to meet such excellent company
         In the other world?

BOSOLA   Yet, methinks,
         The manner of your death should much afflict you:
         This cord should terrify you.

DUCHESS   Not a whit: 210
         What would it pleasure me to have my throat cut
         With diamonds? Or to be smoteréd
         With cassia? Or to be shot to death with pearls?
         I know death hath ten thousand several doors
         For men to take their exits; and 'tis found
         They go on such strange geometrical hinges,
         You may open them both ways; any way, for
                       heaven sake,
         So I were out of your whispering. Tell my brothers
         That I perceive death, now I am well awake,
         Best gift is they can give or I can take.   220
         I would fain put off my last woman's fault,
         I'd not be tedious to you.

I EXECUT.   We are ready.

DUCHESS   Dispose my breath how please you; but my body
         Bestow upon my women, will you?

I EXECUT.   Yes.

DUCHESS   Pull, and pull strongly, for your able strength
         Must pull down heaven upon me –
         Yet stay; heaven-gates are not so highly arched
         As princes' palaces; they that enter there

Must go upon their knees. [*kneels*] – Come,
                      violent death,
Serve for mandragora to make me sleep! –   230
Go tell my brothers, when I am laid out,
They then may feed in quiet.
[*the Executioners strangle the Duchess*]

BOSOLA   Where's the waiting woman?
Fetch her: some other strangle the children.
[*Cariola and children are brought in by the Executioners,
who presently strangle the children*]
Look you, there sleeps your mistress.

CARIOLA   O, you are damned
Perpetually for this! My turn is next,
Is't not so ordered?

BOSOLA   Yes, and I am glad
You are so well prepared for't.

CARIOLA   You are deceived, sir,
I am not prepared for't, I will not die;
I will first come to my answer, and know   240
How I have offended.

BOSOLA   Come, despatch her –
You kept her counsel; now you shall keep ours.

CARIOLA   I will not die, I must not; I am contracted
To a young gentleman.

I EXECUT.   Here's your wedding-ring.

CARIOLA   Let me but speak with the Duke; I'll discover
Treason to his person.

BOSOLA   Delays – throttle her.

I EXECUT.   She bites and scratches.

CARIOLA   If you kill me now,
I am damned; I have not been at confession
This two years.

BOSOLA   [*to Executioners*] When?

CARIOLA   I am quick with child.

BOSOLA   Why, then,
Your credit's saved. [*the Executioners strangle Cariola*]
           Bear her into the next room;   250
Let these lie still.
      [*exeunt the Executioners with the body of Cariola*]

Enter FERDINAND

FERDINAND   Is she dead?
BOSOLA   She is what
          You'd have her. But here begin your pity:
          [*shows the Children strangled*]
          Alas, how have these offended?
FERDINAND   The death
          Of young wolves is never to be pitied.
BOSOLA   Fix your eye here.
FERDINAND   Constantly.
BOSOLA   Do you not weep?
          Other sins only speak; murder shrieks out:
          The element of water moistens the earth,
          But blood flies upwards and bedews the heavens.
FERDINAND Cover her face; mine eyes dazzle: she died young.
BOSOLA   I think not so; her infelicity   260
          Seemed to have years too many.
FERDINAND   She and I were twins;
          And should I die this instant, I had lived
          Her time to a minute.
BOSOLA   It seems she was born first:
          You have bloodily approved the ancient truth,
          That kindred commonly do worse agree
          Than remote strangers.
FERDINAND   Let me see her face
          Again. Why didst not thou pity her? What
          An excellent honest man mightst thou have been,
          If thou hadst borne her to some sanctuary!
          Or, bold in a good cause, opposed thyself,   270
          With thy advancéd sword above thy head,
          Between her innocence and my revenge!
          I bade thee, when I was distracted of my wits,
          Go kill my dearest friend, and thou hast done't.
          For let me but examine well the cause:
          What was the meanness of her match to me?
          Only I must confess I had a hope,
          Had she continued widow, to have gained
          An infinite mass of treasure by her death:
          And what was the main cause? Her marriage,   280

          That drew a stream of gall quite through my heart.
          For thee, as we observe in tragedies
          That a good actor many times is cursed
          For playing a villain's part, I hate thee for't,
          And, for my sake, say, thou hast done much ill well.

BOSOLA   Let me quicken your memory, for I perceive
          You are falling into ingratitude: I challenge
          The reward due to my service.

FERDINAND   I'll tell thee
          What I'll give thee.

BOSOLA   Do.

FERDINAND   I'll give thee a pardon
          For this murder.

BOSOLA   Ha!

FERDINAND   Yes, and 'tis   290
          The largest bounty I can study to do thee.
          By what authority didst thou execute
          This bloody sentence?

BOSOLA   By yours.

FERDINAND   Mine! Was I her judge?
          Did any ceremonial form of law
          Doom her to not-being? Did a complete jury
          Deliver her conviction up i'the court?
          Where shalt thou find this judgment registered,
          Unless in hell? See, like a bloody fool,
          Thou'st forfeited thy life, and thou shalt die for't.

BOSOLA   The office of justice is perverted quite   300
          When one thief hangs another. Who shall dare
          To reveal this?

FERDINAND   O, I'll tell thee;
          The wolf shall find her grave, and scrape it up,
          Not to devour the corpse, but to discover
          The horrid murder.

BOSOLA   You, not I, shall quake for't.

FERDINAND Leave me.

BOSOLA   I will first receive my pension.

FERDINAND You are a villain.

BOSOLA   When your ingratitude
          Is judge, I am so.

FERDINAND O horror, that not the fear of him which binds
          The devils can prescribe man obedience!   310
          Never look upon me more.
BOSOLA   Why, fare thee well.
          Your brother and yourself are worthy men:
          You have a pair of hearts are hollow graves,
          Rotten, and rotting others; and your vengeance,
          Like two chained bullets, still goes arm in arm:
          You may be brothers; for treason, like the plague,
          Doth take much in a blood. I stand like one
          That long hath ta'en a sweet and golden dream:
          I am angry with myself, now that I wake.
FERDINAND Get thee into some unknown part o'the world,   320
          That I may never see thee.
BOSOLA   Let me know
          Wherefore I should be thus neglected. Sir,
          I served your tyranny, and rather strove
          To satisfy yourself than all the world:
          And though I loathed the evil, yet I loved
          You that did counsel it; and rather sought
          To appear a true servant than an honest man.
FERDINAND I'll go hunt the badger by owl-light:
          'Tis a deed of darkness.   [exit
BOSOLA   He's much distracted. Off, my painted honour!   330
          While with vain hopes our faculties we tire,
          We seem to sweat in ice and freeze in fire.
          What would I do, were this to do again?
          I would not change my peace of conscience
          For all the wealth of Europe – She stirs; here's life –
          Return, fair soul, from darkness, and lead mine
          Out of this sensible hell – She's warm, she breathes –
          Upon thy pale lips I will melt my heart,
          To store them with fresh colour – Who's there?
          Some cordial drink! – Alas! I dare not call: 340
          So pity would destroy pity – Her eye opes,
          And heaven in it seems to ope, that late was shut,
          To take me up to mercy.
DUCHESS   Antonio!
BOSOLA   Yes, madam, he is living;

The dead bodies you saw were but feigned statues:
He's reconciled to your brothers; the Pope hath
                              wrought
The atonement.

DUCHESS Mercy! [*dies*]

BOSOLA O, she's gone again! There the cords of life broke.
O sacred innocence, that sweetly sleeps   350
On turtles' feathers, whilst a guilty conscience
Is a black register wherein is writ
All our good deeds and bad, a perspective
That shows us hell! That we cannot be suffered
To do good when we have a mind to it!
This is manly sorrow;
These tears, I am very certain, never grew
In my mother's milk: my estate is sunk
Below the degree of fear: where were
These penitent fountains while she was living?   360
O, they were frozen up! Here is a sight
As direful to my soul as is the sword
Unto a wretch hath slain his father. Come,
I'll bear thee hence,
And execute thy last will; that's deliver
Thy body to the reverend dispose
Of some good women: that the cruel tyrant
Shall not deny me. Then I'll post to Milan,
Where somewhat I will speedily enact
Worth my dejection.   370
                                    [*exit*

ACT 5 SCENE 1

A public place in Milan

Enter ANTONIO and DELIO

ANTONIO What think you of my hope of reconcilement
    To the Arragonian brethren?

DELIO   I misdoubt it;
    For though they have sent their letters of safe-
                                        conduct
    For your repair to Milan, they appear
    But nets to entrap you. The Marquis of Pescara,
    Under whom you hold certain land in cheat,
    Much 'gainst his noble nature hath been moved
    To seize those lands; and some of his dependants
    Are at this instant making it their suit
    To be invested in your revenues.   10
    I cannot think they mean well to your life
    That do deprive you of your means of life,
    Your living.

ANTONIO   You are still an heretic
    To any safety I can shape myself.

DELIO   Here comes the marquis: I will make myself
    Petitioner for some part of your land,
    To know whither it is flying.

ANTONIO   I pray do.   [withdraws

Enter PESCARA

DELIO Sir, I have a suit to you.

PESCARA   To me?

DELIO   An easy one:
    There is the citadel of Saint Bennet,
    With some demesnes, of late in the possession   20
    Of Antonio Bologna – please you bestow them
                                 on me.

PESCARA You are my friend; but this is such a suit,
    Nor fit for me to give, nor you to take.

DELIO No, sir?

PESCARA   I will give you ample reason for't –

Soon in private – here's the Cardinal's mistress.

Enter JULIA

JULIA   My lord, I am grown your poor petitioner,
And should be an ill beggar, had I not
A great man's letter here, the Cardinal's,
[*gives a letter*] To court you in my favour.

PESCARA   He entreats for you
The citadel of Saint Bennet, that belonged   30
To the banished Bologna.

JULIA   Yes.

PESCARA   I could not have thought of a friend I could rather
Pleasure with it: 'tis yours.

JULIA   Sir, I thank you;
And he shall know how doubly I am engaged
Both in your gift, and speediness of giving,
Which makes your grant the greater.   [*exit*

ANTONIO   [*aside*]   How they fortify
Themselves with my ruin!

DELIO   Sir, I am little bound to you.

PESCARA   Why?

DELIO   Because you denied this suit to me, and gave't
To such a creature.

PESCARA   Do you know what it was?   40
It was Antonio's land; not forfeited
By course of law, but ravished from his throat
By the Cardinal's entreaty: it were not fit
I should bestow so main a piece of wrong
Upon my friend; 'tis a gratification
Only due to a strumpet, for it is injustice.
Shall I sprinkle the pure blood of innocents
To make those followers I call my friends
Look ruddier upon me? I am glad
This land, ta'en from the owner by such wrong,   50
Returns again unto so foul an use
As salary for his lust. Learn, good Delio,
To ask noble things of me, and you shall find
I'll be a noble giver.

DELIO   You instruct me well.

ANTONIO   [*aside*] Why, here's a man now would fright impudence
          From sauciest beggars.
PESCARA   Prince Ferdinand's come to Milan,
          Sick, as they give out, of an apoplexy;
          But some say 'tis a frenzy: I am going
          To visit him.   [*exit*
ANTONIO   'Tis a noble old fellow.
DELIO   What course do you mean to take, Antonio?   60
ANTONIO   This night I mean to venture all my fortune,
          Which is no more than a poor lingering life,
          To the Cardinal's worst of malice: I have got
          Private access to his chamber; and intend
          To visit him about the mid of night,
          As once his brother did our noble Duchess.
          It may be that the sudden apprehension
          Of danger – for I'll go in mine own shape –
          When he shall see it fraught with love and duty,
          May draw the poison out of him, and work   70
          A friendly reconcilement: if it fail,
          Yet it shall rid me of this infamous calling;
          For better fall once than be ever falling.
DELIO   I'll second you in all danger; and, howe'er,
          My life keeps rank with yours.
ANTONIO   You are still my loved and best friend.

                                                    [*exeunt*

                          SCENE 2

          A gallery in the Cardinal's palace at Milan

                  Enter PESCARA *and Doctor*

PESCARA   Now, doctor, may I visit your patient?
DOCTOR   If't please your lordship: but he's instantly
          To take the air here in the gallery
          By my direction.
PESCARA   Pray thee, what's his disease?
DOCTOR   A very pestilent disease, my lord,
          They call lycanthropia.
PESCARA   What's that?

I need a dictionary to't.

DOCTOR   I'll tell you.
In those that are possessed with't there o'erflows
Such melancholy humour they imagine
Themselves to be transforméd into wolves;   10
Steal forth to churchyards in the dead of night,
And dig dead bodies up: as two nights since
One met the Duke 'bout midnight in a lane
Behind Saint Mark's church, with the leg of a man
Upon his shoulder; and he howled fearfully;
Said he was a wolf, only the difference
Was, a wolf's skin was hairy on the outside,
His on the inside; bade them take their swords,
Rip up his flesh, and try: straight I was sent for,
And, having ministered to him, found his Grace   20
Very well recovered.

PESCARA   I am glad on't.

DOCTOR   Yet not without some fear
Of a relapse. If he grow to his fit again,
I'll go a nearer way to work with him
Than ever Paracelsus dreamed of; if
They'll give me leave, I'll buffet his madness
                              out of him.
Stand aside; he comes.

Enter FERDINAND, CARDINAL, MALATESTI *and* BOSOLA

FERDINAND Leave me.

MALATESTI Why doth your lordship love this solitariness?

FERDINAND Eagles commonly fly alone: they are crows, daws, and   30
starlings that flock together. Look, what's that follows
me?

MALATESTI Nothing, my lord.

FERDINAND Yes.

MALATESTI 'Tis your shadow.

FERDINAND Stay it; let it not haunt me.

MALATESTI Impossible, if you move, and the sun shine.

FERDINAND I will throttle it. [*throws himself down on his shadow*]

MALATESTI O, my lord, you are angry with nothing.

FERDINAND You are a fool: how is't possible I should catch my   40
shadow, unless I fall upon't? When I go to hell, I mean

              to carry a bribe; for, look you, good gifts evermore
              make way for the worst persons.

PESCARA   Rise, good my lord.

FERDINAND I am studying the art of patience.

PESCARA   'Tis a noble virtue.

FERDINAND To drive six snails before me from this town to Moscow;
              neither use goad nor whip to them, but let them take
              their own time – the patient'st man i'the world match
              me for an experiment – and I'll crawl after like a sheep-   50
              biter.

CARDINAL Force him up. [*they raise him*]

FERDINAND Use me well, you were best. What I have done, I have
              done: I'll confess nothing.

DOCTOR   Now let me come to him. Are you mad, my lord?
              Are you out of your princely wits?

FERDINAND   What's he?

PESCARA   Your doctor.

FERDINAND Let me have his beard sawed off, and his eyebrows
              filed more civil.

DOCTOR   I must do mad tricks with him, for that's the only way   60
              on't. I have brought your grace a salamander's skin to
              keep you from sun-burning.

FERDINAND I have cruel sore eyes.

DOCTOR   The white of a cockatrix's egg is present remedy.

FERDINAND Let it be a new laid one, you were best –
              Hide me from him: physicians are like kings,
              They brook no contradiction.

DOCTOR   Now he begins
              To fear me: now let me alone with him.

CARDINAL How now! Put off your gown!

DOCTOR   Let me have some forty urinals filled with rosewater: he   70
              and I'll go pelt one another with them – Now he begins
              to fear me – Can you fetch a frisk, sir? – Let him go, let
              him go, upon my peril: I find by his eye he stands in
              awe of me; I'll make him as tame as a dormouse.

FERDINAND Can you fetch your frisks, sir? I will stamp him into a
              cullis, flay off his skin, to cover one of the anatomies this
              rogue hath set i'the cold yonder in Barber-Surgeon's
              Hall. Hence, hence! You are all of you like beasts for

sacrifice: there's nothing left of you but tongue and
belly, flattery and lechery.   [*exit* 80

PESCARA   Doctor, he did not fear you throughly.

DOCTOR   True; I was somewhat too forward.

BOSOLA   Mercy upon me, what a fatal judgment
Hath fall'n upon this Ferdinand!

PESCARA   Knows your grace
What accident hath brought unto the prince
This strange distraction?

CARDINAL   [*aside*] I must feign somewhat – Thus they say
                                                it grew.
You have heard it rumoured, for these many years,
None of our family dies but there is seen
The shape of an old woman, which is given   90
By tradition to us to have been murdered
By her nephews for her riches. Such a figure
One night, as the prince sat up late at's book,
Appeared to him; when crying out for help,
The gentlemen of's chamber found his grace
All on a cold sweat, altered much in face
And language: since which apparition,
He hath grown worse and worse, and I much fear
He cannot live.

BOSOLA   Sir, I would speak with you.

PESCARA   We'll leave your grace,   100
Wishing to the sick prince, our noble lord,
All health of mind and body.

CARDINAL   You are most welcome.
                    [*exeunt Pescara, Malatesti and Doctor*
Are you come? So. [*aside*] This fellow must not know
By any means I had intelligence
In our Duchess' death; for, though I counselled it,
The full of all the engagement seemed to grow
From Ferdinand – Now, sir, how fares our sister?
I do not think but sorrow makes her look
Like to an oft-dyed garment: she shall now
Taste comfort from me. Why do you look so wildly?   110
O, the fortune of your master here the prince
Dejects you; but be you of happy comfort:

	If you'll do one thing for me I'll entreat,
	Though he had a cold tombstone o'er his bones,
	I'd make you what you would be.
BOSOLA	Any thing;
	Give it me in a breath, and let me fly to't:
	They that think long small expedition win,
	For musing much o'the end, cannot begin.

Enter JULIA

JULIA	Sir, will you come in to supper?
CARDINAL	I am busy; leave me.
JULIA	[*aside*] What an excellent shape hath that fellow! [*exit* 120
CARDINAL	'Tis thus. Antonio lurks here in Milan:
	Inquire him out, and kill him. While he lives,
	Our sister cannot marry; and I have thought
	Of an excellent match for her. Do this,
	And style me thy advancement.
BOSOLA	But by what means shall I find him out?
CARDINAL	There is a gentleman called Delio
	Here in the camp, that hath been long approved
	His loyal friend. Set eye upon that fellow;
	Follow him to mass; may be Antonio, 130
	Although he do account religion
	But a school-name, for fashion of the world
	May accompany him; or else go inquire out
	Delio's confessor, and see if you can bribe
	Him to reveal it. There are a thousand ways
	A man might find to trace him; as to know
	What fellows haunt the Jews for taking up
	Great sums of money, for sure he's in want;
	Or else to go to the picture-makers, and learn
	Who bought her picture lately: some of these 140
	Happily may take.
BOSOLA	Well, I'll not freeze i'the business:
	I would see that wretched thing, Antonio,
	Above all sights i'the world.
CARDINAL	Do, and be happy. [*exit*
BOSOLA	This fellow doth breed basilisks in's eyes,
	He's nothing else but murder; yet he seems
	Not to have notice of the Duchess' death.

'Tis his cunning: I must follow his example;
There cannot be a surer way to trace
Than that of an old fox.

Re-enter JULIA, *with a pistol*

JULIA   So, sir, you are well met.

BOSOLA   How now!

JULIA   Nay, the doors are fast enough: 150
Now, sir, I will make you confess your treachery.

BOSOLA   Treachery?

JULIA   Yes, confess to me
Which of my women 'twas you hired to put
Love-powder into my drink?

BOSOLA   Love-powder!

JULIA   Yes, when I was at Malfi.
Why should I fall in love with such a face else?
I have already suffered for thee so much pain,
The only remedy to do me good
Is to kill my longing.

BOSOLA   Sure, your pistol holds nothing but perfumes   160
Or kissing-comfits. Excellent lady,
You have a pretty way on't to discover
Your longing. Come, come, I'll disarm you,
And arm you thus: yet this is wondrous strange.

JULIA   Compare thy form and my eyes together,
You'll find my love no such great miracle.
Now you'll say
I am wanton: this nice modesty in ladies
Is but a troublesome familiar
That haunts them.   170

BOSOLA   Know you me, I am a blunt soldier.

JULIA   The better:
Sure, there wants fire where there are no lively sparks
Of roughness.

BOSOLA   And I want compliment.

JULIA   Why, ignorance
In courtship cannot make you do amiss,
If you have a heart to do well.

BOSOLA   You are very fair.

JULIA   Nay, if you lay beauty to my charge,
           I must plead unguilty.

BOSOLA   Your bright eyes
           Carry a quiver of darts in them sharper
           Than sunbeams.

JULIA   You will mar me with commendation,
           Put yourself to the charge of courting me,   180
           Whereas now I woo you.

BOSOLA   [aside] I have it, I will work upon this creature:
           Let us grow most amorously familiar –
           If the great Cardinal now should see me thus,
           Would he not count me a villain?

JULIA   No; he might count me a wanton,
           Not lay a scruple of offence on you;
           For if I see and steal a diamond,
           The fault is not i'the stone, but in me the thief
           That purloins it. I am sudden with you: 190
           We that are great women of pleasure use to cut off
           These uncertain wishes and unquiet longings,
           And in an instant join the sweet delight
           And the pretty excuse together. Had you been
                                              i'the street,
           Under my chamber-window, even there
           I should have courted you.

BOSOLA   O, you are an excellent lady!

JULIA   Bid me do somewhat for you presently
           To express I love you.

BOSOLA   I will; and if you love me,
           Fail not to effect it.
           The Cardinal is grown wondrous melancholy;   200
           Demand the cause, let him not put you off
           With feigned excuse; discover the main ground on't.

JULIA   Why would you know this?

BOSOLA   I have depended on him,
           And I hear that he is fall'n in some disgrace
           With the emperor: if he be, like the mice
           That forsake falling houses, I would shift
           To other dependence.

JULIA   You shall not need

Follow the wars: I'll be your maintenance.

BOSOLA   And I your loyal servant: but I cannot
Leave my calling.

JULIA   Not leave an ungrateful   210
General for the love of a sweet lady!
You are like some cannot sleep in feather-beds,
But must have blocks for their pillows.

BOSOLA   Will you do this?

JULIA   Cunningly.

BOSOLA   Tomorrow I'll expect the intelligence.

JULIA   Tomorrow! Get you into my cabinet;
You shall have it with you. Do not delay me,
No more than I do you: I am like one
That is condemned; I have my pardon promised,
But I would see it sealed. Go, get you in:
You shall see me wind my tongue about his heart   220
Like a skein of silk.   [exit Bosola

Re-enter CARDINAL

CARDINAL   Where are you?

Enter Servants

SERVANTS   Here.

CARDINAL   Let none, upon your lives, have conference
With the Prince Ferdinand, unless I know it. –
[*aside*] In this distraction he may reveal the murder.
                              [*exeunt Servants*
Yond's my lingering consumption: I am weary
Of her, and by any means would be quit of.

JULIA   How now, my lord! What ails you?

CARDINAL Nothing.

JULIA   O, you are much altered:
Come, I must be your secretary, and remove   230
This lead from off your bosom: what's the matter?

CARDINAL I may not tell you.

JULIA   Are you so far in love with sorrow
You cannot part with part of it? Or think you
I cannot love your grace when you are sad
As well as merry? Or do you suspect
I that have been a secret to your heart

These many winters, cannot be the same
Unto your tongue?

CARDINAL   Satisfy thy longing –
The only way to make thee keep my counsel   240
Is, not to tell thee.

JULIA   Tell your echo this –
Or flatterers, that like echoes still report
What they hear though most imperfect – and not me;
For if that you be true unto yourself,
I'll know.

CARDINAL   Will you rack me?

JULIA   No, judgment shall
Draw it from you: it is an equal fault,
To tell one's secrets unto all or none.

CARDINAL The first argues folly.

JULIA   But the last tyranny.

CARDINAL Very well: why, imagine I have committed
Some secret deed which I desire the world   250
May never hear of.

JULIA   Therefore may not I know it?
You have concealed for me as great a sin
As adultery. Sir, never was occasion
For perfect trial of my constancy
Till now: sir, I beseech you –

CARDINAL   You'll repent it.

JULIA   Never.

CARDINAL It hurries thee to ruin: I'll not tell thee.
Be well advised, and think what danger 'tis
To receive a prince's secrets: they that do,
Had need have their breasts hooped with adamant
To contain them. I pray thee, yet be satisfied;   260
Examine thine own frailty; 'tis more easy
To tie knots than unloose them: 'tis a secret
That, like a lingering poison, may chance lie
Spread in thy veins, and kill thee seven year hence.

JULIA Now you dally with me.

CARDINAL   No more; thou shalt know it.
By my appointment the great Duchess of Malfi
And two of her young children, four nights since,

Were strangled.

JULIA   O Heaven! Sir, what have you done!

CARDINAL How now? How settles this? Think you your bosom
          Will be a grave dark and obscure enough   270
          For such a secret?

JULIA   You have undone yourself, sir.

CARDINAL Why?

JULIA   It lies not in me to conceal it.

CARDINAL   No?
          Come, I will swear you to't upon this book.

JULIA   Most religiously.

CARDINAL   Kiss it. [*she kisses the book*]
          Now you shall never utter it; thy curiosity
          Hath undone thee: thou'rt poisoned with that book;
          Because I knew thou couldst not keep my counsel,
          I have bound thee to't by death.

                    Re-enter BOSOLA

BOSOLA   For pity-sake, hold!

CARDINAL   Ha, Bosola!

JULIA   I forgive you
          This equal piece of justice you have done;   280
          For I betrayed your counsel to that fellow:
          He overheard it; that was the cause I said
          It lay not in me to conceal it.

BOSOLA   O foolish woman,
          Couldst not thou have poisoned him?

JULIA   'Tis weakness,
          Too much to think what should have been done. I go,
          I know not whither. [*dies*]

CARDINAL   Wherefore com'st thou hither?

BOSOLA   That I might find a great man like yourself,
          Not out of his wits as the Lord Ferdinand,
          To remember my service.

CARDINAL I'll have thee hewed in pieces.   290

BOSOLA   Make not yourself such promise of that life
          Which is not yours to dispose of.

CARDINAL   Who placed thee here?

BOSOLA   Her lust, as she intended.

CARDINAL   Very well:

Now you know me for your fellow-murderer.

BOSOLA   And wherefore should you lay fair marble colours
            Upon your rotten purposes to me?
            Unless you imitate some that do plot great treasons,
            And when they have done, go hide themselves
                                          i'the graves
            Of those were actors in't?

CARDINAL   No more; there is a fortune attends thee.   300

BOSOLA   Shall I go sue to Fortune any longer?
            'Tis the fool's pilgrimage.

CARDINAL   I have honours in store for thee.

BOSOLA   There are many ways that conduct to
                                          seeming honour,
            And some of them very dirty ones.

CARDINAL   Throw to the devil
            Thy melancholy. The fire burns well;
            What need we keep a stirring of't, and make
            A greater smother? Thou wilt kill Antonio?

BOSOLA   Yes.

CARDINAL   Take up that body.

BOSOLA   I think I shall
            Shortly grow the common bier for churchyards.

CARDINAL   I will allow thee some dozen of attendants   310
            To aid thee in the murder.

BOSOLA   O, by no means. Physicians that apply horse-leeches to
            any rank swelling use to cut off their tails, that the
            blood may run through them the faster: let me have
            no train when I go to shed blood, lest it make me have
            a greater when I ride to the gallows.

CARDINAL   Come to me after midnight, to help to remove
            That body to her own lodging: I'll give out
            She died o'the plague; 'twill breed the less inquiry
            After her death.

BOSOLA   Where's Castruccio her husband?   320

CARDINAL   He's rode to Naples, to take possession
            Of Antonio's citadel.

BOSOLA   Believe me, you have done a very happy turn.

CARDINAL   Fail not to come: there is the master-key
            Of our lodgings; and by that you may conceive

What trust I plant in you.

BOSOLA   You shall find me ready.

[exit Cardinal

O poor Antonio, though nothing be so needful
To thy estate as pity, yet I find
Nothing so dangerous; I must look to my footing:
In such slippery ice-pavements men had need   330
To be frost-nailed well, they may break their
                               necks else;
The precedent's here afore me. How this man
Bears up in blood! Seems fearless! Why, 'tis well:
Security some men call the suburbs of hell,
Only a dead wall between. Well, good Antonio,
I'll seek thee out; and all my care shall be
To put thee into safety from the reach
Of these most cruel biters that have got
Some of thy blood already. It may be,
I'll join with thee in a most just revenge: 340
The weakest arm is strong enough that strikes
With the sword of justice. Still methinks the Duchess
Haunts me: there, there – 'tis nothing but my
                              melancholy.
O Penitence, let me truly taste thy cup,
That throws men down only to raise them up!

[exit

SCENE 3

A fortification at Milan

Enter ANTONIO *and* DELIO

DELIO   Yond's the Cardinal's window. This fortification
             Grew from the ruins of an ancient abbey;
             And to yond side o'the river lies a wall,
             Piece of a cloister, which in my opinion
             Gives the best echo that you ever heard,
             So hollow and so dismal, and withal
             So plain in the distinction of our words,
             That many have supposed it is a spirit
             That answers.

ANTONIO   I do love these ancient ruins.
             We never tread upon them but we set   10
             Our foot upon some reverend history:
             And, questionless, here in this open court,
             Which now lies naked to the injuries
             Of stormy weather, some men lie interred
             Loved the church so well, and gave so largely to't,
             They thought it should have canopied their bones
             Till doomsday; but all things have their end: churches
             And cities, which have diseases like to men,
             Must have like death that we have.

ECHO   'Like death that we have.'

DELIO   Now the echo hath caught you.   20

ANTONIO   It groaned, methought, and gave
             A very deadly accent.

ECHO   'Deadly accent.'

DELIO   I told you 'twas a pretty one: you may make it
             A huntsman, or a falconer, a musician,
             Or a thing of sorrow.

ECHO   'A thing of sorrow.'

ANTONIO   Ay, sure, that suits it best.

ECHO   'That suits it best.'

ANTONIO   'Tis very like my wife's voice.

ECHO   'Ay, wife's voice.'

DELIO   Come, let us walk further from't. I would not have

	You go to the Cardinal's tonight: do not.	
ECHO	'Do not.'	30
DELIO	Wisdom doth not more moderate wasting sorrow	
	Than time: take time for't; be mindful of thy safety.	
ECHO	'Be mindful of thy safety.'	
ANTONIO	Necessity compels me:	

Make scrutiny throughout the passages
Of your own life, you'll find it impossible
To fly your fate.

ECHO   'O, fly your fate.'

DELIO   Hark! The dead stones seem to have pity on you,
And give you good counsel.

ANTONIO   Echo, I will not talk with thee,
For thou art a dead thing.

ECHO   'Thou art a dead thing.'

ANTONIO   My duchess is asleep now,   40
And her little ones, I hope sweetly: O Heaven,
Shall I never see her more?

ECHO   'Never see her more.'

ANTONIO   I marked not one repetition of the echo
But that; and on the sudden a clear light
presented me a face folded in sorrow.

DELIO   Your fancy merely.

ANTONIO   Come, I'll be out of this ague,
For to live thus is not indeed to live;
It is a mockery and abuse of life:
I will not henceforth save myself by halves;
Lose all, or nothing.

DELIO   Your own virtue save you!   50
I'll fetch your eldest son, and second you:
It may be that the sight of his own blood
Spread in so sweet a figure may beget
The more compassion. However, fare you well.
Though in our miseries Fortune have a part,
Yet in our noble sufferings she hath none:
Contempt of pain, that we may call our own.

                                    [exeunt

SCENE 4

An apartment in the Cardinal's palace

Enter CARDINAL, PESCARA, MALATESTI, RODERIGO, *and* GRISOLAN

CARDINAL You shall not watch tonight by the sick prince;
    His Grace is very well recoveréd.

MALATESTI Good my lord, suffer us.

CARDINAL   O, by no means;
    The noise, and change of object in his eye,
    Doth more distract him: I pray, all to bed;
    And though you hear him in his violent fit,
    Do not rise, I entreat you.

PESCARA   So, sir; we shall not.

CARDINAL Nay, I must have you promise
    Upon your honours, for I was enjoined to't
    By himself; and he seemed to urge it sensibly.   10

PESCARA Let our honours bind this trifle.

CARDINAL Nor any of your followers.

MALATESTI   Neither.

CARDINAL It may be, to make trial of your promise.
    When he's asleep, myself will rise and feign
    Some of his mad tricks, and cry out for help,
    And feign myself in danger.

MALATESTI   If your throat were cutting,
    I'd not come at you, now I have protested against it.

CARDINAL Why, I thank you.

GRISOLAN   'Twas a foul storm tonight.

RODERIGO The Lord Ferdinand's chamber shook like an osier.

MALATESTI 'Twas nothing but pure kindness in the devil,   20
    To rock his own child.   [*exeunt all except the Cardinal*

CARDINAL The reason why I would not suffer these
    About my brother, is, because at midnight
    I may with better privacy convey
    Julia's body to her own lodging. O, my conscience!
    I would pray now; but the devil takes away my heart
    For having any confidence in prayer.
    About this hour I appointed Bosola
    To fetch the body: when he hath served my turn,

He dies.   [*exit* 30

Enter BOSOLA

BOSOLA   Ha! 'Twas the Cardinal's voice; I heard him name
            Bosola and my death. Listen; I hear one's footing.

Enter FERDINAND

FERDINAND Strangling is a very quiet death.

BOSOLA   [*aside*] Nay, then, I see I must stand upon my guard.

FERDINAND What say you to that? Whisper softly; do you agree
            to't? So; it must be done i'the dark: the Cardinal
            would not for a thousand pounds the doctor should
            see it.   [*exit*

BOSOLA   My death is plotted; here's the consequence of murder.
            We value not desert nor Christian breath,
            When we know black deeds must be cured
                                            with death.   40

Enter ANTONIO *and Servant*

SERVANT   Here stay, sir, and be confident, I pray:
            I'll fetch you a dark lantern.   [*exit*

ANTONIO   Could I take him
            At his prayers, there were hope of pardon.

BOSOLA   Fall right, my sword! [*stabs him*]
            I'll not give thee so much leisure as to pray.

ANTONIO   O, I am gone! Thou hast ended a long suit
            In a minute.

BOSOLA   What art thou?

ANTONIO   A most wretched thing,
            That only have thy benefit in death,
            To appear myself.

Re-enter Servant with a lantern

SERVANT   Where are you, sir?

ANTONIO   Very near my home – Bosola!

SERVANT   O, misfortune!   50

BOSOLA   Smother thy pity, thou art dead else – Antonio!
            The man I would have saved 'bove mine own life!
            We are merely the stars' tennis-balls, struck
                                            and bandied
            Which way please them – O good Antonio,

	I'll whisper one thing in thy dying ear

I'll whisper one thing in thy dying ear
Shall make thy heart break quickly! Thy fair Duchess
And two sweet children —

ANTONIO Their very names kindle a little life in me.

BOSOLA Are murderéd.

ANTONIO   Some men have wished to die
At the hearing of sad things; I am glad   60
That I shall do't in sadness: I would not now
Wish my wounds balmed nor healed, for I have
                                        no use
To put my life to. In all our quest of greatness,
Like wanton boys, whose pastime is their care,
We follow after bubbles blown in the air.
Pleasure of life, what is't? Only the good hours
Of an ague; merely a preparative to rest,
To endure vexation. I do ask
The process of my death; only commend me
To Delio.   70

BOSOLA Break, heart!

ANTONIO   And let my son fly the courts of princes.
                                            [dies]

BOSOLA Thou seem'st to have loved Antonio?

SERVANT   I brought him hither,
To have reconciled him to the Cardinal.

BOSOLA I do not ask thee that.
Take him up, if thou tender thine own life,
And bear him where the lady Julia
Was wont to lodge — O, my fate moves swift;
I have this Cardinal in the forge already;
Now I'll bring him to the hammer. O direful
                                        misprision!
I will not imitate things glorious,   80
No more than base; I'll be mine own example —
On, on! And look thou represent, for silence,
The thing thou bear'st.
                                        [exeunt

SCENE 5

Another apartment in the same

Enter Cardinal, with a book

CARDINAL   I am puzzled in a question about hell:
He says, in hell there's one material fire,
And yet it shall not burn all men alike.
Lay him by. How tedious is a guilty conscience!
When I look into the fish-ponds in my garden,
Methinks I see a thing armed with a rake,
That seems to strike at me.

Enter BOSOLA, *and Servant bearing* ANTONIO'*s body*

                          Now, art thou come?
Thou look'st ghastly:
There sits in thy face some great determination
Mixed with some fear.

BOSOLA   Thus it lightens into action: 10
I am come to kill thee.

CARDINAL   Ha! Help! Our guard!

BOSOLA   Thou art deceived; they are out of thy howling.

CARDINAL   Hold; and I will faithfully divide
Revenues with thee.

BOSOLA   Thy prayers and proffers
Are both unseasonable.

CARDINAL   Raise the watch!
We are betrayed!

BOSOLA   I have confined your flight:
I'll suffer your retreat to Julia's chamber,
But no further.

CARDINAL   Help! We are betrayed!

Enter, above, PESCARA, MALATESTI, RODERIGO *and* GRISOLAN

MALATESTI   Listen.

CARDINAL   My dukedom for rescue!

RODERIGO   Fie upon his counterfeiting!

MALATESTI   Why, 'tis not the Cardinal.

RODERIGO   Yes, yes, 'tis he: 20
But I'll see him hanged ere I'll go down to him.

CARDINAL	Here's a plot upon me; I am assaulted! I am lost,
	Unless some rescue.
GRISOLAN	He doth this pretty well;
	But it will not serve to laugh me out of mine honour.
CARDINAL	The sword's at my throat!
RODERIGO	You would not bawl so loud then.
MALATESTI	Come, come, let's go
	To bed: he told us thus much aforehand.
PESCARA	He wished you should not come at him; but, believe't,
	The accent of the voice sounds not in jest:
	I'll down to him, howsoever, and with engines 30
	Force ope the doors. [*exit above*
RODERIGO	Let's follow him aloof,
	And note how the Cardinal will laugh at him.
	[*exeunt, above, Malatesti, Roderigo and Grisolan*
BOSOLA	There's for you first, [*kills the Servant*]
	'Cause you shall not unbarricade the door
	To let in rescue.
CARDINAL	What cause hast thou to pursue my life?
BOSOLA	Look there.
CARDINAL	Antonio!
BOSOLA	Slain by my hand unwittingly.
	Pray, and be sudden: when thou killed'st thy sister,
	Thou took'st from Justice her most equal balance,
	And left her naught but her sword.
CARDINAL	O, mercy! 40
BOSOLA	Now it seems thy greatness was only outward;
	For thou fall'st faster of thyself than calamity
	Can drive thee. I'll not waste longer time; there!
	[*stabs him*]
CARDINAL	Thou hast hurt me.
BOSOLA	Again! [*stabs him again*]
CARDINAL	Shall I die like a leveret,
	Without any resistance? – Help, help, help! I am slain!

Enter FERDINAND

FERDINAND The alarum! Give me a fresh horse; rally the vaunt-
guard, or the day is lost. Yield, yield! I give you the
honour of arms, shake my sword over you; will you
yield?

CARDINAL Help me; I am your brother!   50
FERDINAND The devil! My brother fight upon the adverse party!
          [*he wounds the Cardinal, and, in the scuffle, gives Bosola
          his death-wound*]
          There flies your ransom.
CARDINAL   O Justice!
          I suffer now for what hath former been:
          Sorrow is held the eldest child of sin.
FERDINAND Now you're brave fellows. Caesar's fortune was harder
          than Pompey's; Caesar died in the arms of prosperity,
          Pompey at the feet of disgrace. You both died in the
          field. The pain's nothing: pain many times is taken
          away with the apprehension of greater, as the tooth-
          ache with the sight of the barber that comes to pull it 60
          out: there's philosophy for you.
BOSOLA   Now my revenge is perfect. Sink, thou main cause
          [*kills Ferdinand*]
          Of my undoing! The last part of my life
          Hath done me best service.
FERDINAND Give me some wet hay; I am broken-winded.
          I do account this world but a dog kennel:
          I will vault credit and affect high pleasures
          Beyond death.
BOSOLA   He seems to come to himself,
          Now he's so near the bottom.
FERDINAND My sister, O my sister! There's the cause on't.   70
          Whether we fall by ambition, blood, or lust,
          Like diamonds we are cut with our own dust. [*dies*]
CARDINAL Thou hast thy payment too.
BOSOLA   Yes, I hold my weary soul in my teeth;
          'Tis ready to part from me. I do glory
          That thou, which stood'st like a huge pyramid
          Begun upon a large and ample base,
          Shalt end in a little point, a kind of nothing.

          Enter below, PESCARA, MALATESTI, RODERIGO *and* GRISOLAN

PESCARA   How now, my lord!
MALATESTI   O sad disaster!
RODERIGO   How comes this?
BOSOLA   Revenge for the Duchess of Malfi murdered   80

By the Arragonian brethren; for Antonio
Slain by this hand; for lustful Julia
Poisoned by this man; and lastly for myself,
That was an actor in the main of all
Much 'gainst mine own good nature, yet i'the end
Neglected.

PESCARA   How now, my lord!

CARDINAL   Look to my brother:
He gave us these large wounds, as we were struggling
Here i'the rushes. And now, I pray, let me
Be laid by and never thought of. [*dies*]

PESCARA   How fatally, it seems, he did withstand   90
His own rescue!

MALATESTI   Thou wretched thing of blood,
How came Antonio by his death?

BOSOLA   In a mist; I know not how:
Such a mistake as I have often seen
In a play. O, I am gone!
We are only like dead walls or vaulted graves,
That, ruined, yield no echo. Fare you well.
It may be pain, but no harm, to me to die
In so good a quarrel. O, this gloomy world!
In what a shadow, or deep pit of darkness,   100
Doth womanish and fearful mankind live!
Let worthy minds ne'er stagger in distrust
To suffer death or shame for what is just:
Mine is another voyage. [*dies*]

PESCARA   The noble Delio, as I came to the palace,
Told me of Antonio's being here, and showed me
A pretty gentleman, his son and heir.

                    Enter DELIO *and* ANTONIO'S *son*

MALATESTI O sir, you come too late!

DELIO   I heard so, and
Was armed for't, ere I came. Let us make noble use
Of this great ruin; and join all our force   110
To establish this young hopeful gentleman
In's mother's right. These wretched eminent things
Leave no more fame behind 'em, than should one
Fall in a frost, and leave his print in snow;

As soon as the sun shines, it ever melts,
Both form and matter. I have ever thought
Nature doth nothing so great for great men
As when she's pleased to make them lords of truth:
Integrity of life is fame's best friend,
Which nobly, beyond death, shall crown the end.   120

                                        [*exeunt*

THE CHANGELING

INTRODUCTION

The Changeling was first performed in 1622–3 and not published until 1653. It was written by Thomas Middleton, probably in collaboration with William Rowley (*c.*1585–1626). Little is known of Rowley, but he appears to have collaborated with many of the important dramatists in the reign of James I.

The play tells the story of Beatrice Joanna, the beautiful but naive and spoilt daughter of Vermandero, governor of the castle of Alicante. She is due to marry an important courtier, Alonzo de Piracquo, but finds herself desiring the favours of Alsemero, a Valencian nobleman, whom she sees when leaving church. Unbeknown to her, Beatrice Joanna is herself desired by De Flores, a hideous and deformed gentleman of evil disposition in her father's service. Beatrice loathes the sight of him and constantly confesses that she wishes him dead. Alsemero and Beatrice communicate by letter through his friend Jasperino, who is in love with Diaphanta, Beatrice's maid. Beatrice asks for her wedding to be postponed for three days, which arouses the suspicions of Alonzo's brother, Tomazo. The lovers meet in secret. Alsemero suggests that he challenge his rival to a duel, but Beatrice is fearful of his chances of success. Instead she plans to use De Flores to murder Alonzo.

De Flores has been watching Alsemero and Beatrice, and has worked out that her affections have changed. His hope is that she will degenerate so far that she may finally agree to become the lover of one as hideous as himself. He readily agrees to commit the crime when asked. He takes Alonzo on a tour of the city, and lures him into a dark corner where he murders him and cuts off his finger as proof. Beatrice is shocked now the deed has been done; the ring was the first gift she gave him. She is even more shocked when De Flores demands that she become his lover and refuses all attempts to buy him off. The murder makes them partners in crime and so they should become sexual partners.

During the entertainments for Beatrice's wedding her father expresses surprise at the sudden disappearance of the bridegroom. Beatrice is able to marry Alsemero in his stead. As De Flores follows the bridal procession anticipating his triumph, he is disturbed by the appearance of Alonzo's ghost displaying the hand with the severed finger. Beatrice is now dreading her wedding night, as she will have to deceive an honourable man. She finds a key and so enters her husband's secret room. She discovers a laboratory, and a manuscript entitled *The Book of Experiment, Called the Secrets in Nature*, which tells the reader how to find out whether a woman is pregnant and whether she is a virgin. Beatrice decides to substitute Diaphanta for herself. In this way she is able to pass the tests and seemingly answer Alsemero's fears generated by the gossip at court.

However, Diaphanta appears to enjoy the wedding night with Alsemero rather too much. Beatrice becomes jealous and appeals to De Flores to help. He sets fire to Diaphanta's room and then murders her when she returns. However, Alsemero and his friend Jasperino discover De Flores and Beatrice in the garden and the game is up. Claiming that all was done for Alsemero's sake, Beatrice confesses to murder and adultery. De Flores confirms her story. Alsemero delivers the real murderers to Vermandero. Off-stage, De Flores stabs Beatrice, then himself.

The sub-plot, probably written by Rowley, concerns the attempts of Antonio, aided by his servant Franciscus, to woo Isabella, who is married to Alibius, an elderly and extremely jealous doctor who runs a sanatorium for the insane. Their foolishness nearly leads to their deaths when they are suspected of having murdered Alonzo, but all ends happily.

The Changeling is a powerful and subtle play. The title refers to a child switched at birth. The play asks the audience to consider what happens when people are born into vastly different circumstances. Do human beings inherit characteristics which determine their personalities from birth, or do the accidents of their very different lives mould them? Is De Flores evil because he is deformed and hence always doomed to be an outsider? If so, then why is the beautiful Beatrice Joanna also evil, or is it that she becomes so because of her way of life? De Flores pointedly reminds her that, like him, she is 'the deed's creature', and that she cannot ignore what he regards as their natural union. The horrific ending of the play, as the couple's love-making offstage is taken for cries of murder before they are sent down to hell, is a vivid image of beauty and the beast. But we are forced to consider who is really the more culpable of the two.

The Changeling has to be read in terms of the increasingly polarised religious debates of the early seventeenth century leading up to the English Civil War. On one side were the Calvinists who believed that mankind had no free will to act because God *had* planned all future events; on the other were the Armenians, who argued the opposite case, that God had granted mankind free will to act and that his omniscience did not limit the choice of human beings to be good or evil. Middleton's play suggests that its author was more familiar with the arguments of the Calvinists, but the questions it poses so brilliantly are not given definitive answers. The overall impression *The Changeling* leaves is that once anyone has started on the road to damnation it is very hard to turn back.

CHARACTERS IN THE PLAY

VERMANDERO, *father to Beatrice*

TOMAZO DE PIRACQUO, *a noble lord*

ALONZO DE PIRACQUO, *his brother, suitor to Beatrice*

ALSEMERO, *a nobleman, afterwards married to Beatrice*

JASPERINO, *his friend*

ALIBIUS, *a jealous doctor*

LOLLIO, *his man*

PEDRO, *friend to Antonio*

ANTONIO, *the changeling*

FRANCISCUS, *the counterfeit madman*

DE FLORES, *servant to Vermandero*

Madmen

Servants

BEATRICE, *daughter to Vermandero*

DIAPHANTA, *her waiting-woman*

ISABELLA, *wife to Alibius*

The Scene: Alicant

THE CHANGELING

Enter ALSEMERO

ALSEMERO 'Twas in the temple where I first beheld her,
And now again the same; what omen yet
Follows of that? None but imaginary.
Why should my hopes or fate be timorous?
The place is holy, so is my intent;
I love her beauties to the holy purpose,
And that, methinks, admits comparison
With man's first creation, the place blessed,
And is his right home back, if he achieve it.
The church hath first begun our interview,   10
And that's the place must join us into one,
So there's beginning and perfection too.

Enter JASPERINO

JASPERINO Oh, sir, are you here? Come, the wind's fair with you,
Y'are like to have a swift and pleasant passage.
ALSEMERO Sure, y'are deceived, friend, 'tis contrary
In my best judgment.
JASPERINO   What, for Malta?
If you could buy a gale amongst the witches,
They could not serve you such a lucky pennyworth
As comes a'God's name.
ALSEMERO   Even now I observed
The temple's vane to turn full in my face.   20
I know 'tis against me.
JASPERINO   Against you?
Then you know not where you are.
ALSEMERO   Not well, indeed.
JASPERINO Are you not well, sir?
ALSEMERO   Yes, Jasperino;
Unless there be some hidden malady
Within me, that I understand not.
JASPERINO   And that
I begin to doubt, sir. I never knew

> Your inclination to travels at a pause,
> With any cause to hinder it, till now.
> Ashore you were wont to call your servants up,
> And help to trap your horses for the speed;   30
> At sea I have seen you weigh the anchor with 'em,
> Hoist sails for fear to lose the foremost breath,
> Be in continual prayers for fair winds,
> And have you changed your orisons?

ALSEMERO   No, friend,
> I keep the same church, same devotion.

JASPERINO Lover I'm sure y'are none, the stoic was
> Found in you long ago. Your mother nor
> Best friends, who have set snares of beauty – ay,
> And choice ones too – could never trap you that way.
> What might be the cause?

ALSEMERO   Lord, how violent   40
> Thou art! I was but meditating of
> Somewhat I heard within the temple.

JASPERINO Is this violence? 'Tis but idleness
> Compared with your haste yesterday.

ALSEMERO I'm all this while a-going, man.

Enter Servants

JASPERINO Backwards, I think, sir. Look, your servants.

SERVANT The seamen call; shall we board your trunks?

ALSEMERO No, not today.

JASPERINO 'Tis the critical day, it seems, and the sign in Aquarius.

I SERVANT [*aside*] We must not to sea today; this smoke will 50
> bring forth fire!

ALSEMERO Keep all on shore; I do not know the end
> (Which needs I must do) of an affair in hand
> Ere I can go to sea.

I SERVANT Well, your pleasure.

2 SERVANT [*aside*] Let him e'en take his leisure too, we are safer
> on land.   [*exeunt Servants*

Enter BEATRICE, DIAPHANTA, *and Servants.*
> ALSEMERO *greets* BEATRICE *and kisses her*

JASPERINO [*aside*] How now! The laws of the Medes are changed
> sure! Salute a woman? He kisses too; wonderful! Where

learnt he this? And does it perfectly too; in my con- 60
science he ne'er rehearsed it before. Nay, go on, this
will be stranger and better news at Valencia than if
he had ransomed half Greece from the Turk.

BEATRICE   You are a scholar, sir?

ALSEMERO   A weak one, lady.

BEATRICE   Which of the sciences is this love you speak of?

ALSEMERO   From your tongue, I take it to be music.

BEATRICE   You are skilful in't, can sing at first sight.

ALSEMERO   And I have showed you all my skill at once.
I want more words to express me further,
And must be forced to repetition: 70
I love you dearly.

BEATRICE   Be better advised, sir;
Our eyes are sentinels unto our judgments,
And should give certain judgment what they see;
But they are rash sometimes and tell us wonders
Of common things, which, when our judgments
                                   find,
They then can check the eyes and call them blind.

ALSEMERO   But I am further, lady; yesterday
Was mine eyes' employment, and hither now
They brought my judgment, where are both agreed.
Both houses then consenting, 'tis agreed;   80
Only there wants the confirmation
By the hand royal – that's your part, lady.

BEATRICE   Oh, there's one above me, sir. [aside] For five
                                   days past
To be recalled! Sure, mine eyes were mistaken,
This was the man was meant me – That he
                              should come
So near his time, and miss it!

JASPERINO   [aside] We might have come by the carriers from
Valencia, I see, and saved all our sea provision; we are
at farthest sure. Methinks I should do something too;
I meant to be a venturer in this voyage. Yonder's 90
another vessel, I'll board her; if she be lawful prize,
down goes her top sail! [approaches Diaphanta]

Enter DE FLORES

DE FLORES   Lady, your father –
BEATRICE   Is in health, I hope.
DE FLORES   Your eye shall instantly instruct you, lady.
             He's coming hitherward.
BEATRICE   What needed then
             Your duteous preface? I had rather
             He had come unexpected; you must stall
             A good presence with unnecessary blabbing;
             And how welcome for your part you are,
             I'm sure you know.
DE FLORES   [*aside*] Will't never mend, this scorn,   100
             One side nor other? Must I be enjoined
             To follow still whilst she flies from me? Well,
             Fates do your worst, I'll please myself with sight
             Of her, at all opportunities,
             If but to spite her anger; I know she had
             Rather see me dead than living, and yet
             She knows no cause for't but a peevish will.
ALSEMERO   You seemed displeaséd, lady, on the sudden.
BEATRICE   Your pardon, sir, 'tis my infirmity;
             Nor can I other reason render you   110
             Than his or hers, of some particular thing
             They must abandon as a deadly poison,
             Which to a thousand other tastes were wholesome;
             Such to mine eyes is that same fellow there,
             The same that report speaks of the basilisk.
ALSEMERO   This is a frequent frailty in our nature;
             There's scarce a man among a thousand sound,
             But hath his imperfection: one distastes
             The scent of roses, which to infinites
             Most pleasing is, and odoriferous;   120
             One oil, the enemy of poison,
             Another wine, the cheerer of the heart,
             And lively refresher of the countenance.
             Indeed, this fault, if so it be, is general;
             There's scarce a thing but is both loved and loathed;
             Myself, I must confess, have the same frailty.

BEATRICE	And what may be your poison, sir? I am bold
	with you.
ALSEMERO	What might be your desire, perhaps; a cherry.
BEATRICE	I am no enemy to any creature
	My memory has, but yon gentleman. 130
ALSEMERO	He does ill to tempt your sight, if he knew it.
BEATRICE	He cannot be ignorant of that, sir,
	I have not spared to tell him so; and I want
	To help myself, since he's a gentleman
	In good respect with my father, and follows him.
ALSEMERO	He's out of his place then now. [they talk apart]
JASPERINO	I am a mad wag, wench.
DIAPHANTA	So methinks; but for your comfort I can tell you, we
	have a doctor in the city that undertakes the cure of such.
JASPERINO	Tush, I know what physic is best for the state of mine 140
	own body.
DIAPHANTA	'Tis scarce a well governed state, I believe.
JASPERINO	I could show thee such a thing with an ingredient that
	we two would compound together, and if it did not
	tame the maddest blood i'th'town for two hours after,
	I'll ne'er profess physic again.
DIAPHANTA	A little poppy, sir, were good to cause you sleep.
JASPERINO	Poppy? I'll give thee a pop i'th'lips for that first, and
	begin there; poppy is one simple indeed, and cuckoo
	(what you call't) another. I'll discover no more now, 150
	another time I'll show thee all.
BEATRICE	My father, sir.

Enter VERMANDERO *and Servants*

VERMAND.	Oh Joanna, I came to meet thee;
	Your devotion's ended?
BEATRICE	For this time, sir –
	[aside] I shall change my saint, I fear me; I find
	A giddy turning in me – Sir, this while
	I am beholding to this gentleman,
	Who left his own way to keep me company,
	And in discourse I find him much desirous
	To see your castle; he hath deserved it, sir, 160
	If ye please to grant it.
VERMAND.	With all my heart, sir.

Yet there's an article between: I must know
Your country; we use not to give survey
Of our chief strengths to strangers; our citadels
Are placed conspicuous to outward view,
On promonts' tops; but within are secrets.

ALSEMERO   A Valencian, sir.

VERMAND.   A Valencian?
That's native, sir; of what name, I beseech you?

ALSEMERO   Alsemero, sir.

VERMAND.   Alsemero; not the son
Of John de Alsemero?

ALSEMERO   The same, sir.   170

VERMAND.   My best love bids you welcome.

BEATRICE   [aside]   He was wont
To call me so, and then he speaks a most
Unfeignéd truth.

VERMAND.   Oh, sir, I knew your father;
We two were in acquaintance long ago,
Before our chins were worth Iulan down,
And so continued till the stamp of time
Had coined us into silver. Well, he's gone;
A good soldier went with him.

ALSEMERO   You went together in that, sir.

VERMAND.   No, by Saint Jaques, I came behind him.   180
Yet I have done somewhat too; an unhappy day
Swallowed him at last at Gibraltar
In fight with those rebellious Hollanders,
Was it not so?

ALSEMERO   Whose death I had revenged,
Or followed him in fate, had not the late league
Prevented me.

VERMAND.   Ay, ay, 'twas time to breathe –
Oh Joanna, I should ha' told thee news,
I saw Piracquo lately.

BEATRICE   [aside]   That's ill news.

VERMAND.   He's hot preparing for this day of triumph:
Thou must be a bride within this sennight.

ALSEMERO   [aside]   Ha!   190

BEATRICE   Nay, good sir, be not so violent; with speed

I cannot render satisfaction
Unto the dear companion of my soul,
Virginity, whom I thus long have lived with,
And part with it so rude and suddenly;
Can such friends divide, never to meet again,
Without a solemn farewell?

VERMAND.   Tush, tush! There's a toy.

ALSEMERO [*aside*] I must now part, and never meet again
With any joy on earth – Sir, your pardon,
My affairs call on me.

VERMAND.   How, sir? By no means;   200
Not changed so soon, I hope. You must see
                                    my castle,
And her best entertainment, ere we part;
I shall think myself unkindly uséd else.
Come, come, let's on; I had good hope your stay
Had been a while with us in Alicant;
I might have bid you to my daughter's wedding.

ALSEMERO [*aside*] He means to feast me, and poisons me
                                beforehand –
I should be dearly glad to be there, sir,
Did my occasions suit as I could wish.

BEATRICE I shall be sorry if you be not there   210
When it is done, sir – but not so suddenly.

VERMAND. I tell you, sir, the gentleman's complete,
A courtier and a gallant, enriched
With many fair and noble ornaments;
I would not change him for a son-in-law
For any he in Spain, the proudest he,
And we have great ones, that you know.

ALSEMERO   He's much
Bound to you, sir.

VERMAND.   He shall be bound to me,
As fast as this tie can hold him; I'll want
My will else.

BEATRICE [*aside*]   I shall want mine if you do it.   220

VERMAND. But come, by the way I'll tell you more of him.

ALSEMERO [*aside*] How shall I dare to venture in his castle,
When he discharges murderers at the gate?

	But I must on, for back I cannot go.
BEATRICE	[aside] Not this serpent gone yet? [drops a glove]
VERMAND.	Look, girl, thy glove's fall'n.
	Stay, stay; De Flores, help a little.

             [exeunt Vermandero, Alsemero, Jasperino and Servants

DE FLORES	[offers the glove] Here, lady.
BEATRICE	Mischief on your officious forwardness!
	Who bade you stoop? They touch my hand no more.
	There! For t'other's sake I part with this; 230
	[takes off the other glove and throws it down]
	Take 'em and draw thine own skin off with 'em.

             [exeunt Beatrice and Diaphanta

DE FLORES	Here's a favour come, with a mischief! Now I know
	She had rather wear my pelt tanned in a pair
	Of dancing pumps than I should thrust my fingers
	Into her sockets here; I know she hates me,
	Yet cannot choose but love her;
	No matter; if but to vex her, I'll haunt her still;
	Though I get nothing else, I'll have my will.

             [exit

SCENE 2

Enter ALIBIUS *and* LOLLIO

ALIBIUS	Lollio, I must trust thee with a secret,
	But thou must keep it.
LOLLIO	I was ever close to a secret, sir.
ALIBIUS	The diligence that I have found in thee,
	The care and industry already past,
	Assures me of thy good continuance.
	Lollio, I have a wife.
LOLLIO	Fie, sir, 'tis too late to keep her secret, she's known to
	be married all the town and country over.
ALIBIUS	Thou goest too fast, my Lollio; that knowledge 10
	I allow no man can be barred it;
	But there is a knowledge which is nearer,
	Deeper, and sweeter, Lollio.

LOLLIO	Well, sir, let us handle that between you and I.
ALIBIUS	'Tis that I go about, man. Lollio, My wife is young.
LOLLIO	So much the worse to be kept secret, sir.
ALIBIUS	Why, now thou meet'st the substance of the point; I am old, Lollio.
LOLLIO	No, sir, 'tis I am old Lollio. 20
ALIBIUS	Yet why may not this concord and sympathize? Old trees and young plants often grow together, Well enough agreeing.
LOLLIO	Ay, sir, but the old trees raise themselves higher and broader than the young plants.
ALIBIUS	Shrewd application! There's the fear, man: I would wear my ring on my own finger; Whilst it is borrowed it is none of mine, But his that useth it.
LOLLIO	You must keep it on still then; if it but lie by, 30 One or other will be thrusting into't.
ALIBIUS	Thou conceiv'st me, Lollio; here thy watchful eye Must have employment; I cannot always be At home.
LOLLIO	I dare swear you cannot.
ALIBIUS	I must look out.
LOLLIO	I know't; you must look out, 'tis every man's case.
ALIBIUS	Here, I do say, must thy employment be: To watch her treadings, and in my absence Supply my place. 40
LOLLIO	I'll do my best, sir; yet surely I cannot see who you should have cause to be jealous of.
ALIBIUS	Thy reason for that, Lollio? 'Tis a comfortable question.
LOLLIO	We have but two sorts of people in the house, and both under the whip, that's fools and madmen; the one has not wit enough to be knaves, and the other not knavery enough to be fools.
ALIBIUS	Ay, those are all my patients, Lollio. I do profess the cure of either sort; My trade, my living 'tis, I thrive by it; 50 But here's the care that mixes with my thrift:

The daily visitants, that come to see
My brainsick patients, I would not have
To see my wife: gallants I do observe
Of quick enticing eyes, rich in habits,
Of stature and proportion very comely:
These are most shrewd temptations, Lollio.

LOLLIO   They maybe easily answered, sir; if they come to see
the fools and madmen, you and I may serve the turn,
and let my mistress alone, she's of neither sort.   60

ALIBIUS   'Tis a good ward; indeed, come they to see
Our madmen or our fools, let 'em see no more
Than what they come for; by that consequent
They must not see her, I'm sure she's no fool.

LOLLIO   And I'm sure she's no madman.

ALIBIUS   Hold that buckler fast, Lollio, my trust
Is on thee, and I account it firm and strong.
What hour is't, Lollio?

LOLLIO   Towards belly-hour, sir.

ALIBIUS   Dinner time? Thou mean'st twelve o'clock?   70

LOLLIO   Yes, sir, for every part has his hour: we wake at six and
look about us, that's eye-hour; at seven we should pray,
that's knee-hour; at eight walk, that's leg-hour; at nine
gather flowers and pluck a rose, that's nose-hour; at ten
we drink, that's mouth-hour; at eleven lay about us for
victuals, that's hand-hour; at twelve go to dinner, that's
belly-hour.

ALIBIUS   Profoundly, Lollio! It will be long
Ere all thy scholars learn this lesson, and
I did look to have a new one entered – stay,   80
I think my expectation is come home.

Enter PEDRO *and* ANTONIO *like an idiot*

PEDRO   Save you, sir; my business speaks itself,
This sight takes off the labour of my tongue.

ALIBIUS   Ay, ay, sir,
'Tis plain enough; you mean him for my patient.

PEDRO   And if your pains prove but commodious, to give but
some little strength to the sick and weak part of nature
in him, these are but patterns [*gives him money*] to show
you of the whole pieces that will follow to you, beside

	the charge of diet, washing and other necessaries fully 90 defrayed.
ALIBIUS	Believe it, sir, there shall no care be wanting.
LOLLIO	Sir, an officer in this place may deserve something; the trouble will pass through my hands.
PEDRO	'Tis fit something should come to your hands then, sir. [*gives him money*]
LOLLIO	Yes, sir, 'tis I must keep him sweet, and read to him; what is his name?
PEDRO	His name is Antonio; marry, we use but half to him, only Tony. 100
LOLLIO	Tony, Tony; 'tis enough, and a very good name for a fool; what's your name, Tony?
ANTONIO	He, he, he! Well, I thank you, cousin; he, he, he!
LOLLIO	Good boy! Hold up your head. He can laugh; I perceive by that he is no beast.
PEDRO	Well, sir, If you can raise him but to any height, Any degree of wit, might he attain (As I might say) to creep but on all four Towards the chair of wit, or walk on crutches, 110 'Twould add an honour to your worthy pains, And a great family might pray for you, To which he should be heir, had he discretion To claim and guide his own; assure you, sir, He is a gentleman.
LOLLIO	Nay, there's nobody doubted that; at first sight I knew him for a gentleman, he looks no other yet.
PEDRO	Let him have good attendance and sweet lodging.
LOLLIO	As good as my mistress lies in, sir; and as you allow us time and means, we can raise him to the higher degree 120 of discretion.
PEDRO	Nay, there shall no cost want, sir.
LOLLIO	He will hardly be stretched up to the wit of a magnifico.
PEDRO	Oh no, that's not to be expected, far shorter will be enough.
LOLLIO	I'll warrant you [I'll] make him fit to bear office in five weeks; I'll undertake to wind him up to the wit of constable.

PEDRO	If it be lower than that it might serve turn.
LOLLIO	No, fie, to level him with a headborough, beadle, or 130 watchman were but little better than he is; constable I'll able him; if he do come to be a justice afterwards, let him thank the keeper. Or I'll go further with you; say I do bring him up to my own pitch, say I make him as wise as myself.
PEDRO	Why, there I would have it.
LOLLIO	Well, go to; either I'll be as arrant a fool as he, or he shall be as wise as I, and then I think 'twill serve his turn.
PEDRO	Nay, I do like thy wit passing well.
LOLLIO	Yes, you may; yet if I had not been a fool, I had had 140 more wit than I have too; remember what state you find me in.
PEDRO	I will, and so leave you; your best cares, I beseech you.
	[exit Pedro
ALIBIUS	Take you none with you; leave 'em all with us.
ANTONIO	Oh, my cousin's gone, cousin, cousin, oh!
LOLLIO	Peace, peace, Tony; you must not cry, child, you must be whipped if you do; your cousin is here still; I am your cousin, Tony.
ANTONIO	He, he! Then I'll not cry, if thou be'st my cousin; he, he, he! 150
LOLLIO	I were best try his wit a little, that I may know what form to place him in.
ALIBIUS	Ay, do, Lollio, do.
LOLLIO	I must ask him easy questions at first; Tony, how many true fingers has a tailor on his right hand?
ANTONIO	As many as on his left, cousin.
LOLLIO	Good; and how many on both?
ANTONIO	Two less than a deuce, cousin.
LOLLIO	Very well answered; I come to you again, cousin Tony; how many fools goes to a wise man? 160
ANTONIO	Forty in a day sometimes, cousin.
LOLLIO	Forty in a day? How prove you that?
ANTONIO	All that fall out amongst themselves, and go to a lawyer to be made friends.
LOLLIO	A parlous fool! He must sit in the fourth form at least, I

	perceive that; I come again, Tony; how many knaves make an honest man?
ANTONIO	I know not that, cousin.
LOLLIO	No, the question is too hard for you: I'll tell you, cousin, there's three knaves may make an honest man, 170 a sergeant, a jailer, and a beadle; the sergeant catches him, the jailer holds him and the beadle lashes him; and if he be not honest then, the hangman must cure him.
ANTONIO	Ha, ha, ha! That's fine sport, cousin.
ALIBIUS	This was too deep a question for the fool, Lollio.
LOLLIO	Yes, this might have served yourself, though I say't; once more, and you shall go play, Tony.
ANTONIO	Ay, play at push-pin, cousin; ha, he!
LOLLIO	So thou shalt; say how many fools are here –
ANTONIO	Two, cousin, thou and I. 180
LOLLIO	Nay, y'are too forward there, Tony; mark my question: how many fools and knaves are here? A fool before a knave, a fool behind a knave, between every two fools a knave; how many fools, how many knaves?
ANTONIO	I never learnt so far, cousin.
ALIBIUS	Thou putt'st too hard questions to him, Lollio.
LOLLIO	I'll make him understand it easily. Cousin, stand there.
ANTONIO	Ay, cousin.
LOLLIO	Master, stand you next the fool.
ALIBIUS	Well, Lollio? 190
LOLLIO	Here's my place. Mark now, Tony, there['s] a fool before a knave.
ANTONIO	That's I, cousin.
LOLLIO	Here's a fool behind a knave, that's I; and between us two fools there is a knave, that's my master; 'tis but we three, that's all.
ANTONIO	We three, we three, cousin.
MADMAN	[Madmen within] Put's head i'th'pillory, the bread's too little.
MADMAN	Fly, fly, and he catches the swallow.
MADMAN	Give her more onion, or the devil put the rope about 200 her crag.
LOLLIO	You may hear what time of day it is, the chimes of Bedlam goes.

ALIBIUS   Peace, peace, or the wire comes!

3 MADMAN Cat whore, cat whore, her parmasant, her parmasant!

ALIBIUS   Peace, I say! Their hour's come, they must be fed, Lollio.

LOLLIO   There's no hope of recovery of that Welsh madman, was undone by a mouse that spoiled him a parmasant; lost his wits for't.   210

ALIBIUS   Go to your charge, Lollio, I'll to mine.

LOLLIO   Go you to your madmen's ward, let me alone with your fools.

ALIBIUS   And remember my last charge, Lollio.   [exit

LOLLIO   Of which your patients do you think I am? Come, Tony, you must amongst your school-fellows now; there's pretty scholars amongst 'em, I can tell you, there's some of 'em at *stultus, stulta, stultum*.

ANTONIO   I would see the madmen, cousin, if they would not bite me.   220

LOLLIO   No, they shall not bite thee, Tony.

ANTONIO   They bite when they are at dinner, do they not, coz?

LOLLIO   They bite at dinner, indeed, Tony. Well, I hope to get credit by thee; I like thee the best of all the scholars that ever I brought up, and thou shalt prove a wise man, or I'll prove a fool myself.

                                                          [*exeunt*

ACT 2 SCENE 1

Enter BEATRICE *and* JASPERINO *severally*

BEATRICE   Oh, sir, I'm ready now for that fair service
      Which makes the name of friend sit glorious on you.
      Good angels and this conduct be your guide;
      [*gives a paper*] Fitness of time and place is there
                              set down, sir.

JASPERINO   The joy I shall return rewards my service.   [*exit*

BEATRICE   How wise is Alsemero in his friend!
      It is a sign he makes his choice with judgment.
      Then I appear in nothing more approved
      Than making choice of him;
      For 'tis a principle, he that can choose   10
      That bosom well, who of his thoughts partakes,
      Proves most discreet in every choice he makes.
      Methinks I love now with the eyes of judgment,
      And see the way to merit, clearly see it.
      A true deserver like a diamond sparkles,
      In darkness you may see him, that's in absence,
      Which is the greatest darkness falls on love;
      Yet he is best discerned then
      With intellectual eyesight. 'What's Piracquo
      My father spends his breath for? And his blessing   20
      Is only mine as I regard his name,
      Else it goes from me, and turns head against me,
      Transformed into a curse; some speedy way
      Must be remembered; he's so forward too,
      So urgent that way, scarce allows me breath
      To speak to my new comforts.

Enter DE FLORES

DE FLORES   [*aside*]   Yonder's she.
      Whatever ails me, now alate especially,
      I can as well be hanged as refrain seeing her;
      Some twenty times a day, nay, not so little,
      Do I force errands, frame ways and excuses   30
      To come into her sight, and I have small reason for't,
      And less encouragement; for she baits me still

Every time worse than other, does profess herself
The cruellest enemy to my face in town,
At no hand can abide the sight of me,
As if danger or ill luck hung in my looks.
I must confess my face is bad enough,
But I know far worse has better fortune,
And not endured alone, but doted on;
And yet such pick-haired faces, chins like witches',   40
Here and there five hairs, whispering in a corner,
As if they grew in fear one of another,
Wrinkles like troughs, where swine-deformity swills
The tears of perjury that lie there like wash
Fallen from the slimy and dishonest eye;
Yet such a one plucks sweets without restraint,
And has the grace of beauty to his sweet.
Though my hard fate has thrust me out to servitude,
I tumbled into th'world a gentleman.
She turns her blessed eye upon me now,   50
And I'll endure all storms before I part with't.

BEATRICE   [aside] Again!
This ominous ill-faced fellow more disturbs me
Than all my other passions.

DE FLORES   [aside]   Now't begins again;
I'll stand this storm of hail though the stones pelt me.

BEATRICE   Thy business? What's thy business?

DE FLORES   [aside]   Soft and fair,
I cannot part so soon now.

BEATRICE   [aside]   The villain's fixed –
Thou standing toad-pool!

DE FLORES   [aside]   The shower falls amain now.

BEATRICE   Who sent thee? What's thy errand? Leave my sight.

DE FLORES   My lord your father charged me to deliver   60
A message to you.

BEATRICE   What, another since?
Do't and be hanged then; let me be rid of thee.

DE FLORES   True service merits mercy.

BEATRICE   What's thy message?

DE FLORES   Let beauty settle but in patience,

You shall hear all.

BEATRICE   A dallying, trifling torment!

DE FLORES Signor Alonzo de Piracquo, lady,
Sole brother to Tomazo de Piracquo –

BEATRICE Slave, when wilt make an end?

DE FLORES   Too soon I shall.

BEATRICE What all this while of him?

DE FLORES   The said Alonzo,
With the foresaid Tomazo –

BEATRICE   Yet again?   70

DE FLORES Is new alighted.

BEATRICE   Vengeance strike the news!
Thou thing most loathed, what cause was there in this
To bring thee to my sight?

DE FLORES   My lord your father
Charged me to seek you out.

BEATRICE   Is there no other
To send his errand by?

DE FLORES   It seems 'tis my luck
To be i'th'way still.

BEATRICE   Get thee from me.

DE FLORES [aside]   So!
Why, am not I an ass to devise ways
Thus to be railed at? I must see her still!
I shall have a mad qualm within this hour again,
I know't, and, like a common garden-bull,   80
I do but take breath to be lugged again.
What this may bode I know not; I'll despair the less,
Because there's daily precedents of bad faces
Beloved beyond all reason; these foul chops
May come into favour one day 'mongst his fellows;
Wrangling has proved the mistress of good pastime;
As children cry themselves asleep, I ha' seen
Women have chid themselves abed to men.
                                    [exit de Flores

BEATRICE I never see this fellow, but I think
Of some harm towards me, danger's in my mind still;   90
I scarce leave trembling of an hour after.
The next good mood I find my father in,

           I'll get him quite discarded. Oh, I was
           Lost in this small disturbance, and forgot
           Affliction's fiercer torrent that now comes
           To bear down all my comforts.

             Enter VERMANDERO, ALONZO, TOMAZO

VERMAND.   Y'are both welcome,
           But an especial one belongs to you, sir,
           To whose most noble name our love presents
           The addition of a son, our son Alonzo.
ALONZO   The treasury of honour cannot bring forth   100
           A title I should more rejoice in, sir.
VERMAND. You have improved it well; daughter, prepare,
           The day will steal upon thee suddenly.
BEATRICE   [*aside*] Howe'er, I will be sure to keep the night,
           If it should come so near me.
           [*Beatrice and Vermandero talk apart*]
TOMAZO   Alonzo.
ALONZO   Brother?
TOMAZO   In troth I see small welcome in her eye.
ALONZO   Fie, you are too severe a censurer
           Of love in all points, there's no bringing on you;
           If lovers should mark everything a fault,
           Affection would be like an ill-set book,   110
           Whose faults might prove as big as half the volume.
BEATRICE   That's all I do entreat.
VERMAND.   It is but reasonable,
           I'll see what my son says to't: son Alonzo,
           Here's a motion made but to reprieve
           A maidenhead three days longer; the request
           Is not far out of reason, for indeed
           The former time is pinching.
ALONZO   Though my joys
           Be set back so much time as I could wish
           They had been forward, yet since she desires it,
           The time is set as pleasing as before,   120
           I find no gladness wanting.
VERMAND.   May I ever
           Meet it in that point still! Y'are nobly welcome, sirs.
           [*exeunt Vermandero and Beatrice*

TOMAZO	So: did you mark the dulness of her parting now?
ALONZO	What dulness? Thou art so exceptious still!
TOMAZO	Why, let it go then, I am but a fool
	To mark your harms so heedfully.
ALONZO	Where's the oversight?
TOMAZO	Come, your faith's cozened in her, strongly cozened;
	Unsettle your affection with all speed
	Wisdom can bring it to, your peace is ruined else.
	Think what a torment 'tis to marry one 130
	Whose heart is leaped into another's bosom;
	If ever pleasure she receive from thee,
	It comes not in thy name, or of thy gift;
	She lies but with another in thine arms,
	He the half-father unto all thy children
	In the conception; if he get 'em not,
	She helps to get 'em for him, and how dangerous
	And shameful her restraint may go in time to,
	It is not to be thought on without sufferings.
ALONZO	You speak as if she loved some other, then. 140
TOMAZO	Do you apprehend so slowly?
ALONZO	Nay, an that
	Be your fear only, I am safe enough.
	Preserve your friendship and your counsel, brother,
	For time of more distress; I should depart
	An enemy, a dangerous, deadly one,
	To any but thyself, that should but think
	She knew the meaning of inconstancy,
	Much less the use and practice; yet we are friends;
	Pray, let no more be urged; I can endure
	Much, till I meet an injury to her, 150
	Then I am not myself. Farewell, sweet brother;
	How much we are bound to heaven to depart lovingly.
	[exit
TOMAZO	Why, here is love's tame madness; thus a man
	Quickly steals into his vexation.
	[exit

SCENE 2

Enter DIAPHANTA *and* ALSEMERO

DIAPHANTA The place is my charge, you have kept your hour,
And the reward of a just meeting bless you.
I hear my lady coming; complete gentleman,
I dare not be too busy with my praises,
Th'are dangerous things to deal with.   [*exit*

ALSEMERO   This goes well;
These women are the ladies' cabinets,
Things of most precious trust are locked into 'em.

Enter BEATRICE

BEATRICE I have within my eye all my desires;
Requests that holy prayers ascend heaven for,
And bring 'em down to furnish our defects,   10
Come not more sweet to our necessities
Than thou unto my wishes.

ALSEMERO   We are so like
In our expressions, lady, that unless I borrow
The same words, I shall never find their equals.

BEATRICE How happy were this meeting, this embrace,
If it were free from envy! This poor kiss,
It has an enemy, a hateful one,
That wishes poison to't; how well were I now
If there were none such name known as Piracquo,
Nor no such tie as the command of parents!   20
I should be but too much blessed.

ALSEMERO   One good service
Would strike off both your fears, and I'll go near
                                        it too,
Since you are so distressed; remove the cause,
The command ceases, so there's two fears blown out
With one and the same blast.

BEATRICE   Pray, let me find you, sir.
What might that service be so strangely happy?

ALSEMERO The honourablest piece 'bout man, valour.
I'll send a challenge to Piracquo instantly.

BEATRICE How? Call you that extinguishing of fear,

When 'tis the only way to keep it flaming?   30
Are not you ventured in the action,
That's all my joys and comforts? Pray, no more, sir.
Say you prevailed, y'are dangerous and not mine then;
The law would claim you from me, or obscurity
Be made the grave to bury you alive.
I'm glad these thoughts come forth; oh, keep not one
Of this condition, sir; here was a course
Found to bring sorrow on her way to death;
The tears would ne'er ha' dried till dust had
                        choked 'em.

Blood-guiltiness becomes a fouler visage –   40
[*aside*] And now I think on one. I was to blame,
I ha' marred so good a market with my scorn;
'T had been done questionless; the ugliest creature
Creation framed for some use, yet to see
I could not mark so much where it should be!

ALSEMERO Lady –
BEATRICE [*aside*]   Why, men of art make much of poison,
Keep one to expel another; where was my art?
ALSEMERO Lady, you hear not me.
BEATRICE   I do especially, sir;
The present times are not so sure of our side
As those hereafter may be; we must use 'em then   50
As thrifty folk their wealth, sparingly now,
Till the time opens.
ALSEMERO   You teach wisdom, lady.
BEATRICE Within there! Diaphanta!

Enter DIAPHANTA

DIAPHANTA   Do you call, madam?
BEATRICE Perfect your service, and conduct this gentleman
The private way you brought him.
DIAPHANTA   I shall, madam.
ALSEMERO My love's as firm as love e'er built upon.
                [*exeunt Diaphanta and Alsemero*

Enter DE FLORES

DE FLORES [*aside*] I have watched this meeting, and do
                      wonder much

What shall become of t'other; I'm sure both
Cannot be served unless she transgress; happily
Then I'll put in for one; for if a woman   60
Fly from one point, from him she makes a husband,
She spreads and mounts then like arithmetic,
One, ten, a hundred, a thousand, ten thousand,
Proves in time sutler to an army royal.
Now do I look to be most richly railed at,
Yet I must see her.

BEATRICE   [*aside*]   Why, put case I loathed him
As much as youth and beauty hates a sepulchre,
Must I needs show it? Cannot I keep that secret
And serve my turn upon him? – See, he's here.
De Flores!

DE FLORES   [*aside*]   Ha, I shall run mad with joy!   70
She called me fairly by my name, De Flores,
And neither rogue nor rascal.

BEATRICE   What ha' you done
To your face a–late? Y'have met with some
                      good physician;
Y'have pruned yourself, methinks; you were
                      not wont
To look so amorously.

DE FLORES   [*aside*] Not I.
'Tis the same physnomy, to a hair and pimple,
Which she called scurvy scarce an hour ago;
How is this?

BEATRICE   Come hither; nearer, man.

DE FLORES   [*aside*] I'm up to the chin in heaven!

BEATRICE   Turn, let me see;
Faugh, 'tis but the heat of the liver, I perceiv't;   80
I thought it had been worse.

DE FLORES   [*aside*]   Her fingers touched me!
She smells all amber.

BEATRICE   I'll make a water for you shall cleanse this
Within a fortnight.

DE FLORES   With your own hands, lady?

BEATRICE   Yes, mine own, sir; in a work of cure

                I'll trust no other.

DE FLORES   [*aside*]   'Tis half an act of pleasure
                To hear her talk thus to me.

BEATRICE   When we are used
                To a hard face, 'tis not so unpleasing;
                It mends still in opinion, hourly mends,
                I see it by experience.

DE FLORES   [*aside*]   I was blessed   90
                To light upon this minute; I'll make use on't.

BEATRICE   Hardness becomes the visage of a man well,
                It argues service, resolution, manhood,
                If cause were of employment.

DE FLORES   'Twould be soon seen,
                If e'er your ladyship had cause to use it.
                I would but wish the honour of a service
                So happy as that mounts to.

BEATRICE   We shall try you –
                O my De Flores!

DE FLORES   [*aside*]   How's that? She calls me hers
                Already, my De Flores! – You were about
                To sigh out somewhat, madam?

BEATRICE   No, was I?   100
                I forgot – Oh!

DE FLORES   There 'tis again, the very fellow on't.

BEATRICE   You are too quick, sir.

DE FLORES   There's no excuse for't now; I heard it twice, madam;
                That sigh would fain have utterance, take pity on't,
                And lend it a free word; 'las, how it labours
                For liberty! I hear the murmur yet
                Beat at your bosom.

BEATRICE   Would creation –

DE FLORES   Ay, well said, that's it.

BEATRICE   Had formed me man!

DE FLORES   Nay, that's not it.

BEATRICE   Oh, 'tis the soul of freedom!
                I should not then be forced to marry one   110
                I hate beyond all depths; I should have power
                Then to oppose my loathings, nay, remove 'em
                For ever from my sight.

DE FLORES [*aside*]   O blest occasion!
Without change to your sex, you have your wishes.
Claim so much man in me.

BEATRICE   In thee, De Flores?
There's small cause for that.

DE FLORES   Put it not from me;
[*kneels*] It's a service that I kneel for to you.

BEATRICE You are too violent to mean faithfully;
There's horror in my service, blood and danger;
Can those be things to sue for?

DE FLORES   If you knew   120
How sweet it were to me to be employed
In any act of yours, you would say then
I failed, and used not reverence enough
When I receive the charge on't.

BEATRICE [*aside*]   This is much, methinks;
Belike his wants are greedy, and to such
Gold tastes like angel's food – Rise.

DE FLORES I'll have the work first.

BEATRICE [*aside*]   Possible his need
Is strong upon him – There's to encourage thee;
[*gives him money*]
As thou art forward and thy service dangerous,
Thy reward shall be precious.

DE FLORES   That I have thought on; 130
I have assured myself of that beforehand,
And know it will be precious; the thought ravishes.

BEATRICE Then take him to thy fury!

DE FLORES   I thirst for him.

BEATRICE Alonzo de Piracquo!

DE FLORES   His end's upon him;
He shall be seen no more.

BEATRICE   How lovely now
Dost thou appear to me! Never was man
Dearlier rewarded.

DE FLORES   I do think of that.

BEATRICE Be wondrous careful in the execution.

DE FLORES Why, are not both our lives upon the cast?

BEATRICE Then I throw all my fears upon thy service.   140

DE FLORES   They ne'er shall rise to hurt you.
BEATRICE   When the deed's done,
            I'll furnish thee with all things for thy flight;
            Thou may'st live bravely in another country.
DE FLORES   Ay, ay, we'll talk of that hereafter.
BEATRICE   [aside]   I shall rid myself
            Of two inveterate loathings at one time,
            Piracquo, and his dog-face.   [exit
DE FLORES   O my blood!
            Methinks I feel her in my arms already,
            Her wanton fingers combing out this beard,
            And, being pleased, praising this bad face.
            Hunger and pleasure, they'll commend sometimes   150
            Slovenly dishes, and feed heartily on 'em,
            Nay, which is stranger, refuse daintier for 'em.
            Some women are odd feeders – I'm too loud.
            Here comes the man goes supperless to bed,
            Yet shall not rise tomorrow to his dinner.

                        Enter ALONZO

ALONZO   De Flores.
DE FLORES   My kind, honourable lord?
ALONZO   I am glad I ha' met with thee.
DE FLORES   Sir?
ALONZO   Thou canst show me
            The full strength of the castle?
DE FLORES   That I can, sir.
ALONZO   I much desire it.
DE FLORES   And if the ways and straits
            Of some of the passages be not too tedious for you,   160
            I will assure you, worth your time and sight, my lord.
ALONZO   Push, that shall be no hindrance.
DE FLORES   I'm your servant then.
            'Tis now near dinner time; 'gainst your lordship's
                                                       rising
            I'll have the keys about me.
ALONZO   Thanks, kind De Flores.
DE FLORES   [aside] He's safely thrust upon me beyond hopes.
                                                    [exeunt

ACT 3 SCENE I

Enter ALONZO *and* DE FLORES
(*In the act-time* DE FLORES *hides a naked rapier*)

DE FLORES   Yes, here are all the keys; I was afraid, my lord,
            I'd wanted for the postern, this is it.
            I've all, I've all, my lord; this for the sconce.

ALONZO   'Tis a most spacious and impregnable fort.

DE FLORES   You'll tell me more, my lord: this descent
            Is somewhat narrow, we shall never pass
            Well with our weapons, they'll but trouble us.

ALONZO   Thou say'st true.

DE FLORES   Pray let me help your lordship.

ALONZO   'Tis done. Thanks, kind De Flores.

DE FLORES   Here are hooks, my lord,
            To hang such things on purpose.
            [*he hangs up the swords*]

ALONZO   Lead, I'll follow thee.   10
                           [*exeunt at one door and enter at the other*

SCENE 2

DE FLORES   All this is nothing; you shall see anon
            A place you little dream on.

ALONZO   I am glad
            I have this leisure; all your master's house
            Imagine I ha' taken a gondola.

DE FLORES   All but myself, sir – [*aside*] which makes up
                                                  my safety.
            My lord, I'll place you at a casement here
            Will show you the full strength of all the castle.
            Look, spend your eye awhile upon that object.

ALONZO   Here's rich variety, De Flores.

DE FLORES   Yes, sir.

ALONZO   Goodly munition.

DE FLORES   Ay, there's ordnance, sir,   10
            No bastard metal, will ring you a peal like bells

         At great men's funerals; keep your eye straight,
                                   my lord;
         Take special notice of that sconce before you,
         There you may dwell awhile. [*takes up the rapier*]

ALONZO   I am upon't.

DE FLORES   And so am I. [*stabs him*]

ALONZO   De Flores! O, De Flores!
         Whose malice hast thou put on?

DE FLORES   Do you question
         A work of secrecy? I must silence you. [*stabs him*]

ALONZO   Oh, oh, oh!

DE FLORES   I must silence you. [*stabs him*]
         So here's an undertaking well accomplished.
         This vault serves to good use now – Ha, what's that   20
         Threw sparkles in my eye? Oh, 'tis a diamond
         He wears upon his finger; it was well found,
         This will approve the work. What, so fast on?
         Not part in death? I'll take a speedy course then,
         Finger and all shall off [*cuts off the finger*] So now
                                   I'll clear
         The passages from all suspect or fear.

                                 [*exit with body*

SCENE 3

Enter ISABELLA *and* LOLLIO

ISABELLA   Why, sirrah? Whence have you commission
         To fetter the doors against me? If you
         Keep me in a cage, pray whistle to me,
         Let me be doing something.

LOLLIO   You shall be doing, if it please you; I'll whistle to you
         if you'll pipe after.

ISABELLA   Is it your master's pleasure or your own,
         To keep me in this pinfold?

LOLLIO   'Tis for my master's pleasure, lest being taken in another
         man's corn, you might be pounded in another place.   10

ISABELLA   'Tis very well, and he'll prove very wise.

LOLLIO   He says you have company enough in the house, if you please to be sociable, of all sorts of people.

ISABELLA   Of all sorts? Why, here's none but fools and madmen.

LOLLIO   Very well; and where will you find any other, if you
            should go abroad? There's my master and I to boot
            too.

ISABELLA   Of either sort one, a madman and a fool.

LOLLIO   I would even participate of both then, if I were as you;
            I know y'are half mad already, be half foolish too.   20

ISABELLA   Y'are a brave, saucy rascal! Come on, sir,
            Afford me then the pleasure of your bedlam;
            You were commending once today to me
            Your last-come lunatic; what a proper
            Body there was without brains to guide it,
            And what a pitiful delight appeared
            In that defect, as if your wisdom had found
            A mirth in madness; pray, sir, let me partake,
            If there be such a pleasure.

LOLLIO   If I do not show you the handsomest, discreetest   30
            madman, one that I may call the understanding mad-
            man, then say I am a fool.

ISABELLA   Well, a match, I will say so.

LOLLIO   When you have a taste of the madman, you shall, if
            you please, see Fools' College, o'th'side; I seldom
            lock there, 'tis but shooting a bolt or two, and you are
            amongst 'em.   [exit
            [enter presently] Come on, sir, let me see how hand-
            somely you'll behave yourself now.

Enter FRANCISCUS

FRANCISC.   How sweetly she looks! Oh, but there's a wrinkle in   40
            her brow as deep as philosophy. Anacreon, drink to my
            mistress' health, I'll pledge it; stay, stay, there's a spider
            in the cup! No, 'tis but a grape-stone; swallow it, fear
            nothing, poet; so, so, lift higher.

ISABELLA   Alack, alack, 'tis too full of pity
            To be laughed at. How fell he mad? Canst thou tell?

LOLLIO   For love, mistress; he was a pretty poet too, and that
            set him forwards first; the Muses then forsook him; he
            ran mad for a chambermaid, yet she was but a dwarf
            neither.   50

FRANCISC.   Hail, bright Titania!
          Why stand'st thou idle on these flow'ry banks?
          Oberon is dancing with his Dryades;
          I'll gather daisies, primrose, violets,
          And bind them in a verse of poesie.

LOLLIO   Not too near; you see your danger. [shows the whip]

FRANCISC.   Oh, hold thy hand, great Diomed!
          Thou feed'st thy horses well, they shall obey thee;
          Get up, Bucephalus kneels. [kneels]

LOLLIO   You see how I awe my flock; a shepherd has not his 60
          dog at more obedience.

ISABELLA   His conscience is unquiet; sure that was
          The cause of this. A proper gentleman.

FRANCISC.   Come hither, Esculapius; hide the poison.

LOLLIO   Well, 'tis hid. [hides the whip]

FRANCISC.   Didst thou never hear of one Tiresias,
          A famous poet?

LOLLIO   Yes, that kept tame wild geese.

FRANCISC.   That's he; I am the man.

LOLLIO   No!   70

FRANCISC.   Yes, but make no words on't; I was a man
          Seven years ago.

LOLLIO   A stripling I think you might.

FRANCISC.   Now I'm a woman, all feminine.

LOLLIO   I would I might see that.

FRANCISC.   Juno struck me blind.

LOLLIO   I'll ne'er believe that; for a woman, they say, has an
          eye more than a man.

FRANCISC.   I say she struck me blind.

LOLLIO   And Luna made you mad; you have two trades to beg 80
          with.

FRANCISC.   Luna is now big-bellied, and there's room
          For both of us to ride with Hecate;
          I'll drag thee up into her silver sphere,
          And there we'll kick the dog, and beat the bush,
          That barks against the witches of the night,
          The swift lycanthropi that walk the round,
          We'll tear their wolvish skins and save the sheep.
          [tries to seize Lollio]

LOLLIO	Is't come to this? Nay, then my poison comes forth again [*shows the whip*]; mad slave, indeed, abuse your 90 keeper!
ISABELLA	I prithee, hence with him, now he grows dangerous.
FRANCISC.	[*sings*] Sweet love, pity me.
	Give me leave to lie with thee.
LOLLIO	No, I'll see you wiser first; to your kennel.
FRANCISC.	No noise, she sleeps, draw all the curtains round,
	Let no soft sound molest the pretty soul
	But love, and love creeps in at a mouse-hole.
LOLLIO	I would you would get into your hole! [*exit Franciscus*
	Now, mistress, I will bring you another sort, you shall 100 be fooled another while; Tony, come hither, Tony; look who's yonder, Tony.

Enter ANTONIO

ANTONIO	Cousin, is it not my aunt?
LOLLIO	Yes, 'tis one of 'em, Tony.
ANTONIO	He, he! How do you, uncle?
LOLLIO	Fear him not, mistress, 'tis a gentle nigget; you may play with him, as safely with him as with his bauble.
ISABELLA	How long hast thou been a fool?
ANTONIO	Ever since I came hither, cousin.
ISABELLA	Cousin? I'm none of thy cousins, fool. 110
LOLLIO	O mistress, fools have always so much wit as to claim their kindred.
MADMAN	[*within*] Bounce, bounce, he falls, he falls!
ISABELLA	Hark you, your scholars in the upper room
	Are out of order.
LOLLIO	Must I come amongst you there? Keep you the fool, mistress; I'll go up and play left-handed Orlando amongst the madmen. [*exit*
ISABELLA	Well, sir.
ANTONIO	'Tis opportuneful now, sweet lady! Nay, 120
	Cast no amazing eye upon this change.
ISABELLA	Ha!
ANTONIO	This shape of folly shrouds your dearest love,
	The truest servant to your powerful beauties,
	Whose magic had this force thus to transform me.

ISABELLA   You are a fine fool indeed.
ANTONIO   Oh, 'tis not strange;
            Love has an intellect that runs through all
            The scrutinous sciences, and like
            A cunning poet catches a quantity
            Of every knowledge, yet brings all home   130
            Into one mystery, into one secret
            That he proceeds in.
ISABELLA   Y'are a parlous fool.
ANTONIO   No danger in me; I bring naught but love
            And his soft-wounding shafts to strike you with.
            Try but one arrow; if it hurt you,
            I'll stand you twenty back in recompense. [kisses her]
ISABELLA   A forward fool too!
ANTONIO   This was love's teaching
            A thousand ways he fashioned out my way,
            And this I found the safest and [the] nearest
            To tread the Galaxia to my star.   140
ISABELLA   Profound, withal! Certain, you dreamed of this;
            Love never taught it waking.
ANTONIO   Take no acquaintance
            Of these outward follies; there is within
            A gentleman that loves you.
ISABELLA   When I see him,
            I'll speak with him; so in the meantime keep
            Your habit, it becomes you well enough.
            As you are a gentleman, I'll not discover you;
            That's all the favour that you must expect;
            When you are weary, you may leave the school,
            For all this while you have but played the fool.   150

                        Enter LOLLIO

ANTONIO   And must again – He, he! I thank you, cousin;
            I'll be your Valentine tomorrow morning.
LOLLIO   How do you like the fool, mistress?
ISABELLA   Passing well, sir.
LOLLIO   Is he not witty, pretty well for a fool?
ISABELLA   If he hold on as he begins, he is like
            To come to something.

LOLLIO	Ay, thank a good tutor; you may put him to't; he begins to answer pretty hard questions. Tony, how many is five times six?

160

ANTONIO	Five times six is six times five.
LOLLIO	What arithmetician could have answered better? How many is one hundred and seven?
ANTONIO	One hundred and seven is seven hundred and one, cousin.
LOLLIO	This is no wit to speak on; will you be rid of the fool now?
ISABELLA	By no means, let him stay a little.
MADMAN	[*within*] Catch there, catch the last couple in hell!
LOLLIO	Again! Must I come amongst you? Would my master were come home! I am not able to govern both these wards together. [*exit*

170

ANTONIO	Why should a minute of love's hour be lost?
ISABELLA	Fie, out again! I had rather you kept Your other posture; you become not your tongue When you speak from your clothes.
ANTONIO	How can he freeze, Lives near so sweet a warmth? Shall I alone Walk though the orchard of the Hesperides, And cowardly not dare to pull an apple? This with the red cheeks I must venture for. [*tries to kiss her*]

180

Enter LOLLIO *above*

ISABELLA	Take heed, there's giants keep 'em.
LOLLIO	[*aside*] How now, fool, are you good at that? Have you read Lipsius? He's past *Ars Amandi*; I believe I must put harder questions to him, I perceive that.
ISABELLA	You are bold without fear too.
ANTONIO	What should I fear, Having all joys about me? Do you smile, And love shall play the wanton on your lip, Meet and retire, retire and meet again; Look you but cheerfully, and in your eyes I shall behold mine own deformity, And dress myself up fairer; I know this shape

190

Becomes me not, but in those bright mirrors
I shall array me handsomely.

LOLLIO   Cuckoo, cuckoo!   [exit

Enter Madmen above, some as birds, other as beasts

ANTONIO   What are these?
ISABELLA   Of fear enough to part us;
Yet they are but our school of lunatics,
That act their fantasies in any shapes
Suiting their present thoughts; if sad, they cry;
If mirth by their conceit, they laugh again.
Sometimes they imitate the beasts and birds,   200
Singing, or howling, braying, barking; all
As their wild fancies prompt 'em.

Enter LOLLIO

ANTONIO   These are no fears.
ISABELLA   But here's a large one, my man.
ANTONIO   Ha, he! That's fine sport indeed, cousin.
LOLLIO   I would my master were come home, 'tis too much for
one shepherd to govern two of these flocks; nor can I
believe that one churchman can instruct two benefices
at once; there will be some incurable mad of the one
side, and very fools on the other. Come, Tony.
ANTONIO   Prithee, cousin, let me stay here still.   210
LOLLIO   No, you must to your book now, you have played
sufficiently.
ISABELLA   Your fool is grown wondrous witty.
LOLLIO   Well, I'll say nothing; but I do not think but he will
put you down one of these days.
                                        [*exeunt Lollio and Antonio*
ISABELLA   Here the restrainéd current might make breach,
Spite of the watchful bankers; would a woman stray,
She need not gad abroad to seek her sin,
It would be brought home one ways or other:
The needle's point will to the fixéd north;   220
Such drawing arctics women's beauties are.

Enter LOLLIO

LOLLIO   How dost thou, sweet rogue?

ISABELLA	How now?
LOLLIO	Come, there are degrees, one fool may be better than another.
ISABELLA	What's the matter?
LOLLIO	Nay, if thou giv'st thy mind to fool's-flesh, have at thee! [*tries to kiss her*]
ISABELLA	You bold slave, you!
LOLLIO	I could follow now as t'other fool did: 230

'What should I fear,
Having all joys about me? Do you but smile,
And love shall play the wanton on your lip,
Meet and retire, retire and meet again;
Look you but cheerfully, and in your eyes
I shall behold my own deformity,
And dress myself up fairer; I know this shape
Becomes me not – '

and so as it follows, but is not this the more foolish
way? Come, sweet rogue; kiss me, my little Lace- 240
demonian. Let me feel how thy pulses beat; thou hast
a thing about thee would do a man pleasure, I'll lay
my hand on't.

ISABELLA	Sirrah, no more! I see you have discovered

This love's knight-errant, who hath made adventure
For purchase of my love; be silent, mute,
Mute as a statue, or his injunction,
For me enjoying, shall be to cut thy throat;
I'll do it, though for no other purpose,
And be sure he'll not refuse it.   250

LOLLIO	My share, that's all; I'll have my fool's part with you.
ISABELLA	No more! Your master.

Enter ALIBIUS

ALIBIUS	Sweet, how dost thou?
ISABELLA	Your bounden servant, sir.
ALIBIUS	Fie, fie, sweetheart, No more of that.
ISABELLA	You were best lock me up.
ALIBIUS	In my arms and bosom, my sweet Isabella, I'll lock thee up most nearly. Lollio,

We have employment, we have task in hand;
At noble Vermandero's, our castle captain,
There is a nuptial to be solemnised –
Beatrice-Joanna, his fair daughter, bride –   260
For which the gentleman hath bespoke our pains,
A mixture of our madmen and our fools,
To finish, as it were, and make the fag
Of all the revels, the third night from the first;
Only an unexpected passage over,
To make a frightful pleasure, that is all,
But not the all I aim at; could we so act it,
To teach it in a wild, distracted measure,
Though out of form and figure, breaking time's head,
It were no matter, 'twould be healed again   270
In one age or other, if not in this.
This, this, Lollio; there's a good reward begun,
And will beget a bounty be it known.

LOLLIO   This is easy, sir, I'll warrant you; you have about you
fools and madmen that can dance very well, and 'tis
no wonder, your best dancers are not the wisest men;
the reason is, with often jumping they jolt their brains
down into their feet, that their wits lie more in their
heels than in their heads.

ALIBIUS   Honest Lollio, thou givest me a good reason   280
And a comfort in it.

ISABELLA   Y'have a fine trade on't,
Madmen and fools are a staple commodity.

ALIBIUS   O wife, we must eat, wear clothes, and live;
Just at the lawyer's haven we arrive,
By madmen and by fools we both do thrive.

                                        [*exeunt*

SCENE 4

Enter VERMANDERO, ALSEMERO, JASPERINO *and* BEATRICE

VERMAND.	Valencia speaks so nobly of you, sir,
	I wish I had a daughter now for you.
ALSEMERO	The fellow of this creature were a partner
	For a king's love.
VERMAND.	I had her fellow once, sir,
	But Heaven has married her to joys eternal;
	'Twere sin to wish her in this vale again.
	Come, sir, your friend and you shall see the pleasures
	Which my health chiefly joys in.
ALSEMERO	I hear the beauty of this seat largely.
VERMAND.	It falls much short of that. *[exeunt, Beatrice remains*
BEATRICE	So, here's one step 10
	Into my father's favour; time will fix him.
	I have got him now the liberty of the house;
	So wisdom by degrees works out her freedom;
	And if that eye be darkened that offends me –
	I wait but that eclipse – this gentleman
	Shall soon shine glorious in my father's liking,
	Though the refulgent virtue of my love.

Enter DE FLORES

DE FLORES	[*aside*] My thoughts are at a banquet; for the deed,
	I feel no weight in't, 'tis but light and cheap
	For the sweet recompense that I set down for't. 20
BEATRICE	De Flores.
DE FLORES	Lady?
BEATRICE	Thy looks promise cheerfully.
DE FLORES	All things are answerable: time, circumstance,
	Your wishes, and my service.
BEATRICE	Is it done then?
DE FLORES	Piracquo is no more.
BEATRICE	My joys start at mine eyes; our sweet'st delights
	Are evermore born weeping.
DE FLORES	I've a token for you.
BEATRICE	For me?
DE FLORES	But it was sent somewhat unwillingly,

I could not get the ring without the finger.
[shows her the finger]

BEATRICE Bless me! 'What hast thou done?

DE FLORES   Why, is that more
Than killing the whole man? I cut his heart-strings. 30
A greedy hand thrust in a dish at court
In a mistake hath had as much as this.

BEATRICE 'Tis the first token my father made me send him.

DE FLORES And I [have] made him send it back again
For his last token; I was loath to leave it,
And I'm sure dead men have no use of jewels.
He was as loath to part with't, for it stuck
As if the flesh and it were both one substance.

BEATRICE At the stag's fall the keeper has his fees;
'Tis soon applied, all dead men's fees are yours, sir. 40
I pray, bury the finger, but the stone
You may make use on shortly; the true value,
Take't of my truth, is near three hundred ducats.

DE FLORES 'Twill hardly buy a capcase for one's
             conscience, though,
To keep it from the worm, as fine as 'tis.
Well, being my fees, I'll take it;
Great men have taught me that, or else my merit
Would scorn the way on't.

BEATRICE   It might justly, sir;
Why, thou mistak'st, De Flores, 'tis not given
In state of recompense.

DE FLORES   No, I hope so, lady, 50
You should soon witness my contempt to't then.

BEATRICE Prithee, thou look'st as if thou wert offended.

DE FLORES That were strange, lady; 'tis not possible
My service should draw such a cause from you.
Offended? Could you think so? That were much
For one of my performance, and so warm
Yet in my service.

BEATRICE 'Twere misery in me to give you cause, sir.

DE FLORES I know so much, it were so, misery
In her most sharp condition.

BEATRICE   'Tis resolved then; 60

Look you, sir, here's three thousand golden forms;
I have not meanly thought upon thy merit.

DE FLORES What, salary? Now you move me.

BEATRICE   How, De Flores?

DE FLORES Do you place me in the rank of verminous fellows,
To destroy things for wages? Offer gold?
The life blood of man! Is anything
Valued too precious for my recompense?

BEATRICE I understand thee not.

DE FLORES   I could ha' hired
A journeyman in murder at this rate,
And mine own conscience might have [slept at ease],   70
And have had the work brought home.

BEATRICE [aside]   I'm in a labyrinth;
What will content him? I would fain be rid of him –
I'll double the sum, sir.

DE FLORES   You take a course
To double my vexation, that's the good you do.

BEATRICE [aside] Bless me! I am now in worse plight than I was;
I know not what will please him – For my
                                        fear's sake,
I prithee make away with all speed possible.
And if thou be'st so modest not to name
The sum that will content thee, paper blushes not;
Send thy demand in writing, it shall follow thee,   80
But prithee take thy flight.

DE FLORES   You must fly too then.

BEATRICE I?

DE FLORES   I'll not stir a foot else.

BEATRICE   What's your meaning?

DE FLORES Why, are you not as guilty – in, I'm sure,
As deep as I? And we should stick together.
Come, your fears counsel you but ill; my absence
Would draw suspect upon you instantly;
There were no rescue for you.

BEATRICE [aside]   He speaks home.

DE FLORES Nor is it fit we two engaged so jointly,
Should part and live asunder.

BEATRICE   How now, sir?

This shows not well.

DE FLORES   What makes your lip so strange? 90
This must not be betwixt us.

BEATRICE [aside]   The man talks wildly.

DE FLORES Come, kiss me with a zeal now.

BEATRICE [aside]   Heaven, I doubt him!

DE FLORES I will not stand so long to beg 'em shortly.

BEATRICE Take heed, De Flores, of forgetfulness,
'Twill soon betray us.

DE FLORES   Take you heed first;
Faith, y'are grown much forgetful, y'are to blame in't.

BEATRICE [aside] He's bold, and I am blamed for't!

DE FLORES   I have eased
You of your trouble, think on't, I'm in pain,
And must be eased of you; 'tis a charity,
Justice invites your blood to understand me.   100

BEATRICE I dare not.

DE FLORES   Quickly!

BEATRICE   Oh, I never shall!
Speak it yet further off that I may lose
What has been spoken, and no sound remain on't.
I would not hear so much offence again
For such another deed.

DE FLORES   Soft, lady, soft;
The last is not yet paid for. Oh, this act
Has put me into spirit; I was as greedy on't
As the parched earth of moisture, when the
                              clouds weep.
Did you not mark, I wrought myself into't,
Nay, sued and kneeled for't? Why was all that
                              pains took? 110
You see I have thrown contempt upon your gold,
Not that I want it [not], for I do piteously;
In order I will come unto't, and make use on't,
But 'twas not held so precious to begin with;
For I place wealth after the heels of pleasure,
And were I not resolved in my belief
That thy virginity were perfect in thee,
I should but take my recompense with grudging,

As if I had but half my hopes I agreed for.
BEATRICE   Why, 'tis impossible thou canst be so wicked,   120
            Or shelter such a cunning cruelty,
            To make his death the murderer of my honour!
            Thy language is so bold and vicious,
            I cannot see which way I can forgive it
            With any modesty.
DE FLORES   Push! You forget yourself!
            A woman dipped in blood, and talk of modesty!
BEATRICE   O misery of sin! Would I had been bound
            Perpetually unto my living hate
            In that Piracquo, than to hear these words.
            Think but upon the distance that creation   130
            Set 'twixt thy blood and mine, and keep thee there.
DE FLORES   Look but in your conscience, read me there,
            'Tis a true book, you'll find me there your equal.
            Push! Fly not to your birth, but settle you
            In what the act has made you, y'are no more now.
            You must forget your parentage to me:
            Y'are the deed's creature; by that name
            You lost your first condition, and I challenge you,
            As peace and innocency has turned you out,
            And made you one with me.
BEATRICE   With thee, foul villain?   140
DE FLORES   Yes, my fair murderess; do you urge me?
            Though thou writ'st maid, thou whore in thy affection!
            'Twas changed from thy first love, and that's a kind
            Of whoredom in thy heart; and he's changed now,
            To bring thy second on, thy Alsemero,
            Whom (by all sweets that ever darkness tasted)
            If I enjoy thee not, thou ne'er enjoy'st;
            I'll blast the hopes and joys of marriage.
            I'll confess all; my life I rate at nothing.
BEATRICE   De Flores!   150
DE FLORES   I shall rest from all lovers' plagues then;
            I live in pain now; that shooting eye
            Will burn my heart to cinders.
BEATRICE   O sir, hear me.
DE FLORES   She that in life and love refuses me,

In death and shame my partner she shall be.

BEATRICE   [*kneels*] Stay, hear me once for all; I make thee master
Of all the wealth I have in gold and jewels;
Let me go poor unto my bed with honour,
And I am rich in all things.

DE FLORES   Let this silence thee:
The wealth of all Valencia shall not buy   160
My pleasure from me;
Can you weep Fate from its determined purpose?
So soon may [you] weep me.

BEATRICE   Vengeance begins;
Murder, I see, is followed by more sins.
Was my creation in the womb so cursed,
It must engender with a viper first?

DE FLORES   Come, rise, and shroud your blushes in my bosom;
[*raises her*] Silence is one of pleasure's best receipts;
Thy peace is wrought for ever in this yielding.
'Las, how the turtle pants! Thou'lt love anon   170
What thou so fear'st and faint'st to venture on.

[*exeunt*

ACT 4 SCENE I

Dumb show

Enter GENTLEMEN, VERMANDERO *meeting them with action of wonderment at the flight of* PIRACQUO. *Enter* ALSEMERO, *with* JASPERINO *and* GALLANTS; VERMANDERO *points to him, the* GENTLEMAN *seeming to applaud the choice.* [*exeunt*] ALSEMERO, JASPERINO *and* GENTLEMEN; BEATRICE *the bride following in great state, accompanied with* DIAPHANTA, ISABELLA, *and other* GENTLEWOMAN; DE FLORES *after all, smiling at the accident;* ALONZO'S *ghost appears to* DE FLORES *in the midst of his smile, startles him, showing him the hand whose finger he had cut off. They pass over in great solemnity.*

Enter BEATRICE

BEATRICE   This fellow has undone me endlessly;
        Never was bride so fearfully distressed.
        The more I think upon th'ensuing night,
        And whom I am to cope with in embraces,
        One who's ennobled both in blood and mind,
        So clear in understanding – that's my plague now –
        Before whose judgment will my fault appear
        Like malefactors' crimes before tribunals;
        There is no hiding on't, the more I dive
        Into my own distress; how a wise man   10
        Stands for a great calamity! There's no venturing
        Into his bed, what course soe'er I light upon,
        Without my shame, which may grow up to danger;
        He cannot but in justice strangle me
        As I lie by him, as a cheater use me;
        'Tis a precious craft to play with a false die
        Before a cunning gamester. Here's his closet,
        The key left in't, and he abroad i'th'park?
        Sure 'twas forgot; I'll be so bold as look in't.
        [*opens closet*] Bless me! A right physician's closet 'tis,   20
        Set round with vials, every one her mark too.
        Sure he does practise physic for his own use,
        Which may be safely called your great man's wisdom.

What manuscript lies here? *The Book of Experiment,*
Called Secrets in Nature; so 'tis, 'tis so;
'How to know whether a woman be with child or no;
I hope I am not yet; if he should try though!
Let me see, folio forty-five. Here 'tis;
The leaf tucked down upon't, the place suspicious:
'If you would know whether a woman be with child   30
or not, give her two spoonfuls of the white water in
glass C' –
Where's that glass C? Oh, yonder, I see't now –
'and if she be with child she sleeps full twelve hours
after; if not, not.'
None of that water comes into my belly.
I'll know you from a hundred; I could break you now,
Or turn you into milk, and so beguile
The master of the mystery, but I'll look to you.
Ha! That which is next is ten times worse: 40
'How to know whether a woman be a maid or not.'
If that should be applied, what would become of me?
Belike he has a strong faith of my purity,
That never yet made proof; but this he calls
'A merry sleight, but true experiment, the author
Antonius Mizaldus. Give the party you suspect the
quantity of a spoonful of the water in glass M, which,
upon her that is a maid, makes three several effects:
'twill make her incontinently gape, then fall into a
sudden sneezing, last into a violent laughing; else dull,   50
heavy, and lumpish.'
Where had I been?
I fear it, yet 'tis seven hours to bedtime.

Enter DIAPHANTA

DIAPHANTA   Cuds, madam, are you here?
BEATRICE   [*aside*]   Seeing that wench now,
A trick comes in my mind; 'tis a nice piece
Gold cannot purchase – I come hither, wench,
To look my lord.
DIAPHANTA   [*aside*]   Would I had such a cause
To look him too! – Why, he's i'th'park, madam.

BEATRICE There let him be.

DIAPHANTA   Ay, madam, let him compass
Whole parks and forests, as great rangers do;   60
At roosting time a little lodge can hold 'em.
Earth-conquering Alexander, that thought the world
Too narrow for him, in the end had but his pit-hole.

BEATRICE I fear thou art not modest, Diaphanta.

DIAPHANTA Your thoughts are so unwilling to be known, madam;
'Tis ever the bride's fashion towards bed time
To set light by her joys, as if she owed 'em not.

BEATRICE Her joys? Her fears, thou would'st say.

DIAPHANTA   Fear of what?

BEATRICE Art thou a maid, and talk'st so to a maid?
You leave a blushing business behind,   70
Beshrew your heart for't!

DIAPHANTA   Do you mean good sooth, madam?

BEATRICE Well, if I'd thought upon the fear at first,
Man should have been unknown.

DIAPHANTA   Is't possible?

BEATRICE I will give a thousand ducats to that woman
Would try what my fear were, and tell me true
Tomorrow, when she gets from't; as she likes,
I might perhaps be drawn to't.

DIAPHANTA   Are you in earnest?

BEATRICE Do you get the woman, then challenge me,
And see if I'll fly from't; but I must tell you
This by the way, she must be a true maid,   80
Else there's no trial, my fears are not hers else.

DIAPHANTA Nay, she that I would put into your hands, madam,
Shall be a maid.

BEATRICE   You know I should be shamed else,
Because she lies for me.

DIAPHANTA   'Tis a strange humour;
But are you serious still? Would you resign
Your first night's pleasure, and give money too?

BEATRICE As willingly as live — [aside] alas, the gold
Is but a by-bet to wedge in the honour.

DIAPHANTA I do not know how the world goes abroad
For faith or honesty, there's both required in this.   90

                Madam, what say you to me, and stray no further?
                I've a good mind, in troth, to earn your money.
BEATRICE   Y'are too quick, I fear, to be a maid.
DIAPHANTA   How? Not a maid? Nay, then you urge me, madam;
                Your honourable self is not a truer
                With all your fears upon you —
BEATRICE   [aside]   Bad enough then.
DIAPHANTA   Than I with all my lightsome joys about me.
BEATRICE   I'm glad to hear't; then you dare put your honesty
                Upon an easy trial?
DIAPHANTA   Easy? Anything.
BEATRICE   I'll come to you straight. [goes to the closet]   100
DIAPHANTA   [aside] She will not search me, will she,
                Like the forewoman of a female jury?
BEATRICE   Glass M; ay, this is it; look, Diaphanta,
                You take no worse than I do. [drinks]
DIAPHANTA   And in so doing,
                I will not question what 'tis, but take it. [drinks]
BEATRICE   [aside] Now if the experiment be true, 'twill
                                              praise itself,
                And give me noble ease — Begins already;
                [Diaphanta gapes]
                There's the first symptom; and what haste it makes
                To fall into the second, there by this time!
                [Diaphanta sneezes]
                Most admirable secret! On the contrary,   110
                It stirs me not a whit, which most concerns it.
DIAPHANTA   Ha, ha, ha!
BEATRICE   [aside]   Just in all things and in order,
                As if 'twere circumscribed; one accident
                Gives way unto another.
DIAPHANTA   Ha, ha, ha!
BEATRICE   How now, wench?
DIAPHANTA   Ha, ha, ha! I am so, so light
                At heart — ha, ha, ha! — so pleasurable.
                But one swig more, sweet madam.
BEATRICE   Ay, tomorrow;
                We shall have time to sit by't.
DIAPHANTA   Now I'm sad again.

BEATRICE   [*aside*] It lays itself so gently, too! Come, wench,
             Most honest Diaphanta I dare call thee now.   120
DIAPHANTA   Pray tell me, madam, what trick call you this?
BEATRICE   I'll tell thee all hereafter; we must study
             The carriage of this business.
DIAPHANTA   I shall carry't well,
             Because I love the burthen.
BEATRICE   About midnight
             You must not fail to steal forth gently,
             That I may use the place.
DIAPHANTA   O, fear not, madam,
             I shall be cool by that time – the bride's place,
             And with a thousand ducats! I'm for a justice now,
             I bring a portion with me; I scorn small fools.
                                                            [*exeunt*

SCENE 2

Enter VERMANDERO *and* SERVANT

VERMAND.   I tell thee, knave, mine honour is in question,
             A thing till now free from suspicion,
             Nor ever was there cause; who of my gentlemen
             Are absent? Tell me, and truly, how many and who.
SERVANT   Antonio, sir, and Franciscus.
VERMAND.   When did they leave the castle?
SERVANT   Some ten days since, sir, the one intending to Bria-
             mata, th'other for Valencia.
VERMAND.   The time accuses 'em; a charge of murder
             Is brought within my castle gate, Piracquo's murder;   10
             I dare not answer faithfully their absence;
             A strict command of apprehension
             Shall pursue 'em suddenly, and either wipe
             The stain off clear, or openly discover it.
             Provide me winged warrants for the purpose.
                                                        [*exit Servant*
             See, I am set on again.

Enter TOMAZO

TOMAZO   I claim a brother of you.
VERMAND.   Y'are too hot,

Seek him not here.

TOMAZO　　　　　　　　　　　Yes, 'mongst your dearest bloods,
If my peace find no fairer satisfaction;
This is the place must yield account for him,　　　　　20
For here I left him, and the hasty tie
Of this snatched marriage gives strong testimony
Of his most certain ruin.

VERMAND.　　　　　　　　　Certain falsehood!
This is the place indeed; his breach of faith
Has too much marred both my abuséd love,
The honourable love I reserved for him,
And mocked my daughter's joy; the prepared morning
Blushed at his infidelity; he left
Contempt and scorn to throw upon those friends
Whose belief hurt 'em; O, 'twas most ignoble　　　　　30
To take his flight so unexpectedly,
And throw such public wrongs on those that
　　　　　　　　　　　　　　　loved him.

TOMAZO　Then this is all your answer?

VERMAND.　　　　　　　　　'Tis too fair
For one of his alliance; and I warn you
That this place no more see you.　　　　　　　[exit

　　　　　　　　　Enter DE FLORES

TOMAZO　　　　　　　　　　　The best is,
There is more ground to meet a man's revenge on.
Honest De Flores —

DE FLORES　　　　　That's my name indeed.
Saw you the bride? Good sweet sir, which way
　　　　　　　　　　　　　　took she?

TOMAZO　I have blessed mine eyes from seeing such a false one.

DE FLORES　[aside] I'd fain get off, this man's not for my company, 40
I smell his brother's blood when I come near him.

TOMAZO　Come hither, kind and true one; I remember
My brother loved thee well.

DE FLORES　　　　　Oh, purely, dear sir!
[aside] Methinks I am now again a-killing on him,
He brings it so fresh to me.

TOMAZO　　　　　　Thou canst guess, sirrah —

One honest friend has an instinct of jealousy –
At some foul guilty person?

DE FLORES   'Las, sir,
I am so charitable I think none
Worse than myself – You did not see the bride then?

TOMAZO   I prithee name her not. Is she not wicked?   50

DE FLORES   No, no, a pretty, easy, round-packed sinner,
As your most ladies are, else you might think
I flattered her; but, sir, at no hand wicked,
Till th'are so old their chins and noses meet,
And they salute witches. I am called, I think, sir.
[aside] His company ev'n o'erlays my conscience.

                                                   [exit

TOMAZO   That De Flores has a wondrous honest heart;
He'll bring it out in time, I'm assured on't.
Oh, here's the glorious master of the day's joy;
'Twill not be long till he and I do reckon.   60

                        Enter ALSEMERO

Sir!

ALSEMERO   You are most welcome.

TOMAZO   You may call that word back;
I do not think I am, nor wish to be.

ALSEMERO   'Tis strange you found your way to this house then.

TOMAZO   Would I'd ne'er known the cause! I'm none of
                                              those, sir,
That come to give you joy and swill your wine;
'Tis a more precious liquor that must lay
The fiery thirst I bring.

ALSEMERO   Your words and you
Appear to me great strangers.

TOMAZO   Time and our swords
May make us more acquainted; this the business:
I should have a brother in your place;   70
How treachery and malice have disposed of him,
I'm bound to inquire of him which holds his right,
Which never could come fairly.

ALSEMERO   You must look
To answer for that word, sir.

TOMAZO   Fear you not,

I'll have it ready drawn at our next meeting.
Keep your day solemn. Farewell, I disturb it not;
I'll bear the smart with patience for a time.   [*exit*

ALSEMERO 'Tis somewhat ominous this, a quarrel entered
Upon this day; my innocence relieves me,

Enter JASPERINO

I should be wondrous sad else. Jasperino,   80
I have news to tell thee, strange news.

JASPERINO   I ha' some too,
I think as strange as yours; would I might keep
Mine, so my faith and friendship might be kept in't!
Faith, sir, dispense a little with my zeal,
And let it cool in this.

ALSEMERO   This puts me on,
And blames thee for thy slowness.

JASPERINO   All may prove nothing,
Only a friendly fear that leapt from me, sir.

ALSEMERO No question it may prove nothing; let's partake
                                          it, though.

JASPERINO 'Twas Diaphanta's chance (for to that wench
I pretend honest love, and she deserves it)   90
To leave me in a back part of the house,
A place we chose for private conference;
She was no sooner gone, but instantly
I heard your bride's voice in the next room to me;
And, lending more attention, found De Flores
Louder than she.

ALSEMERO   De Flores? Thou art out now.

JASPERINO You'll tell me more anon.

ALSEMERO   Still I'll prevent thee;
The very sight of him is poison to her.

JASPERINO That made me stagger too, but Diaphanta
At her return confirmed it.

ALSEMERO   Diaphanta!   100

JASPERINO Then fell we both to listen, and words passed
Like those that challenge interest in a woman.

ALSEMERO Peace! Quench thy zeal; 'tis dangerous to thy bosom.

JASPERINO Then truth is full of peril.

ALSEMERO   Such truths are —

O, were she the sole glory of the earth,
Had eyes that could shoot fire into kings' breasts,
And touched, she sleeps not here! Yet I have time,
Though night be near, to be resolved hereof;
And, prithee, do not weigh me by my passions.

JASPERINO   I never weighed friend so.

ALSEMERO   Done charitably!   110
That key will lead thee to a pretty secret,
By a Chaldean taught me, and I have
My study upon some. Bring from my closet
A glass incribed there with the letter M,
And question not my purpose.

JASPERINO   It shall be done, sir. [exit

ALSEMERO   How can this hang together? Not an hour since,
Her woman came pleading her lady's fears,
Delivered her for the most timorous virgin
That ever shrunk at man's name, and so modest,
She charged her weep out her request to me   120
That she might come obscurely to my bosom.

Enter BEATRICE

BEATRICE   [aside] All things go well; my woman's preparing
                                                  yonder
For her sweet voyage, which grieves me to lose;
Necessity compels it; I lose all else.

ALSEMERO   [aside] Push! Modesty's shrine is set in yonder
                                                  forehead,
I cannot be too sure though – My Joanna!

BEATRICE   Sir, I was bold to weep a message to you;
Pardon my modest fears.

ALSEMERO   [aside]   The dove's not meeker;
She's abused, questionless.

Enter JASPERINO

                              Oh, are you come, sir?

BEATRICE   [aside] The glass, upon my life! I see the letter.   130

JASPERINO   Sir, this is M.

ALSEMERO   'Tis it.

BEATRICE   [aside]   I am suspected.

ALSEMERO   How fitly our bride comes to partake with us!

BEATRICE   What is't, my lord?
ALSEMERO   No hurt.
BEATRICE   Sir, pardon me,
            I seldom taste of any composition.
ALSEMERO   But this, upon my warrant, you shall venture on.
BEATRICE   I fear 'twill make me ill.
ALSEMERO   Heaven forbid that!
BEATRICE   [aside] I'm put now to my cunning; th'effects I know,
            If I can now but feign 'em handsomely. [drinks]
ALSEMERO   [to Jasperino] It has that secret virtue it ne'er
                                                    missed, sir,
            Upon a virgin.
JASPERINO   Treble qualitied?   140
            [Beatrice gapes, then sneezes]
ALSEMERO   By all that's virtuous, it takes there, proceeds!
JASPERINO   This is the strangest trick to know a maid by.
BEATRICE   Ha, ha, ha!
            You have given me joy of heart to drink, my lord.
ALSEMERO   No, thou hast given me such joy of heart,
            That never can be blasted.
BEATRICE   What's the matter, sir?
ALSEMERO   [to Jasperino] See, now 'tis settled in a melancholy,
            Keep[s] both the time and method – My Joanna,
            Chaste as the breath of heaven, or morning's womb,
            That brings the day forth, thus my love encloses thee. 150
                                                    [exeunt

SCENE 3

Enter ISABELLA *and* LOLLIO

ISABELLA   O heaven! Is this the waning moon?
        Does love turn fool, run mad, and all at once?
        Sirrah, here's a madman, akin to the fool too,
        A lunatic lover.

LOLLIO   No, no, not he I brought the letter from?

ISABELLA   Compare his inside with his out, and tell me.

LOLLIO   The out's mad, I'm sure of that; I had a taste on't. 'To
        the bright Andromeda, chief chambermaid to the
        Knight of the Sun, at the sign of Scorpio, in the
        middle region, sent by the bellows-mender of Aeolus.   10
        Pay the post.' This is stark madness.

ISABELLA   Now mark the inside. [*reads*] 'Sweet lady, having now
        cast off this counterfeit cover of a madman, I appear
        to your best judgment a true and faithful lover of your
        beauty.'

LOLLIO   He is mad still.

ISABELLA   'If any fault you find, chide those perfections in you
        which have made me imperfect; 'tis the same sun that
        causeth to grow and enforceth to wither' –

LOLLIO   O rogue!   20

ISABELLA   – 'Shapes and transhapes, destroys and builds again;
        I come in winter to you dismantled of my proper
        ornaments; by the sweet splendour of your cheerful
        smiles, I spring and live a lover.'

LOLLIO   Mad rascal still!

ISABELLA   'Tread him not under foot, that shall appear an hon-
        our to your bounties. I remain – mad till I speak with
        you, from whom I expect my cure – Yours all, or one
        beside himself, Franciscus.'

LOLLIO   You are like to have a fine time on't; my master and I   30
        may give over our professions, I do not think but you
        can cure fools and madmen faster than we, with little
        pains too.

ISABELLA   Very likely.

LOLLIO   One thing I must tell you, mistress: you perceive that

	I am privy to your skill; if I find you minister once and set up the trade, I put in for my thirds, I shall be mad or fool else.
ISABELLA	The first place is thine, believe it, Lollio, If I do fall —
LOLLIO	I fall upon you.
ISABELLA	So.
LOLLIO	Well, I stand to my venture.
ISABELLA	But thy counsel now, how shall I deal with 'em?
LOLLIO	Why, do you mean to deal with 'em?
ISABELLA	Nay, the fair understanding, how to use 'em.
LOLLIO	Abuse 'em! That's the way to mad the fool, and make a fool of the madman, and then you use 'em kindly.
ISABELLA	'Tis easy, I'll practise; do thou observe it; The key of thy wardrobe.
LOLLIO	There; fit yourself for 'em, and I'll fit 'em both for you. [gives her the key]
ISABELLA	Take thou no further notice than the outside. [exit
LOLLIO	Not an inch; I'll put you to the inside.

40

50

Enter ALIBIUS

ALIBIUS	Lollio, art there? Will all be perfect, think'st thou? Tomorrow night, as if to close up the solemnity, Vermandero expects us.
LOLLIO	I mistrust the madmen most; the fools will do well enough; I have taken pains with them.
ALIBIUS	Tush, they cannot miss; the more absurdity, The more commends it, so no rough behaviours Affright the ladies; they are nice things, thou know'st.
LOLLIO	You need not fear, sir; so long as we are there with our commanding pizzles, they'll be as tame as the ladies themselves.
ALIBIUS	I will see them once more rehearse before they go.
LOLLIO	I was about it, sir; look you to the madmen's morris, and let me alone with the other; there is one or two that I mistrust their fooling; I'll instruct them, and then they shall rehearse the whole measure.
ALIBIUS	Do so; I'll see the music prepared; but, Lollio, By the way, how does my wife brook her restraint? Does she not grudge at it?

60

70

LOLLIO	So, so; she takes some pleasure in the house, she would abroad else; you must allow her a little more length, she's kept too short.
ALIBIUS	She shall along to Vermandero's with us; That will serve her for a month's liberty.
LOLLIO	What's that on your face, sir?
ALIBIUS	Where, Lollio? I see nothing.
LOLLIO	Cry you mercy, sir, 'tis your nose; it showed like the 80 trunk of a young elephant.
ALIBIUS	Away, rascal! I'll prepare the music, Lollio.

[exit Alibius

| LOLLIO | Do, sir, and I'll dance the whilst. Tony, where art thou, Tony? |

Enter ANTONIO

ANTONIO	Here, cousin; where art thou?
LOLLIO	Come, Tony, the footmanship I taught you.
ANTONIO	I had rather ride, cousin.
LOLLIO	Ay, a whip take you; but I'll keep you out. Vault in; look you, Tony: fa, la, la, la, la. *[dances]*
ANTONIO	Fa, la, la, la, la. *[dances]* 90
LOLLIO	There, an honour.
ANTONIO	Is this an honour, coz?
LOLLIO	Yes, an it please your worship.
ANTONIO	Does honour bend in the hams, coz?
LOLLIO	Marry, does it, as low as worship, squireship, nay, yeomanry itself sometimes, from whence it first stiffened; there, rise, a caper.
ANTONIO	Caper after an honour, coz?
LOLLIO	Very proper; for honour is but a caper, rises as fast and high, has a knee or two, and falls to the ground again. 100 You can remember your figure, Tony?
ANTONIO	Yes, cousin; when I see thy figure, I can remember mine.

Enter Isabella [like a madwoman]

| ISABELLA | Hey, how he treads the air! Shough, shough, t'other way! He burns his wings else; here's wax enough below, Icarus, more than will be cancelled these eighteen moons; |

He's down, he's down! What a terrible fall he had!
Stand up, thou son of Cretan Dedalus,
And let us tread the lower labyrinth;   110
I'll bring thee to the clue.

ANTONIO   Prithee, coz, let me alone.

ISABELLA   Art thou not drowned?
About thy head I saw a heap of clouds,
Wrapped like a Turkish turban; on thy back
A crooked chameleon-coloured rainbow hung
Like a tiara down unto thy hams.
Let me suck out those billows in thy belly;
Hark how they roar and rumble in the straits!
Bless thee from the pirates.

ANTONIO   Pox upon you; let me alone!   120

ISABELLA   Why shouldst thou mount so high as Mercury,
Unless thou hadst reversion of his place?
Stay in the moon with me, Endymion,
And we will rule these wild, rebellious waves,
That would have drowned my love.

ANTONIO   I'll kick thee if again thou touch me,
Thou wild unshapen antic; I am no fool,
You bedlam!

ISABELLA   But you are, as sure as I am, mad.
Have I put on this habit of a frantic,
With love as full of fury, to beguile   130
The nimble eye of watchful jealousy,
And am I thus rewarded? [*reveals herself*]

ANTONIO   Ha, dearest beauty!

ISABELLA   No, I have no beauty now,
Nor ever had, but what was in my garments.
You, a quick-sighted lover? Come not near me!
Keep your caparisons, y'are aptly clad;
I came a feigner to return stark mad.   [*exit*

Enter LOLLIO

ANTONIO   Stay, or I shall change condition,
And become as you are.

LOLLIO   Why, Tony, whither now? Why, fool?   140

ANTONIO   Whose fool, usher of idiots? You coxcomb!
I have fooled too much.

LOLLIO	You were best be mad another while then.
ANTONIO	So I am, stark mad; I have cause enough;
	And I could throw the full effects on thee,
	And beat thee like a fury.
LOLLIO	Do not, do not; I shall not forbear the gentleman
	under the fool, if you do; alas, I saw through your
	fox-skin before now! Come, I can give you comfort;
	my mistress loves you, and there is as arrant a madman 150
	i'th'house as you are a fool, your rival, whom she
	loves not; if after the masque we can rid her of him,
	you earn her love, she says, and the fool shall ride her.
ANTONIO	May I believe thee?
LOLLIO	Yes, or you may choose whether you will or no.
ANTONIO	She's eased of him; I have a good quarrel on't.
LOLLIO	Well, keep your old station yet, and be quiet.
ANTONIO	Tell her I will deserve her love. [exit
LOLLIO	And you are like to have your desire.

Enter FRANCISCUS

FRANCISC.	[*sings*] 'Down, down, down a-down a-down' and 160
	then with a horse-trick,
	To kick Latona's forehead, and break her bowstring.
LOLLIO	This is t'other counterfeit; I'll put him out of his
	humour. [*takes out letter and reads*] 'Sweet lady, having
	now cast [off] this counterfeit cover of a madman, I
	appear to your best judgment a true and faithful lover
	of your beauty.' This is pretty well for a madman.
FRANCISC.	Ha! What's that?
LOLLIO	'Chide those perfections in you which [have] made
	me imperfect.' 170
FRANCISC.	I am discovered to the fool.
LOLLIO	I hope to discover the fool in you, ere I have done
	with you. 'Yours all, or one beside himself, Franciscus.'
	This madman will mend sure.
FRANCISC.	What do you read, sirrah?
LOLLIO	Your destiny, sir; you'll be hanged for this trick, and
	another that I know.
FRANCISC.	Art thou of counsel with thy mistress?
LOLLIO	Next her apron strings.
FRANCISC.	Give me thy hand. 180

LOLLIO　　　Stay, let me put yours in my pocket first [*puts away the letter*]; your hand is true, is it not? It will not pick? I partly fear it, because I think it does lie.

FRANCISC.　　Not in a syllable.

LOLLIO　　　So; if you love my mistress so well as you have handled the matter here, you are like to be cured of your madness.

FRANCISC.　　And none but she can cure it.

LOLLIO　　　Well, I'll give you over then, and she shall cast your water next.　　　　　　　　　　　　　　　　　　　　190

FRANCISC.　　Take for thy pains past. [*gives him money*]

LOLLIO　　　I shall deserve more, I hope; my mistress loves you, but must have some proof of your love to her.

FRANCISC.　　There I meet my wishes.

LOLLIO　　　That will not serve, you must meet her enemy and yours.

FRANCISC.　　He's dead already!

LOLLIO　　　Will you tell me that, and I parted but now with him?

FRANCISC.　　Show me the man.

LOLLIO　　　Ay, that's a right course now; see him before you kill　200 him in any case, and yet it needs not go so far neither; 'tis but a fool that haunts the house and my mistress in the shape of an idiot; bang but his fool's coat well-favouredly, and 'tis well.

FRANCISC.　　Soundly, soundly!

LOLLIO　　　Only reserve him till the masque be past; and if you find him not now in the dance yourself, I'll show you. In, in! My master!

FRANCISC.　　He handles him like a feather. Hey!　　　[*exit dancing*

Enter ALIBIUS

ALIBIUS　　　Well said; in a readiness, Lollio?　　　　　　　　210

LOLLIO　　　Yes, sir.

ALIBIUS　　　Away then, and guide them in, Lollio;
　　　　　　Entreat your mistress to see this sight.
　　　　　　Hark, is there not one incurable fool
　　　　　　That might be begged? I have friends.

LOLLIO　　　I have him for you, one that shall deserve it too. [*exit*

ALIBIUS　　　Good boy, Lollio.

Enter ISABELLA, *then* LOLLIO *with Madmen and Fools.*
The madmen and fools dance.

ALIBIUS   'Tis perfect; well, fit but once these strains,
         We shall have coin and credit for our pains.

                                                     [exeunt

Enter BEATRICE. *A clock strikes one.*

BEATRICE One struck, and yet she lies by't! – Oh, my fears!
This strumpet serves her own ends, 'tis apparent
                                                    now,
Devours the pleasure with a greedy appetite,
And never minds my honour or my peace,
Makes havoc of my right; but she pays dearly for't:
No trusting of her life with such a secret,
That cannot rule her blood to keep her promise.
Beside, I have some suspicion of her faith to me,
Because I was suspected of my lord,
And it must come from her. Hark! By my horrors,   10
Another clock strikes. [*strikes two*] Two!

Enter DE FLORES

DE FLORES   Pist, where are you?
BEATRICE De Flores?
DE FLORES   Ay; is she not come from him yet?
BEATRICE As I am a living soul, not.
DE FLORES   Sure the devil
Hath sowed his itch within her; who'd trust
A waiting-woman?
BEATRICE   I must trust somebody.
DE FLORES Push! They are termagants;
Especially when they fall upon their masters,
And have their ladies' first-fruits; th'are mad whelps,
You cannot stave 'em off from game royal; then
You are so harsh and hardy, ask no counsel,   20
And I could have helped you to an apothecary's
                                              daughter,
Would have fall'n off before eleven, and thanked
                                              you too.
BEATRICE O me, not yet? This whore forgets herself.
DE FLORES The rascal fares so well; look, y'are undone,
The day-star, by this hand! See Phosphorus plain
                                              yonder.

BEATRICE	Advise me now to fall upon some ruin,
	There is no counsel safe else.
DE FLORES	Peace, I ha't now;

BEATRICE Advise me now to fall upon some ruin,
There is no counsel safe else.
DE FLORES   Peace, I ha't now;
For we must force a rising, there's no remedy.
BEATRICE How? Take heed of that.
DE FLORES Tush, be you quiet, or else give over all.   30
BEATRICE Prithee, I ha' done then.
DE FLORES   This is my reach: I'll set
Some part afire of Diaphanta's chamber.
BEATRICE How? Fire, sir? That may endanger the whole house.
DE FLORES You talk of danger when your fame's on fire?
BEATRICE That's true; do what thou wilt now.
DE FLORES   Push! I aim
At a most rich success strikes all dead sure;
The chimney being afire, and some light parcels
Of the least danger in her chamber only,
If Diaphanta should be met by chance then,
Far from her lodging – which is now suspicious –   40
It would be thought her fears and affrights then
Drove her to seek for succour; if not seen
Or met at all, as that's the likeliest,
For her own shame she'll hasten towards her lodging;
I will be ready with a piece high-charged,
As 'twere to cleanse the chimney; there 'tis
                          proper now,
But she shall be the mark.
BEATRICE   I'm forced to love thee now,
'Cause thou provid'st so carefully for my honour.
DE FLORES 'Slid, it concerns the safety of us both,
Our pleasure and continuance.
BEATRICE   One word now,   50
Prithee; how for the servants?
DE FLORES   I'll despatch them
Some one way, some another in the hurry,
For buckets, hooks, ladders; fear not you;
The deed shall find its time; and I've thought since
Upon a safe conveyance for the body too.
How this fire purifies wit! Watch you your minute.
BEATRICE Fear keeps my soul upon't, I cannot stray from't.

Enter ALONZO'S ghost

DE FLORES   Ha! What art thou that tak'st away the light
                'Twixt that star and me? I dread thee not;
                'Twas but a mist of conscience – All's clear again.   60
                                                          [*exit*

BEATRICE   Who's that, De Flores? Bless me! It slides by;
                                                  [*exit ghost*
                Some ill thing haunts the house; 't has left behind it
                A shivering sweat upon me; I'm afraid now;
                This night has been so tedious. O, this strumpet!
                Had she a thousand lives, he should not leave her
                Till he had destroyed the last – List! O, my terrors!
                [*struck three o'clock*] Three struck by Saint Sebastian's!
WITHIN   Fire, fire, fire!
BEATRICE   Already! How rare is that man's speed!
                How heartily he serves me! His face loathes one,
                But look upon his care, who would not love him?   70
                The east is not more beauteous than his service.
WITHIN   Fire, fire, fire!

           Enter DE FLORES; *Servants pass over, ring a bell*

DE FLORES   Away, despatch! Hooks, buckets, ladders! That's
                                                      well said;
                The fire-bell rings, the chimney works; my charge;
                The piece is ready.   [*exit*
BEATRICE   Here's a man worth loving –

                   Enter DIAPHANTA

                O, y'are a jewel!
DIAPHANTA   Pardon frailty, madam;
                In troth I was so well, I ev'n forgot myself.
BEATRICE   Y'have made trim work.
DIAPHANTA   What?
BEATRICE   Hie quickly to your chamber;
                Your reward follows you.
DIAPHANTA   I never made
                So sweet a bargain.   [*exit*
                   Enter ALSEMERO
ALSEMERO   O my dear Joanna,   80

Alas, art thou risen too? I was coming,
My absolute treasure.

BEATRICE   When I missed you,
I could not choose but follow.

ALSEMERO   Th'art all sweetness;
The fire is not so dangerous.

BEATRICE   Think you so, sir?

ALSEMERO   I prithee tremble not; believe me, 'tis not.

       Enter VERMANDERO *and* JASPERINO

VERMAND.   O, bless my house and me!

ALSEMERO   My lord your father.

       Enter DE FLORES *with a piece*

VERMAND.   Knave, whither goes that piece?

DE FLORES   To scour the chimney.

                                           [exit

VERMAND.   Oh, well said, well said;
That fellow's good on all occasions.

BEATRICE   A wondrous necessary man, my lord.   90

VERMAND.   He hath a ready wit, he's worth 'em all, sir;
Dog at a house of fire; I ha' seen him singed ere now.
[the piece goes off] – Ha, there he goes.

BEATRICE   'Tis done.

ALSEMERO   Come, sweet, to bed now;
Alas, thou wilt get cold.

BEATRICE   Alas, the fear keeps that out;
My heart will find no quiet till I hear
How Diaphanta, my poor woman, fares;
It is her chamber, sir, her lodging chamber.

VERMAND.   How should the fire come there?

BEATRICE   As good a soul as ever lady countenanced,
But in her chamber negligent and heavy;   100
She 'scaped a mine twice.

VERMAND.   Twice?

BEATRICE   Strangely twice, sir.

VERMAND.   Those sleepy sluts are dangerous in a house,
An they be ne'er so good.

Enter DE FLORES

DE FLORES   O poor virginity,
Thou hast paid dearly for't!
VERMAND.   Bless us! What's that?
DE FLORES A thing you all knew once – Diaphanta's burnt.
BEATRICE My woman, O, my woman!
DE FLORES   Now the flames
Are greedy of her; burnt, burnt, burnt to death, sir!
BEATRICE O, my presaging soul!
ALSEMERO   Not a tear more;
I charge you by the last embrace I gave you
In bed before this raised us.
BEATRICE   Now you tie me;   110
Were it my sister, now she gets no more.

Enter Servant

VERMAND. How now?
SERVANT All danger's past; you may now take your rests, my
lords, the fire is throughly quenched; ah, poor gentle-
woman, how soon was she stifled!
BEATRICE De Flores, what is left of her inter,
And as we mourners all will follow her;
I will entreat that honour to my servant,
Ev'n of my lord himself.
ALSEMERO   Command it, sweetness.
BEATRICE Which of you spied the fire first?
DE FLORES   'Twas I, madam.   120
BEATRICE And took such pains in't too? A double goodness!
'Twere well he were rewarded.
VERMAND.   He shall be;
De Flores, call upon me.
ALSEMERO   And upon me, sir.
                    [*exeunt all, except De Flores*
DE FLORES Rewarded? Precious! Here's a trick beyond me;
I see in all bouts both of sport and wit,
Always a woman strives for the last hit.
                                              [*exit*

SCENE 2

Enter TOMAZO

TOMAZO　I cannot taste the benefits of life
With the same relish I was wont to do.
Man I grow weary of, and hold his fellowship
A treacherous, bloody friendship; and because
I am ignorant in whom my wrath should settle,
I must think all men villains, and the next
I meet, whoe'er he be, the murderer
Of my most worthy brother – Ha! What's he?

Enter DE FLORES, *passes over the stage*

Oh, the fellow that some call honest De Flores;
But methinks honesty was hard bested　　　　　10
To come there for a lodging, as if a queen
Should make her palace of a pest-house.
I find a contrariety in nature
Betwixt that face and me; the least occasion
Would give me game upon him; yet he's so foul
One would scarce touch him with a sword he loved
And made account of; so most deadly venomous,
He would go near to poison any weapon
That should draw blood on him; one must resolve
Never to use that sword again in fight,　　　　　20
In way of honest manhood, that strikes him;
Some river must devour't, 'twere not fit
That any man should find it – What, again?

Enter DE FLORES

He walks a'purpose by, sure, to choke me up,
To infect my blood.

DE FLORES　　　　　　　　My worthy noble lord!

TOMAZO　Dost offer to come near and breathe upon me?
[*strikes him*]

DE FLORES　A blow! [*draws his sword*]

TOMAZO　　　　　Yea, are you so prepared?
I'll rather, like a soldier, die by th'sword [*draws*]
Than like a politician by thy poison.

DE FLORES	Hold, my lord, as you are honourable. 30
TOMAZO	All slaves that kill by poison are still cowards.
DE FLORES	[aside] I cannot strike; I see his brother's wounds

Fresh bleeding in his eye, as in a crystal –
I will not question this; I know y'are noble;
I take my injury with thanks given, sir,
Like a wise lawyer; and as a favour
Will wear it for the worthy hand that gave it. –
[aside] Why this from him that yesterday appeared
So strangely loving to me?
O, but instinct is of a subtler strain;   40
Guilt must not walk so near his lodge again;
He came near me now.   [exit

TOMAZO   All league with mankind I renounce for ever
Till I find this murderer; not so much
As common courtesy, but I'll lock up;
For in the state of ignorance I live in,
A brother may salute his brother's murderer,
And wish good speed to th'villain in a greeting.

Enter VERMANDERO, ALIBIUS, *and* ISABELLA

VERMAND.   Noble Piracquo!
TOMAZO   Pray keep on your way, sir,
I've nothing to say to you.
VERMAND.   Comforts bless you, sir.   50
TOMAZO   I have forsworn compliment, in troth I have, sir;
As you are merely man, I have not left
A good wish for you, nor any here.
VERMAND.   Unless you be so far in love with grief
You will not part from't upon any terms,
We bring that news will make a welcome for us.
TOMAZO   What news can that be?
VERMAND.   Throw no scornful smile
Upon the zeal I bring you, 'tis worth more, sir.
Two of the chiefest men I kept about me
I hide not from the law or your just vengeance.   60
TOMAZO   Ha!
VERMAND.   To give your peace more ample satisfaction,
Thank these discoverers.
TOMAZO   If you bring that calm,

Name but the manner I shall ask forgiveness in
For that contemptuous smile upon you:
I'll perfect it with reverence that belongs
Unto a sacred altar. [*kneels*]

VERMAND.   Good sir, rise;
Why, now you overdo so much o'this hand
As you fell short o't'other. Speak, Alibius.

ALIBIUS   'Twas my wife's fortune, as she is most lucky   70
At a discovery, to find out lately
Within our hospital of fools and madmen
Two counterfeits slipped into these disguises:
Their names Franciscus and Antonio.

VERMAND.   Both mine, sir, and I ask no favour for 'em.

ALIBIUS   Now that which draws suspicion to their habits,
The time of their disguisings, agrees justly
With the day of the murder.

TOMAZO   O blest revelation!

VERMAND.   Nay more, nay more, sir – I'll not spare mine own
In way of justice – they both feigned a journey   80
To Briamata, and so wrought out their leaves;
My love was so abused in't.

TOMAZO   Time's too precious
To run in waste now; you have brought a peace
The riches of five kingdoms could not purchase.
Be my most happy conduct; I thirst for 'em;
Like subtle lightning will I wind about 'em,
And melt their marrow in 'em.

                                              [*exeunt*

SCENE 3

Enter ALSEMERO *and* JASPERINO

JASPERINO Your confidence, I'm sure, is now of proof.
The prospect from the garden has showed
Enough for deep suspicion.

ALSEMERO   The black mask
That so continually was worn upon't
Condemns the face for ugly ere't be seen;

Her despite to him, and so seeming bottomless.

JASPERINO Touch it home then; 'tis not a shallow probe
Can search this ulcer soundly; I fear you'll find it
Full of corruption; 'tis fit I leave you,
She meets you opportunely from that walk;   10
She took the back door at his parting with her.

[exit Jasperino

ALSEMERO Did my fate wait for this unhappy stroke
At my first sight of woman? – She's here.

Enter BEATRICE

BEATRICE Alsemero!
ALSEMERO   How do you?
BEATRICE   How do I?
Alas! How do you? You look not well.
ALSEMERO You read me well enough, I am not well.
BEATRICE Not well, sir? Is't in my power to better you?
ALSEMERO Yes.
BEATRICE   Nay, then y'are cured again.
ALSEMERO Pray resolve me one question, lady.
BEATRICE   If I can.
ALSEMERO None can so sure. Are you honest?   20
BEATRICE Ha, ha, ha! That's a broad question, my lord.
ALSEMERO But that's not a modest answer, my lady.
Do you laugh? My doubts are strong upon me.
BEATRICE 'Tis innocence that smiles, and no rough brow
Can take away the dimple in her cheek.
Say I should strain a tear to fill the vault,
Which would you give the better faith to?
ALSEMERO 'Twere but hypocrisy of a sadder colour,
But the same stuff; neither your smiles nor tears
Shall move or flatter me from my belief: 30
You are a whore!
BEATRICE   What a horrid sound it hath!
It blasts a beauty to deformity;
Upon what face soever that breath falls,
It strikes it ugly; O, you have ruined
What you can ne'er repair again.
ALSEMERO   I'll all

Demolish, and seek out truth within you,
If there be any left; let your sweet tongue
Prevent your heart's rifling; there I'll ransack
And tear out my suspicion.

BEATRICE   You may, sir,
'Tis an easy passage; yet, if you please,   40
Show me the ground whereon you lost your love;
My spotless virtue may but tread on that
Before I perish.

ALSEMERO   Unanswerable!
A ground you cannot stand on; you fall down
Beneath all grace and goodness when you set
Your ticklish heel on't; there was a visor
O'er that cunning face, and that became you;
Now impudence in triumph rides upon't;
How comes this reconcilement else
'Twixt you and your despite, your rancorous loathing, 50
De Flores? He that your eye was sore at sight of,
He's now become your arm's supporter, your
Lip's saint!

BEATRICE   Is there the cause?

ALSEMERO   Worse; your lust's devil,
Your adultery!

BEATRICE   Would any but yourself say that,
'Twould turn him to a villain.

ALSEMERO   'Twas witnessed
By the counsel of your bosom, Diaphanta.

BEATRICE Is your witness dead then?

ALSEMERO   'Tis to be feared
It was the wages of her knowledge; poor soul,
She lived not long after the discovery.

BEATRICE Then hear a story of not much less horror   60
Than this your false suspicion is beguiled with;
To your bed's scandal I stand up innocence,
Which even the guilt of one black other deed
Will stand for proof of: your love has made me
A cruel murderess.

ALSEMERO   Ha!

BEATRICE   A bloody one;

I have kissed poison for't, stroked a serpent:
That thing of hate, worthy in my esteem
Of no better employment, and him most worthy
To be so employed, I caused to murder
That innocent Piracquo, having no   70
Better means than that worst, to assure
Yourself to me.

ALSEMERO   O, the place itself e'er since
Has crying been for vengeance, the temple
Where blood and beauty first unlawfully
Fired their devotion and quenched the right one;
'Twas in my fears at first, 'twill have it now;
O, thou art all deformed!

BEATRICE   Forget not, sir,
It for your sake was done; shall greater dangers
Make the less welcome?

ALSEMERO   O, thou shouldst have gone
A thousand leagues about to have avoided   80
This dangerous bridge of blood! Here we are lost.

BEATRICE   Remember I am true unto your bed.

ALSEMERO   The bed itself's a charnel, the sheets shrouds
For murdered carcasses. It must ask pause
What I must do in this; meantime you shall
Be my prisoner only. Enter my closet;   [exit Beatrice
I'll be your keeper yet. O, in what part
Of this sad story shall I first begin? – Ha!
This same fellow has put me in –

Enter DE FLORES

                    De Flores!

DE FLORES   Noble Alsemero!

ALSEMERO   I can tell you
News, sir; my wife has her commended to you.   90

DE FLORES   That's news indeed, my lord; I think she would
Commend me to the gallows if she could,
She ever loved me so well; I thank her.

ALSEMERO   What's this blood upon your hand, De Flores?

DE FLORES   Blood? No, sure, 'twas washed since.

ALSEMERO   Since when, man?

DE FLORES   Since t'other day I got a knock
            In a sword-and-dagger school; I think 'tis out.
ALSEMERO   Yes, 'tis almost out, but 'tis perceived though.
            I had forgot my message; this it is:
            What price goes murder?
DE FLORES   How sir?
ALSEMERO   I ask you, sir;   100
            My wife's behindhand with you; she tells me,
            For a brave bloody blow you gave for her sake
            Upon Piracquo.
DE FLORES   Upon? 'Twas quite through him, sure;
            Has she confessed it?
ALSEMERO   As sure as death to both of you,
            And much more than that.
DE FLORES   It could not be much more;
            'Twas but one thing, and that – she's a whore.
ALSEMERO   It could not choose but follow; O, cunning devils!
            How should blind men know you from fair-faced
                                                        saints?
BEATRICE   [within] He lies, the villain does belie me!
DE FLORES   Let me go to her, sir.
ALSEMERO   Nay, you shall to her.   110
            Peace, crying crocodile, your sounds are heard!
            Take your prey to you, get you in to her, sir.
                                           [exit De Flores
            I'll be your pander now; rehearse again
            Your scene of lust, that you may be perfect
            When you shall come to act it to the black audience
            Where howls and gnashings shall be music to you.
            Clip your adulteress freely, 'tis the pilot
            Will guide you to the Mare Mortuum,
            Where you shall sink to fathoms bottomless.

            Enter VERMANDERO, ALIBIUS, ISABELLA, TOMAZO,
                  FRANCISCUS and ANTONIO

VERMAND.   O, Alsemero, I have a wonder for you.   120
ALSEMERO   No, sir, 'tis I, I have a wonder for you.
VERMAND.   I have suspicion near as proof itself
            For Piracquo's murder.
ALSEMERO   Sir, I have proof

           Beyond suspicion for Piracquo's murder.

VERMAND. Beseech you, hear me; these two have been disguised
           E'er since the deed was done.

ALSEMERO   I have two other
           That were more close disguised than your two could be
           E'er since the deed was done.

VERMAND. You'll hear me – these mine own servants –

ALSEMERO Hear me: those nearer than your servants,   130
           That shall acquit them and prove them guiltless.

FRANCISC. That may be done with easy truth, sir.

TOMAZO How is my cause bandied through your delays!
           'Tis urgent in my blood and calls for haste;
           Give me a brother alive or dead;
           Alive, a wife with him; if dead, for both
           A recompense for murder and adultery.

BEATRICE [within] Oh, oh, oh!

ALSEMERO   Hark! 'Tis coming to you.

DE FLORES [within] Nay, I'll along for company.

BEATRICE [within]   Oh, oh!

VERMAND. What horrid sounds are these?   140

ALSEMERO Come forth, you twins of mischief.

       Enter DE FLORES, *bringing in* BEATRICE [*wounded*]

DE FLORES Here we are; if you have any more
           To say to us speak quickly, I shall not
           Give you the hearing else; I am so stout yet,
           And so, I think, that broken rib of mankind.

VERMAND. A host of enemies entered my citadel
           Could not amaze like this: Joanna! Beatrice-Joanna!

BEATRICE O, come not near me, sir, I shall defile you;
           I am that of your blood was taken from you
           For your better health; look no more upon't,   150
           But cast it to the ground regardlessly,
           Let the common sewer take it from distinction.
           Beneath the stars, upon yon meteor
           Ever hung my fate, 'mongst things corruptible;
           I ne'er could pluck it from him; my loathing
           Was prophet to the rest, but ne'er believed;
           Mine honour fell with him, and now my life.
           Alsemero, I am a stranger to your bed,

Your bed was cozened on the nuptial night,
For which your false bride died.

ALSEMERO   Diaphanta!   160

DE FLORES Yes, and the while I coupled with your mate
At barley-break; now we are left in hell.

VERMAND. We are all there, it circumscribes [us] here.

DE FLORES I loved this woman in spite of her heart;
Her love I earned out of Piracquo's murder.

TOMAZO Ha! My brother's murderer?

DE FLORES   Yes, and her honour's prize
Was my reward; I thank life for nothing
But that pleasure; it was so sweet to me
That I have drunk up all, left none behind
For any man to pledge me.

VERMAND.   Horrid villain!   170
Keep life in him for further tortures.

DE FLORES   No!
I can prevent you; here's my penknife still;
It is but one thread more, [stabs himself] and now
                                        'tis cut.
Make haste, Joanna, by that token to thee,
Canst not forget, so lately put in mind;
I would not go to leave thee far behind. [dies]

BEATRICE Forgive me, Alsemero, all forgive;
'Tis time to die when 'tis a shame to live. [dies]

VERMAND. O, my name is entered now in that record,
Where till this fatal hour 'twas never read.   180

ALSEMERO Let it be blotted out; let your heart lose it,
And it can never look you in the face,
Nor tell a tale behind the back of life
To your dishonour; justice hath so right
The guilty hit that innocence is quit
By proclamation, and may joy again.
Sir, you are sensible of what truth hath done;
'Tis the best comfort that your grief can find.

TOMAZO Sir, I am satisfied; my injuries
Lie dead before me; I can exact no more,   190
Unless my soul were loose, and could o'ertake
Those black fugitives that are fled from thence,

To take a second vengeance; but there are wraths
Deeper than mine, 'tis to be feared, about 'em.

ALSEMERO   What an opacous body had that moon
That last changed on us! Here's beauty changed
To ugly whoredom; here, servant obedience
To a master-sin, imperious murder;
I, a supposed husband, changed embraces
With wantonness, but that was paid before;   200
Your change is come too, from an ignorant wrath
To knowing friendship. Are there any more on's?

ANTONIO   Yes, sir, I was changed too, from a little ass as I was to
a great fool as I am, and had like to ha'been changed
to the gallows, but that you know my innocence
always excuses me.

FRANCISC. I was changed from a little wit to be stark mad,
Almost for the same purpose.

ISABELLA   Your change is still behind,
But deserve best your transformation:
You are a jealous coxcomb, keep schools of folly,   210
And teach your scholars how to break your own head.

ALIBIUS   I see all apparent, wife, and will change now
Into a better husband, and never keep
Scholars that shall be wiser than myself.

ALSEMERO   Sir, you have yet a son's duty living,
Please you accept it; let that your sorrow,
As it goes from your eye, go from your heart;
Man and his sorrow at the grave must part.

EPILOGUE

ALSEMERO   All we can do to comfort one another,
To stay a brother's sorrow for a brother,   220
To dry a child from the kind father's eyes,
Is to no purpose, it rather multiplies;
Your only smiles have power to cause relive
The dead again, or in their rooms to give
Brother a new brother, father a child;
If these appear, all griefs are reconciled.

                                        [exeunt omnes

WOMEN BEWARE WOMEN

INTRODUCTION

Women Beware Women, the last of the plays collected here, was written just before the end of the Jacobean era. It was probably first performed in 1625, the year of James I's death. The title is deeply ironic. Although it is ostensibly true that women have to beware other women, as in *The White Devil*, their real enemies are men. As in Middleton's other tragedies, the characters are complex and tormented, often driven by psychological forces they cannot understand or account for. The play itself moves from a web of intrigue towards a climax which is as ridiculous as it is tragic, a feature of much Jacobean tragedy, especially towards the end of the period. Like *The Revenger's Tragedy* and *The Duchess of Malfi*, the audience is constantly reminded of the heavily eroticised atmosphere at court, where everyone is looking for a sexual opportunity. Even more than in those two plays, one is constantly reminded that both sexes are driven by depraved lust if their senses are awakened.

Like Webster's Italian-based plays, *Women Beware Women* is based on a true story, that of Francesco de Medici, who also appears in *The White Devil*. However, either Middleton or a lost source appears to have taken a number of liberties with the story. Among the more important of these, Livia is an invention of Middleton's, and the Cardinal appears to have been rather less innocent in real life than he is in Middleton's story. Middleton probably relied on Italian sources for all the plot-strands he draws together in his play.

Bianca, a young and naive noblewoman from Venice, marries Leantio, an honest but rather dull Florentine merchant's clerk. She moves into Leantio's house which is shared with his decent but unsophisticated mother. She is soon invited to court, and starts to tire of the restricted life she has been forced to lead after her marriage. Livia, a cynical and powerful woman at court who enjoys manipulating others, has plans for her. The lecherous Duke of Florence is attracted to Bianca. He seduces her in his private chambers at court, having shown her a series of erotic paintings which inflame Bianca's base desires. Livia is at the same time furthering her brother Hippolito's adulterous lust for their niece, Isabella.

Livia's cynicism is suspended for a brief moment when she encounters Leantio and they become lovers. However, the Duke, criticised for his adultery by his brother, the Cardinal, decides to solve his problem by having Leantio murdered and marrying Bianca. He discovers that Livia and Leantio are lovers and lets Hippolito discover the truth of his sister's passion. Hippolito murders Leantio, and Livia takes her immediate revenge by announcing her brother's incest to the court. The climax of the play is reached in the performance of a masque to celebrate the nuptials of the Duke and Bianca, a conclusion which recalls the ending of *The Spanish Tragedy*, where a similar event enabled the wronged father to dispose of his enemies. A series of mistaken and bungled murder attempts result in the deaths of all the protagonists. The Duke drinks poisoned wine; Livia succumbs to poisoned incense; Isabella is shot by flaming gold; Hippolito is shot by a series of Cupids. Bianca, realising the fate of her new husband, drinks out of the same poisoned cup and expires blaming women for the tragedy: 'O the deadly snares / That women set for women, without pity / Either to soul or honour!' A debatable conclusion. The Cardinal, in this play a virtuous figure unlike his counterparts in Webster's two tragedies, is left to conclude, rather inadequately: 'So where lust reigns, that prince cannot reign long.'

The play is a brilliant work, which demonstrates a number of the most fascinating features of Jacobean tragedy. Middleton combines psychological insight and tragic action in the first half of the play with a farcical explosion of plots and action in the last two acts. This divided structure can be read as an exhaustion of a form which was maintained in earlier plays, the unbearable atmosphere of the most intense tragedy descending into ridiculousness. However this would be a naive view of the play. It is more likely that Middleton, acutely aware of the formulae of Jacobean tragedy, was showing that he could use the form to say as much as any other writer, but had recognised its excesses and clichés, which he duly satirised. In a way, the over-indulgent ending, with the stage yet again littered with the bodies of the truly guilty, comes as something of a relief to the audience after the unbearable sexual tension of the first half of the play.

The play raises the interesting question of the roles of the sexes in the same way that Webster does in *The White Devil*. Bianca's descent into depravity resembles the route away from virtue taken by Beatrice Joanna in Middleton's slightly earlier play, *The Changeling*. The question we have to ask is, how culpable is she? It is true that she dies blaming other women, probably because she was helped on her way by Livia, the key figure at court, who is able to control the action until she loses her detached stance when she falls for Leantio. But is Livia really in control? Is she not just as much a victim of a corrupt court as the woman she ruins? Looked at another way, what happens in the main plot strands in the play is that the women serve the lusts of men. Livia procures Bianca for the Duke, Isabella for Hippolito and herself for Leantio. The women may blame themselves, but that does not mean that the audience has to take their judgments at face value. They merely participate in a system which serves to satisfy male – and, it has to be said, their own – lust.

Virtually everyone in the play can be seen as a whore, but it is only the women who are regarded in this light. To give one example: there are a number of encounters between Leantio and Bianca after their marriage has effectively ended. At first Leantio is crushed by the loss of his wife. It is easy for the audience to feel sympathy for his pitiful laments and his conclusion that 'All preferment / That springs from sin and lust, it shoots up quickly, / As gardeners' crops do in the rottenest grounds; / So is all means raised from base prostitution' (3, 2, 47–50). The cuckolded Leantio is able to assume the role of the virtuous outsider looking in on the vile corruption of the court, which has claimed his wife. A few scenes later, however, after he has been taken up by Livia, Leantio continues in his moral discourse when he encounters his wife again. He relishes the confrontation, as does Bianca. Leantio boasts that he longs 'to see how my despiser looks, / Now she's come here to court' (4, 1, 41–2). This is a far cry from his earlier self-pity, now that he has become part of the corrupt society he affected to despise before. He finds nothing odd in describing his former wife as a 'whore' and sneering at her new riches, when he has behaved in exactly the same way. Bianca describes him as a 'silk-worm' in his new clothes. Indeed, Leantio's desire to take revenge for Bianca's former assumption of superiority leads to his downfall. He cannot resist boasting that he is now the lover of Livia. This has the desired effect in shocking Bianca, but the end result is the Duke's decision to have Leantio murdered.

This strand of the plot shows how keenly *Women Beware Women* comments on the question of class and status. Leantio will always be a vulgar outsider, whatever clothes he disguises himself in. He will never match the insouciant arrogance of the Duke, who will always be able to assume his own superiority. Leantio's mother, a minor but significant character, who initially cares for and worries about the fate of her son, reveals that she can easily be bought by the wealth and riches on offer. When Leantio begs Bianca not to go to the Duke, his mother, who has been with her daughter-in-law, shows just how easily she can be bought: 'I'll first obey the Duke, / And taste of a good banquet' (3, 1, 265–6). Once characters are caught up in the web of deceit which characterises court society, it is hard for them to stand outside and remember their original moral sense. All those who enter this world find themselves trapped: Bianca, Leantio and the mother. They make errors which lead to their deaths, but then so do characters who exist at ease in this vile world. One way of reading *Women Beware Women* is to regard it as almost a parody of the types of assumptions made in Jacobean tragedy – or rather, as a work which pushes generic expectations to the limit, indicating how familiar the themes and conventions of such plays had become.

Upon the tragedy of my familiar acquaintance
THO. MIDDLETON

Women beware Women: 'tis a true text
Never to be forgot. Drabs of state vexed
Have plots, poisons, mischiefs that seldom miss
To murther virtue with a venom kiss –
Witness this worthy tragedy, expressed
By him that well deserved amongst the best
Of poets in his time. He knew the rage,
Madness of women crossed; and for the stage
Fitted their humours, hell-bred malice, strife
Acted in state, presented to the life.
I that have seen't can say, having just cause,
Never came tragedy off with more applause.

NATH. RICHARDS

CHARACTERS IN THE PLAY

DUKE OF FLORENCE

LORD CARDINAL, *brother to the Duke*

TWO CARDINALS *more*

A LORD

FABRITIO, *father to Isabella*

HIPPOLITO, *brother to Fabritio*

GUARDIANO, *uncle to the foolish Ward*

THE WARD, *a rich young heir*

LEANTIO, *a factor, husband to Bianca*

SORDIDO, *the Ward's man*

LIVIA, *sister to Fabritio*

ISABELLA, *niece to Livia*

BIANCA, *Leantio's wife*

THE WIDOW, *Leantio's mother*

States of Florence, Citizens, a 'Prentice,

Boys, Messenger, Servants

[*Two Ladies, other Lords, Pages, Guard*]

The Scene: Florence

WOMEN BEWARE WOMEN

ACT I SCENE I

Enter LEANTIO *with* BIANCA *and* MOTHER

MOTHER   Thy sight was never yet more precious to me;
Welcome, with all the affection of a mother,
That comfort can express from natural love:
Since thy birth-joy – a mother's chiefest gladness
After sh'as undergone her curse of sorrows –
Thou wast not more dear to me than this hour
Presents thee to my heart. Welcome again.

LEANTIO   'Las, poor affectionate soul, how her joys speak to me!
I have observed it often, and I know it is
The fortune commonly of knavish children   10
To have the loving'st mothers.

MOTHER   What's this gentlewoman?

LEANTIO   O, you have named the most unvalued'st purchase
That youth of man had ever knowledge of.
As often as I look upon that treasure,
And know it to be mine – there lies the blessing –
It joys me that I ever was ordained
To have a being, and to live 'mongst men;
Which is a fearful living, and a poor one,
Let a man truly think on't,
To have the toil and griefs of fourscore years   20
Put up in a white sheet, tied with two knots.
Methinks it should strike earthquakes in adulterers,
When even the very sheets they commit sin in,
May prove, for aught they know, all their
                          last garments.
O what a mark were there for women then!
But beauty able to content a conqueror
Whom earth could scarce content, keeps me
                          in compass;
I find no wish in me bent sinfully,
To this man's sister or to that man's wife:
In love's name let 'em keep their honesties,   30

And cleave to their own husbands, 'tis their duties.
Now when I go to church, I can pray handsomely,
Nor come like gallants only to see faces,
As if lust went to market still on Sundays.
I must confess I am guilty of one sin, mother,
More than I brought into the world with me;
But that I glory in: 'tis theft, but noble
As ever greatness yet shot up withal.

MOTHER How's that?

LEANTIO   Never to be repented, mother,
Though sin be death! I had died, if I had not sinned,   40
And here's my masterpiece. Do you now behold her!
Look on her well, she's mine; look on her better —
Now say, if't be not the best piece of theft
That ever was committed. And I have my pardon for't:
'Tis sealed from Heaven by marriage.

MOTHER   Married to her!

LEANTIO You must keep counsel, mother, I am undone else;
If it be known, I have lost her. Do but think now
What that loss is — life's but a trifle to't.
From Venice her consent and I have brought her,
From parents great in wealth, more now in rage;   50
But let storms spend their furies. Now we have got
A shelter o'er our quiet innocent loves,
We are contented. Little money sh'as brought me:
View but her face, you may see all her dowry,
Save that which lies locked up in hidden virtues,
Like jewels kept in cabinets.

MOTHER   Y'are to blame,
If your obedience will give way to a check,
To wrong such a perfection.

LEANTIO   How?

MOTHER   Such a creature,
To draw her from her fortune, which no doubt,
At the full time, might have proved rich and noble: 60
You know not what you have done. My life
                              can give you
But little helps, and my death lesser hopes;
And hitherto your own means has but made shift

To keep you single, and that hardly too.
What ableness have you to do her right, then,
In maintenance fitting her birth and virtues,
Which every woman of necessity looks for,
And most to go above it, not confined
By their conditions, virtues, bloods, or births,
But flowing to affections, wills and humours?   70

LEANTIO   Speak low, sweet mother; you are able to spoil as many
As come within the hearing; if it be not
Your fortune to mar all, I have much marvel.
I pray do not you teach her to rebel,
When she's in a good way to obedience –
To rise with other women in commotion
Against their husbands, for six gowns a year,
And so maintain their cause, when they're once up,
In all things else that require cost enough.
They are all of 'em a kind of spirits – soon raised,   80
But not so soon laid, mother. As for example,
A woman's belly is got up in a trice:
A simple charge ere it be laid down again:
So ever in all their quarrels, and their courses.
And I'm a proud man, I hear nothing of 'em;
They're very still, I thank my happiness,
And sound asleep; pray let not your tongue wake 'em.
If you can but rest quiet, she's contented
With all conditions that my fortunes bring her to:
To keep close as a wife that loves her husband;   90
To go after the rate of my ability,
Not the licentious swinge of her own will,
Like some of her old schoolfellows. She intends
To take out other works in a new sampler,
And frame the fashion of an honest love,
Which knows no wants but, mocking poverty,
Brings forth more children, to make rich men wonder
At divine Providence, that feeds mouths of infants,
And sends them none to feed, but stuffs their rooms
With fruitful bags, their beds with barren wombs.   100
Good mother, make not you things worse
                         than they are

Out of your too much openness – pray take
heed on't –
Nor imitate the envy of old people,
That strive to mar good sport, because they are perfect.
I would have you more pitiful to youth,
Especially to your own flesh and blood.
I'll prove an excellent husband – here's my hand –
Lay in provision, follow my business roundly,
And make you a grandmother in forty weeks!
Go, pray salute her, bid her welcome cheerfully.   110

MOTHER   Gentlewoman, thus much is a debt of courtesy
[*she kisses Bianca*]
Which fashionable strangers pay each other
At a kind meeting; then there's more than one,
Due to the knowledge I have of your nearness;
I am bold to come again, and now salute you
By th'name of daughter, which may challenge more
Than ordinary respect.

LEANTIO   Why, this is well now,
And I think few mothers of threescore will mend it.

MOTHER   What I can bid you welcome to, is mean;
But make it all your own: we are full of wants,   120
And cannot welcome worth.

LEANTIO   Now this is scurvy,
And spoke as if a woman lacked her teeth!
These old folks talk of nothing but defects,
Because they grow so full of 'em themselves.

BIANCA   Kind mother, there is nothing can be wanting
To her that does enjoy all her desires.
Heaven send a quiet peace with this man's love,
And I am as rich, as virtue can be poor –
Which were enough, after the rate of mind,
To erect temples for content placed here.   130
I have forsook friends, fortunes, and my country;
And hourly I rejoice in't. Here's my friends,
And few is the good number. Thy successes,
Howe'er they look, I will still name my fortunes;
Hopeful or spiteful, they shall all be welcome:
Who invites many guests, has of all sorts

As he that traffics much, drinks of all fortunes:
Yet they must all be welcome, and used well.
I'll call this place the place of my birth now –
And rightly too, for here my love was born,   140
And that's the birthday of a woman's joys.
You have not bid me welcome since I came.

LEANTIO   That I did, questionless.

BIANCA   No sure, how was't?
I have quite forgot it.

LEANTIO   Thus. [*kisses her*]

BIANCA   O sir, 'tis true,
Now I remember well: I have done thee wrong,
Pray take't again, sir. [*kisses him*]

LEANTIO   How many of these wrongs
Could I put up in an hour? And turn up the glass
For twice as many more.

MOTHER   Will't please you to walk in, daughter?

BIANCA   Thanks, sweet mother;
The voice of her that bare me is not more pleasing.   150

                      [*exeunt Mother and Bianca*]

LEANTIO   Though my own care and my rich master's trust
Lay their commands both on my factorship,
This day and night I'll know no other business
But her and her dear welcome. 'Tis a bitterness
To think upon tomorrow, that I must leave her
Still to the sweet hopes of the week's end.
That pleasure should be so restrained and curbed
After the course of a rich workmaster,
That never pays till Saturday night!
Marry, it comes together in a round sum then,   160
And does more good, you'll say.

                      O fair-eyed Florence!
Didst thou but know what a most matchless jewel
Thou now art mistress of, a pride would take thee
Able to shoot destruction through the bloods
Of all thy youthful sons! But 'tis great policy
To keep choice treasures in obscurest places:
Should we show thieves our wealth, 'twould
                        make 'em bolder.

Temptation is a devil will not stick
To fasten upon a saint – take heed of that.
The jewel is cased up from all men's eyes: 170
Who could imagine now a gem were kept,
Of that great value, under this plain roof?
But how in times of absence – what assurance
Of this restraint then? Yes, yes – there's one with her!
Old mothers know the world; and such as these,
When sons lock chests, are good to look to keys.

                                                        [*exit*

SCENE 2

Enter GUARDIANO, FABRITIO *and* LIVIA *with* SERVANT

GUARD'O   What, has your daughter seen him yet?

                                     Know you that?

FABRITIO   No matter – she shall love him.

GUARD'O   Nay, let's have fair play!
He has been now my ward some fifteen year,
And 'tis my purpose, as time calls upon me,
By custom seconded, and such moral virtues,
To tender him a wife; now, sir, this wife
I'd fain elect out of a daughter of yours.
You see my meaning's fair. If now this daughter,
So tendered – let me come to your own phrase, sir –
Should offer to refuse him, I were handselled.   10
[*aside*] Thus am I fain to calculate all my words
For the meridian of a foolish old man,
To take his understanding! [*aloud*] What do you
                                                        answer, sir?

FABRITIO   I say still, she shall love him.

GUARD'O   Yet again?
And shall she have no reason for this love?

FABRITIO   Why, do you think that women love with reason?

GUARD'O   I perceive fools are not at all hours foolish,
No more than wise men wise.

FABRITIO   I had a wife;
She ran mad for me; she had no reason for't
For aught I could perceive. What think you,   20

      Lady sister?

GUARD'O [*aside*]   – 'Twas a fit match that,
      Being both out of their wits! [*aloud*] A loving
                wife, 'seemed,
      She strove to come as near you as she could.

FABRITIO And if her daughter prove not mad for love too,
      She takes not after her – nor after me,
      If she prefer reason before my pleasure.
      You're an experienced widow, lady sister;
      I pray let your opinion come amongst us.

LIVIA   I must offend you then, if truth will do't,
      And take my niece's part, and call't injustice   30
      To force her love to one she never saw.
      Maids should both see and like – all little enough:
      If they love truly after that, 'tis well.
      Counting the time, she takes one man till death,
      That's a hard task, I tell you; but one may
      Enquire at three years' end amongst young wives,
      And mark how the game goes.

FABRITIO   Why, is not man
      Tied to the same observance, lady sister,
      And in one woman?

LIVIA   'Tis enough for him;
      Besides, he tastes of many sundry dishes   40
      That we poor wretches never lay our lips to –
      As obedience, forsooth, subjection, duty, and
                such kickshaws,
      All of our making, but served in to them;
      And if we lick a finger then, sometimes,
      We are not to blame; your best cooks use it.

FABRITIO Th'art a sweet lady, sister, and a witty.

LIVIA   A witty! Oh, the bud of commendation,
      Fit for a girl of sixteen! I am blown, man!
      I should be wise by this time – and, for instance,
      I have buried my two husbands in good fashion, 50
      And never mean more to marry.

GUARD'O   No, why so, lady?

LIVIA   Because the third shall never bury me:
      I think I am more than witty. How think you, sir?

FABRITIO   I have paid often fees to a counsellor
           Has had a weaker brain.

LIVIA   Then I must tell you,
           Your money was soon parted.

GUARD'O   Light her now, brother!

LIVIA   Where is my niece? Let her be sent for straight.
                                              [exit Servant
           If you have any hope 'twill prove a wedding,
           'Tis fit i'faith she should have one sight of him,
           And stop upon't, and not be joined in haste,   60
           As if they went to stock a new found land.

FABRITIO   Look out her uncle, and y'are sure of her,
           Those two are never asunder; they've been heard
           In argument at midnight, moonshine nights
           Are noondays with them; they walk out their sleeps –
           Or rather at those hours appear like those
           That walk in 'em, for so they did to me.
           Look you, I told you truth: they're like a chain,
           Draw but one link, all follows.

                   Enter HIPPOLITO and ISABELLA the niece

GUARD'O   Oh affinity,
           What piece of excellent workmanship art thou?   70
           'Tis work clean wrought, for there's no lust,
                                              but love in't,
           And that abundantly – when in stranger things
           There is no love at all, but what lust brings.

FABRITIO   On with your mask, for 'tis your part to see now,
           And not be seen. Go to, make use of your time;
           See what you mean to like – nay, and I charge you,
           Like what you see. Do you hear me? There's
                                              no dallying.
           The gentleman's almost twenty, and 'tis time
           He were getting lawful heirs, and you a-breeding
                                              on 'em.

ISABELLA   Good father!

FABRITIO   Tell not me of tongues and rumours!   80
           You'll say the gentleman is somewhat simple –
           The better for a husband, were you wise:
           For those that marry fools, live ladies' lives.

On with the mask, I'll hear no more; he's rich:
The fool's hid under bushels.

LIVIA   Not so hid neither,
But here's a foul great piece of him, methinks:
What will he be, when he comes altogether?

Enter the WARD *with a trapstick, and* SORDIDO *his man*

WARD   Beat him?
           I beat him out o'th'field with his own cat-stick,
           Yet gave him the first hand.

SORDIDO   Oh strange!
WARD   I did it,   90
           Then he set jacks on me.

SORDIDO   What, my lady's tailor?
WARD   Ay, and I beat him too.

SORDIDO   Nay, that's no wonder,
           He's used to beating.

WARD   Nay, I tickled him
           When I came once to my tippings.

SORDIDO   Now you talk on 'em,
           There was a poulterer's wife made a great complaint
           of you last night to your guardianer, that you struck a
           bump in her child's head, as big as an egg.

WARD   An egg may prove a chicken, then in time the poulter-
           er's wife will get by't. When I am in game, I am
           furious; came my mother's eyes in my way, I would not   100
           lose a fair end – no, were she alive, but with one tooth
           in her head, I should venture the striking out of that. I
           think of nobody, when I am in play, I am so earnest.
           Coads me, my guardianer! Prithee lay up my cat and
           cat-stick safe.

SORDIDO   Where sir, i'th'chimney-corner?
WARD   Chimney-corner!
SORDIDO   Yes sir, your cats are always safe i'th'chimney-corner,
           unless they burn their coats.

WARD   Marry, that I am afraid on.   110
SORDIDO   Why then, I will bestow your cat i'th'gutter,
           And there she's safe, I am sure.

WARD   If I but live

To keep a house, I'll make thee a great man —
If meat and drink can do't. I can stoop gallantly,
And pitch out when I list; I'm dog at a hole.
I mar'l my guardianer does not seek a wife for me;
I protest, I'll have a bout with the maids else,
Or contract myself at midnight to the larder-woman
In presence of a fool or a sack-posset.

GUARD'O   Ward!
WARD   I feel myself after any exercise   120
Horribly prone: let me but ride, I'm lusty —
A cockhorse straight, i'faith.
GUARD'O   Why, ward I say.
WARD   I'll forswear eating eggs in moon-shine nights;
There's never a one I eat, but turns into a cock
In four-and-twenty hours; if my hot blood
Be not took down in time, sure 'twill crow shortly.
GUARD'O   Do you hear, sir? Follow me; I must new school you.
WARD   School me? I scorn that now; I am past schooling.
I am not so base to learn to write and read;
I was born to better fortunes in my cradle.   130
                    [exit Ward, Sordido and Guardiano
FABRITIO   How do you like him, girl? This is your husband.
Like him or like him not, wench, you shall have him,
And you shall love him.
LIVIA   Oh, soft there, brother! Though you be a justice,
Your warrant cannot be served out of your liberty.
You may compel, out of the power of father,
Things merely harsh to a maid's flesh and blood;
But when you come to love, there the soil alters;
Y'are in another country, where your laws
Are no more set by, than the cacklings of geese   140
In Rome's great Capitol.
FABRITIO   Marry him she shall then;
Let her agree upon love afterwards.   [exit
LIVIA   You speak now, brother, like an honest mortal
That walks upon th'earth with a staff;
You were up i'th'clouds before; you'd
                              command love —
And so do most old folks that go without it.

My best and dearest brother, I could dwell here;
There is not such another seat on earth
Where all good parts better express themselves.
HIPPOLITO   You'll make me blush anon.   150
LIVIA   'Tis but like saying grace before a feast, then,
And that's most comely; thou art all a feast,
And she that has thee, a most happy guest.
Prithee cheer up thy niece with special counsel.   [*exit*
HIPPOLITO   I would 'twere fit to speak to her what I would, but
'Twas not a thing ordained; Heaven has forbid it,
And 'tis most meet that I should rather perish
Than the decree divine receive least blemish.
Feed inward, you my sorrows, make no noise;
Consume me silent, let me be stark dead   160
Ere the world know I'm sick. You see my honesty,
If you befriend me – so.
ISABELLA   Marry a fool!
Can there be greater misery to a woman
That means to keep her days true to her husband,
And know no other man, so virtue wills it!
Why, how can I obey and honour him,
But I must needs commit idolatry?
A fool is but the image of a man,
And that but ill made neither. Oh the heartbreakings
Of miserable maids, where love's enforced!   170
The best condition is but bad enough:
When women have their choices, commonly
They do but buy their thraldoms, and bring
                                        great portions
To men to keep 'em in subjection:
As if a fearful prisoner should bribe
The keeper to be good to him, yet lies in still,
And glad of a good usage, a good look
Sometimes. By'r Lady, no misery surmounts
                                        a woman's!
Men buy their slaves, but women buy their masters.
Yet honesty and love makes all this happy   180
And, next to angels', the most blest estate.
That Providence, that has made every poison

Good for some use, and sets four warring elements
At peace in man, can make a harmony
In things that are most strange to human reason.
Oh but this marriage! What, are you sad too, uncle?
'Faith, then there's a whole household down together:
Where shall I go to seek my comfort now
When my best friend's distressed? What is't
                                             afflicts you, sir?

HIPPOLITO 'Faith, nothing but one grief that will not leave me,   190
And now 'tis welcome; every man has something
To bring him to his end, and this will serve,
Joined with your father's cruelty to you –
That helps it forward.

ISABELLA   Oh be cheered, sweet uncle!
How long has't been upon you? I never spied it;
What a dull sight have I! How long, I pray sir?

HIPPOLITO Since I first saw you, niece, and left Bologna.

ISABELLA And could you deal so unkindly with my heart,
To keep it up so long hid from my pity?
Alas, how shall I trust your love hereafter!   200
Have we passed through so many arguments,
And missed of that still the most needful one?
Walked out whole nights together in discourses,
And the main point forgot? We are to blame both;
This is an obstinate wilful forgetfulness,
And faulty on both parts. Let's lose no time now.
Begin, good uncle, you that feel't; what is it?

HIPPOLITO You of all creatures, niece, must never hear on't;
'Tis not a thing ordained for you to know.

ISABELLA Not I, sir! All my joys that word cuts off;   210
You made profession once you loved me best –
'Twas but profession!

HIPPOLITO   Yes, I do't too truly,
And fear I shall be chid for't. Know the worst then:
I love thee dearlier than an uncle can.

ISABELLA Why, so you ever said, and I believed it.

HIPPOLITO So simple is the goodness of her thoughts
They understand not yet th'unhallowed language
Of a near sinner: I must yet be forced

(Though blushes be my venture) to come nearer.
As a man loves his wife, so love I thee.

ISABELLA   What's that?   220
Methought I heard ill news come toward me,
Which commonly we understand too soon,
Than over-quick at hearing. I'll prevent it,
Though my joys fare the harder; welcome it –
It shall never come so near mine ear again.
Farewell all friendly solaces and discourses;
I'll learn to live without ye, for your dangers
Are greater than your comforts. What's become
Of truth in love, if such we cannot trust.
When blood that should be love is mixed with lust!   230

                                                   [exit

HIPPOLITO The worst can be but death, and let it come;
He that lives joyless, every day's his doom.

                                                   [exit

SCENE 3

Enter LEANTIO *alone*

LEANTIO Methinks I'm even as dull now at departure
As men observe great gallants the next day
After a revels; you shall see 'em look
Much of my fashion, if you mark 'em well.
'Tis even a second hell to part from pleasure
When man has got a smack on't. As many holidays
Coming together makes your poor heads idle
A great while after, and are said to stick
Fast in their fingers' ends, even so does game
In a new-married couple for the time;   10
It spoils all thrift, and indeed lies a-bed

        Enter BIANCA *and* MOTHER *above*

To invent all the new ways for great expenses.
See, and she be not got on purpose now
Into the window to look after me!

I have no power to go now and I should be hanged.
Farewell all business! I desire no more
Than I see yonder. Let the goods at quay
Look to themselves; why should I toil my youth out?
It is but begging two or three year sooner,
And stay with her continually: is't a match?   20
Oh fie, what a religion have I leaped into!
Get out again, for shame! The man loves best
When his care's most – that shows his zeal to love.
Fondness is but the idiot to affection,
That plays at hot-cockles with rich merchants' wives –
Good to make sport withal when the chest's full,
And the long warehouse cracks. 'Tis time of day
For us to be more wise; 'tis early with us,
And if they lose the morning of their affairs,
They commonly lose the best part of the day.   30
Those that are wealthy and have got enough,
'Tis after sunset with 'em; they may rest,
Grow fat with ease, banquet, and toy and play,
When such as I enter the heat o'th'day;
And I'll do't cheerfully.

BIANCA   I perceive, sir,
Y'are not gone yet; I have good hope you'll stay now.

LEANTIO   Farewell, I must not.

BIANCA   Come, come; pray return.
Tomorrow, adding but a little care more,
Will dispatch all as well – believe me, 'twill sir.

LEANTIO   I could well wish myself where you would have me;   40
But love that's wanton must be ruled awhile
By that that's careful, or all goes to ruin.
As fitting is a government in love
As in a kingdom; where 'tis all mere lust,
'Tis like an insurrection in the people
That, raised in self-will, wars against all reason:
But love that is respective of increase
Is like a good king, that keeps all in peace.
Once more, farewell.

BIANCA   But this one night, I prithee.

LEANTIO   Alas, I'm in for twenty, if I stay,   50

And then for forty more, I have such luck to flesh:
I never bought a horse, but he bore double.
If I stay any longer, I shall turn
An everlasting spendthrift; as you love
To be maintained well, do not call me again,
For then I shall not care which end goes forward.
Again, farewell to thee.   [exit

BIANCA   Since it must, farewell too.
MOTHER   'Faith daughter, y'are to blame; you take the course
To make him an ill husband, troth you do,
And that disease is catching, I can tell you –   60
Ay, and soon taken by a young man's blood,
And that with little urging. Nay, fie, see now –
What cause have you to weep? Would I had
                         no more,
That have lived threescore years; there were a cause
And 'twere well thought on. Trust me, y'are
                         to blame;
His absence cannot last five days at utmost.
Why should those tears be fetched forth?
                         Cannot love
Be even as well expressed in a good look,
But it must see her face still in a fountain?
It shows like a country maid dressing her head   70
By a dish of water. Come, 'tis an old custom
To weep for love.

Enter two or three BOYS *and a* CITIZEN *or two, with an* APPRENTICE

BOYS   Now they come! Now they come!
BOY   The duke!
BOY   The state!
CITIZEN   How near, boy?
BOY   I'th'next street sir, hard at hand.
CITIZEN   You sirra, get a standing for your mistress,
The best in all the city.
APPRENTICE   I have't for her, sir.
'Twas a thing I provided for her overnight,
'Tis ready at her pleasure.
CITIZEN   Fetch her to't then;

Away sir!

BIANCA   What's the meaning of this hurry,
Can you tell, mother?

MOTHER   What a memory   80
Have I! I see by that years come upon me.
Why, 'tis a yearly custom and solemnity,
Religiously observed by th'duke and state,
To St Mark's temple, the fifteenth of April.
See if my dull brains had not quite forgot it!
'Twas happily questioned of thee; I had gone
                              down else,
Sat like a drone below, and never thought on't.
I would not to be ten years younger again
That you had lost the sight; now you shall see
Our duke, a goodly gentleman of his years.   90

BIANCA Is he old then?

MOTHER   About some fifty-five.

BIANCA That's no great age in man; he's then at best
For wisdom and for judgement.

MOTHER   The lord Cardinal,
His noble brother – there's a comely gentleman,
And greater in devotion than in blood.

BIANCA He's worthy to be marked.

MOTHER   You shall behold
All our chief states of Florence; you came fortunately
Against this solemn day.

BIANCA   I hope so always.

                      Music

MOTHER I hear 'em near us now; do you stand easily?

BIANCA Exceeding well, good mother.

MOTHER   Take this stool.   100

BIANCA I need it not, I thank you.

MOTHER   Use your will, then.

Enter in great solemnity six KNIGHTS *bare-headed, then two*
CARDINALS, *and then the* LORD CARDINAL, *then the* DUKE;
after him the STATES OF FLORENCE *by two and two,*
with variety of music and song; then exeunt all

MOTHER   How like you, daughter?
BIANCA   'Tis a noble state.
         Methinks my soul could dwell upon the reverence
         Of such a solemn and most worthy custom.
         Did not the duke look up? Methought he saw us.
MOTHER   That's everyone's conceit that sees a duke:
         If he look steadfastly, he looks straight at them —
         When he perhaps, good careful gentleman,
         Never minds any, but the look he casts
         Is at his own intentions, and his object
         Only the public good.   110
BIANCA   Most likely so.
MOTHER   Come, come, we'll end this argument below.
                                              [exeunt

ACT 2 SCENE 1

Enter HIPPOLITO *and* LADY LIVIA *the widow*

LIVIA   A strange affection, brother, when I think on't!
I wonder how thou cam'st by't.

HIPPOLITO   Even as easily
As man comes by destruction, which oft-times
He wears in his own bosom.

LIVIA   Is the world
So populous in women, and creation
So prodigal in beauty and so various,
Yet does love turn thy point to thine own blood?
'Tis somewhat too unkindly. Must thy eye
Dwell evilly on the fairness of thy kindred,
And seek not where it should? It is confined   10
Now in a narrower prison than was made for't:
It is allowed a stranger; and where bounty
Is made the great man's honour, 'tis ill husbandry
To spare, and servants shall have small thanks for't.
So he heaven's bounty seems to scorn and mock,
That spares free means, and spends of his own stock.

HIPPOLITO   Never was man's misery so soon sewed up,
Counting how truly.

LIVIA   Nay, I love you so,
That I shall venture much to keep a change from you
So fearful as this grief will bring upon you —   20
'Faith, it even kills me, when I see you faint
Under a reprehension; and I'll leave it,
Though I know nothing can be better for you.
Prithee, sweet brother, let not passion waste
The goodness of thy time and of thy fortune;
Thou keep'st the treasure of that life I love
As dearly as mine own; and if you think
My former words too bitter, which were ministered
By truth and zeal — 'tis but a hazarding
Of grace and virtue, and I can bring forth   30
As pleasant fruits as sensuality wishes
In all her teeming longings. This I can do.

HIPPOLITO   Oh nothing that can make my wishes perfect!

LIVIA   I would that love of yours were pawned to 't, brother,
And as soon lost that way as I could win.
Sir, I could give as shrewd a lift to chastity
As any she that wears a tongue in Florence:
Sh'ad need be a good horsewoman and sit fast
Whom my strong argument could not fling at last.
Prithee take courage, man; though I should counsel   40
Another to despair, yet I am pitiful
To thy afflictions, and will venture hard –
I will not name for what, 'tis not handsome;
Find you the proof, and praise me.

HIPPOLITO   Then I fear me,
I shall not praise you in haste.

LIVIA   This is the comfort:
You are not the first, brother, has attempted
Things more forbidden than this seems to be.
I'll minister all cordials now to you,
Because I'll cheer you up, sir.

HIPPOLITO   I am past hope.

LIVIA   Love, thou shalt see me do a strange cure then,   50
As e'er was wrought on a disease so mortal
And near akin to shame. When shall you see her?

HIPPOLITO   Never in comfort more.

LIVIA   Y'are so impatient too.

HIPPOLITO   Will you believe – 'death, sh'as forsworn my company,
And sealed it with a blush.

LIVIA   So, I perceive
All lies upon my hands, then; well, the more glory
When the work's finished.

Enter SERVANT

           How now, sir, the news?

SERVANT   Madam, your niece, the virtuous Isabella,
Is 'lighted now to see you.

LIVIA   That's great fortune.
Sir, your stars bless you simply. Lead her in.   60
                     [*exit Servant*

HIPPOLITO   What's this to me?

LIVIA   Your absence, gentle brother;

I must bestir my wits for you.

HIPPOLITO   Ay, to great purpose.

                                         [*exit Hippolito*

LIVIA   Beshrew you, would I loved you not so well!
I'll go to bed, and leave this deed undone;
I am the fondest where I once affect,
The carefull'st of their healths, and of their
                                         ease, forsooth,
That I look still but slenderly to mine own.
I take a course to pity him so much now,
That I have none left for modesty and myself.
This 'tis to grow so liberal — y'have few sisters   70
That love their brother's ease 'bove their
                                         own honesties:
But if you question my affections,
That will be found my fault.

                Enter ISABELLA *the* NIECE

                                    Niece, your love's welcome.
Alas, what draws that paleness to thy cheeks?
This enforced marriage towards?

ISABELLA   It helps, good aunt,
Amongst some other griefs — but those I'll keep
Locked up in modest silence; for they're sorrows
Would shame the tongue more than they grieve
                                         the thought.

LIVIA   Indeed, the ward is simple.

ISABELLA   Simple! That were well:
Why, one might make good shift with such a husband. 80
But he's a fool entailed, he halts downright in't.

LIVIA   And knowing this, I hope 'tis at your choice
To take or refuse, niece.

ISABELLA   You see it is not.
I loathe him more than beauty can hate death,
Or age, her spiteful neighbour.

LIVIA   Let't appear, then.

ISABELLA   How can I, being born with that obedience
That must submit unto a father's will?
If he command, I must of force consent.

LIVIA   Alas, poor soul! Be not offended, prithee,

	If I set by the name of niece awhile,	90
	And bring in pity in a stranger fashion.	
	It lies here in this breast, would cross this match.	
ISABELLA	How, cross it, aunt?	
LIVIA	Ay, and give thee more liberty	
	Than thou hast reason yet to apprehend,	
ISABELLA	Sweet aunt, in goodness keep not hid from me	
	What may befriend my life.	
LIVIA	Yes, yes, I must,	
	When I return to reputation,	
	And think upon the solemn vow I made	
	To your dead mother, my most loving sister . . .	
	As long as I have her memory 'twixt mine eyelids,	100
	Look for no pity, now.	
ISABELLA	Kind, sweet, dear aunt –	
LIVIA	No, 'twas a secret I have took special care of,	
	Delivered by your mother on her deathbed –	
	That's nine years now – and I'll not part from't yet,	
	Though never was fitter time nor greater cause for't.	
ISABELLA	As you desire the praises of a virgin –	
LIVIA	Good sorrow! I would do thee any kindness,	
	Not wronging secrecy or reputation –	
ISABELLA	Neither of which, as I have hope of fruit[ful]ness,	
	Shall receive wrong from me.	
LIVIA	Nay, 'twould be your own wrong	110
	As much as any's, should it come to that once.	
ISABELLA	I need no better means to work persuasion then.	
LIVIA	Let it suffice, you may refuse this fool,	
	Or you may take him, as you see occasion	
	For your advantage: the best wits will do't.	
	Y'have liberty enough in your own will;	
	You cannot be enforced – there grows the flower,	
	If you could pick it out, makes whole life sweet to you.	
	That which you call your father's command's nothing:	
	Then your obedience must needs be as little.	120
	If you can make shift here to taste your happiness,	
	Or pick out aught that likes you, much good do you.	
	You see your cheer, I'll make you no set dinner.	
ISABELLA	And trust me, I may starve for all the good	

I can find yet in this! Sweet aunt, deal plainlier.

LIVIA   Say I should trust you now upon an oath,
             And give you in a secret that would start you;
             How am I sure of you, in faith and silence?

ISABELLA   Equal assurance may I find in mercy,
             As you for that in me.

LIVIA   It shall suffice.   130
             Then know, however custom has made good,
             For reputation's sake, the names of niece
             And aunt 'twixt you and I, w'are nothing less.

ISABELLA   How's that!

LIVIA   I told you I should start your blood.
             You are no more allied to any of us –
             Save what the courtesy of opinion casts
             Upon your mother's memory and your name –
             Than the merest stranger is, or one begot
             At Naples when the husband lies at Rome;
             There's so much odds betwixt us. Since your
                                              knowledge   140
             Wished more instruction, and I have your oath
             In pledge for silence, it makes me talk the freelier.
             Did never the report of that famed Spaniard,
             Marquess of Coria, since your time was ripe
             For understanding, fill your ear with wonder?

ISABELLA   Yes, what of him? I have heard his deeds of honour
             Often related when we lived in Naples.

LIVIA   You heard the praises of your father then.

ISABELLA   My father!

LIVIA   That was he; but all the business
             So carefully and so discreetly carried   150
             That fame received no spot by't, not a blemish.
             Your mother was so wary to her end,
             None knew it but her conscience, and her friend,
             Till penitent confession made it mine,
             And now my pity, yours: it had been long else,
             And I hope care and love alike in you,
             Made good by oath, will see it take no wrong now.
             How weak his commands now, whom you call father!
             How vain all his enforcements, your obedience!

And what a largeness in your will and liberty   160
To take or to reject – or to do both?
For fools will serve to father wise men's children –
All this y'have time to think on. Oh my wench,
Nothing o'erthrows our sex but indiscretion!
We might do well else of a brittle people
As any under the great canopy.
I pray forget not but to call me aunt still –
Take heed of that, it may be marked in time else.
But keep your thoughts to yourself, from all the world,
Kindred or dearest friend – nay, I entreat you,   170
From him that all this while you have called uncle;
And though you love him dearly, as I know
His deserts claim as much even from a stranger,
Yet let not him know this, I prithee do not;
As ever thou hast hope of second pity
If thou shouldst stand in need on't, do not do't.

ISABELLA   Believe my oath, I will not.

LIVIA   Why, well said.
[aside] Who shows more craft t'undo a maidenhead,
I'll resign my part to her.

Enter HIPPOLITO

                              She's thine own, go.   [*exit*

HIPPOLITO   Alas, fair flattery cannot cure my sorrows!   180

ISABELLA   [aside] Have I passed so much time in ignorance,
And never had the means to know myself
Till this blest hour! Thanks to her virtuous pity
That brought it now to light – would I had known it
But one day sooner! He had then received
In favours what, poor gentleman, he took
In bitter words – a slight and harsh reward
For one of his deserts.

HIPPOLITO   [aside]   There seems to me now
More anger and distraction in her looks.
I'm gone, I'll not endure a second storm;   190
The memory of the first is not past yet.

ISABELLA   [aside] Are you returned, you comforts of my life,
In this man's presence? I will keep you fast now,
And sooner part eternally from the world

Than my good joys in you. [*to Hippolito*] Prithee,
                                        forgive me.
I did but chide in jest; the best loves use it
Sometimes; it sets an edge upon affection.
When we invite our best friends to a feast,
'Tis not all sweetmeats that we set before them;
There's somewhat sharp and salt, both to whet   200
                                        appetite
And make 'em taste their wine well: so, methinks,
After a friendly, sharp, and savoury chiding,
A kiss tastes wondrous well and full o'th'grape –
[*kisses him*] How think'st thou, does't not?

HIPPOLITO   'Tis so excellent,
I know not how to praise it, what to say to't!

ISABELLA   This marriage shall go forward.

HIPPOLITO   With the ward!
Are you in earnest?

ISABELLA   'Twould be ill for us else.

HIPPOLITO   [*aside*] For us! How means she that?

ISABELLA   [*aside*]   Troth, I begin
To be so well, methinks, within this hour –
For all this match able to kill one's heart –   210
Nothing can pull me down now; should my father
Provide a worse fool yet (which I should think
Were a hard thing to compass) I'd have him either:
The worse the better; none can come amiss now
If he want wit enough. So discretion love me,
Desert and judgement, I have content sufficient.
[*aside*] She that comes once to be a housekeeper
Must not look every day to fare well, sir,
Like a young waiting gentlewoman in service;
For she feeds commonly as her lady does,   220
No good bit passes her but she gets a taste on't;
But when she comes to keep house for herself,
She's glad of some choice cates then once a week,
Or twice at most, and glad if she can get 'em:
So must affection learn to fare with thankfulness.
Pray make your love no stranger, sir, that's all –
[*aside*] Though you be one yourself, and know not on't,

And I have sworn you must not.   [*exit*

HIPPOLITO   This is beyond me!
Never came joys so unexpectedly
To meet desires in man. How came she thus?   230
What has she done to her, can any tell?
'Tis beyond sorcery, this, drugs or love-powders;
Some art that has no name, sure; strange to me
Of all the wonders I ere met withal
Throughout my ten years' travels. But I'm
                                        thankful for't.
This marriage now must of necessity forward:
It is the only veil wit can devise
To keep our acts hid from sin-piercing eyes.
                                              [*exit*

SCENE 2

Enter GUARDIANO AND LIVIA

LIVIA   How, sir, a gentlewoman so young, so fair,
          As you set forth, spied from the widow's window?
GUARD'O   She!
LIVIA   Our Sunday-dinner woman?
GUARD'O   And Thursday-supper woman, the same still.
          I know not how she came by her, but I'll swear
          She's the prime gallant for a face in Florence,
          And no doubt other parts follow their leader.
          The duke himself first spied her at the window,
          Then in a rapture, as if admiration   10
          Were poor when it were single, beckoned me,
          And pointed to the wonder warily,
          As one that feared she would draw in her splendour
          Too soon, if too much gazed at. I never knew him
          So infinitely taken with a woman;
          Nor can I blame his appetite, or tax
          His raptures of slight folly; she's a creature
          Able to draw a state from serious business,
          And make it their best piece to do her service.
          What course shall we devise? H'as spoke twice now.   20

LIVIA   Twice?
GUARD'O   'Tis beyond your apprehension
             How strangely that one look has catched his heart!
             'Twould prove but too much worth in wealth
                                        and favour
             To those should work his peace.
LIVIA   And if I do't not,
             Or at least come as near it (if your art
             Will take a little pains and second me)
             As any wench in Florence of my standing,
             I'll quite give o'er, and shut up shop in cunning.
GUARD'O   'Tis for the duke; and if I fail your purpose,
             All means to come by riches or advancement,   30
             Miss me and skip me over!
LIVIA   Let the old woman then
             Be sent for with all speed; then I'll begin.
GUARD'O   A good conclusion follow, and a sweet one,
             After this stale beginning with old ware.
             Within there!

                    Enter SERVANT

SERVANT   Sir, do you call?
GUARD'O   Come near, list hither.
LIVIA   I long myself to see this absolute creature
             That wins the heart of love and praise so much.
GUARD'O   Go sir, make haste.
LIVIA   Say I entreat her company;
             Do you hear, sir?
SERVANT   Yes, madam.   [*exit*
LIVIA   That brings her quickly.
GUARD'O   I would 'twere done; the Duke waits the good hour,   40
             And I wait the good fortune that may spring from't:
             I have had a lucky hand these fifteen year
             At such court-passage with three dice in a dish.

                    Enter FABRITIO

             Signor Fabritio!
FABRITIO   Oh sir, I bring an alteration in my mouth now.
GUARD'O   [*aside*] An alteration! No wise speech, I hope;
             He means not to talk wisely does he, trow?

	[*to Fabritio*] Good! What's the change, I pray sir?
FABRITIO	A new change.
GUARD'O	Another yet! 'Faith, there's enough already.
FABRITIO	My daughter loves him now.
GUARD'O	What, does she, sir? 50
FABRITIO	Affects him beyond thought – who but the
	ward, forsooth!
	No talk but of the ward; she would have him
	To choose 'bove all the men she ever saw.
	My will goes not so fast as her consent now;
	Her duty gets before my command still.
GUARD'O	Why then sir, if you'll have me speak my thoughts,
	I smell 'twill be a match.
FABRITIO	Ay, and a sweet young couple,
	If I have any judgement.
GUARD'O	[*aside*] 'Faith, that's little.
	[*to Fabritio*] Let her be sent tomorrow before noon,
	And handsomely tricked up, for 'bout that time 60
	I mean to bring her in and tender her to him.
FABRITIO	I warrant you for handsome; I will see
	Her things laid ready, every one in order,
	And have some part of her tricked up tonight.
GUARD'O	Why, well said.
FABRITIO	'Twas a use her mother had
	When she was invited to an early wedding;
	She'd dress her head o'ernight, sponge up herself,
	And give her neck three lathers.
GUARD'O	[*aside*] Ne'er a halter?
FABRITIO	On with her chain of pearl, her ruby bracelets,
	Lay ready all her tricks and jiggambobs. 70
GUARD'O	So must your daughter.
FABRITIO	I'll about it straight, sir.
	[*exit Fabritio*
LIVIA	How he sweats in the foolish zeal of fatherhood
	After six ounces an hour, and seems
	To toil as much as if his cares were wise ones!
GUARD'O	Y'have let his folly blood in the right vein, lady.
LIVIA	And here comes his sweet son-in-law that shall be.
	They're both allied in wit before the marriage;

What will they be hereafter, when they are nearer?
Yet they can go no further than the fool:
There's the word's end in both of 'em.

Enter WARD *and* SORDIDO, *one with a shuttlecock,*
the other a battledore

GUARD'O   Now, young heir! 80

WARD   What's the next business after shuttlecock, now?

GUARD'O   Tomorrow you shall see the gentlewoman
Must be your wife.

WARD   There's ev'n another thing too
Must be kept up with a pair of battledores.
My wife! What can she do?

GUARD'O   Nay, that's a question
You should ask yourself, ward, when y'are
                                   alone together.

WARD   That's as I list! A wife's to be asked anywhere, I hope;
I'll ask her in a congregation, if I have a mind to't,
and so save a licence. — My guardianer has no more
wit than an herb-woman, that sells away all her sweet 90
herbs and nosegays, and keeps a stinking breath for
her own pottage.

SORDIDO   Let me be at the choosing of your beloved,
If you desire a woman of good parts.

WARD   Thou shalt, sweet Sordido.

SORDIDO   I have a plaguey guess;
Let me alone to see what she is. If I
But look upon her — 'way, I know all the faults
To a hair that you may refuse her for.

WARD   Dost thou?
I prithee let me hear 'em, Sordido.

SORDIDO   Well, mark 'em then; I have 'em all in rhyme. 100
The wife your guardianer ought to tender,
Should be pretty, straight and slender;
Her hair not short, her foot not long,
Her hand not huge, nor too too loud her tongue;
No pearl in eye nor ruby in her nose,
No burn or cut but what the catalogue shows.
She must have teeth, and that no black ones,
And kiss most sweet when she does smack once:

Her skin must be both white and plumped,
Her body straight, not hopper-rumped,   110
Or wriggle sideways like a crab.
She must be neither slut nor drab,
Nor go too splay-foot with her shoes
To make her smock lick up the dews.
And two things more which I forgot to tell ye:
She neither must have bump in back nor belly.
These are the faults that will not make her pass.

WARD   And if I spy not these I am a rank ass!

SORDIDO Nay, more — by right, sir, you should see her naked,
For that's the ancient order.

WARD   See her naked?   120
That were good sport, i'faith. I'll have the books
                                    turned over,
And if I find her naked on record
She shall not have a rag on — but stay, stay!
How if she should desire to see me so too?
I were in a sweet case then; such a foul skin!

SORDIDO But y'have a clean shirt, and that makes amends, sir.

WARD   I will not see her naked for that trick, though.   [exit

SORDIDO Then take her with all faults with her clothes on,
And they may hide a number with a bum-roll.
'Faith, choosing of a wench in a huge farthingale   130
Is like the buying of ware under a great penthouse:
What with the deceit of one,
And the false light of th'other, mark my speeches,
He may have a diseased wench in's bed
And rotten stuff in's breeches.   [exit

GUARD'O It may take handsomely.

LIVIA   I see small hindrance.
How now, so soon returned?

Enter SERVANT *with* MOTHER

GUARD'O   She's come.

LIVIA   That's well.
Widow, come, come; I have a great quarrel to you,
'Faith, I must chide you, that you must be sent for!
You make yourself so strange, never come at us,   140
And yet so near a neighbour, and so unkind!

	Troth, y'are to blame; you cannot be more welcome
	To any house in Florence, that I'll tell you.
MOTHER	My thanks must needs acknowledge so much, madam.
LIVIA	How can you be so strange then? I sit here
	Sometime whole days together without company
	When business draws this gentleman from home,
	And should be happy in society
	Which I so well affect as that of yours.
	I know y'are alone too; why should not we, 150
	Like two kind neighbours, then, supply the wants
	Of one another, having tongue-discourse,
	Experience in the world, and such kind helps
	To laugh down time, and meet age merrily?
MOTHER	Age, madam! You speak mirth; 'tis at my door,
	But a long journey from your ladyship yet.
LIVIA	My faith, I'm nine-and-thirty, every stroke, wench;
	And 'tis a general observation
	'Mongst knights' wives or widows, we account
	Ourselves then old, when young men's eyes
	leave looking at's: 160
	'Tis a true rule amongst us, and ne'er failed yet
	In any but in one that I remember;
	Indeed, she had a friend at nine-and-forty!
	Marry, she paid well for him; and in th'end
	He kept a quean or two with her own money,
	That robbed her of her plate and cut her throat.
MOTHER	She had her punishment in this world, madam;
	And a fair warning to all other women
	That they live chaste at fifty.
LIVIA	Ay, or never, wench.
	Come, now I have thy company I'll not part with't 170
	Till after supper.
MOTHER	Yes, I must crave pardon, madam.
LIVIA	I swear you shall stay supper; we have no
	strangers, woman,
	None but my sojourners and I – this gentleman
	And the young heir, his ward. You know
	our company.
MOTHER	Some other time I will make bold with you, madam.

GUARD'O Nay, pray stay, widow.
LIVIA   'Faith, she shall not go.
         Do you think I'll be forsworn?

                        Table, and chess

MOTHER   'Tis a great while
         Till supper-time; I'll take my leave then, now, madam,
         And come again i'th'evening, since your ladyship
         Will have it so.
LIVIA   I'th'evening! By my troth, wench,   180
         I'll keep you while I have you; you have
                                      great business, sure,
         To sit alone at home. I wonder strangely
         What pleasure you take in't! Were't to me now,
         I should be ever at one neighbour's house
         Or other all day long, having no charge,
         Or none to chide you if you go or stay.
         Who may live merrier – ay, or more at heart's ease?
         Come, we'll to chess or draughts; there are
                                      an hundred tricks
         To drive out time till supper, never fear't, wench.
MOTHER   I'll but make one step home and return
                                      straight, madam.   190
LIVIA   Come, I'll not trust you; you use more excuses
         To your kind friends than ever I knew any.
         What business can you have, if you be sure
         Y'have locked the doors? And that being all you have,
         I know y'are careful on't. One afternoon
         So much to spend here! Say I should entreat you now
         To lie a night or two, or a week, with me,
         Or leave your own house for a month together –
         It were a kindness that long neighbourhood
         And friendship might well hope to prevail in –   200
         Would you deny such a request? I'faith,
         Speak truth, and freely.
MOTHER   I were then uncivil, madam.
LIVIA   Go to, then, set your men; we'll have whole nights
         Of mirth together ere we be much older, wench.
MOTHER   [*aside*] As good now tell her, then, for she will know't;
         I have always found her a most friendly lady.

LIVIA	Why widow, where's your mind?
MOTHER	Troth, even at home, madam.
	To tell you truth, I left a gentlewoman
	Even sitting all alone, which is uncomfortable,
	Especially to young bloods.
LIVIA	Another excuse!
MOTHER	No, as I hope for health, madam, that's a truth.
	Please you to send and see.
LIVIA	What gentlewoman? Pish!
MOTHER	Wife to my son, indeed, but not known, madam,
	To any but yourself.
LIVIA	Now I beshrew you!
	Could you be so unkind to her and me,
	To come and not bring her? 'Faith, 'tis not friendly!
MOTHER	I feared to be too bold.
LIVIA	Too bold? Oh what's become
	Of the true hearty love was wont to be
	'Mongst neighbours in old time!
MOTHER	And she's a stranger, madam.
LIVIA	The more should be her welcome. When is courtesy
	In better practice than when 'tis employed
	In entertaining strangers? I could chide, i'faith.
	Leave her behind, poor gentlewoman, alone too!
	Make some amends, and send for her betimes; go.
MOTHER	Please you command one of your servants, madam.
LIVIA	Within there!

Enter Servant

SERVANT	Madam?
LIVIA	Attend the gentlewoman.
MOTHER	[*aside*] It must be carried wondrous privately
	From my son's knowledge; he'll break out in
	storms else.
	[*to Servant*] Hark you sir. [*she gives instructions*]
	[*exit Servant*
LIVIA	[*to Guardiano*] Now comes in the heat of your part.
GUARD'O	True, I know it, lady; and if I be out,
	May the duke banish me from all employments,
	Wanton or serious.
LIVIA	So, have you sent, widow?

210

220

230

MOTHER   Yes madam, he's almost at home by this.
LIVIA   And 'faith, let me entreat you, that henceforward
              All such unkind faults may be swept from friendship,
              Which does but dim the lustre. And think thus much:
              It is a wrong to me, that have ability
              To bid friends welcome, when you keep 'em from me;
              You cannot set greater dishonour near me,
              For bounty is the credit and the glory   240
              Of those that have enough. I see y'are sorry,
              And the good 'mends is made by't.
MOTHER   Here she's, madam.

              Enter BIANCA, *and Servant, who shows her in, then goes off*

BIANCA   [*aside*] I wonder how she comes to send for me now?
LIVIA   Gentlewoman, y'are most welcome, trust me y'are,
              As courtesy can make one, or respect
              Due to the presence of you.
BIANCA   I give you thanks, lady.
LIVIA   I heard you were alone, and't had appeared
              An ill condition in me, though I knew you not,
              Nor ever saw you (yet humanity
              Thinks every case her own) to have kept your company 250
              Here from you and left you all solitary.
              I rather ventured upon boldness then
              As the least fault, and wished your presence here –
              A thing most happily motioned of that gentleman,
              Whom I request you, for his care and pity,
              To honour and reward with your acquaintance;
              A gentleman that ladies' rights stands for:
              That's his profession.
BIANCA   'Tis a noble one,
              And honours my acquaintance.
GUARD'O   All my intentions
              Are servants to such mistresses.
BIANCA   'Tis your modesty,   260
              It seems, that makes your deserts speak so low, sir.
LIVIA   Come widow – look you, lady, here's our business;
              Are we not well employed, think you? An old quarrel
              Between us, that will never be at an end.
BIANCA   No?

	And methinks there's men enough to part you, lady.
LIVIA	Ho – but they set us on, let us come off
	As well as we can, poor souls; men care no farther.
	I pray sit down, forsooth, if you have the patience
	To look upon two weak and tedious gamesters.
GUARD'O	'Faith madam, set these by till evening; 270
	You'll have enough on't then. The gentlewoman,
	Being a stranger, would take more delight
	To see your rooms and pictures.
LIVIA	Marry, good sir,
	And well remembered! I beseech you show 'em her,
	That will beguile time well; pray heartily, do sir –
	I'll do as much for you; here, take these keys,
	Show her the monument too – and that's a thing
	Everyone sees not; you can witness that, widow.
MOTHER	And that's worth sight indeed, madam.
BIANCA	Kind lady,
	I fear I came to be a trouble to you. 280
LIVIA	Oh, nothing less, forsooth.
BIANCA	And to this courteous gentleman,
	That wears a kindness in his breast so noble
	And bounteous to the welcome of a stranger.
GUARD'O	If you but give acceptance to my service,
	You do the greatest grace and honour to me
	That courtesy can merit.
BIANCA	I were to blame else,
	And out of fashion much; I pray you lead, sir.
LIVIA	After a game or two we're for you, gentlefolk.
GUARD'O	We wish no better seconds in society
	Than your discourses, madam, and your partner's there. 290
MOTHER	I thank your praise. I listened to you, sir,
	Though when you spoke there came a paltry rook
	Full in my way, and chokes up all my game.
	[exit Guardiano and Bianca
LIVIA	Alas, poor widow, I shall be too hard for thee.
MOTHER	Y'are cunning at the game, I'll be sworn, madam.
LIVIA	It will be found so, ere I give you over.
	She that can place her man well –
MOTHER	As you do, madam –

LIVIA   As I shall, wench – can never lose her game.
              Nay, nay, the black king's mine.
MOTHER   Cry you mercy, madam.
LIVIA   And this my queen.
MOTHER   I see't now.
LIVIA   Here's a duke   300
              Will strike a sure stroke for the game anon;
              Your pawn cannot come back to relieve itself.
MOTHER   I know that, madam.
LIVIA   You play well the whilst;
              How she belies her skill! I hold two ducats
              I give you check and mate to your white king,
              Simplicity itself, your saintish king there.
MOTHER   Well, ere now, lady,
              I have seen the fall of subtlety. Jest on.
LIVIA   Ay, but simplicity receives two for one.
MOTHER   What remedy but patience!

              Enter above GUARDIANO *and* BIANCA

BIANCA   Trust me, sir,   310
              Mine eye never met with fairer ornaments.
GUARD'O   Nay, livelier, I'm persuaded, neither Florence
              Nor Venice can produce.
BIANCA   Sir, my opinion
              Takes your part highly.
GUARD'O   There's a better piece
              Yet than all these.

              Enter DUKE *above*

BIANCA   Not possible, sir.
GUARD'O   Believe it;
              You'll say so when you see't. Turn but your
                                                eye now,
              Y'are upon it presently.   [*exit*
BIANCA   O sir!
DUKE   He's gone, beauty!
              Pish, look not after him, he's but a vapour
              That when the sun appears is seen no more.
BIANCA   Oh treachery to honour!
DUKE   Prithee tremble not.   320

    I feel thy breast shake like a turtle panting
    Under a loving hand that makes much on't.
    Why art so fearful? As I'm friend to brightness,
    There's nothing but respect and honour near thee.
    You know me, you have seen me; here's a heart
    Can witness I have seen thee.

BIANCA   The more's my danger.

DUKE   The more's thy happiness. Pish, strive not, sweet!
    This strength were excellent employed in love, now,
    But here 'tis spent amiss. Strive not to seek
    Thy liberty and keep me still in prison.   330
    I'faith, you shall not out till I'm released now.
    We'll both be freed together, or stay still by't;
    So is captivity pleasant.

BIANCA   O my lord!

DUKE   I am not here in vain: have but the leisure
    To think on that, and thou'lt be soon resolved.
    The lifting of thy voice is but like one
    That does exalt his enemy, who, proving high,
    Lays all the plots to confound him that raised him.
    Take warning, I beseech thee; thou seem'st to me
    A creature so composed of gentleness   340
    And delicate meekness, such as bless the faces
    Of figures that are drawn for goddesses
    And make art proud to look upon her work.
    I should be sorry the least force should lay
    An unkind touch upon thee.

BIANCA   O my extremity!
    My lord, what seek you?

DUKE   Love.

BIANCA   'Tis gone already;
    I have a husband.

DUKE   That's a single comfort;
    Take a friend to him.

BIANCA   That's a double mischief,
    Or else there's no religion.

DUKE   Do not tremble
    At fears of thine own making.

BIANCA   Nor, great lord,   350

Make me not bold with death and deeds of ruin
Because they fear not you; me they must fright,
Then am I best in health. Should thunder speak
And none regard it, it had lost the name,
And were as good be still. I'm not like those
That take their soundest sleeps in greatest tempests;
Then wake I most, the weather fearfullest,
And call for strength to virtue.

DUKE   Sure I think
Thou know'st the way to please me; I affect
A passionate pleading 'bove an easy yielding –   360
But never pitied any: they deserve none
That will not pity me. I can command:
Think upon that. Yet if thou truly knewest
The infinite pleasure my affection takes
In gentle, fair entreatings, when love's businesses
Are carried courteously 'twixt heart and heart,
You'd make more haste to please me.

BIANCA   Why should you seek, sir,
To take away that you can never give?

DUKE   But I give better in exchange – wealth, honour.
She that is fortunate in a duke's favour   370
Lights on a tree that bears all women's wishes:
If your own mother saw you pluck fruit there,
She would commend your wit, and praise the time
Of your nativity. Take hold of glory.
Do not I know y'have cast away your life
Upon necessities, means merely doubtful
To keep you in indifferent health and fashion
(A thing I heard too lately and soon pitied)?
And can you be so much your beauty's enemy
To kiss away a month or two in wedlock,   380
And weep whole years in wants for ever after?
Come, play the wise wench, and provide for ever:
Let storms come when they list, they find thee
                                sheltered;
Should any doubt arise, let nothing trouble thee.
Put trust in our love for the managing
Of all to thy heart's peace. We'll walk together,

And show a thankful joy for both our fortunes.

                                    [exit both above

LIVIA   Did not I say my duke would fetch you over, widow?

MOTHER   I think you spoke in earnest when you said it, madam.

LIVIA   And my black king makes all the haste he can, too.   390

MOTHER   Well, madam, we may meet with him in time yet.

LIVIA   I have given thee blind mate twice.

MOTHER   You may see, madam,
My eyes begin to fail.

LIVIA   I'll swear they do, wench.

                    Enter GUARDIANO

GUARD'O I can but smile as often as I think on't!
How prettily the poor fool was beguiled,
How unexpectedly! It's a witty age;
Never were finer snares for women's honesties
Than are devised in these days; no spider's web
Made of a daintier thread than are now practised
To catch love's flesh-fly by the silver wing.   400
Yet to prepare her stomach by degrees
To Cupid's feast, because I saw 'twas queasy,
I showed her naked pictures by the way –
A bit to stay the appetite. Well, advancement,
I venture hard to find thee; if thou com'st
With a greater title set upon thy crest,
I'll take that first cross patiently, and wait
Until some other comes greater than that.
I'll endure all.

LIVIA   The game's even at the best now; you may see, widow,   410
How all things draw to an end.

MOTHER   Even so do I, madam.

LIVIA   I pray take some of your neighbours along with you.

MOTHER   They must be those are almost twice your years, then,
If they be chose fit matches for my time, madam.

LIVIA   Has not my duke bestirred himself?

MOTHER   Yes, 'faith madam,
Was done me all the mischief in this game.

LIVIA   H'as showed himself in's kind.

MOTHER   In's kind, call you it?

I may swear that.

LIVIA   Yes 'faith, and keep your oath.

GUARD'O   Hark, list! There's somebody coming down; 'tis she.

Enter BIANCA

BIANCA   [aside] Now bless me from a blasting! I saw that now   420
Fearful for any woman's eye to look on.
Infectious mists and mildews hang at's eyes,
The weather of a doomsday dwells upon him.
Yet since mine honour's leprous, why should I
Preserve that fair that caused the leprosy?
Come, poison all at once! [to Guardiano] Thou in
                                   whose baseness
The bane of virtue broods, I'm bound in soul
Eternally to curse thy smooth-browed treachery
That wore the fair veil of a friendly welcome,
And I a stranger; think upon't, 'tis worth it.   430
Murders piled up upon a guilty spirit
At his last breath will not lie heavier
Than this betraying act upon thy conscience.
Beware of offering the first-fruits to sin:
His weight is deadly who commits with strumpets
After they have been abased and made for use;
If they offend to th'death, as wise men know,
How much more they, then, that first make 'em so?
I give thee that to feed on. I'm made bold now,
I thank thy treachery; sin and I'm acquainted,   440
No couple greater; and I'm like that great one
Who, making politic use of a base villain,
'He likes the treason well, but hates the traitor';
So I hate thee, slave.

GUARD'O   Well, so the duke love me,
I fare not much amiss then; two great feasts
Do seldom come together in one day.
We must not look for 'em.

BIANCA   What, at it still, mother?

MOTHER   You see we sit by't; are you so soon returned?

LIVIA   So lively and so cheerful! A good sign, that.

MOTHER   You have not seen all since, sure?

BIANCA   That have I, mother,   450

The monument and all: I'm so beholding
To this kind, honest, courteous gentleman.
You'd little think it, mother – showed me all,
Had me from place to place so fashionably;
The kindness of some people, how't exceeds!
'Faith, I have seen that I little thought to see
I'th'morning when I rose.

MOTHER   Nay, so I told you
Before you saw't, it would prove worth your sight.
I give you great thanks for my daughter, sir,
And all your kindness towards her.

GUARD'O   Oh good widow!   460
Much good may't do her – [aside] forty weeks
                                   hence, i'faith.

                    Enter Servant

LIVIA   Now, sir?
SERVANT   May't please you, madam, to walk in;
Supper's upon the table.
LIVIA   Yes, we come.
Will't please you, gentlewoman?
BIANCA   Thanks, virtuous lady –
Y'are a damned bawd! I'll follow you, forsooth;
Pray take my mother in – [aside] an old ass go
                                   with you –
[aloud] This gentleman and I vow not to part.
LIVIA   Then get you both before.
BIANCA   There lies his art.
                    [exeunt Bianca and Guardiano
LIVIA   Widow, I'll follow you.   [exit mother
                    Is't so, 'damned bawd'!
Are you so bitter? 'Tis but want of use;   470
Her tender modesty is sea-sick a little,
Being not accustomed to the breaking billow
Of woman's wavering faith, blown with temptations.
'Tis but a qualm of honour, 'twill away;
A little bitter for the time, but lasts not.
Sin tastes at the first draught like wormwood water,
But drunk again, 'tis nectar ever after.
                                   [exit

Enter MOTHER

MOTHER   I would my son would either keep at home
          Or I were in my grave!
          She was but one day abroad, but ever since
          She's grown so cutted, there's no speaking to her.
          Whether the sight of great cheer at my lady's,
          And such mean fare at home, work discontent in her,
          I know not; but I'm sure she's strangely altered.
          I'll never keep daughter-in-law i'th'house with me
          Again, if I had an hundred. When read I of any
          That agreed long together, but she and her mother   10
          Fell out in the first quarter – nay, sometime
          A grudging of a scolding the first week, by'r Lady.
          So takes the new disease, methinks, in my house.
          I'm weary of my part, there's nothing likes her;
          I know not how to please her here o'late.
          And here she comes.

Enter BIANCA

BIANCA   This is the strangest house
          For all defects, as ever gentlewoman
          Made shift withal to pass away her love in!
          Why is there not a cushion-cloth of drawn work,
          Or some fair cut-work pinned up in my bed-chamber, 20
          A silver-and-gilt casting-bottle hung by't?
          Nay, since I am content to be so kind to you,
          To spare you for a silver basin and ewer
          (Which one of my fashion looks for of duty)
          She's never offered under, where she sleeps.
MOTHER   She talks of things here my whole state's not worth.
BIANCA   Never a green silk quilt is there i'th'house, mother,
          To cast upon my bed?
MOTHER   No, by troth, is there,
          Nor orange-tawny neither.
BIANCA   Here's a house
          For a young gentlewoman to be got with child in!   30
MOTHER   Yes, simple though you make it, there has been three

Got in a year in't – since you move me to't –
And all as sweet-faced children and as lovely
As you'll be mother of: I will not spare you.
What, cannot children be begot, think you,
Without gilt casting-bottles? Yes, and as sweet ones:
The miller's daughter brings forth as white boys
As she that bathes herself with milk and bean-flour.
'Tis an old saying 'one may keep good cheer
In a mean house': so may true love affect   40
After the rate of princes, in a cottage.

BIANCA   Troth, you speak wondrous well for your old
                                                house here;
'Twill shortly fall down at your feet to thank you,
Or stoop when you go to bed, like a good child,
To ask you blessing. Must I live in want,
Because my fortune matched me with your son?
Wives do not give away themselves to husbands
To the end to be quite cast away; they look
To be the better used and tendered rather,
Highlier respected, and maintained the richer;   50
They're well rewarded else for the free gift
Of their whole life to a husband. I ask less now
Than what I had at home when I was a maid
And at my father's house, kept short of that
Which a wife knows she must have – nay, and will –
Will, mother, if she be not a fool born.
And report went of me that I could wrangle
For what I wanted when I was two hours old;
And by that copy, this land still I hold.
You hear me, mother.   [exit

MOTHER   Ay, too plain, methinks;   60
And were I somewhat deafer when you spake
'Twere never a whit the worse for my quietness.
'Tis the most sudden'st, strangest alteration,
And the most subtlest that ever wit at threescore
Was puzzled to find out. I know no cause for't; but
She's no more like the gentlewoman at first
Than I am like her that never lay with man yet,
And she's a very young thing where'er she be.

When she first lighted here, I told her then
How mean she should find all things; she was
                              pleased, forsooth,   70
None better: I laid open all defects to her,
She was contented still. But the devil's in her,
Nothing contents her now. Tonight my son
Promised to be at home; would he were come once,
For I'm weary of my charge, and life too.
She'd be served all in silver, by her good will,
By night and day; she hates the name of pewter
More than sick men the noise, or diseased bones
That quake at fall o'th'hammer, seeming to have
A fellow-feeling with't at every blow.   80
What course shall I think on? She frets me so.
[*withdraws to back of stage*]

Enter LEANTIO

LEANTIO   How near am I now to a happiness
That earth exceeds not – not another like it!
The treasures of the deep are not so precious
As are the concealed comforts of a man,
Locked up in woman's love. I scent the air
Of blessings when I come but near the house.
What a delicious breath marriage sends forth;
The violet-bed's not sweeter. Honest wedlock
Is like a banqueting-house built in a garden,   90
On which the spring's chaste flowers take delight
To cast their modest odours – when base lust,
With all her powders, paintings and best pride,
Is but a fair house built by a ditch side.
When I behold a glorious dangerous strumpet,
Sparkling in beauty and destruction too,
Both at a twinkling, I do liken straight
Her beautified body to a goodly temple
That's built on vaults where carcasses lie rotting:
And so by little and little I shrink back again,   100
And quench desire with a cool meditation;
And I'm as well, methinks. Now for a welcome
Able to draw men's envies upon man:
A kiss now that will hang upon my lip

As sweet as morning dew upon a rose,
And full as long. After a five days' fast
She'll be so greedy now, and cling about me,
I take care how I shall be rid of her;
And here't begins.

Enter BIANCA; MOTHER *comes forward*

BIANCA	Oh sir, y'are welcome home.
MOTHER	Oh, is he come? I am glad on't.
LEANTIO	Is that all? 110

Why this? As dreadful now as sudden death
To some rich man that flatters all his sins
With promise of repentance when he's old,
And dies in the midway before he comes to't.
Sure y'are not well, Bianca! How dost, prithee?

BIANCA   I have been better than I am at this time.

LEANTIO   Alas, I thought so.

BIANCA   Nay, I have been worse too
Than now you see me, sir.

LEANTIO   I'm glad thou mend'st yet;
I feel my heart mend too. How came it to thee?
Has anything disliked thee in my absence?   120

BIANCA   No, certain; I have had the best content
That Florence can afford.

LEANTIO   Thou makest the best on't;
Speak mother, what's the cause? You must
                    needs know.

MOTHER   Troth, I know none, son; let her speak herself —
[*aside*] Unless it be the same gave Lucifer
A tumbling cast, that's pride.

BIANCA   Methinks this house stands nothing to my mind.
I'd have some pleasant lodging i'th'high street, sir;
Or if 'twere near the court, sir, that were much better —
'Tis a sweet recreation for a gentlewoman   130
To stand in a bay-window and see gallants.

LEANTIO   Now I have another temper, a mere stranger
To that of yours, it seems; I should delight
To see none but yourself.

BIANCA   I praise not that:
Too fond is as unseemly as too churlish.

I would not have a husband of that proneness
To kiss me before company, for a world!
Beside, 'tis tedious to see one thing still, sir,
Be it the best that ever heart affected –
Nay, were't yourself, whose love had power, you know, 140
To bring me from my friends, I would not stand thus
And gaze upon you always; troth, I could not, sir.
As good be blind and have no use of sight
As look on one thing still: what's the eye's treasure
But change of objects? You are learned, sir,
And know I speak not ill. 'Tis full as virtuous
For woman's eye to look on several men,
As for her heart, sir, to be fixed on one.

LEANTIO Now thou com'st home to me; a kiss for that word.

BIANCA No matter for a kiss, sir; let it pass; 150
'Tis but a toy, we'll not so much as mind it.
Let's talk of other business and forget it.
What news now of the pirates; any stirring?
Prithee discourse a little.

MOTHER [aside]   I am glad he's here yet
To see her tricks himself; I had lied monstrously
If I had told 'em first.

LEANTIO   Speak, what's the humour, sweet,
You make your lip so strange? This was not wont.

BIANCA Is there no kindness betwixt man and wife
Unless they make a pigeon-house of friendship
And be still billing? 'Tis the idlest fondness 160
That ever was invented, and 'tis pity
It's grown a fashion for poor gentlewomen;
There's many a disease kissed in a year by't,
And a French curtsy made to't. Alas, sir,
Think of the world, how we shall live, grow serious;
We have been married a whole fortnight now.

LEANTIO How? A whole fortnight! Why, is that so long?

BIANCA 'Tis time to leave off dalliance; 'tis a doctrine
Of your own teaching, if you be remembered,
And I was bound to obey it.

MOTHER [aside]   Here's one fits him! 170
This was well catched, i'faith, son – like a fellow

That rids another country of a plague
And brings it home with him to his own house.

Knock within

Who knocks?
LEANTIO   Who's there now? Withdraw you, Bianca;
Thou art a gem no stranger's eye must see,
However thou please now to look dull on me.

                                        [*exit Bianca*

Enter Messenger

Y'are welcome sir; to whom your business, pray?
MESSENGER To one I see not here now.
LEANTIO   Who should that be, sir?
MESSENGER A young gentlewoman I was sent to.
LEANTIO A young gentlewoman?
MESSENGER   Ay sir, about sixteen.   180
Why look you wildly sir?
LEANTIO   At your strange error;
Y'have mistook the house, sir, there's none such here,
I assure you.
MESSENGER   I assure you too:
The man that sent me cannot be mistook.
LEANTIO Why, who is't sent you, sir?
MESSENGER   The Duke.
LEANTIO   The Duke!
MESSENGER Yes, he entreats her company at a banquet
At Lady Livia's house.
LEANTIO   Troth, shall I tell you, sir,
It is the most erroneous business
That ere your honest pains was abused with.
I pray forgive me if I smile a little –   190
I cannot choose, i'faith, sir – at an error
So comical as this; I mean no harm, though.
His grace has been most wondrous ill informed;
Pray so return it, sir. What should her name be?
MESSENGER That I shall tell you straight too: Bianca Capello.
LEANTIO How sir, Bianca? What do you call th'other?
MESSENGER Capello. Sir, it seems you know no such, then?
LEANTIO Who should this be? I never heard o'th'name.

MESSENGER   Then 'tis a sure mistake.

LEANTIO   What if you enquired
In the next street, sir? I saw gallants there   200
In the new houses that are built of late.
Ten to one, there you find her.

MESSENGER   Nay, no matter,
I will return the mistake and seek no further.

LEANTIO   Use your own will and pleasure sir; y'are welcome.

[*exit Messenger*

What shall I think of first? Come forth, Bianca.
Thou art betrayed, I fear me.

Enter BIANCA

BIANCA   Betrayed? How sir?

LEANTIO   The Duke knows thee.

BIANCA   Knows me! How know you that, sir?

LEANTIO   Has got thy name.

BIANCA   [*aside*]   Ay, and my good name too,
That's worse o'th'twain.

LEANTIO   How comes this work about?

BIANCA   How should the Duke know me? Can you guess,
                        mother?   210

MOTHER   Not I with all my wits; sure, we kept house close.

LEANTIO   Kept close! Not all the locks in Italy
Can keep you women so. You have been gadding,
And ventured out at twilight to th'court-green yonder,
And met the gallant bowlers coming home,
Without your masks too, both of you; I'll be
                      hanged else!
Thou hast been seen, Bianca, by some stranger;
Never excuse it.

BIANCA   I'll not seek the way, sir.
Do you think y'have married me to mew me up,
Not to be seen; what would you make of me?   220

LEANTIO   A good wife, nothing else.

BIANCA   Why, so are some
That are seen every day, else the devil take 'em.

LEANTIO   No more then: I believe all virtuous in thee
Without an argument. 'Twas but thy hard chance
To be seen somewhere; there lies all the mischief,

But I have devised a riddance.

MOTHER   Now I can tell you, son,
The time and place.

LEANTIO   When? Where?

MOTHER   What wits have I!
When you last took your leave, if you remember,
You left us both at window.

LEANTIO   Right, I know that.

MOTHER And not the third part of an hour after   230
The Duke passed by in a great solemnity
To St Mark's temple; and to my apprehension
He looked up twice to th'window.

LEANTIO   Oh, there quickened
The mischief of this hour.

BIANCA [aside]   If you call't mischief,
It is a thing I fear I am conceived with.

LEANTIO Looked he up twice, and could you take no warning?

MOTHER Why, once may do as much harm, son, as a thousand:
Do not you know one spark has fired an house
As well as a whole furnace?

LEANTIO   My heart flames for't!
Yet let's be wise and keep all smothered closely;   240
I have bethought a means. Is the door fast?

MOTHER I locked it myself after him.

LEANTIO   You know, mother,
At the end of the dark parlour there's a place
So artificially contrived for a conveyance
No search could ever find it − when my father
Kept in for manslaughter, it was his sanctuary:
There will I lock my life's best treasure up.
Bianca!

BIANCA   Would you keep me closer yet?
Have you the conscience? Y'are best ev'n choke
                                    me up, sir!
You make me fearful of your health and wits,   250
You cleave to such wild courses. What's the matter?

LEANTIO Why, are you so insensible of your danger
To ask that now? The Duke himself has sent for you
To Lady Livia's, to a banquet forsooth.

BIANCA   Now I beshrew you heartily. Has he so?
            And you the man would never yet vouchsafe
            To tell me on't till now! You show your loyalty
            And honesty at once; and so farewell, sir.

LEANTIO   Bianca, whither now?

BIANCA   Why, to the Duke, sir.
            You say he sent for me.

LEANTIO   But thou dost not mean   260
            To go, I hope.

BIANCA   No? I shall prove unmannerly,
            Rude and uncivil, mad, and imitate you?
            Come, mother, come; follow his humour no longer.
            We shall be all executed for treason shortly.

MOTHER   Not I, i'faith; I'll first obey the Duke,
            And taste of a good banquet; I'm of thy mind.
            I'll step but up and fetch two handkerchiefs,
            To pocket up some sweetmeats, and o'ertake thee.
                                                        [*exit*

BIANCA   [*aside*] Why, here's an old wench would trot into
                                            a bawd now
            For some dry sucket or a colt in marchpane.   [*exit* 270

LEANTIO   O, thou the ripe time of man's misery, wedlock,
            When all his thoughts, like over-laden trees,
            Crack with the fruits they bear, in cares, in jealousies —
            Oh, that's a fruit that ripens hastily
            After 'tis knit to marriage: it begins
            As soon as the sun shines upon the bride
            A little to show colour. Blessed powers, ·
            Whence comes this alteration? The distractions,
            The fears and doubts it brings are numberless,
            And yet the cause I know not. What a peace   280
            Has he that never marries! If he knew
            The benefit he enjoyed, or had the fortune
            To come and speak with me, he should know then
            The infinite wealth he had, and discern rightly
            The greatness of his treasure by my loss.
            Nay, what a quietness has he 'bove mine,
            That wears his youth out in a strumpet's arms,
            And never spends more care upon a woman

Than at the time of lust; but walks away,
And if he finds her dead at his return,   290
His pity is soon done: he breaks a sigh
In many parts, and gives her but a piece on't.
But all the fears, shames, jealousies, costs and troubles,
And still renewed cares of a marriage bed
Live in the issue when the wife is dead.

Enter MESSENGER

MESSENGER A good perfection to your thoughts.
LEANTIO   The news, sir?
MESSENGER Though you were pleased of late to pin an error on me,
You must not shift another in your stead too:
The Duke has sent me for you.
LEANTIO   How, for me, sir?
[*aside*] I see then 'tis my theft; we're both betrayed.   300
Well, I'm not the first has stol'n away a maid:
My countrymen have used it. I'll along with you, sir.
                                               [*exeunt*

SCENE 2

A banquet prepared

Enter GUARDIANO *and* WARD

GUARD'O Take you especial note of such a gentlewoman,
She's here on purpose; I have invited her,
Her father and her uncle, to this banquet.
Mark her behaviour well, it does concern you;
And what her good parts are, as far as time
And place can modestly require a knowledge of,
Shall be laid open to your understanding.
You know I'm both your guardian and your uncle:
My care of you is double – ward and nephew –
And I'll express it here.
WARD   'Faith, I should know her   10
Now, by her mark, among a thousand women:
A little, pretty, deft and tidy thing, you say?
GUARD'O Right.
WARD   With a lusty sprouting sprig in her hair?

GUARD'O   Thou goest the right way still; take one mark more:
          Thou shalt never find her hand out of her uncle's,
          Or else his out of hers, if she be near him:
          The love of kindred never yet stuck closer
          Than their's to one another; he that weds her
          Marries her uncle's heart too.

                              Cornets

WARD   Say you so, sir;
          Then I'll be asked i'th'church to both of 'em.   20
GUARD'O   Fall back, here comes the Duke.
WARD   He brings a gentlewoman,
          I should fall forward rather,

          Enter DUKE, BIANCA, FABRITIO, HIPPOLITO, LIVIA,
                MOTHER, ISABELLA, *and Attendants*

DUKE   Come, Bianca,
          Of purpose sent into the world to show
          Perfection once in woman; I'll believe
          Henceforward they have every one a soul too,
          'Gainst all the uncourteous opinions
          That man's uncivil rudeness ever held of 'em.
          Glory of Florence, light into mine arms!

                          Enter LEANTIO

BIANCA   Yon comes a grudging man will chide you, sir.
          The storm is now in's heart, and would get nearer   30
          And fall here if it durst; it pours down yonder.
DUKE   If that be he, the weather shall soon clear;
          List and I'll tell thee how. [*whispers to Bianca*]
LEANTIO   A-kissing too?
          I see 'tis plain lust now, adultery boldened.
          What will it prove anon, when 'tis stuffed full
          Of wine and sweetmeats, being so impudent fasting?
DUKE   We have heard of your good parts, sir, which
                                        we honour
          With our embrace and love. Is not the captainship
          Of Rouens' citadel, since the late deceased,
          Supplied by any yet?
GENT.   By none, my lord.   40

DUKE	Take it, the place is yours then; [*Leantio kneels*]
	and as faithfulness
	And desert grows, our favour shall grow with't:
	Rise now the captain of our fort at Rouens.
LEANTIO	The service of whole life give your grace thanks.
DUKE	Come, sit, Bianca.
LEANTIO	This is some good yet,
	And more than ever I looked for − a fine bit
	To stay a cuckold's stomach! All preferment
	That springs from sin and lust, it shoots up quickly,
	As gardeners' crops do in the rottenest grounds:
	So is all means raised from base prostitution 50
	Even like a sallet growing upon a dunghill.
	I'm like a thing that never was yet heard of,
	Half merry and half mad − much like a fellow
	That eats his meat with a good appetite,
	And wears a plague-sore that would fright a country;
	Or rather like the barren hardened ass,
	That feeds on thistles till he bleeds again.
	And such is the condition of my misery.
LIVIA	Is that your son, widow?
MOTHER	Yes, did your ladyship
	Never know that till now?
LIVIA	No, trust me, did I. 60
	[*aside*] Nor ever truly felt the power of love
	And pity to a man, till now I knew him.
	I have enough to buy me my desires,
	And yet to spare, that's one good comfort. Hark you?
	Pray let me speak with you, sir, before you go.
LEANTIO	With me, lady? You shall; I am at your service.
	[*aside*] What will she say now, trow? More
	goodness yet?
WARD	I see her now, I'm sure; the ape's so little,
	I shall scarce feel her! I have seen almost
	As tall as she sold in the fair for tenpence. 70
	See how she simpers it − as if marmalade
	Would not melt in her mouth! She might have
	the kindness, i'faith,
	To send me a gilded bull from her own trencher,

A ram, a goat, or somewhat to be nibbling;
These women, when they come to sweet things once,
They forget all their friends, they grow so greedy –
Nay, oftentimes their husbands.

DUKE   Here's a health now, gallants,
To the best beauty at this day in Florence.

BIANCA   Whoe'er she be, she shall not go unpledged, sir.

DUKE   Nay, you're excused for this.

BIANCA   Who, I, my lord?   80

DUKE   Yes, by the law of Bacchus; plead your benefit:
You are not bound to pledge your own health, lady.

BIANCA   That's a good way, my lord, to keep me dry.

DUKE   Nay then, I will not offend Venus so much;
Let Bacchus seek his 'mends in another court.
Here's to thyself, Bianca.

BIANCA   Nothing comes
More welcome to that name than your grace.

LEANTIO   So, so!
Here stands the poor thief now that stole the treasure,
And he's not thought on. Ours is near kin now
To a twin misery born into the world: 90
First the hard-conscienced worldling – he hoards
                       wealth up:
Then comes the next, and he feasts all upon't;
One's damned for getting, th'other for spending on't.
O equal justice, thou hast met my sin
With a full weight; I'm rightly now oppressed:
All her friends' heavy hearts lie in my breast.

DUKE   Methinks there is no spirit amongst us, gallants,
But what divinely sparkles from the eyes
Of bright Bianca; we sat all in darkness
But for that splendour. Who was't told us lately   100
Of a match-making rite, a marriage-tender?

GUARD'O   'Twas I, my lord.

DUKE   'Twas you indeed. Where is she?

GUARD'O   This is the gentlewoman.

FABRITIO   My lord, my daughter.

DUKE   Why, here's some stirring yet.

FABRITIO   She's a dear child to me.

DUKE   That must needs be, you say she is your daughter.
FABRITIO   Nay my good lord, dear to my purse, I mean,
              Beside my person; I never reckoned that.
              She has the full qualities of a gentlewoman;
              I have brought her up to music, dancing, what not,
              That may commend her sex and stir her husband.   110
DUKE   And which is he now?
GUARD'O   This young heir, my lord.
DUKE   What is he brought up to?
HIPPOLITO   To cat and trap.
GUARD'O   My lord, he's a great ward, wealthy but simple;
              His parts consist in acres.
DUKE   Oh, wise-acres!
GUARD'O   Y'have spoke him in a word, sir.
BIANCA   'Las, poor gentlewoman,
              She's ill bestead, unless sh'as dealt the wiselier
              And laid in more provision for her youth:
              Fools will not keep in summer.
LEANTIO   [aside]   No, nor such wives
              From whores in winter.
DUKE   Yea, the voice too, sir?
FABRITIO   Ay, and a sweet breast too, my lord, I hope,   120
              Or I have cast away my money wisely;
              She took her pricksong earlier, my lord,
              Than any of her kindred ever did.
              A rare child, though I say't – but I'd not have
              The baggage hear so much; 'twould make her
                                                    swell straight,
              And maids of all things must not be puffed up.
DUKE   Let's turn us to a better banquet, then;
              For music bids the soul of man to a feast,
              And that's indeed a noble entertainment
              Worthy Bianca's self. You shall perceive, beauty,   130
              Our Florentine damsels are not brought up idly.
BIANCA   They're wiser of themselves, it seems, my lord,
              And can take gifts, when goodness offers 'em.

                            Music

LEANTIO   [aside] True; and damnation has taught you that wisdom,

	You can take gifts too. Oh, that music mocks me!
LIVIA	[aside] I am as dumb to any language now
	But love's, as one that never learned to speak!
	I am not yet so old, but he may think of me.
	My own fault – I have been idle a long time;
	But I'll begin the week and paint tomorrow,
	So follow my true labour day by day:
	I never thrived so well as when I used it.
ISABELLA	[sings]
	What harder chance can fall to woman,
	Who was born to cleave to some man,
	Than to bestow her time, youth, beauty,
	Life's observance, honour, duty,
	On a thing for no use good,
	But to make physic work, or blood
	Force fresh in an old lady's cheek?
	She that would be
	Mother of fools, let her compound with me.
WARD	Here's a tune indeed! Pish! I had rather hear one ballad
	sung i'th'nose now, of the lamentable drowning of fat
	sheep and oxen, than all these simpering tunes played
	upon cats-guts and sung by little kitlings.
FABRITIO	How like you her breast now, my lord?
BIANCA	Her breast!
	He talks as if his daughter had given suck
	Before she were married, as her betters have;
	The next he praises sure will be her nipples.
DUKE	Methinks now, such a voice to such a husband
	Is like a jewel of unvalued worth
	Hung at a fool's ear.
FABRITIO	May it please your grace
	To give her leave to show another quality?
DUKE	Marry, as many good ones as you will, sir,
	The more the better welcome.
LEANTIO	[aside] But the less
	The better practised. That soul's black indeed
	That cannot commend virtue. But who keeps it?
	The extortioner will say to a sick beggar
	'Heaven comfort thee', though he give none himself.

140

150

160

This good is common.

FABRITIO   Will it please you now, sir,   170
To entreat your ward to take her by the hand
And lead her in a dance before the Duke?

GUARD'O That will I, sir; 'tis needful. Hark you, nephew.

FABRITIO Nay you shall see, young heir, what y'have for
                                        your money,
Without fraud or imposture.

WARD   Dance with her!
Not I, sweet guardianer, do not urge my heart to't,
'Tis clean against my blood; dance with a stranger!
Let whos' will do't, I'll not begin first with her.

HIPPOLITO [aside] No, fear't not, fool; sh'as took a better order.

GUARD'O Why, who shall take her, then?

WARD   Some other gentleman –   180
Look, there's her uncle, a fine-timbered reveller;
Perhaps he knows the manner of her dancing too;
I'll have him do't before me. I have sworn, guardianer;
Then may I learn the better.

GUARD'O   Thou'lt be an ass still.

WARD Ay, all that 'uncle' shall not fool me out:
Pish, I stick closer to myself than so.

GUARD'O I must entreat you, sir, to take your niece
And dance with her; my ward's a little wilful,
He would have you show him the way.

HIPPOLITO   Me sir?
He shall command it at all hours; pray tell him so.   190

GUARD'O I thank you for him; he has not wit himself, sir.

HIPPOLITO Come, my life's peace, [aside] I have a strange office
                         on't here!
'Tis some man's luck to keep the joys he likes
Concealed for his own bosom; but my fortune
To set 'em out now for another's liking:
Like the mad misery of necessitous man,
That parts from his good horse with many praises,
And goes on foot himself. Need must be obeyed
In every action, it mars man and maid.

Music. A dance, making honours to the Duke and
curtsy to themselves, both before and after

DUKE   Signor Fabritio, y'are a happy father;   200
                 Your cares and pains are fortunate; you see
                 Your cost bears noble fruits. Hippolito, thanks.

FABRITIO   Here's some amends for all my charges yet;
                 She wins both prick and praise where'er she comes.

DUKE   How lik'st, Bianca?

BIANCA   All things well, my lord,
                 But this poor gentlewoman's fortune, that's the worst.

DUKE   There is no doubt, Bianca, she'll find leisure
                 To make that good enough; he's rich and simple.

BIANCA   She has the better hope o'th'upper hand, indeed,
                 Which women strive for most.

GUARD'O   Do't when I bid you, sir. 210

WARD   I'll venture but a hornpipe with her, guardianer,
                 Or some such married man's dance.

GUARD'O   Well, venture something, sir.

WARD   I have rhyme for what I do.

GUARD'O   But little reason, I think.

WARD   Plain men dance the measures, the cinquepace the gay;
                 Cuckolds dance the hornpipe, and farmers dance
                                   the hay;
                 Your soldiers dance the round, and maidens that
                                     grow big;
                 Your drunkards, the canaries; your whore and bawd,
                                     the jig.
                 Here's your eight kind of dancers – he that finds
                                     the ninth,
                 Let him pay the minstrels.

DUKE   Oh, here he appears once in his own person! 220
                 I thought he would have married her by attorney,
                 And lain with her so too.

BIANCA   Nay, my kind lord,
                 There's very seldom any found so foolish
                 To give away his part there.

LEANTIO   [aside]   Bitter scoff!
                 Yet I must do't. With what a cruel pride
                 The glory of her sin strikes by my afflictions!

           Music. The Ward and Isabella dance;
             he ridiculously imitates Hippolito

DUKE   This thing will make shift, sirs, to make a husband,
For aught I see in him; how think'st, Bianca?

BIANCA   'Faith, an ill-favoured shift, my lord. Methinks
If he would take some voyage when he's married,   230
Dangerous or long enough, and scarce be seen
Once in nine year together, a wife then
Might make indifferent shift to be content with him.

DUKE   A kiss! That wit deserves to be made much on.
Come, our caroche!

GUARD'O   Stands ready for your grace.

DUKE   My thanks to all your loves. Come, fair Bianca;
We have took special care of you, and provided
Your lodging near us now.

BIANCA   Your love is great, my lord.

DUKE   Once more, our thanks to all.

OMNES   All blest honours guard you.

                 [exeunt all but Leantio and Livia

             Cornets flourish

LEANTIO   Oh, hast thou left me then, Bianca, utterly?   240
Bianca! Now I miss thee – O, return,
And save the faith of woman. I never felt
The loss of thee till now; 'tis an affliction
Of greater weight than youth was made to bear –
As if a punishment of after-life
Were fallen upon man here, so new it is
To flesh and blood; so strange, so insupportable
A torment – even mistook, as if a body
Whose death were drowning, must needs
                     therefore suffer it
In scalding oil.

LIVIA   Sweet sir!

LEANTIO   [*aside*]   As long as mine eye saw thee,   250
I half enjoyed thee.

LIVIA   Sir?

LEANTIO   [*aside*]   Canst thou forget
The dear pains my love took, how it has watched
Whole nights together in all weathers for thee,
Yet stood in heart more merry than the tempests
That sung about mine ears, like dangerous flatterers

	That can set all their mischiefs to sweet tunes;
	And then received thee from thy father's window
	Into these arms at midnight, when we embraced
	As if we had been statues only made for't,
	To show art's life, so silent were our comforts, 260
	And kissed as if our lips had grown together.

LIVIA   [*aside*] This makes me madder to enjoy him now.

LEANTIO   [*aside*] Canst thou forget all this? And better joys
That we met after this, which then new kisses
Took pride to praise?

LIVIA   [*aside*]   I shall grow madder yet. Sir!

LEANTIO   [*aside*] This cannot be but of some close
                                    bawd's working.
[*aloud*] Cry mercy, lady! What would you say to me?
My sorrow makes me so unmannerly,
So comfort bless me, I had quite forgot you.

LIVIA   Nothing, but even in pity to that passion,   270
Would give your grief good counsel.

LEANTIO   Marry, and welcome;
It never could come better, lady;

LIVIA   Then first, sir,
To make away all your good thoughts at once of her,
Know most assuredly she is a strumpet.

LEANTIO   Ha! Most assuredly! Speak not a thing
So vile so certainly; leave it more doubtful.

LIVIA   Then I must leave all truth, and spare my knowledge
A sin which I too lately found and wept for.

LEANTIO   Found you it?

LIVIA   Ay, with wet eyes.

LEANTIO   Oh perjurious friendship!

LIVIA   You missed your fortunes when you met with her, sir.   280
Young gentlemen that only love for beauty,
They love not wisely; such a marriage rather
Proves the destruction of affection:
It brings on want, and want's the key of whoredom.
I think y'had small means with her?

LEANTIO   Oh, not any, lady.

LIVIA   Alas, poor gentleman! What mean'st thou, sir,
Quite to undo thyself with thine own kind heart?

Thou art too good and pitiful to woman.
Marry sir, thank thy stars for this blest fortune
That rids the summer of thy youth so well   290
From many beggars, that had lain a-sunning
In thy beams only else, till thou hadst wasted
The whole days of thy life in heat and labour.
What would you say now to a creature found
As pitiful to you, and as it were
Even sent on purpose from the whole sex general
To requite all that kindness you have shown to't?

LEANTIO   What's that, madam?

LIVIA   Nay, a gentlewoman,
And one able to reward good things; ay,
And bears a conscience to't. Couldst thou love
                                        such a one   300
That, blow all fortunes, would never see thee want?
Nay more, maintain thee to thine enemy's envy;
And shalt not spend a care for't, stir a thought,
Nor break a sleep – unless love's music waked thee,
No storm of fortune should. Look upon me,
And know that woman.

LEANTIO   Oh my life's wealth, Bianca!

LIVIA   Still with her name? Will nothing wear it out?
That deep sigh went but for a strumpet, sir.

LEANTIO   It can go for no other that loves me.

LIVIA   [aside] He's vexed in mind. I came too soon to him;   310
Where's my discretion now, my skill, my judgement?
I'm cunning in all arts but my own love.
'Tis as unseasonable to tempt him now,
So soon, as a widow to be courted
Following her husband's corse, or to make bargain
By the grave-side, and take a young man there:
Her strange departure stands like a hearse yet
Before his eyes, which time will take down shortly.
                                                  [exit

LEANTIO   Is she my wife till death, yet no more mine?
That's a hard measure. Then what's marriage good for?   320
Methinks by right I should not now be living,
And then 'twere all well. What a happiness

Had I been made of, had I never seen her!
For nothing makes man's loss grievous to him
But knowledge of the worth of what he loses:
For what he never had, he never misses.
She's gone for ever – utterly; there is
As much redemption of a soul from hell
As a fair woman's body from his palace.
Why should my love last longer than her truth?   330
What is there good in woman to be loved
When only that which makes her so has left her?
I cannot love her now, but I must like
Her sin and my own shame too, and be guilty
Of law's breach with her, and mine own abusing;
All which were monstrous. Then my safest course,
For health of mind and body, is to turn
My heart and hate her, most extremely hate her!
I have no other way. Those virtuous powers
Which were chaste witnesses of both our troths   340
Can witness she breaks first – and I'm rewarded
With captainship o'th'fort! A place of credit,
I must confess, but poor; my factorship
Shall not exchange means with't; he that died last in't,
He was no drunkard, yet he died a beggar
For all his thrift. Besides, the place not fits me:
It suits my resolution, not my breeding.

Enter LIVIA

LIVIA   [*aside*] I have tried all ways I can, and have not power
To keep from sight of him. [*aloud*] How are you
                                        now, sir?

LEANTIO   I feel a better ease, madam.
LIVIA   Thanks to blessedness!   350
You will do well, I warrant you, fear it not, sir.
Join but your own good will to't; he's not wise
That loves his pain or sickness, or grows fond
Of a disease whose property is to vex him
And spitefully drink his blood up. Out upon't, sir,
Youth knows no greater loss. I pray let's walk, sir.
You never saw the beauty of my house yet,
Nor how abundantly fortune has blessed me

In worldly treasure; trust me, I have enough, sir,
To make my friend a rich man in my life,   360
A great man at my death – yourself will say so.
If you want anything and spare to speak,
Troth, I'll condemn you for a wilful man, sir.
LEANTIO   Why sure, this can be but the flattery of some dream.
LIVIA   Now by this kiss, my love, my soul and riches,
'Tis all true substance.
          Come, you shall see my wealth, take what you list;
          The gallanter you go, the more you please me.
          I will allow you, too, your page and footman,
          Your racehorses, or any various pleasure   370
          Exercised youth delights in: but to me
          Only, sir, wear your heart of constant stuff.
          Do but you love enough, I'll give enough.
LEANTIO   Troth then, I'll love enough and take enough.
LIVIA   Then we are both pleased enough.

                                                   [exeunt

                        SCENE 3

            Enter GUARDIANO and ISABELLA at one door,
                 the WARD and SORDIDO at another

GUARD'O   Now nephew, here's the gentlewoman again.
WARD   Mass, here she's come again; mark her now, Sordido.
GUARD'O   This is the maid my love and care has chose
          Out for your wife, and so I tender her to you.
          Yourself has been eye-witness of some qualities
          That speak a courtly breeding and are costly.
          I bring you both to talk together now,
          'Tis time you grew familiar in your tongues:
          Tomorrow you join hands, and one ring ties you;
          And one bed holds you, if you like the choice.   10
          Her father and her friends are i'th'next room
          And stay to see the contract ere they part;
          Therefore dispatch, good ward, be sweet and short.
          Like her or like her not – there's but two ways;
          And one your body, th'other your purse pays.

WARD	I warrant you guardianer, I'll not stand all day
	thrumming,
	But quickly shoot my bolt at your next coming.
GUARD'O	Well said! Good fortune to your birding then. [*exit*
WARD	I never missed mark yet.
SORDIDO	Troth I think, master, if the truth were known, 20
	You never shot at any but the kitchen-wench,
	And that was a she-woodcock, a mere innocent,
	That was oft lost and cried at eight-and-twenty.
WARD	No more of that meat, Sordido, here's eggs
	O'th'spit now; we must turn gingerly. Draw out
	The catalogue of all the faults of women.
SORDIDO	How, all the faults! Have you so little reason
	To think so much paper will lie in my breeches?
	Why, ten carts will not carry it, if you set down
	But the bawds. All the faults! Pray let's be content 30
	With a few of 'em; and if they were less,
	You would find 'em enough, I warrant you.
	Look you, sir.
ISABELLA	[*aside*] But that I have th'advantage of the fool
	As much as woman's heart can wish and joy at,
	What an infernal torment 'twere to be
	Thus bought and sold and turned and pried into;
	when alas
	The worst bit is too good for him! And the comfort is,
	H'as but a cater's place on't, and provides
	All for another's table – yet how curious
	The ass is, like some nice professor on't, 40
	That buys up all the daintiest food i'th'markets
	And seldom licks his lips after a taste on't.
SORDIDO	Now to her, now y'have scanned all her parts over.
WARD	But at what end shall I begin now, Sordido?
SORDIDO	Oh, ever at a woman's lip, while you live, sir; do you
	ask that question?
WARD	Methinks, Sordido, sh'as but a crabbed face to begin
	with.
SORDIDO	A crabbed face? That will save money.
WARD	How, save money, Sordido? 50
SORDIDO	Ay sir; for having a crabbed face of her own, she'll eat

the less verjuice with her mutton – 'twill save verjuice
at year's end, sir.

WARD   Nay, and your jests begin to be saucy once, I'll make
you eat your meat without mustard.

SORDIDO   And that in some kind is a punishment.

WARD   Gentlewoman, they say 'tis your pleasure to be my
wife; and you shall know shortly whether it be mine
or no to be your husband. And thereupon thus I first
enter upon you. [kisses her] O most delicious scent!   60
Methinks it tasted as if a man had stepped into a
comfit-maker's shop to let a cart go by, all the while I
kissed her. It is reported, gentlewoman, you'll run mad
for me, if you have me not.

ISABELLA   I should be in great danger of my wits, sir,
For being so forward – [aside] should this ass
                                        kick backward now!

WARD   Alas, poor soul. And is that hair your own?

ISABELLA   Mine own? Yes sure, sir; I owe nothing for't.

WARD   'Tis a good hearing; I shall have the less to pay when I
have married you. Look, does her eyes stand well?   70

SORDIDO   They cannot stand better than in her head, I think;
where would you have them? And for her nose, 'tis of
a very good last.

WARD   I have known as good as that has not lasted a year,
though.

SORDIDO   That's in the using of a thing; will not any strong
bridge fall down in time, if we do nothing but beat at
the bottom? A nose of buff would not last always, sir,
especially if it came into th'camp once.

WARD   But Sordido, how shall we do to make her laugh, that   80
I may see what teeth she has – for I'll not bate her a
tooth, nor take a black one into th'bargain.

SORDIDO   Why, do but you fall in talk with her; you cannot
choose but one time or other make her laugh, sir.

WARD   It shall go hard, but I will. Pray what qualities have you
beside singing and dancing? Can you play at shuttlecock, forsooth?

ISABELLA   Ay, and at stool-ball too, sir; I have great luck at it.

WARD   Why, can you catch a ball well?

ISABELLA   I have catched two in my lap at one game.   90
WARD   What, have you, woman? I must have you learn to
           play at trap too, then y'are full and whole.
ISABELLA   Anything that you please to bring me up to I shall
           take pains to practise.
WARD   'Twill not do, Sordido; we shall never get her mouth
           opened wide enough.
SORDIDO   No sir? That's strange; then here's a trick for your
           learning.
           [he yawns. Isabella yawns too, but covers her mouth]
           Look now, look now! Quick, quick there.
WARD   Pox of that scurvy mannerly trick with handkerchief; 100
           it hindered me a little, but I am satisfied. When a fair
           woman gapes and stops her mouth so, it shows like a
           cloth stopple in a cream-pot. I have fair hope of her
           teeth now, Sordido.
SORDIDO   Why, then y'have all well, sir, for aught I see. She's
           right and straight enough now, as she stands – they'll
           commonly lie crooked, that's no matter; wise game-
           sters never find fault with that, let 'em lie still so.
WARD   I'd fain mark how she goes, and then I have all – for
           of all creatures I cannot abide a splay-footed woman: 110
           she's an unlucky thing to meet in a morning; her heels
           keep together so, as if she were beginning an Irish
           dance still, and the wriggling of her bum playing the
           tune to't. But I have bethought a cleanly shift to find
           it: dab down as you see me, and peep of one side
           when her back's toward you; I'll show you the way.
SORDIDO   And you shall find me apt enough to peeping!
           I have been one of them has seen mad sights
           Under your scaffolds.
WARD   Will it please you walk, forsooth,
           A turn or two by yourself? You are so pleasing to me, 120
           I take delight to view you on both sides.
ISABELLA   I shall be glad to fetch a walk to your love, sir,
           'Twill get affection a good stomach, sir –
           [aside] Which I had need have, to fall to such coarse
                                           victuals. [she walks about]
WARD   Now go thy ways for a clean-treading wench,

As ever man in modesty peeped under!

SORDIDO   I see the sweetest sight to please my master!
Never went Frenchman righter upon ropes
Than she on Florentine rushes.

WARD   'Tis enough, forsooth.

ISABELLA   And how do you like me now, sir?

WARD   'Faith, so well   130
I never mean to part with thee, sweetheart,
Under some sixteen children, and all boys.

ISABELLA   You'll be at simple pains, if you prove kind,
And breed 'em all in your teeth.

WARD   Nay, by my faith,
What serves your belly for? 'Twould make my cheeks
Look like blown bagpipes.

Enter GUARDIANO

GUARD'O   How now, ward and nephew,
Gentlewoman and niece! Speak, is it so or not?

WARD   'Tis so; we are both agreed, sir.

GUARD'O   In to your kindred, then;
There's friends, and wine and music, waits to
                                             welcome you.

WARD   Then I'll be drunk for joy.

SORDIDO   And I for company;   140
I cannot break my nose in a better action.

                                             [*exeunt*

ACT 4 SCENE I

Enter BIANCA *attended by two* LADIES

BIANCA	How goes your watches, ladies; what's o'clock now?
1 LADY	By mine, full nine.
2 LADY	By mine, a quarter past.
1 LADY	I set mine by St Mark's.
2 LADY	St Antony's,
	They say, goes truer.
1 LADY	That's but your opinion, madam,
	Because you love a gentleman o'th'name.
2 LADY	He's a true gentleman, then.
1 LADY	So may he be
	That comes to me tonight, for aught you know.
BIANCA	I'll end this strife straight. I set mine by the sun;
	I love to set by th'best, one shall not then
	Be troubled to set often.
2 LADY	You do wisely in't.

10

BIANCA	If I should set my watch as some girls do
	By every clock i'th'town, 'twould never go true;
	And too much turning of the dial's point,
	Or tampering with the spring, might in small time
	Spoil the whole work too. Here it wants of nine now.
1 LADY	It does indeed, forsooth; mine's nearest truth yet.
2 LADY	Yet I have found her lying with an advocate,
	which showed
	Like two false clocks together in one parish.
BIANCA	So now I thank you ladies. I desire
	Awhile to be alone.
1 LADY	And I am nobody,

20

	Methinks, unless I have one or other with me;
	'Faith, my desire and hers will never be sisters.

[exeunt Ladies

BIANCA	How strangely woman's fortune comes about!
	This was the farthest way to come to me,
	All would have judged, that knew me born in Venice
	And there with many jealous eyes brought up,
	That never thought they had me sure enough

But when they were upon me; yet my hap
To meet it here, so far off from my birthplace,
My friends or kindred. 'Tis not good, in sadness,   30
To keep a maid so strict in her young days.
Restraint breeds wandering thoughts, as many
                              fasting days
A great desire to see flesh stirring again.
I'll never use any girl of mine so strictly;
However they're kept, their fortunes find 'em out –
I see't in me. If they be got in court
I'll never forbid 'em the country; nor the court,
Though they be born i'th'country. They will
                              come to't,
And fetch their falls a thousand mile about,
Where one would little think on't.   40

Enter LEANTIO

LEANTIO   I long to see how my despiser looks
Now she's come here to court; these are her lodgings!
She's simply now advanced! I took her out
Of no such window, I remember, first;
That was a great deal lower, and less carved.

BIANCA   How now? What silkworm's this, i'th'name of pride;
What, is it he?

LEANTIO   A bow i'th'ham to your greatness;
You must have now three legs, I take it, must you not?

BIANCA   Then I must take another, I shall want else
The service I should have; you have but two there,   50

LEANTIO   Y'are richly placed.

BIANCA   Methinks y'are wondrous brave, sir.

LEANTIO   A sumptuous lodging!

BIANCA   Y'have an excellent suit there.

LEANTIO   A chair of velvet!

BIANCA   Is your cloak lined through, sir?

LEANTIO   Y'are very stately here.

BIANCA   'Faith, something proud, sir.

LEANTIO   Stay, stay; let's see your cloth-of-silver slippers.

BIANCA   Who's your shoemaker? H'as made you a neat boot.

LEANTIO   Will you have a pair? The duke will lend you spurs.

BIANCA   Yes, when I ride.

LEANTIO   'Tis a brave life you lead.

BIANCA   I could never see you in such good clothes
In my time.

LEANTIO   In your time?

BIANCA   Sure I think, sir,   60
We both thrive best asunder.

LEANTIO   Y'are a whore.

BIANCA   Fear nothing, sir.

LEANTIO   An impudent, spiteful strumpet.

BIANCA   Oh sir, you give me thanks for your captainship;
I thought you had forgot all your good manners.

LEANTIO   And to spite thee as much, look there, there read!
[*shows her a letter*]Vex! Gnaw! Thou shalt find
                       there I am not love-starved.
The world was never yet so cold or pitiless
But there was ever still more charity found out
Than at one proud fool's door; and 'twere hard, 'faith,
If I could not pass that. Read to thy shame, there –   70
A cheerful and a beauteous benefactor too,
As ever erected the good works of love.

BIANCA   Lady Livia!
[*aside*] Is't possible? Her worship was my pandress.
She dote and send and give, and all to him!
Why, here's a bawd-plagued home! [*aside*] Y'are
                       simply happy, sir,
Yet I'll not envy you.

LEANTIO   No, court-saint, not thou!
You keep some friend of a new fashion.
There's no harm in your devil, he's a suckling;
But he will breed teeth shortly, will he not?

BIANCA   Take heed you play not then too long with him.   80

LEANTIO   Yes, and the great one too. I shall find time
To play a hot religious bout with some of you,
And perhaps drive you and your course of sins
To their eternal kennels. I speak softly now –
'Tis manners in a noblewoman's lodgings,
And I well know all my degrees of duty –
But come I to your everlasting parting once,

	Thunder shall seem soft music to that tempest.
BIANCA	'Twas said last week there would be change of weather
	When the moon hung so; and belike you heard it. 90
LEANTIO	Why, here's sin made, and never a conscience put to't,
	A monster with all forehead and no eyes!
	Why do I talk to thee of sense or virtue,
	That art as dark as death? And as much madness
	To set light before thee, as to lead blind folks
	To see the monuments which they may smell as soon
	As they behold – marry, oft-times their heads,
	For want of light, may feel the hardness of 'em:
	So shall thy blind pride my revenge and anger,
	That canst not see it now; and it may fall 100
	At such an hour when thou least see'st of all.
	So to an ignorance darker than thy womb
	I leave thy perjured soul. A plague will come! [exit
BIANCA	Get you gone first, and then I fear no greater –
	Nor thee will I fear long! I'll have this sauciness
	Soon banished from these lodgings, and the rooms
	Perfumed well after the corrupt air it leaves.
	His breath has made me almost sick, in troth.
	A poor base start-up! 'Life – because h'as got
	Fair clothes by foul means, comes to rail and
	show 'em! 110

Enter the DUKE

DUKE	Who's that?
BIANCA	Cry you mercy, sir.
DUKE	Prithee, who's that?
BIANCA	The former thing, my lord, to whom you gave
	The captainship; he eats his meat with grudging still.
DUKE	Still!
BIANCA	He comes vaunting here of his new love –
	And the new clothes she gave him – Lady Livia;
	Who but she now his mistress!
DUKE	Lady Livia?
	Be sure of what you say.
BIANCA	He showed me her name, sir,
	In perfumed paper – her vows, her letter –

With an intent to spite me: so his heart said,
And his threats made it good; they were as spiteful   120
As ever malice uttered; and as dangerous,
Should his hand follow the copy.

DUKE   But that must not.
Do not you vex your mind; prithee to bed, go.
All shall be well and quiet.

BIANCA   I love peace, sir.

DUKE   And so do all that love; take you no care for't,
It shall be still provided to your hand.   [exit Bianca
Who's near us there?

Enter MESSENGER

MESSENGER   My lord?

DUKE   Seek out Hippolito,
Brother to Lady Livia, with all speed.

MESSENGER He was the last man I saw, my lord.   [exit

DUKE   Make haste.
He is a blood soon stirred; and as he's quick   130
To apprehend a wrong, he's bold and sudden
In bringing forth a ruin. I know likewise
The reputation of his sister's honour's
As dear to him as life-blood to his heart;
Beside, I'll flatter him with a goodness to her
Which I now thought on – but never meant to practise
Because I know her base; and that wind drives him.
The ulcerous reputation feels the poise
Of lightest wrongs, as sores are vexed with flies.
He comes. Hippolito, welcome.

Enter HIPPOLITO

HIPPOLITO   My loved lord.   140

DUKE   How does that lusty widow, thy kind sister?
Is she not sped yet of a second husband?
A bed-fellow she has, I ask not that;
I know she's sped of him.

HIPPOLITO   Of him, my lord?

DUKE   Yes, of a bed-fellow. Is the news so strange to you?

HIPPOLITO I hope 'tis so to all.

DUKE   I wish it were, sir,

But 'tis confessed too fast. Her ignorant pleasures,
Only by lust instructed, have received
Into their services an impudent boaster,
One that does raise his glory from her shame,   150
And tells the midday sun what's done in darkness.
Yet blinded with her appetite, wastes her wealth;
Buys her disgraces at a dearer rate
Than bounteous housekeepers purchase their honour.
Nothing sads me so much, as that in love
To thee and to thy blood, I had picked out
A worthy match for her, the great Vincentio,
High in our favour and in all men's thoughts.

HIPPOLITO Oh thou destruction of all happy fortunes,
Unsated blood! Know you the name, my lord,   160
Of her abuser?

DUKE   One Leantio.

HIPPOLITO He's a factor!

DUKE   He never made so brave a voyage
By his own talk.

HIPPOLITO   The poor old widow's son!
I humbly take my leave.

DUKE   [aside]   I see 'tis done.
[aloud] Give her good counsel, make her see her error;
I know she'll harken to you.

HIPPOLITO   Yes, my lord,
I make no doubt – as I shall take the course
Which she shall never know till it be acted;
And when she wakes to honour, then she'll
                                        thank me for't.
I'll imitate the pities of old surgeons   170
To this lost limb, who ere they show their art
Cast one asleep, then cut the diseased part:
So out of love to her I pity most,
She shall not feel him going till he's lost;
Then she'll commend the cure.   [exit

DUKE   The great cure's past.
I count this done already; his wrath's sure,
And speaks an injury deep. Farewell, Leantio;
This place will never hear thee murmur more.

Enter LORD CARDINAL, *attended*

          Our noble brother, welcome!
CARDINAL   Set those lights down.
          Depart till you be called.   [*exit Attendant*
DUKE   [*aside*]   There's serious business   180
          Fixed in his look – nay, it inclines a little
          To the dark colour of a discontentment.
          [*aloud*] Brother, what is't commands your eye so
                                             powerfully?
          Speak, you seem lost.
CARDINAL   The thing I look on seems so,
          To my eyes lost for ever.
DUKE   You look on me.
CARDINAL What a grief 'tis to a religious feeling
          To think a man should have a friend so goodly,
          So wise, so noble – nay, a duke, a brother –
          And all this certainly damned!
DUKE   How!
CARDINAL   'Tis no wonder,
          If your great sin can do't. Dare you look up,   190
          For thinking of a vengeance? Dare you sleep,
          For fear of never waking but to death?
          And dedicate unto a strumpet's love
          The strength of your affections, zeal and health?
          Here you stand now: can you assure your pleasures
          You shall once more enjoy her – but once more?
          Alas, you cannot! What a misery 'tis, then,
          To be more certain of eternal death
          Than of a next embrace. Nay, shall I show you
          How more unfortunate you stand in sin,   200
          Than the low private man: all his offences,
          Like enclosed grounds, keep but about himself
          And seldom stretch beyond his own soul's bounds;
          And when a man grows miserable, 'tis some comfort
          When he's no further charged than with himself:
          'Tis a sweet ease to wretchedness. But, great man,
          Every sin thou commit'st shows like a flame
          Upon a mountain; 'tis seen far about,
          And with a big wind made of popular breath

The sparkles fly through cities; here one takes,   210
Another catches there, and in short time
Waste all to cinders: but remember still,
What burnt the valleys, first came from the hill.
Every offence draws his particular pain;
But 'tis example proves the great man's bane.
The sins of mean men lie like scattered parcels
Of an unperfect bill; but when such fall,
Then comes example, and that sums up all.
And this your reason grants: if men of good lives,
Who by their virtuous actions stir up others   220
To noble and religious imitation,
Receive the greater glory after death –
As sin must needs confess – what may they feel
In height of torments and in weight of vengeance;
Not only they themselves not doing well,
But sets a light up to show men to hell?

DUKE If you have done, I have. No more, sweet brother.
CARDINAL I know time spent in goodness is too tedious;
This had not been a moment's space in lust, now.
How dare you venture on eternal pain,   230
That cannot bear a minute's reprehension?
Methinks you should endure to hear that talked of
Which you so strive to suffer. Oh my brother!
What were you, if you were taken now?
My heart weeps blood to think on't; 'tis a work
Of infinite mercy you can never merit,
That yet you are not death-struck – no, not yet . . .
I dare not stay you long, for fear you should not
Have time enough allowed you to repent in.
There's but this wall betwixt you and destruction   240
When y'are at strongest – and but poor thin clay.
Think upon't, brother! Can you come so near it
For a fair strumpet's love, and fall into
A torment that knows neither end nor bottom
For beauty but the deepness of a skin,
And that not of their own neither? Is she a thing
Whom sickness dare not visit, or age look on,
Or death resist? Does the worm shun her grave?

If not (as your soul knows it) why should lust
Bring man to lasting pain, for rotten dust?   250

DUKE   Brother of spotless honour, let me weep
The first of my repentance in thy bosom,
And show the blest fruits of a thankful spirit;
And if I ere keep woman more unlawfully,
May I want penitence at my greatest need:
And wise men know there is no barren place
Threatens more famine, than a dearth in grace.

CARDINAL   Why, here's a conversion is at this time, brother,
Sung for a hymn in heaven; and at this instant,
The powers of darkness groan, makes all hell sorry.   260
First, I praise heaven; then in my work I glory.
Who's there attends without?

Enter SERVANTS

SERVANT   My lord?

CARDINAL   Take up those lights; there was a thicker darkness
When they came first. The peace of a fair soul
Keep with my noble brother.   [*exit Cardinal, etc.*

DUKE   Joys be with you, sir.
She lies alone tonight for't; and must still,
Though it be hard to conquer. But I have vowed
Never to know her as a strumpet more,
And I must save my oath. If fury fail not,
Her husband dies tonight, or at the most   270
Lives not to see the morning spent tomorrow;
Then will I make her lawfully mine own,
Without this sin and horror. Now I'm chidden
For what I shall enjoy then unforbidden,
And I'll not freeze in stoves; 'tis but a while
Live like a hopeful bridegroom, chaste from flesh,
And pleasure then will seem new, fair and fresh.

                                       [*exit*

SCENE 2

Enter HIPPOLITO

HIPPOLITO The morning so far wasted, yet his baseness
So impudent? See if the very sun do not blush at him!
Dare he do thus much, and know me alive!
Put case one must be vicious – as I know myself
Monstrously guilty – there's a blind time made for't;
He might use only that, 'twere conscionable;
Art, silence, closeness, subtlety and darkness
Are fit for such a business: but there's no pity
To be bestowed on an apparent sinner,
An impudent daylight lecher! The great zeal   10
I bear to her advancement in this match
With Lord Vincentio, as the Duke has wrought it,
To the perpetual honour of our house,
Puts fire into my blood, to purge the air
Of this corruption, fear it spread too far
And poison the whole hopes of this fair fortune.
I love her good so dearly, that no brother
Shall venture farther for a sister's glory
Than I for her preferment.

Enter LEANTIO *and a* PAGE

LEANTIO   Once again
I'll see that glistering whore shines like a serpent,   20
Now the court sun's upon her. Page!

PAGE   Anon sir!

LEANTIO I'll go in state too; see the coach be ready.   [*exit Page*
I'll hurry away presently.

HIPPOLITO   Yes, you shall hurry,
And the devil after you; take that at setting forth!
[*strikes him*]
Now, and you'll draw, we are upon equal terms, sir.
Thou took'st advantage of my name in honour
Upon my sister; I never saw the stroke
Come, till I found my reputation bleeding;
And therefore count it I no sin to valour
To serve thy lust so. Now we are of even hand,   30

             Take your best course against me. You must die.

LEANTIO   How close sticks envy to man's happiness!
             When I was poor, and little cared for life,
             I had no such means offered me to die,
             No man's wrath minded me. Slave, I turn this to thee,
             To call thee to account for a wound lately
             Of a base stamp upon me.

HIPPOLITO   'Twas most fit
             For a base metal. Come and fetch one now
             More noble, then; for I will use thee fairer
             Than thou hast done thine own soul or our honour.   40
             [*they fight, and Leantio is fatally wounded*]
             And there I think 'tis for thee.

VOICES WITHIN   Help, help! O part 'em.

LEANTIO   False wife, I feel now th'hast paid heartily for me.
             Rise, strumpet, by my fall! Thy lust may reign now;
             My heart-string and the marriage-knot that tied thee
             Breaks both together. [*dies*]

HIPPOLITO   There I heard the sound on't,
             And never liked string better.

      Enter GUARDIANO, LIVIA, ISABELLA, WARD, *and* SORDIDO

LIVIA   'Tis my brother!
             Are you hurt, sir?

HIPPOLITO   Not anything.

LIVIA   Blessed fortune!
             Shift for thyself; what is he thou hast killed?

HIPPOLITO Our honour's enemy.

GUARD'O   Know you this man, lady?

LIVIA   Leantio! My love's joy! Wounds stick upon thee   50
             As deadly as thy sins! Art thou not hurt?
             The devil take thy fortune. And he dead!
             Drop plagues into thy bowels without voice,
             Secret and fearful. Run for officers!
             Let him be apprehended with all speed,
             For fear he 'scape away; lay hands on him,
             We cannot be too sure. 'Tis wilful murder!
             You do heaven's vengeance and the law just service;
             You know him not as I do – he's a villain,
             As monstrous as a prodigy, and as dreadful.   60

HIPPOLITO   Will you but entertain a noble patience
            Till you but hear the reason, worthy sister!
LIVIA   The reason! That's a jest hell falls a-laughing at!
            Is there a reason found for the destruction
            Of our more lawful loves? And was there none
            To kill the black lust 'twixt thy niece and thee
            That has kept close so long?
GUARD'O   How's that, good madam?
LIVIA   Too true, sir! There she stands, let her deny't;
            The deed cries shortly in the midwife's arms,
            Unless the parents' sins strike it still-born.   70
            And if you be not deaf and ignorant,
            You'll hear strange notes ere long. Look upon
                                              me, wench!
            'Twas I betrayed thy honour subtly to him
            Under a false tale; it lights upon me now!
            His arm has paid me home upon thy breast,
            My sweet, beloved Leantio!
GUARD'O   Was my judgement
            And care in choice so devilishly abused,
            So beyond-shamefully? All the world will grin at me!
WARD   Oh Sordido, Sordido, I'm damned, I'm damned!
SORDIDO   Damned! Why, sir?
WARD   One of the wicked; dost not see't?   80
            A cuckold, a plain reprobate cuckold!
SORDIDO   Nay, and you be damned for that, be of good cheer,
            sir — y'have gallant company of all professions; I'll
            have a wife next Sunday too, because I'll along with
            you myself.
WARD   That will be some comfort yet.
LIVIA   You, sir, that bear your load of injuries
            As I of sorrows, lend me your grieved strength
            To this sad burthen who, in life, wore actions
            Flames were not nimbler. We will talk of things   90
            May have the luck to break our hearts together.
GUARD'O   I'll list to nothing but revenge and anger,
            Whose counsels I will follow.
                                    [*exeunt Livia and Guardiano,*
                                      carrying Leantio's body

SORDIDO A wife, quoth'a! Here's a sweet plum-tree of your guardianer's grafting!

WARD Nay, there's a worse name belongs to this fruit yet, and you could hit on't – a more open one! For he that marries a whore looks like a fellow bound all his lifetime to a medlar-tree; and that's good stuff – 'tis no sooner ripe but it looks rotten; and so do some queans at nineteen. A pox on't, I thought there was some knavery abroach, for something stirred in her belly the first night I lay with her.

SORDIDO What, what sir!

WARD This is she brought up so courtly! Can sing and dance – and tumble too, methinks! I'll never marry wife again that has so many qualities.

SORDIDO Indeed, they are seldom good, master. For likely when they are taught so many, they will have one trick more of their own finding out. Well, give me a wench but with one good quality, to lie with none but her husband, and that's bringing-up enough for any woman breathing.

WARD This was the fault when she was tendered to me; you never looked to this.

SORDIDO Alas, how would you have me see through a great farthingale, sir! I cannot peep through a millstone, or in the going, to see what's done i'th'bottom.

WARD Her father praised her breast! Sh'ad the voice, forsooth! I marvell'd she sung so small, indeed, being no maid; now I perceive there's a young chorister in her belly – this breeds a singing in my head, I'm sure.

SORDIDO 'Tis but the tune of your wives' cinquepace danced in a featherbed. 'Faith, go lie down, master – but take heed your horns do not make holes in the pillowberes! [*aside*] I would not batter brows with him for a hogshead of angels; he would prick my skull as full of holes as a scrivener's sandbox. [*exeunt Ward and Sordido*

ISABELLA Was ever maid so cruelly beguiled,
To the confusion of life, soul and honour,
All of one woman's murdering! I'd fain bring
Her name no nearer to my blood than woman,

And 'tis too much of that. Oh shame and horror!
In that small distance from yon man to me
Lies sin enough to make a whole world perish.
'Tis time we parted, sir, and left the sight
Of one another; nothing can be worse
To hurt repentance — for our very eyes
Are far more poisonous to religion
Than basilisks to them. If any goodness   140
Rest in you, hope of comforts, fear of judgements,
My request is, I never may see you more;
And so I turn me from you everlastingly,
So is my hope to miss you. But for her,
That durst so dally with a sin so dangerous,
And lay a snare so spitefully for my youth —
If the least means but favour my revenge,
That I may practise the like cruel cunning
Upon her life, as she has on mine honour,
I'll act it without pity.

HIPPOLITO   Here's a care   150
Of reputation and a sister's fortune
Sweetly rewarded by her! Would a silence,
As great as that which keeps among the graves,
Had everlastingly chained up her tongue.
My love to her has made mine miserable.

Enter GUARDIANO *and* LIVIA

GUARD'O   [*to Livia*] If you can but dissemble your heart's
                                                griefs now,
           Be but a woman so far.
LIVIA   [*to Guardiano*]   Peace! I'll strive, sir.
GUARD'O   [*to Livia*] As I can wear my injuries in a smile.
           Here's an occasion offered, that gives anger
           Both liberty and safety to perform   160
           Things worth the fire it holds, without the fear
           Of danger or of law; for mischiefs acted
           Under the privilege of a marriage-triumph
           At the duke's hasty nuptials, will be thought
           Things merely accidental, all's by chance,
           Not got of their own natures.
LIVIA   [*to Guardiano*]   I conceive you, sir,

Even to a longing for performance on't;
And here behold some fruits.
[kneels before Hippolito and Isabella]
                                   Forgive me both!
What I am now, returned to sense and judgement,
Is not the same rage and distraction   170
Presented lately to you; that rude form
Is gone for ever. I am now myself,
That speaks all peace and friendship; and these tears
Are the true springs of hearty, penitent sorrow
For those foul wrongs which my forgetful fury
Slandered your virtues with. This gentleman
Is well resolved now.

GUARD'O   I was never otherways.
I knew, alas, 'twas but your anger spake it,
And I never thought on't more.

HIPPOLITO   Pray rise, good sister.

ISABELLA *[aside]* Here's even as sweet amends made for a
                                        wrong now   180
As one that gives a wound, and pays the surgeon –
All the smart's nothing, the great loss of blood,
Or time of hindrance! Well, I had a mother,
I can dissemble too. *[aloud]* What wrongs have slipped
Through anger's ignorance, aunt, my heart forgives.

GUARD'O Why, this is tuneful now.

HIPPOLITO   And what I did, sister,
Was all for honour's cause, which time to come
Will approve to you.

LIVIA   Being awaked to goodness,
I understand so much, sir, and praise now
The fortune of your arm and of your safety;   190
For by his death y'have rid me of a sin
As costly as ever woman doted on.
'T has pleased the Duke so well too that, behold sir,
H'as sent you here your pardon, which I kissed
With most affectionate comfort; when 'twas brought,
Then was my fit just past – it came so well, methought,
To glad my heart.

HIPPOLITO   I see his grace thinks on me.

LIVIA	There's no talk now but of the preparation
	For the great marriage.
HIPPOLITO	Does he marry her, then?
LIVIA	With all speed, suddenly, as fast as cost 200
	Can be laid on with many thousand hands.
	This gentleman and I had once a purpose
	To have honoured the first marriage of the Duke
	With an invention of his own; 'twas ready,
	The pains well past, most of the charge bestowed on't –
	Then came the death of your good mother, niece,
	And turned the glory of it all to black.
	'Tis a device would fit these times so well, too,
	Art's treasury not better. If you'll join,
	It shall be done; the cost shall all be mine. 210
HIPPOLITO	Y'have my voice first: 'twill well approve my
	thankfulness
	For the Duke's love and favour.
LIVIA	What say you, niece?
ISABELLA	I am content to make one.
GUARD'O	The plot's full, then;
	Your pages, madam, will make shift for cupids.
LIVIA	That will they, sir.
GUARD'O	You'll play your old part still?
LIVIA	What is't? Good troth, I have even forgot it!
GUARD'O	Why, Juno Pronuba, the marriage goddess.
LIVIA	'Tis right, indeed.
GUARD'O	And you shall play the nymph
	That offers sacrifice to appease her wrath.
ISABELLA	Sacrifice, good sir?
LIVIA	Must I be appeased, then? 220
GUARD'O	That's as you list yourself, as you see cause.
LIVIA	Methinks 'twould show the more state in her deity
	To be incensed.
ISABELLA	'Twould – but my sacrifice
	Shall take a course to appease you, or I'll fail in't –
	[aside] And teach a sinful bawd to play a goddess.
GUARD'O	For our parts we'll not be ambitious, sir;
	Please you walk in and see the project drawn,

Then take your choice.

HIPPOLITO   I weigh not, so I have one.

                              [*exeunt all except Livia*

LIVIA   How much ado have I to restrain fury
          From breaking into curses! Oh how painful 'tis   230
          To keep great sorrow smothered! Sure I think
          'Tis harder to dissemble grief than love.
          Leantio, here the weight of thy loss lies,
          Which nothing but destruction can suffice.

                                                    [*exit*

SCENE 3

Hoboys

Enter in great state the DUKE *and* BIANCA, *richly attired,*
with LORDS, CARDINALS, LADIES, *and other* ATTENDANTS.
They pass solemnly over. Enter LORD CARDINAL *in a rage,*
seeming to break off the ceremony

CARDINAL   Cease, cease! Religious honours done to sin
           Disparage virtue's reverence, and will pull
           Heaven's thunder upon Florence; holy ceremonies
           Were made for sacred uses, not for sinful.
           Are these the fruits of your repentance, brother?
           Better it had been you had never sorrowed
           Than to abuse the benefit, and return
           To worse than where sin left you.
           Vowed you then never to keep strumpet more,
           And are you now so swift in your desires   10
           To knit your honours and your life fast to her?
           Is not sin sure enough to wretched man
           But he must bind himself in chains to't? Worse!
           Must marriage, that immaculate robe of honour
           That renders virtue glorious, fair and fruitful
           To her great Master, be now made the garment
           Of leprosy and foulness? Is this penitence,
           To sanctify hot lust? What is it otherways
           Than worship done to devils? Is this the best
           Amends that sin can make after her riots?   20

As if a drunkard, to appease heaven's wrath,
Should offer up his surfeit for a sacrifice!
If that be comely, then lust's offerings are,
On wedlock's sacred altar.

DUKE   Here y'are bitter
Without cause, brother: what I vowed, I keep
As safe as you your conscience; and this needs not.
I taste more wrath in't than I do religion,
And envy more than goodness. The path now
I tread, is honest – leads to lawful love
Which virtue in her strictness would not check.   30
I vowed no more to keep a sensual woman:
'Tis done; I mean to make a lawful wife of her.

CARDINAL He that taught you that craft,
Call him not master long, he will undo you.
Grow not too cunning for your soul, good brother.
Is it enough to use adulterous thefts,
And then take sanctuary in marriage?
I grant, so long as an offender keeps
Close in a privileged temple, his life's safe;
But if he ever venture to come out,   40
And so be taken, then he surely dies for't:
So now y'are safe; but when you leave this body,
Man's only privileged temple upon earth,
In which the guilty soul takes sanctuary,
Then you'll perceive what wrongs chaste vows endure
When lust usurps the bed that should be pure.

BIANCA   Sir, I have read you over all this while
In silence, and I find great knowledge in you,
And severe learning; yet 'mongst all your virtues   50
I see not charity written, which some call
The first-born of religion; and I wonder
I cannot see't in yours. Believe it, sir,
There is no virtue can be sooner missed
Or later welcomed; it begins the rest,
And sets 'em all in order. Heaven and angels
Take great delight in a converted sinner:
Why should you, then, a servant and professor,
Differ so much from them? If every woman

That commits evil should be therefore kept
Back in desires of goodness, how should virtue   60
Be known and honoured? From a man that's blind
To take a burning taper, 'tis no wrong,
He never misses it; but to take light
From one that sees, that's injury and spite.
Pray, whether is religion better served
When lives that are licentious are made honest,
Than when they still run through a sinful blood?
'Tis nothing virtue's temple to deface,
But build the ruins, there's a work of grace.

DUKE   I kiss thee for that spirit; thou hast praised thy wit   70
     A modest way. On, on there!

Hoboys

CARDINAL   Lust is bold,
And will have vengeance speak, ere't be controlled.

                                      [exeunt

ACT 5 SCENE I

Enter GUARDIANO *and* WARD

GUARD'O   Speak, hast thou any sense of thy abuse?
      Dost thou know what wrong's done thee?

WARD   I were an ass else;
      I cannot wash my face but I am feeling on't.

GUARD'O   Here, take this caltrop, then; convey it secretly
      Into the place I showed you. Look you, sir,
      This is the trap-door to't.

WARD   I know't of old, uncle,
      Since the last triumph – here rose up a devil
      With one eye, I remember, with a company
      Of fireworks at's tail.

GUARD'O   Prithee leave squibbing now;
      Mark me and fail not – but when thou hear'st me   10
      Give a stamp, down with't; the villain's caught then.

WARD   If I miss you, hang me; I love to catch
      A villain, and your stamp shall go current, I
                             warrant you.
      But how shall I rise up and let him down too,
      All at one hole? That will be a horrible puzzle.
      You know I have a part in't – I play Slander.

GUARD'O   True, but never make you ready for't.

WARD   No?
      But my clothes are bought and all, and a foul fiend's
      Head with a long contumelious tongue i'th'
                         chaps on't,
      A very fit shape for Slander i'th'out-parishes.   20

GUARD'O   It shall not come so far; thou understand'st it not.

WARD   Oh, oh?

GUARD'O   He shall lie deep enough ere that time, and stick first
      Upon those.

WARD   Now I conceive you, guardianer.

GUARD'O   Away; list to the privy stamp, that's all thy part.

WARD   Stamp my horns in a mortar if I miss you,
      And give the powder in white wine to sick cuckolds –
      A very present remedy for the headache.   [*exit Ward*

GUARD'O   If this should any way miscarry now –
       As, if the fool be nimble enough, 'tis certain –
       The pages that present the swift-winged cupids   30
       Are taught to hit him with their shafts of love,
       Fitting his part, which I have cunningly poisoned.
       He cannot 'scape my fury; and those ills
       Will be laid all on fortune, not our wills –
       That's all the sport on't! For who will imagine
       That at the celebration of this night
       Any mischance that haps can flow from spite?

                                           [*exit*

SCENE 2

Flourish. Enter above DUKE, BIANCA, LORD CARDINAL,
FABRITIO, *and other* CARDINALS, LORDS *and* LADIES *in state*

DUKE   Now, our fair Duchess, your delight shall witness
       How y'are beloved and honoured: all the glories
       Bestowed upon the gladness of this night
       Are done for your bright sake.

BIANCA   I am the more
       In debt, my lord, to loves and courtesies
       That offer up themselves so bounteously
       To do me honoured grace, without my merit.

DUKE   A goodness set in greatness! How it sparkles
       Afar off, like pure diamonds set in gold.
       How perfect my desires were, might I witness
       But a fair noble peace 'twixt your two spirits!   10
       The reconcilement would be more sweet to me
       Than longer life to him that fears to die.
       Good sir!

CARDINAL   I profess peace, and am content.

DUKE   I'll see the seal upon't, and then 'tis firm.

CARDINAL   You shall have all you wish. [*kisses Bianca*]

DUKE   I have all indeed now.

BIANCA   [*aside*] But I have made surer work; this shall
                            not blind me.
       He that begins so early to reprove,

Quickly rid him, or look for little love:
Beware a brother's envy – he's next heir too.   20
Cardinal, you die this night; the plot's laid surely:
In time of sports death may steal in securely.
Then 'tis least thought on:
For he that's most religious, holy friend,
Does not at all hours think upon his end;
He has his times of frailty, and his thoughts
Their transportations too, through flesh and blood,
For all his zeal, his learning, and his light,
As well as we poor souls that sin by night.

DUKE   What's this, Fabritio?

FABRITIO   Marry, my lord, the model   30
Of what's presented.

DUKE   Oh, we thank their loves.
Sweet Duchess, take your seat; list to the argument.
[reads]
There is a nymph that haunts the woods and springs
In love with two at once, and they with her;
Equal it runs; but to decide these things,
The cause to mighty Juno they refer,
She being the marriage-goddess. The two lovers,
They offer sighs; the nymph, a sacrifice –
All to please Juno, who by signs discovers
How the event shall be. So that strife dies.
Then springs a second; for the man refused   40
Grows discontent, and out of love abused
He raises Slander up, like a black fiend,
To disgrace th'other, which pays him i'th'end.

BIANCA   In troth, my lord, a pretty, pleasing argument,
And fits th'occasion well: envy and slander
Are things soon raised against two faithful lovers;
But comfort is, they are not long unrewarded.

Music

DUKE   This music shows they're upon entrance now.
BIANCA   Then enter all my wishes!   50

Enter HYMEN *in yellow,* GANYMEDE *in a blue robe powdered
with stars, and* HEBE *in a white robe with golden stars, with
covered cups in their hands. They dance a short dance,
then bowing to the* DUKE *etc.,* HYMEN *speaks*

HYMEN   To thee, fair bride, Hymen offers up
          Of nuptial joys this the celestial cup;
          Taste it, and thou shalt ever find
          Love in thy bed, peace in thy mind.

BIANCA   We'll taste you, sure; 'twere pity to disgrace
          So pretty a beginning.

DUKE   'Twas spoke nobly.

GANYMEDE Two cups of nectar have we begged from Jove:
          Hebe, give that to Innocence; I this to Love.

        HEBE *gives a cup to the* CARDINAL,
        GANYMEDE *one to the* DUKE; *both drink*

          Take heed of stumbling more, look to your way;
          Remember still the Via Lactea.   60

HEBE   Well Ganymede, you have more faults, though
                             not so known;
          I spilled one cup, but you have filched many a one.

HYMEN   No more, forbear for Hymen's sake;
          In love we met, and so let's parting take.   [*exeunt*

DUKE   But soft! Here's no such persons in the argument
          As these three, Hymen, Hebe, Ganymede;
          The actors that this model here discovers
          Are only four – Juno, a nymph, two lovers.

BIANCA   This is some antemasque belike, my lord,
          To entertain time – now my peace is perfect.   70
          Let sports come on apace; now is their time, my lord,

                    Music

          Hark you, you hear from 'em.

DUKE   The nymph indeed!

Enter two dressed like nymphs, bearing two tapers lighted; then
ISABELLA *dressed with flowers and garlands, bearing a censer
with fire in it. They set the censer and tapers on Juno's
altar with much reverence, this ditty being sung in parts*

Ditty

    Juno, nuptial goddess,
    Thou that rul'st o'er coupled bodies,
    Tiest man to woman, never to forsake her;
    Thou only powerful marriage-maker;
    Pity this amazed affection:
    I love both and both love me;
    Nor know I where to give rejection,
    My heart likes so equally,   80
    Till thou set'st right my peace of life,
    And with thy power conclude this strife.

ISABELLA   Now with my thanks depart, you to the springs,
    I to these wells of love.   *[exeunt the two nymphs*
                        Thou sacred goddess
    And queen of nuptials, daughter to great Saturn,
    Sister and wife to Jove, imperial Juno,
    Pity this passionate conflict in my breast,
    This tedious war 'twixt two affections;
    Crown me with victory, and my heart's at peace.

Enter HIPPOLITO *and* GUARDIANO *like shepherds*

HIPPOLITO   Make me that happy man, thou mighty goddess.   90
GUARD'O   But I live most in hope, if truest love
    Merit the greatest comfort.
ISABELLA   I love both
    With such an even and fair affection,
    I know not which to speak for, which to wish for,
    Till thou, great arbitress 'twixt lovers' hearts,
    By thy auspicious grace design the man:
    Which pity I implore.
HIPPOLITO & GUARDIANO   We all implore it.
ISABELLA   And after sighs, contrition's truest odours,

      LIVIA *descends like Juno, with Cupids*

    I offer to thy powerful deity
    This precious incense; may it ascend peacefully.   100
    [poisoned smoke arises]
    [aside] And if it keep true touch, my good aunt Juno,
    'Twill try your immortality ere't be long;

	I fear you'll never get so nigh heaven again,
	When you're once down.
LIVIA	Though you and your affections
	Seem all as dark to our illustrious brightness
	As night's inheritance, hell, we pity you,
	And your requests are granted. You ask signs:
	They shall be given you; we'll be gracious to you.
	He of those twain which we determine for you,
	Love's arrows shall wound twice; the later wound

I fear you'll never get so nigh heaven again,
When you're once down.

LIVIA   Though you and your affections
Seem all as dark to our illustrious brightness
As night's inheritance, hell, we pity you,
And your requests are granted. You ask signs:
They shall be given you; we'll be gracious to you.
He of those twain which we determine for you,
Love's arrows shall wound twice; the later wound   110
Betokens love in age: for so are all
Whose love continues firmly all their lifetime
Twice wounded at their marriage, else affection
Dies when youth ends – This savour overcomes me!
Now for a sign of wealth and golden days,
Bright-eyed prosperity which all couples love,
Ay, and makes love – take that!
        [*throws flaming gold upon Isabella who falls dead*]
                                    Our brother Jove
Never denies us of his burning treasure
T'express bounty.

DUKE   She falls down upon't;
What's the conceit of that?

FABRITIO   As over-joyed, belike: 120
Too much prosperity overjoys us all,
And she has her lapful, it seems, my lord.

DUKE   This swerves a little from the argument, though:
Look you, my lords.

GUARD'O   [*aside*] All's fast; now comes my part to toll him hither;
Then, with a stamp given, he's dispatched as
                                    cunningly.
        [*Guardiano stamps on the floor; the trapdoor opens and he
        himself falls through it. Hippolito bends over Isabella's body*]

HIPPOLITO   Stark dead! O treachery – cruelly made away!
How's that?

FABRITIO   Look, there's one of the lovers dropped away too.

DUKE   Why sure, this plot's drawn false; here's no such thing.   130

LIVIA   Oh, I am sick to th'death! Let me down quickly.
This fume is deadly. O, 't has poisoned me!

My subtlety is sped; her art has quitted me.
My own ambition pulls me down to ruin. [*dies*]

HIPPOLITO Nay, then I kiss thy cold lips, and applaud
This thy revenge in death. [*Cupids shoot at Hippolito*]

FABRITIO   Look, Juno's down too!
What makes she there? Her pride should keep aloft.
She was wont to scorn the earth in other shows.
Methinks her peacocks' feathers are much pulled.

HIPPOLITO Oh, death runs through my blood in a wild flame too! 140
Plague of those Cupids! Some lay hold on 'em.
Let 'em not 'scape, they have spoiled me; the
                                    shaft's deadly.

DUKE I have lost myself in this quite.

HIPPOLITO My great lords, we are all confounded.

DUKE   How?

HIPPOLITO Dead; and, ay, worse.

FABRITIO   Dead? My girl dead? I hope
My sister Juno has not served me so.

HIPPOLITO Lust and forgetfulness has been amongst us,
And we are brought to nothing. Some blest charity
Lend me the speeding pity of his sword
To quench this fire in blood! Leantio's death   150
Has brought all this upon us – now I taste it –
And made us lay plots to confound each other:
The event so proves it; and man's understanding
Is riper at his fall than all his lifetime.
She, in a madness for her lover's death,
Revealed a fearful lust in our near bloods,
For which I am punished dreadfully and unlooked for;
Proved her own ruin too: vengeance met vengeance
Like a set match: as if the plagues of sin
Had been agreed to meet here altogether.   160
But how her fawning partner fell, I reach not,
Unless caught by some springe of his own setting –
For on my pain, he never dreamed of dying;
The plot was all his own, and he had cunning
Enough to save himself: but 'tis the property
Of guilty deeds to draw your wise men downward.
Therefore the wonder ceases – O this torment!

DUKE   Our guard below there!

Enter a LORD *with a* GUARD

LORD   My lord?

HIPPOLITO   Run and meet death then,
And cut off time and pain. [*runs on Guard's sword*]

LORD   Behold, my lord,
H'as run his breast upon a weapon's point.   170

DUKE   Upon the first night of our nuptial honours
Destruction play her triumph, and great mischiefs
Mask in expected pleasures! 'Tis prodigious!
They're things most fearfully ominous: I like 'em not.
Remove these ruined bodies from our eyes.
                  [*the bodies are taken away*

BIANCA   [*aside*] Not yet? No change? When falls he to
                          the earth?

LORD   Please but your excellence to peruse that paper,
Which is a brief confession from the heart
Of him that fell first, ere his soul departed;
And there the darkness of these deeds speaks plainly: 180
'Tis the full scope, the manner and intent.
His ward, that ignorantly let him down,
Fear put to present flight at the voice of him.

BIANCA   [*aside*] Nor yet?

DUKE   Read, read; for I am lost in sight and strength.

CARDINAL   My noble brother!

BIANCA   Oh the curse of wretchedness!
My deadly hand is fall'n upon my lord.
Destruction take me to thee, give me way –
The pains and plagues of a lost soul upon him
That hinders me a moment!

DUKE   My heart swells bigger yet; help here, break't ope!   190
My breast flies open next. [*dies*]

BIANCA   Oh, with the poison
That was prepared for thee – thee, Cardinal!
'Twas meant for thee!

CARDINAL   Poor prince!

BIANCA   Accursed error!
Give me thy last breath, thou infected bosom,

And wrap two spirits in one poisoned vapour.
Thus, thus, reward thy murderer, and turn death
Into a parting kiss! My soul stands ready at my lips,
Ev'n vexed to stay one minute after thee.

CARDINAL The greatest sorrow and astonishment
That ever struck the general peace of Florence   200
Dwells in this hour.

BIANCA   So . . . my desires are satisfied,
I feel death's power within me!
Thou hast prevailed in something, cursèd poison,
Though thy chief force was spent in my lord's bosom.
But my deformity in spirit's more foul:
A blemished face best fits a leprous soul.
What make I here? These are all strangers to me,
Not known but by their malice, now th'art gone,
Nor do I seek their pities.

CARDINAL   O restrain
Her ignorant, wilful hand.

[Bianca seizes the poisoned cup and drinks from it]

BIANCA   Now do; 'tis done.   210
Leantio, now I feel the breach of marriage
At my heartbreaking! Oh the deadly snares
That women set for women – without pity
Either to soul or honour! Learn by me
To know your foes. In this belief I die:
Like our own sex, we have no enemy.

LORD See, my lord,
What shift sh'as made to be her own destruction.

BIANCA Pride, greatness, honours, beauty, youth, ambition –
You must all down together; there's no help for't.   220
Yet this my gladness is, that I remove,
Tasting the same death in a cup of love. *[dies]*

CARDINAL Sin, what thou art, these ruins show too piteously!
Two kings on one throne cannot sit together
But one must needs down, for his title's wrong:
So where lust reigns, that prince cannot reign long.
                        [exeunt

WORDSWORTH CLASSICS
OF WORLD LITERATURE

REQUESTS FOR INSPECTION COPIES   Lecturers wishing to obtain copies of Wordsworth Classics, Wordsworth Poetry Library or Wordsworth Classics of World Literature titles on inspection are invited to contact: Dennis Hart, Wordsworth Editions Ltd, Crib Street, Ware, Herts SG12 9ET; E-mail: dennis.hart@wordsworth-editions.com. Please quote the author, title and ISBN of the titles in which you are interested, together with your name, academic address, E-mail address, the course on which the books will be used and the expected enrolment.

Teachers wishing to inspect specific core titles for GCSE or A level courses are also invited to contact Wordsworth Editions at the above address.

Inspection copies are sent solely at the discretion of Wordsworth Editions Ltd.

APULEIUS
The Golden Ass

ARISTOTLE
The Nicomachean Ethics

MARCUS AURELIUS
Meditations

FRANCIS BACON
Essays

JAMES BOSWELL
The Life of Samuel Johnson
(UNABRIDGED)

JOHN BUNYAN
The Pilgrim's Progress

BALDESAR CASTIGLIONE
The Book of the Courtier

CATULLUS
Poems

CERVANTES
Don Quixote

CARL VON CLAUSEWITZ
On War
(ABRIDGED)

CONFUCIUS
The Analects

CAPTAIN JAMES COOK
The Voyages of Captain Cook

DANTE
The Inferno

CHARLES DARWIN
The Origin of Species
The Voyage of the Beagle

RENÉ DESCARTES
Key Philosophical Writings

FYODOR DOSTOEVSKY
The Devils

ERASMUS
Praise of Folly

SIGMUND FREUD
The Interpretation of Dreams

EDWARD GIBBON
*The Decline and Fall of the
Roman Empire*
(ABRIDGED)

GUSTAVE FLAUBERT
Sentimental Education

KAHLIL GIBRAN
The Prophet

JOHANN WOLFGANG
VON GOETHE
Faust, Part 1

HERODOTUS
Histories

HOMER
The Iliad and The Odyssey

HORACE
The Odes

BEN JONSON
Volpone and Other Plays

KENKO
Essays in Idleness

WILLIAM LANGLAND
Piers Plowman

LAO TZU
Tao Te Ching

T. E. LAWRENCE
Seven Pillars of Wisdom